Cinema against Spectacle

Film Theory in Media History explores the epistemological and theoretical foundations of the study of film through texts by classical authors as well as anthologies and monographs on key issues and developments in film theory. Adopting a historical perspective, but with a firm eye to the further development of the field, the series provides a platform for ground-breaking new research into film theory and media history and features high-profile editorial projects that offer resources for teaching and scholarship. Combining the book form with open access online publishing the series reaches the broadest possible audience of scholars, students, and other readers with a passion for film and theory.

Film Theory in Media History is published in cooperation with the Permanent Seminar for the History of Film Theories.

Cinema against Spectacle

Technique and Ideology Revisited

By Jean-Louis Comolli

Translated and edited by Daniel Fairfax

Amsterdam University Press

This book is published in print and online through the online OAPEN library (www.oapen.org).

OAPEN (Open Access Publishing in European Networks) is a collaborative initiative to develop and implement a sustainable Open Access publication model for academic books in the Humanities and Social Sciences. The OAPEN Library aims to improve the visibility and usability of high quality academic research by aggregating peer reviewed Open Access publications from across Europe.

Cover illustration: Jean-Louis Comolli

Cover design: Suzan Beijer, Amersfoort
Lay-out: JAPES, Amsterdam

Amsterdam University Press English-language titles are distributed in the US and Canada by the University of Chicago Press.

ISBN 978 90 8964 554 8
e-ISBN 978 90 4851 945 3
NUR 670

Table of Contents

Preface

Philip Rosen

A network of new conceptions, arguments and debates about cinema produced in the 1970s made these years one of the key periods in the history of film theory. With the contemporaneous "take-off" of university film studies in the English-speaking world, these ideas assumed foundational status during a period of expansive professionalization and academic institutionalization. As contested as some became, certain ideas and concepts from 1970s film theory have had staying power. However, many of the most important formulations of 1970s film theory claimed motivation in the politically radical impulses and ideas of the period, which also permeated some of the most important filmmaking of the time.

By the mid-1960s, there were already important claims for a distinctive break with earlier, "classical" film theory. Then, in 1968, a number of political tensions and conflicts erupted in spectacular political disruptions and oppositional public events all over the globe. For a few years after 1968, yearnings for political transformation often intersected with desires for the radical transformation of intellectual sectors, desires which one finds in certain of the initiating texts of 1970s film theory. Among all of these events, May 1968 in France was the time and place where film culture was most famously – and perhaps even mythically – associated with politicized practices and understandings of cinema.

Jean-Louis Comolli was one of the central figures in French film culture at that moment. Very much an *homme du cinéma,* he is a filmmaker as well as critic and theorist. As critic and theorist he has always committed himself to engaging with the very textures of films while simultaneously conceptualizing the broader aesthetic vocations and social possibilities and roles of cinema. In the early 1960s, Comolli had emerged as a writer, and then chief editor, for that most influential of Parisian film journals, *Cahiers du cinéma.*

His articles from the late 1960s and early 1970s are not his only important theoretical and critical work, but they may be counted among the foundational texts of 1970s film theory. In this volume, Daniel Fairfax provides corrected, theoretically and historically informed translations of certain of Comolli's most widely discussed writings dating from the immediate post-1968 years of *Cahiers*. These include two polemical editorials written in 1969 and co-authored with Comolli's fellow *Cahiers* editor Jean Narboni, along with Comolli's most far-reaching, extensive, and consequential work for the history of film theory, "Technique and Ideology," which was written and published serially in 1971-1972 in several issues of *Cahiers*. Fairfax additionally provides a translation of "Cinema against Spectacle," a recent major essay in which Comolli reconsiders the position of cinema some 40 years later, when filmmaking finds itself part of a transformed 21st-century media universe.

Fairfax's extensive introduction gives us a detailed account of the debates and critiques generated by "Technique and Ideology" and the *Cahiers* editorials. In the English-speaking world, the impact of "Technique and Ideology" was all the more remarkable because of the cumbersome, inconvenient way it was distributed. Though rapidly translated into English, it was at first available only in typescript form for discussion and study groups in London. Some contemporaneous British translations of other French film-theoretical polemics were quickly published in the journal *Screen*, the most central English-language journal for 1970s film theory, and they soon became standard texts in Anglophone debates. But strangely, none of the "Technique and Ideology" translation was published in *Screen* or other British venues. Instead, the British translation took on something of an itinerant status. I myself first encountered the text as a xerox of the British typescript as it circulated among certain graduate programs in what was then the small world of US academic film studies in the early 1970s. Eventually, most installments of "Technique and Ideology" as rendered in these British translations were published, but piecemeal and in a variety of venues. Until now the text as a whole has never received an integral English-language publication. Along with Comolli's own retrospective and prospective reconsiderations, Fairfax's new translation and his historical contextualization of "Technique and Ideology" can stimulate a nuanced and contemporary re-evaluation of Comolli's interventions, and of 1970s film theory more broadly.

***

Seen in retrospect, the programmatic *Cahiers* editorials Comolli wrote with Narboni schematically declare what became two of the privileged and defining themes of this 1970s theory. One was a new kind of emphasis on the realist claims of cinema, which entailed interrogating any cinematic "impression of reality" by placing it under political and ideological critique. The second theme was a new kind of approach to spectatorship, which at this point focused on conceptualizing spectatorial recognition, misrecognition and self-recognition, all understood as interconnected with ideology. As the arguments and debates quickly developed, many emphasized claims about contradictory processes underlying structures and experiences of subjectivity, invoking notions of the imaginary in a technical, psychoanalytic sense.

1970s film theory was often more diverse than its opponents allowed, partly because it was formed in a developing network of debates and projects among several writers, and partly because it was often associated with positional journals. One way we might conceive a preliminary mapping of such film-theoretical discussions and debates could be to treat the two themes outlined above as conceptual markers of its general terrain. One finds differing and overlapping accounts of each of these two markers in the major texts of 1970s film theory. These show that the post-1968 critique of realist ontologies and epistemologies in film theory was not grounded in run-of-the-mill social constructionism or representational conventionalism. Rather, it entailed an intricate and radical critical explication of the nature, capacities, and limitations of filmic representation and operations.

On the heels of 1968, Marxism was central to establishing this film-theoretical terrain in France. This was evident in *Cahiers du cinéma* and its key leftist sparring partner, *Cinéthique*. Claims for radical new conceptions of cinema required radical theoretical grounds consonant with the political inspirations and urgencies of the moment. In the Parisian context, this most often led to the theories being developed by Louis Althusser at the same time. This is not the place to rehearse Althusser's conceptions, except to note that they entailed a revision of Marxist notions of historical determination by and within the "complex whole" of a contradictory social formation; that they opened the way for new emphases on the importance and "relative autonomy" of ideological practices within Marxist theory; and that Althusser himself was linking ideology and subject-positioning. Appeals to Althusser as a central reference for film theory overlapped with other major developments in the French theoretical landscape. Thus, by 1968, a self-conscious post-structuralism was being formulated. Comolli himself has recourse to the early work of Jacques Derrida and Julia Kristeva. Meanwhile, those interested in spectatorship were turning to Lacanian psychoanalytic theory, which would very soon become central to many wings of 1970s film theory.

***

Within this heated French discursive arena, there was a certain distinctive thrust in Comolli's contributions. Take the critique of the cinematic impression of reality, which was being defined as a pivotal operation of dominant ideological practices. Comolli consistently refused to treat it as a unitary, monolithic end product, instead seeing it as a complex, ongoing production or process. For Comolli, the cinematic impression of reality never entails a simple submission of the spectator to an illusion, but an *activation* of the spectator. In his view, the cinematic impression of reality is always inadequate to the task of transmitting reality in any absolute sense. This is why the impression of reality can only be completed by spectatorial investment, which means spectatorship is an *activity*. Here is one passage from "Technique and Ideology," where he makes this crucial point in the context of a discussion of silent film:

> It is at the price of a series of blind spots (of disavowals) that the silent image could be accepted as the objective reflection and duplication of "life itself": the denial of color, stereoscopy and sound. Founded on these absences (just as, incidentally, all forms of representation are founded on an absence governing them, on a fault-line lying at the basis of every simulacrum – the spectator, in any case,

very well knows about the artifice, but prefers to believe in it all the same), filmic representation could only be produced, as I have already noted, by working to attenuate their effects, and even masking their real existence. Otherwise, it would have been refused, as being too visibly factitious: it was absolutely necessary for it to facilitate the disavowal of those veritable sensorial castrations which established its specificity, and for it not to stymie this process by re-marking them. *Compromises* were needed in order for the cinema to function as an ideological apparatus, in order for it to act as a lure.[1]

The reference is to Octave Mannoni's comments on Freud's account of fetishism, where fetishism is described as a disavowal.[2] Mannoni's much-noted formula for this disavowal is "I know very well, but all the same..." In Comolli, it summarizes the structure of belief engendered by any signification claiming secure referentiality. In cinema, according to Comolli, "realism is only produced [...] as a denial of filmic reality."[3]

It is worth considering some of the implications of the metaphor of the lure. First, a lure is designed to attract an action from its target; that is, if the target takes the lure, this means it must *do* something in order to take the bait. So the metaphor encompasses the idea of an activation of the spectator. But second, there is always the possibility that the target of the lure might recognize it as an artifice, as mere bait for something else. A fetishistic structure has potential knowledge value – "I *know* very well, but all the same." The possibility of gaining such understanding of the nature of the lure entails the possibility of counteractivity. The lure might be refused, or even destroyed. Or there might be a kind of play with the lure, whereby structures of belief and artifice can be investigated. To put it more generally, this metaphor of the lure designates the cinematic impression of reality as a complex, contradictory process, a kind of balancing act that admits the possibility of comprehending its nature.

***

Within this complexity, Comolli finds the potential to counter cinema's ideological mechanisms. Such an impulse can be found throughout his writings, even in the socially and politically evaluative schematism of "Cinema/Ideology/Criticism (1)" – a text that could too quickly be read as affirming straightforward textual determinism, and therefore a duped or "passive" spectator. The editorial polemically announces that one must begin from the premise that cinema is an ideological practice based on the impression of reality. It even goes so far as to assert that cameras and film

1. Cf. infra, p. 230.
2. Cf. Octave Mannoni, *Clefs pour l'imaginaire ou l'Autre Scène* (Paris: Seuil, 1969).
3. Cf. infra, p. 186.

stocks seem to be made with the goal of presenting a reproduction of reality, such that cinema is a privileged instrument for the naturalization of "bourgeois ideology." Therefore, it proposes, militant film theory must always ask whether films (and probably theories) "are content to be traversed by ideology such as it is, as its site of passage, its transparent mediation, its chosen language, or whether, on the other hand, they attempt to turn it back on itself, to reflect on it, to intervene *into* it, to render it visible and in doing so render its mechanisms visible."[4] At first this seems to be a clear and absolute binary criterion: all sociopolitical evaluations of films are to be based on an opposition between transparency (the impression of reality) and self-reflexive exposure of the inadequacies of the impression of reality. Yet, Narboni and Comolli go on to generate a much-discussed textual typology of films, which is composed of *seven* categories of ideological complicity and/or interventions. We might note the logical strangeness here: a binary opposition generates an odd number of oppositions. This is the consequence of recognizing the importance of mixed cases and contradictions, an arena that would be central to Comolli's subsequent theoretical contributions.

Polemical and unfinished as it was, "Technique and Ideology" can be read as working out the terms and consequences of this complexity in the context of the early, foundational debates establishing 1970s film theory. Fairfax and Comolli himself have much to say about it. Here, I will just make notations on three of its major moves.

First, "Technique and Ideology" begins with Comolli's intervention in foundational debates about the ideological status of cinematic technology, including several formulations that helped establish what is now sometimes called apparatus theory. Mostly written in the years immediately following 1968, many texts of apparatus theory were written with greater or lesser awareness of the distinction attempted by Althusser between science and ideology, and they often focused on the camera and perspectival optics. In his comments on Jean-Patrick Lebel, Marcelin Pleynet and Jean-Louis Baudry (among others), Comolli once again complicates what appears as a binary opposition. As Fairfax points out, Comolli reaffirms the idea that cinema has an ideological vocation, with the crucial proviso that it is more than just this vocation.

One of Comolli's critiques of other participants in the debate is that they make the camera stand in for all cinematic technology. Whether this critique is justified or not, it leads to the more general principle: cinematic technology must be seen as a multiplicity, an assemblage. This is a pluralization of "the" apparatus. It is a way of developing the idea that the impression of reality is a dominant social vocation of cinema, while opening up the possibility – the inevitability – of frictions, contradictions, and changes within that vocation. That is, it leads not only the ideological analysis of cinema as apparatus to history, but also film theory itself to history. It is also related

4. Cf. infra, p. 252.

to a larger theoretical principle: the concepts or identities of objects or processes under discussion must be conceived as a structured multiplicity that shifts over time.

Second, this leads Comolli to conceive of a materialist historicity. Here yet another binary opposition must be surpassed: the hoary but widespread division between theory and history. In "Technique and Ideology" film theory becomes radically historicized, because the components of cinema that this text privileges – cinema technology, depth of field, the impression of reality itself – are historically shifting assemblages rather than immutable identities or unities. Film technology must be conceptualized as a multiplicity whose contents and forms may shift over time depending on the interrelation of economics and ideology. On the other side of the ledger, film history requires self-conscious, reflexively considered concepts and conceptualizations – that is, theory.

Another way of putting it is that film theory must understand cinema in its historical actuality; however, that actuality is not available to any simple, positive empirical investigation. It can only be thought through the construction of a problematic – a structure of concepts and questions – suitable to it. This was one of the noted assertions of Althusser, and it informs the quest for a materialist approach to history in "Technique and Ideology." One can find the effects of this principle at several levels in Comolli's text. For instance, it is manifest in his critique of simply accepting the statements of historical agents such as studio technicians at face value rather than reading them symptomatically. Another example is Comolli's attack on standard practices of writing film history by finding "first times" and producing linear accounts stemming from such alleged origins. His theoretical sources no doubt attuned him to problems in the widespread rhetoric and tropes of "firsts" in film history and theory. After all, Althusser had defined history as a process without origin or end, and in "Technique and Ideology" this dovetails with the contemporaneous post-structuralist critiques of origins, especially in Kristeva. A related example is Comolli's embrace of a notion of differential historical temporalities, which is aligned to his understanding of the multiplicity of assemblages constituting cinema technologies and techniques. These and other of his initiatives for a materialist historiography generated significant discussion in an emergent academic film studies in the 1970s, for which methodological self-consciousness and theoretical innovation were important.

Third, "Technique and Ideology" seeks to subject concepts in film theory to a materialist historicization of film technique and stylistics. The particulars of Comolli's intervention in film theory are structured by another French debate. Once again Comolli seems to define a binary opposition between two of the most ambitious and synthetic of French film theorists, in order to complicate and surpass it: André Bazin, the "idealist" theorist of realism, *versus* Jean Mitry, who presents himself as a more empirical, perceptually constructivist theorist. Aware of Althusser's critique of empiricism in philosophy, Comolli is in many ways more critical of Mitry than Bazin. He argues that Mitry takes technologies and their discourses at face value and too often dismisses the impression of reality as a mistaken question. For Comolli, Bazin has the virtue of foregrounding and interrogating the problem of realism, which is central to the ideological operations of the cinema, even if Bazin's account must be transformed from the perspective of a Marxist theory of ideology. Depth of field is Comolli's privileged example of a stylistic device, precisely because Bazin privileged it as a realist strategy.

According to Comolli, the basic flaw Bazin and Mitry share is their assumption that a concept such as "depth of field" designates a stable identity. Comolli argues that depth of field, whether considered as technological product or as signification, has appeared intermittently and with different import and purposes at different points in film history. It is to be understood as the product and component of historically shifting assemblages of technical practices and stylistic configurations. But not just that. These historically shifting technical and cinematic configurations are themselves components of broader signifying, technological, and social conjunctures.

This brings us back to multiplicities. Comolli wishes to show that "realism" as ideological ambition must be understood as existing in different combinations of elements at different historical moments. On the technological level, these certainly include imaging and photographic techniques, but even these camera manipulations may be composed by varying combinations of focus, lighting, tonality, and so forth. In addition, "realism" includes work that is detached from the camera and the instant of filming, such as changeable practices of color grading and other post-production operations, and, after 1926, sound recording and mixing. At yet another level, the history of film styles and techniques signifying realism and reality in films does not belong just to cinema, even considered only as a technology. Thus, in the final installment, Comolli argues that at any given social and historical conjuncture, techniques and codifications signifying the realism of cinema develop historically in relation to the current state of techniques and codifications in other media technologies and forms. For example, theorists note that depth of field seems to have been less important in the early sound period. Comolli will refuse Mitry's explanations through technological changes (in this case film stock and lighting equipment), but tie it to a more profound, wide-ranging codic shift involving the possibility of guaranteeing cinema's reality-status by the voice as the expression of the human subject.

Thus, in "Technique and Ideology" Comolli sees such formal, stylistic, and codic options in filmmaking as interventions that may sustain, rebalance and/or contest the impression of reality. That is, they are engaged on the field of the lure.

***

Opponents of 1970s film theory often treated it as a monolithic discourse. By the 1980s, some of those affiliated with such different perspectives as the cultural studies movement and cognitivist film theory argued that 1970s film theory *tout court* constructed the spectator as "passive." In fact, such critical accounts rarely if ever thought through the complexities and difficulties of the active-passive distinction, whose genealogy includes theological accounts of the soul and free will. For Comolli, spectatorship and operations of cinema's ideological vocation are contradictory and complex, and his work could suggest another binary opposition must be surpassed, namely active *versus* passive.

From my own perspective, a weakness of some 1970s film theory lies elsewhere but, again, cannot be monolithically applied to the whole period. Some important and productive strands of 1970s theory in practice did not follow Comolli's refusal of the theory-history divide by intertwining theoretical argument with historical analysis. Perhaps the institutionalization of film studies in the university contributed to this. The breakthrough theoretical innovations of the 1970s also helped justify the distinctiveness of film studies, and the academy likes specialization. Conversely, academic film historians have since gone on to reconstruct the history of film with remarkable results, and continue to do so. But this sometimes occurred in a way that bracketed, or even posed itself against, film theory. Interestingly, the onset and diffusion of electronic and digital technologies into film history has stimulated new forms of overcoming the theory-history opposition, something that Comolli already announced as a necessity.

This brings us to the present. From the early 1970s, Comolli argued for the multiplicity and instability of the objects of film history grasped as theoretical concepts, and the non-identical character of theoretical concepts because they must respond to historical complexities and changes. This was connected to his insistence on the potential productivity of the lure (an idea which also was not always sustained in sectors of 1970s theory). These are principles that are sustained in "Cinema against Spectacle," even as the new work proposes that there have been some fundamental changes in the status of cinema as he had approached it after 1968.

Comolli understands films as now existing within a vast multimedia spectacle immersed in a universalizing commodification. He certainly remains admirably committed to critique and to a politics of the cinematic. But his account of the contemporary situation seems to deemphasize the Althusserian Marxism and Kristevan post-structuralism of 1968, while it incorporates other formulations in order to conceptualize and respond to this new media context, with references to figures such as Foucault, Deleuze ("societies of control"), Baudrillard, Rancière, and more. It also appears that the contemporary situation requires of critical thought that it conceive of cinema in somewhat different terms. All of these changes can be exemplified by the appearance of two theoretical concepts that were excluded from "Technique and Ideology."

First, there is alienation, a concept that has no presence of any consequence in "Technique and Ideology." It is true that at points Comolli himself now reads the critique of alienation back into his post-1968 writings, but in fact the term does not appear there. Indeed, there it would have been a theoretically problematic concept. The critique of alienation was foundational in the humanist Marxist tradition that Althusser attacked in the name of a theoretically non-humanist Marxism. But now, the need to develop critiques of universal commodification in the present-day global multimedia spectacle seems to have led Comolli to resuscitate the term. It is striking that not even all of the newer theorists cited in "Cinema against Spectacle" would necessarily embrace this concept, so Comolli's turn to it is an important decision on his part, responding to his perception of the new media context.

The second concept absent from Comolli's previous writings that informs "Cinema against Spectacle" is the concept of the spectacle, as derived from Guy Debord's situationist polemic, *Society of the Spectacle*. The term spectacle does not appear in its Debordian sense in "Technique and Ideology," even though Debord was certainly among the prominent references in the cultural politics of 1968. But again, Debord's definitions of capitalism as universal spectacle were grounded in a critique of universal commodification that appealed to the concept of alienation. Perhaps this is why Debord's concept of the spectacle was nowhere to be found in the Althusser-oriented "Technique and Ideology." In fact, this same absence of Debord was true of 1970s film theory generally.

If Comolli's sense of the contemporary media universe now leads him toward a Debordian notion of the spectacle, he nevertheless criticizes and diverges from Debord on the basis of one of his own central principles: the potential productivity of the impression of reality as lure. This idea does not lose any pertinence but, if anything, gains in critical importance. According to Comolli, Debord does not allow for the multiplicity and frictions that have always been central to cinema, its spectatorship, and its history. We can see their importance in "Cinema against Spectacle" by mentioning just one of its characterizations of the contemporary media spectacle, namely fragmentation. Fragmentation and synthesis constitute the cinema as a machine that produces illusions of movement and continuity, and they are basic to such fundamental filmic operations as editing and framing. How, then, should the cinematic fragmentation-synthesis interplay be deployed within the spectacle? For, according to Comolli, the spectacle works through intensive and constant fragmentation, an impossibly rapid, perpetual blizzard of commodified particles of the world. One of the formal problems for the politics of the cinematic thus becomes addressing the universalizing normalization of fragmentation. This problem leads Comolli to discussions of such fundamental filmmaking elements as framing and camera setups, and what he sees as the changed status of montage. Montage, he argues, could be positively critical and even utopian in earlier leftist filmmaking, but now it may too easily and unproblematically merge into the forms of contemporary spectacle. Thus, the problem for a political, critical cinema is no longer engaging and countering the artifices of the illusion of reality, but countering fragmentation. This changes and revivifies the realist function of cinema, whether fiction or documentary. Comolli here invokes contemporary filmmakers whose films use strategies that slow down and critique the fragmentation on which the spectacle is built, for example, through an emphasis on the engagement of the film with the human body, with a temporality, or with a location.

This is not to revert to a realist aesthetic, or a Bazinian account of the cinema, even if some comparisons are possible. It remains a matter of the impression of reality as lure, but that lure is now a field of critical potentiality. For Comolli, the political task of cinema has always been to work with the lure, against the lure, by staying open to its potential productivity. This is a principle he has consistently maintained, and it might serve as a starting point for rereading 1970s film theory and asking whether it has unexpected kinds of use value in the present. For it is a basis for the challenge Comolli puts forward about the place of cinema in the contemporary multimedia universe. To pose cinema against spectacle is to say that one must exploit regimes of belief and knowledge activated in cinema, in the contradictory processes and play between them.

This can be understood as a paradox, a subtlety, or a dialectic. In a certain sense, this *homme du cinéma* is now arguing that the productivity of the type of lure specific to cinema could be even more important in the contemporary world than after 1968, but now because of the newly positive, critical role it may allow cinema to play in the spectacle. Cinema is one of the components of the spectacle, but there remains the lesson of "Technique and Ideology": it is simultaneously a complex, historically shifting assemblage that we encounter and deploy as an apparatus. Comolli suggests that the multiplicity that constitutes cinema has once again resulted in an unexpected historical and critical turn, giving it new kinds of value in the sociopolitical present.

Introduction

Daniel Fairfax

Published in *Cahiers du cinéma* as the journal entered a politically radicalized phase following the events of May 1968, Jean-Louis Comolli's series of articles "Technique and Ideology" has few equals as far as its "canonical" status within the academic discipline of film studies is concerned. There may thus be no small irony that a work that was produced under the auspices of what Comolli himself has dubbed a "new iconoclasm" – the journal found itself marginalized both politically and within the film world, was excoriated for being "unreadable," and subjected all conventions and institutions it encountered to a bracing "ideological critique" – should be so seamlessly assimilated into the institutional behemoth of the contemporary university. But this irony is inherent to a field which itself only came to be established as such in the wake of the "Prague Spring of academia,"[1] and which was founded precisely on the basis of the structuralist (and later post-structuralist) recasting of theoretical discourse that took place during this historical moment. A more specific matter that is of concern for film and media theorists in the present day, however, is the fact that – as will be explained in greater detail below – the English version of the text that has made its way into this canon is at a distinct remove from Comolli's original work.

Appearing in six installments between May 1971 and September 1972, "Technique and Ideology" represents one of the most rigorous efforts to apply Althusserian Marxist theory to a historical analysis of the development of the cinema. With the claim that the cinema "owes its existence" to the "reciprocal reinforcement" of ideological and economic demands, Comolli engaged in debates with theoretical trends as diverse as Bazin's notion of the cinema's ontological realism, the traditional film historiography projects of Georges Sadoul and Jean Mitry, the "technicism" of Jean-Patrick Lebel, and the Marxism-of-a-different-shade of *Cinéthique*'s Gérard Leblanc and *Tel Quel*'s Marcelin Pleynet, and would carve out a line of reasoning that carefully distinguished itself from all of these approaches while at the same time deftly playing them off against each other.

---

1. The phrase is Dudley Andrew's. Cf. Dudley Andrew, "The 'Three Ages' of Cinema Studies and the Age to Come," *PMLA*, vol. 115 no. 3 (2000), p. 341. Grieveson and Wasson, meanwhile, caution against seeing 1968 as "the birth of the discipline," insisting on the fertile academic work carried out in the field before this moment. Cf. *Inventing Film Studies*, ed. Lee Grieveson and Haidee Wasson (Durham, NC: Duke University Press, 2008), pp. xv-xvi.

Comolli's work would quickly gain resonance within Anglophone film studies, and its translation into English and subsequent (partial) publication soon followed. Its central ideas thus ramified throughout a range of texts and theoretical currents during the 1970s, albeit in ways which were often remote from *Cahiers*' original theoretical conceptions. More recent decades, however, have been less favorable toward "Technique and Ideology." As the scholarly fortunes of "1970s film theory" waned,[2] so too did the standing of the *Cahiers* writers. In the 1980s and 1990s their work was subject to hostile repudiation,[3] while, at the same time, even those more sympathetic to their theoretical lineage admitted that it had undeniably entered into a "crisis."[4] Those clamorous debates may have since died down, but the result has only been to leave works such as "Technique and Ideology" in a state of relative silence. Obligatory reading in film studies departments it may still be, but only as a document of its time: to be looked back on with a mixture of "pride and embarrassment" (as Rodowick memorably put it[5]), and to remain in a frozen state, without much prospect for the types of productive re-readings or lines of research that the writings of a Bazin or a Benjamin have prompted.[6] Against this view, it will be maintained that Comolli's work does indeed warrant such creative exegesis, and it is the aim of the present volume to contribute to a change in this state of affairs.

At least some of the responsibility for this situation lies with the translation itself. Although indispensable for "Technique and Ideology" finding a wider readership in the English-speaking world, the existing translation by Diana Matias exhibits a number of shortcomings: working with a stylistically challenging text under precipitous conditions, the translator frequently has recourse to paraphrase and approximation. For the most part, the broader meaning of Comolli's articles comes through, but many of the subtleties of his text are lost. Furthermore, the drawbacks in the English version of the text are compounded by its publication history. Of the six installments, only the first four have found publication in English, and these have been scattered

---

2. This is the appellation adopted by Philip Rosen to denote the strand of film theory opened up by the work of *Cahiers* and *Cinéthique* in the late 1960s and early 1970s, with Rosen declaring, "Today it is possible to identify something we can call 1970s film theory." Cf., in addition to his preface in the present volume, Philip Rosen, "*Screen* and 1970s Film Theory," in *Inventing Film Studies*, ed. Grieveson and Wasson, *op. cit.*, p. 264.

3. Cf., in particular, *Post-Theory: Reconstructing Film Studies*, ed. David Bordwell and Noël Carroll (Madison: University of Wisconsin Press, 1996). Admittedly the focus of the texts in this volume is more on *Screen* and its legacy in English-language film theory than *Cahiers per se.*

4. Cf. D.N. Rodowick, *The Crisis of Political Modernism*, 2nd edition (Berkeley: University of California Press, 1993). Rodowick's influential account of "political modernism" will be further addressed below.

5. *Ibid.*, p. vii.

6. Of particular note here, with regard to Bazin's work, is the collection *Opening Bazin*, ed. Dudley Andrew and Hervé Joubert-Laurencin (Oxford: Oxford University Press, 2011), as well as Barnard's re-translation of a number of Bazin's key texts, cf. André Bazin, *What Is Cinema?*, trans. and ed. Timothy Barnard (Montreal: Caboose, 2009).

across a number of different anthologies.[7] *Cinema against Spectacle* thus presents, for the first time in English, Comolli's entire text, in a fresh, annotated translation which seeks to avoid the pitfalls of its existing English versions by conveying as faithfully as possible the substance and flavor of his original French.

Such a long necessary project gained added urgency in 2009, when Comolli himself returned to his own texts. While recognizing that they "have not ceased to shape my work,"[8] he confesses to not having read the articles since their original publication. In refreshing contrast to the legion of former radicals (in both France and elsewhere) who would subsequently repudiate their youthful "naïveté," Comolli maintains that the questions addressed in his original text are "still active today, 37 years later." The resulting book, *Cinéma contre spectacle*, thus comprises, as Tom Conley put it, "two panels of almost identical proportions":[9] a re-publication, in full and without any emendations, of "Technique et idéologie," and a theoretical reconsideration of its central argument from the standpoint of the present day, in light of the sweeping changes to the cinema and the world in the era of neo-liberal capitalism and media globalization, the full effects of which, in his view, were barely augured by the French intellectual left in the early 1970s.

Alongside these two texts, the present volume also includes a re-translation of the two-part text "Cinema/Ideology/Criticism" (an indispensable complement to "Technique and Ideology," but one which has suffered its own, perhaps more glaring, translation problems), extracts from the companion piece "Machines of the Visible," and a detailed filmography and bibliography of works by Comolli during his five decades of activity in the cinema. This introduction, meanwhile, will proceed to situate the original text within the twin contexts of, firstly, the historical development of *Cahiers du cinéma* and, secondly, the theoretical/political environment in which the journal intervened, before giving an overview and critical analysis of the arguments coursing through "Technique and Ideology." From that point, its translation history and reception in the English-speaking world will be explored, before "Technique and Ideology" will be related to Comolli's later work in both film theory and filmmaking.[10] Finally, the principles underpinning the current translation effort will be expounded. Together with an appended glossary of terms, this concluding section is intended to help the reader navigate through the lexical difficulties that a theoretical text of this nature poses.

---

7. A fuller account of the text's publication history follows below.

8. Cf. infra, p. 57.

9. Tom Conley, "Comolli Again," paper at Society for Cinema and Media Studies conference, New Orleans, March 2011.

10. For more on Comolli's biographical background, cf. the two-part interview recently published in *Senses of Cinema*, which serves as a pendant to this introduction. Jean-Louis Comolli, interviewed by Daniel Fairfax, "'Yes, we were utopians; in a way, I still am…': An Interview with Jean-Louis Comolli," *Senses of Cinema*, no. 62 and 64 (2012).

The primary impetus behind this undertaking, therefore, is not to entrench the already consecrated status of a landmark work, but to follow through on the invitation presented by Comolli's reprinting of the text in 2009, and "revisit" it in the true sense of the word. In doing so, Comolli beckons us to test out the force of the original propositions, to find out what remains valid and what has become outdated in them, and to think through their implications in original, groundbreaking ways. To put it simply: he invites us to *theorize* the cinema.

Historical Background

Truly coming to grips with the contents of "Technique and Ideology" is impossible without a familiarity with the historical context of the article: both that of France at large and, in what Althusser would call its "differential specificity,"[11] that of *Cahiers du cinéma* itself. This history is well-documented,[12] and Comolli makes ample reference to it in "Cinema against Spectacle." As such, only a bare outline need be given here. Founded in 1951 by Bazin and Jacques Doniol-Valcroze, *Cahiers* quickly gained renown not only for giving expression to Bazin's theories – later characterized as "idealist" by Comolli and his colleagues – but also, and more prominently, for fostering the critical maturation of those figures who would go on to form the core of the *nouvelle vague*, most notably (and in rough order of their "crossing over" to filmmaking): Claude Chabrol, François Truffaut, Jean-Luc Godard, Jacques Rivette and Éric Rohmer. After Bazin's death in 1958, stewardship of the journal was handed to Rohmer, his heir apparent. In the early 1960s, a new generation of young writers would gravitate toward the journal – including Comolli, Narboni and Jean-André Fieschi –

11. Louis Althusser et al., *Reading Capital*, trans. Ben Brewster (London: NLB, 1977), *passim*.

12. Two works focusing on the history of *Cahiers* have been released to date: Antoine de Baecque's two-volume, French-language account (*Cahiers du cinéma: Histoire d'une revue*, vol. I, "À l'assaut du cinéma," and II, "Cinéma, tours détours," Paris: Cahiers du cinéma, 1991); and Emilie Bickerton's more recent, and much briefer, exposition (*A Short History of Cahiers du cinéma* [London: Verso, 2009]). Both adopt a clear narrative line to the periods they cover, but with very different outlooks. Whereas de Baecque sees the journal's initial Bazinian mission as having been lost during the Marxist turn under Comolli and Narboni, only to be recovered with the later stewardship of Toubiana and Daney (his chronicle ends with Daney's departure in 1981), Bickerton views the journal as the "last modernist project," a vocation which continued from its founding in the 1950s up until the mid-1970s, at which point this outlook is progressively abandoned. To these accounts should be added the valuable introductions in the four-volume set of *Cahiers* articles published under the auspices of the BFI. Cf. *Cahiers du cinéma, The 1950s: Neo-Realism, Hollywood, New Wave*, ed. Jim Hillier (Cambridge, MA: Harvard University Press, 1985); *Cahiers du cinéma, 1960-1968: New Wave, New Cinema, Re-evaluating Hollywood*, ed. Jim Hillier (London: Routledge, 1986); *Cahiers du cinéma, 1969-1972: The Politics of Representation*, ed. Nick Browne (London: Routledge, 1990); and *Cahiers du cinéma, 1973-1978: History, Ideology, Cultural Struggle*, ed. David Wilson (London: Routledge, 2000). For a historical overview of the relationship between *Cahiers* (along with French film criticism more broadly) and the political situation of the late 1960s and 1970s, cf. Sylvia Harvey's peerless study *May '68 and Film Culture* (London: BFI, 1978).

and it was their dissatisfaction with the aesthetically conservative direction that *Cahiers* took under Rohmer which led to his ousting and replacement, as editor-in-chief, by Rivette. During this time the journal progressively opened itself up to the "new cinemas" blossoming in countries such as Poland, Czechoslovakia, Italy, Brazil and Japan, and tentatively explored radical currents of critical theory and artistic modernism – as exemplified by lengthy, if not always fruitful, interviews carried out with Roland Barthes, Claude Lévi-Strauss and Pierre Boulez. Rivette, however, always saw his position on the journal as a transitional one: by the time shooting started on his second feature film, *La Religieuse*, in 1965, the baton had been passed to Comolli, who was still in his early twenties at the time.[13] The banning of Rivette's Diderot-adaptation by the Gaullist government became a flashpoint for the journal, and through exposure to the work of Godard, Pasolini and Garrel, among others, their turn to the left had further deepened by 1968.

While fully participating in the protests against Langlois' dismissal from the Cinémathèque française in February, and the social upheaval of May (which included a general strike of the film industry and the convocation of the *États généraux du cinéma*), *Cahiers*' radicalism was still, at this time, a politically and theoretically eclectic one. Open to a wide range of ideas and influences, and not imposing an explicit line on its contributors, the journal was still operating in continuity with its immediate past, even while writers such as Jacques Aumont, Pascal Bonitzer and Jean-Pierre Oudart joined its ranks. "May" for *Cahiers*, therefore, came somewhat belatedly: in October 1969, with the publication of Comolli and Narboni's editorial "Cinema/Ideology/Criticism." Certainly, as Comolli and Narboni themselves recognized, some signs of a more pointedly Marxist orientation had manifested themselves in the months preceding the editorial: the commencement of the exhaustive, 15-month project to translate Eisenstein's writings into French, the theoretical underpinnings of articles such as the "Montage" roundtable (March 1969), Comolli's "Le détour par le direct" (February-April 1969) and Oudart's "La Suture" (April-May 1969), the attitudes expressed in reviews of films such as *Z* and *Shame*, and interviews with, among others, Glauber Rocha, Carmelo Bene and Fernando Solanas. But with its proclamation that "all films are political," and its stated aim of "attempt[ing] the elaboration and application of a critical theory of the cinema, a specific mode of apprehension of rigorously determined objects, with direct reference to the method of dialectical materialism,"[14] the editorial was incandescent enough to prompt the journal's then owner, media tycoon Daniel Filipacchi, to shut down *Cahiers* and attempt to replace the editorial board. Filipacchi's maneuver was thwarted, however: financial assistance from a range of former contributors allowed the journal to be

---

13. After six issues (160-165) as adjunct editor-in-chief, Comolli replaced Rivette with issue no. 166-167 (May-June 1965). Narboni officially joined him as co-editor in October 1968, replacing Jean-Louis Ginibre, whose position at the journal was purely titular in nature.

14. Cf. infra, p. 259.

bought out. After a four-month publication break, *Cahiers* made a triumphant return in March 1970.

The period between the journal's Marxist turn in 1969 and its near-collapse in 1973 tends to be painted as a homogeneous phase of political and aesthetic radicalism. In fact, *Cahiers* themselves, in an early act of retrospection, would distinguish between three broad stages during this time: a structuralist "moment" in 1968-1969, a period of alignment with the PCF (1970-1971), and an "anti-revisionist" turn toward Maoism from late 1971 onwards.[15] But it is more apt to see *Cahiers* as undergoing a state of constant, unremitting tumult during this period, such that texts were no sooner written than central aspects of their arguments would be discarded or politically rejected, and the traumas of these political contortions would leave long-term marks on the journal's writers. Beyond the broader political turmoil in France (with layers of radicalizing youth meeting with intense state repression from a sclerotic Gaullist state[16]), the impetus for this ongoing upheaval came from several quarters. The theoretical vicissitudes of *Cahiers' maîtres à penser*, the pressures of polemical combat with rival journals (whether film-specific, such as *Positif* and *Cinéthique*, or more broadly literary/cultural, such as *Tel Quel* and *La Nouvelle Critique*), and the pressure-cooker atmosphere imposed by their own urge to engage in a radically collectivized approach to intellectual work, all contributed to the journal's overarching state of permanent revolution. In light of these conditions, it is remarkable that this brief period gave rise to texts of the quality and density of "Technique and Ideology," Bonitzer's series "'Réalité' de la dénotation" and Serge Daney/Jean-Pierre Oudart's "Work, Reading, Pleasure," alongside "symptomatic readings" of films such as *Young Mr. Lincoln* (the template for so much later work in film analysis), *Morocco*, *La vie est à nous* and *Intolerance*.

Inevitably, the energy behind these efforts would dissipate. While the shift toward "Marxism-Leninism" initially yielded fertile results (such as an Althusserian analysis of the television show *À armes égales*, the influential comparative study of *Tout va bien* and *Coup pour coup*, and the continuation of "Technique and Ideology"), their politics soon led the *Cahiers* editors to an ascetic dogmatism, which led them to come close to the totalizing rejection of the cinema that they had previously been so careful to avoid. With its texts smothered in *gauchiste* jargon,[17] the journal hemorrhaged readers and exhausted its funds, while its publication frequency decreased

15. Cf. "Intervention à Avignon: premier bilan critique," *Cahiers du cinéma*, no. 241 (1972), pp. 7-16.

16. In accounts of the aftermath of May '68, state repression of left-wing activists tends to be glossed over. In fact, between 1968 and 1972, more than 1000 militants were imprisoned, for "crimes" such as publicly selling banned newspapers. For more on the far left in this era, cf. Kristin Ross, *May 1968 and Its Afterlives* (Chicago: University of Chicago Press, 2002); Christophe Bourseiller, *Les Maoïstes: la folle histoire des gardes rouges français* (Paris: Plon, 1996).

17. A hallmark of this era are the abbreviated terms "GRCPC" for the Chinese cultural revolution and "P'C'F" for the French Communist Party, which recur with incantatory regularity.

such that it had become a monthly in name only – only four issues were published in 1973. With efforts devoted to the establishment of the "*Front culturel*" (an ostensibly broad-based grouping of militants active in the cultural arena), focus shifted away from film theory, and even the cinema as a whole came to be neglected – by this time, only the work of Godard/Gorin and Straub/Huillet still found favor in the pages of *Cahiers*.[18] The texts produced during this period may find their defenders, and they undoubtedly have significance as historical documents, but most will agree that their doctrinaire *langue de bois* has not aged well.

The historical irony was that *Cahiers'* political line had hardened at the precise moment that the far left in France went into decline, with the May 1972 funeral of Maoist militant Pierre Overney marking, as Althusser recognized, a symbolic moment of closure.[19] When the 1973 Avignon conference organized by *Cahiers* in support of their *Front culturel* project met with an underwhelming response, the sense of failure was palpable. Comolli and Narboni distanced themselves from the editorial board, with Daney and Serge Toubiana taking over and leading *Cahiers* gradually back toward the mainstream. While the journal's physical survival was thereby ensured, the political legacy of the "*années rouges*" was progressively diminished. And whereas Narboni stayed within the orbit of the journal for much of the 1970s, subsequently assuming responsibility for its publishing arm, for Comolli the break was more definitive, and for the most part his energies would henceforth be directed toward filmmaking.

Theoretical Context

When asked why *Cahiers* embarked on a rapprochement with the PCF at a time when the party's attitude toward the May '68 protests seemed to have conclusively proven its political regression, Narboni answered with a single word: "Althusser."[20] More than any other figure, Althusser was *the* theoretical mentor for the post-1968 *Cahiers*, and, indeed, many of the other influences on their work at the time – Barthes, Metz, Lacan, Derrida, Kristeva – were either seen with or critiqued through

18. Bonitzer would later state, "During these years, in the most hardened, dogmatic, closed-off militant period, as well as in more open periods, we remained connected to the cinema by not letting go of the red thread that was Godard." Cf. Pascal Bonitzer, "Nos années non-légendaires" (1998), in *Cinéma 68*, ed. Antoine de Baecque, Stéphane Bouquet and Emmanuel Burdeau (Paris: Cahiers du cinéma, 2008), p. 152. As early as February 1971, the journal's editorial diary noted: "We no longer go to the cinema, which is radically true." Cited in: De Baecque, *Histoire d'une revue*, vol. II., *op. cit.*, p. 228.

19. Althusser trenchantly referred to Overney's funeral as the "burial of the extreme left." Cf. Louis Althusser, *The Future Lasts a Long Time*, trans. Richard Veasey (London: Chatto & Windus, 1993), p. 356. Godard similarly categorized the procession as "the last embers of May 68." Cf. Jean-Luc Godard, *Introduction à une véritable histoire du cinéma* (Paris: Albatros, 1980), p. 159.

20. Private conversation, February 2010, in Paris.

an Althusserian optic. This influence was so strong that it continued well after the journal rejected the philosopher's political strategy of reforming the PCF from within, and it can be singularly felt in "Technique and Ideology."

Althusser's role in retrieving French Marxist theory from the sterility of Stalinist dogma can hardly be overstated. His senior position at the École normale supérieure transformed the elite educational institution into a hub of radical critical theory, with Foucault, Rancière, Badiou, Macherey and Balibar numbering among his pupils, along with many of the most prominent *gauchiste* militants of the post-68 period,[21] and his texts allowed for numerous points of intersection between the "Marxist classics" and contemporary French thought, especially Lacanian psychoanalysis.[22] The *Reading Capital* project – whose seminars sought to engage in a "symptomatic reading" of Marx's text, analyzing both its "*vues*" and its "*bévues*" (its insights and its oversights) – included a lengthy outline of his concept of "differential historical temporality,"[23] a notion which Comolli would notably incorporate into the theoretical armory of "Technique and Ideology." In the contemporaneous work *For Marx*, meanwhile, Althusser would borrow the notion of the "epistemological break" from Gaston Bachelard to distinguish between the philosophical writings of the young Marx and the "scientific" nature of his later work.

It is, however, above all for his reworking of the Marxist concept of ideology that Althusser is most well-known, and where his influence on *Cahiers* is most palpable. While a theory of ideology can be found in Marx's writings, the relevant passages stem mostly from his early work, in particular the posthumously published 1846 text *The German Ideology*. In this lacerating assault on the idealist philosophy of the Hegelian tradition, Marx proclaimed that:

> We do not set out from what men say, imagine, conceive, nor from men as narrated, thought of, imagined, conceived, in order to arrive at men in the flesh. We set out from real, active men, and on the basis of their real life-process we demonstrate the development of the ideological reflexes and echoes of this life-process. The phantoms formed in the human brain are also, necessarily, sublimates of

---

21. Notably, the Union de jeunesse communiste marxiste-léniniste (UJCM-L) was largely composed of ENS students. An early Maoist organization, established in the mid-1960s and responsible for the journal *Cahiers marxistes-léninistes*, the UJCM-L collapsed after 1968, but many of the later Maoist organizations were founded by former members of group.

22. Althusser was instrumental in bringing Lacan to the ENS in 1965, and stridently argued for the theoretical compatibility of Marxism and Freudian psychoanalysis. The Althusser-Lacan nexus was mainly a one-sided phenomenon, however, with Lacan never evincing a particularly strong interest in Marxist theory. Cf. Joe Valente, "Lacan's Marxism, Marxism's Lacan (from Žižek to Althusser)," in *The Cambridge Companion to Lacan*, ed. Jean-Michel Rabaté (Cambridge: Cambridge University Press, 2003), pp. 153-172.

23. Cf. Althusser et al., *Reading Capital*, *op. cit.*, pp. 99-106 and *passim*.

their material life-process, which is empirically verifiable and bound to material premises.[24]

A little earlier in the same work, Marx would memorably compare the function of ideology to the workings of a *camera obscura* (a significant predecessor to the film camera), musing: "If in all ideology men and their circumstances appear upside-down as in a *camera obscura*, this phenomenon arises just as much from their historical life-process as the inversion of objects on the retina does from their physical life-process."[25] Along with the economic base/ideological superstructure dichotomy (which only appears cursorily in Marx's own writings), these comparisons – presenting ideology as the reflex, echo, phantom or sublimate of reality, resulting in an "inversion" of historical life-processes – have been widely acknowledged as inadequate for a Marxist theory of ideology, with Althusser explicitly stating "*The German Ideology* does offer us [...] an explicit theory of ideology, but... it is not Marxist,"[26] and dubbing it instead a positivist and historicist thesis akin to the pre-Freudian understanding of dreams.

In the texts collected in *For Marx*, Althusser would seek to replace the base/superstructure "topography" of orthodox Marxism's account of ideology with a relationship of "overdetermination," drawing above all from Freud's analysis of the dream-work in *The Interpretation of Dreams*.[27] It was in this anthology that he would also make the first attempt at a definition of ideology. In "Marxism and Humanism," ideology is viewed as "a system (with its own logic and rigor) of representations (images, myths, ideas or concepts, depending on the case) endowed with a historical existence and role within a given society," and is seen as distinct from science in that "in it the practico-social function is more important than the theoretical function (function as knowledge)."[28] Importantly, Althusser stresses that ideology is "an organic part of

---

24. Karl Marx, *The German Ideology*, in *The Collected Works of Marx and Engels*, vol. V (New York: International Publishers, 1975), p. 36.

25. *Ibid.* This analogy with the *camera obscura* would be the source of a heated rebuke of *Cinéthique* by *Cahiers* in the second part of "Cinema/Ideology/Criticism." Cf. infra, pp. 269-270.

26. Louis Althusser, "Ideology and Ideological State Apparatuses: Notes towards an Investigation," in Althusser, *Lenin and Philosophy and Other Essays*, trans. Ben Brewster (New York: Monthly Review Press, 1971), p. 107.

27. Louis Althusser, "Contradiction and Overdetermination," in Althusser, *For Marx*, trans. Ben Brewster (London: Verso, 1979), pp. 87-128. In addition to Freud, this concept owes a great debt to Mao's text "On Contradiction," for which Comolli has also noted an abiding fondness. Cf. Mao Tse-tung, "On Contradiction" (1937), in *Mao: On Practice and Contradiction*, ed. Slavoj Žižek (London: Verso, 2007), pp. 67-102. Derrida would later declare that "everything Althusser says about overdetermination satisfies me more than the rest – alas, this means that it satisfies me to the detriment of almost all the rest, in particular the 'in the last instance' discourse which I consider the metaphysical anchoring of the whole enterprise." Jacques Derrida and Michael Sprinker, "Politics and Friendship: An Interview with Jacques Derrida," in *Althusser's Legacy*, ed. E. Ann Kaplan and Michael Sprinker (London: Verso, 1993), p. 204.

28. Louis Althusser, "Marxism and Humanism," in *For Marx*, *op. cit.*, p. 231.

every social totality,"[29] such that even a classless society can not hope to be entirely disembarrassed of ideology. Instead, the difference between the divided societies of today and a putative communist future will be that:

> In a class society ideology is the relay whereby, and the element in which, the relation between men and their conditions of existence is settled to the profit of the ruling class. In a classless society ideology is the relay whereby, and the element in which, the relation between men and their conditions of existence is lived to the profit of all men.[30]

This conception of ideology will be substantially revised in the wake of May '68, possibly under the influence of Althusser's "*maoïsant*" students at the ENS.[31] In a text that exists in three substantially different versions, the most well-known of which was a short article published in the PCF-aligned journal *La Pensée* in June 1970,[32] Althusser posited the existence of "Ideological State Apparatuses," which represent the material embodiment of ideology, and whose social function within class-based societies is to ensure the unimpeded reproduction of the labor power of the working classes through their "submission to the rules of the established order."[33] In the same text, ideology is seen to be grounded in the "interpellation" of the individual as a subject (a concept echoing Lacan's notion of specular recognition), and is defined as the "imaginary relationship of individuals to their real conditions of existence."[34] Importantly for the contemporaneous debates on the ideological nature of the cinema in which Comolli intervened, Althusser also draws a strict terminological distinction between "ideolog*ies*" in the specific, historically grounded sense, and "ideology in general," which, in accord with his statements in "Marxism and Humanism," is viewed as eternal and omnipresent. Paradoxically, Althusser can thus maintain that, in its generalized form, "ideology *has no outside* (for itself)," but that, at the same time, "*it is nothing but outside* (for science and reality)."

29. *Ibid.*, p. 232.
30. *Ibid.*, p. 235-236.
31. For more on this, cf. Jason Barker, *Alain Badiou: A Critical Introduction* (London: Pluto, 2002).
32. The first version of the text is a 150-page manuscript composed in early 1969. Although never published, it is currently accessible at the archives of the Institut Mémoires de l'édition contemporaine in Caen. Along with the *La Pensée* article (abridged from this manuscript), an augmented version of the text was posthumously published as *Sur la reproduction* (Paris: PUF, 1995; translated as *On the Reproduction of Capitalism: Ideology and Ideological State Apparatuses*, trans. Geoffrey Goshgarian [London: Verso, 2014]). The initial manuscript was circulating among far left circles before the *La Pensée* article was published, and formed the basis for the 1969 Groupe Dziga Vertov film *Luttes en Italie*, but Comolli affirms that his first exposure to Althusser's text was with its journal publication (private communication, September 2013).
33. Althusser, "Ideology and ISAs," *op. cit.*, p. 89.
34. *Ibid.*, p. 109

The role of art in Althusserian theory, particularly with regards to its position within the science/ideology dichotomy, is a vexed issue. In several moments in "On the Materialist Dialectic," "Marxism and Humanism," and "Ideology and Ideological State Apparatuses," Althusser seems unambiguously to place art within the sphere of ideology, or, alternatively, as part of the "cultural ISA." Prompted by early texts by Alain Badiou and Pierre Macherey pleading for the "autonomy of the aesthetic process," however, he would offer an alternative viewpoint in "A Letter on Art in Reply to André Dastre."[35] Here, Althusser explicitly rejects a standpoint which would rank what he terms "authentic art" among the ideologies. At the same time, however, he views art as being unable to produce knowledge of reality in the scientific sense. Instead, the role of the art work is to "make us *see* and therefore give to us in the form of '*seeing*,' '*perceiving*' and '*feeling*' (which is not the form of *knowing*) the ideology from which it is born, in which it bathes, from which it detaches itself as art, and to which it alludes."[36] Novelists such as Tolstoy, Balzac and Solzhenitsyn thus "make us 'perceive' (but not know) in some sense *from the inside*, by an *internal distance*, the very ideology in which they are held."[37]

Rodowick asserts that the critical theory *Cahiers* developed "privileged Althusser's work on epistemology and ideology at the expense of his and Pierre Macherey's writings on art,"[38] but this ignores both the fact that Macherey (and Badiou) was cited in *Cahiers* on multiple occasions, and that the writings of Comolli and his *confrères* would exhibit contradictions similar to those of their Althusserian mentors. He is nonetheless fully justified on one point: whereas Althusser, Macherey and Badiou largely restricted themselves to commenting on works of literature from the bourgeois realist canon (Tolstoy, Balzac, Dostoyevsky), the primary focus for *Cahiers* – valuable work on classical Hollywood films notwithstanding – would come to be works of what Rodowick has called "epistemological modernism": whether the Soviet avant-gardes (Eisenstein, Vertov) or their more contemporary equivalents. For this side of their work, the influence of *Tel Quel*'s Philippe Sollers – and literary theorists close to him such as Julia Kristeva, Marcelin Pleynet and Jean-Louis Baudry – became far more significant than that of Althusser. Broadly speaking, if Althusser was key to

---

35. Louis Althusser, "A Letter on Art in Reply to André Dastre" (April 1966), in *Lenin and Philosophy, op. cit.*, pp. 151-156. Cf. also "Cremonini, Painter of the Abstract" (August 1966), in *Lenin and Philosophy, op. cit.*, pp. 157-166. By June 1970, Althusser would state that these texts were "already old" and subject to an "internal evolution and displacement giving rise to the new Theses" of his later writings, including the "Ideology and ISAs" article ("Foreword," *Lenin and Philosophy, op. cit.*, p. xv). For the Macherey and Badiou texts, cf. Pierre Macherey, *Pour une théorie de la production littéraire* (Paris: Maspero, 1966), translated as *A Theory of Literary Production*, trans. Geoffrey Wall (London: Routledge, 1978); Alain Badiou, "L'autonomie du processus esthétique," *Cahiers marxistes-léninistes*, no. 12-13 (1966), pp. 77-89.

36. Althusser, "A Letter on Art," *op. cit.*, p. 152.

37. *Ibid.*

38. Rodowick, pp. 82-83.

Cahiers' rapprochement with PCF-aligned intellectuals in 1969, Sollers was decisive in their vitriolic break with the party over the course of 1971. But while the shared political outlook of *Tel Quel*, *Cinéthique* and *Cahiers* would, during this time, lead them to form united fronts against common "enemies" (whether *La Nouvelle Critique* or *Positif*), this would not prevent the journals from engaging in bitter polemics against each other,[39] and in retrospect *Tel Quel*'s turn to Maoism would prove to be far more playfully ironic than that of either *Cahiers* or *Cinéthique*.

Althusser and Sollers were, however, merely two components of the wide range of theoretical influences operative for *Cahiers* at the time. While the high-water mark for the influence of semiotics on film theory had already passed by the time that "Technique and Ideology" was written, Christian Metz and Roland Barthes were still privileged interlocutors for *Cahiers*, and Comolli continues to avow his great debt to Metz to the present day. Lacan, who was actively presenting his "Séminaires" at the ENS at the time, was a formative figure for many of the writers at the journal – Oudart, Bonitzer and Pierre Baudry in particular – and would become even more central when their embryonic theoretical concepts were exported to Anglophone academia under the guise of the "psychoanalytic paradigm" of film theory. Beyond this, figures as diverse as Derrida, Bataille, Brecht, Benjamin and the Russian formalists were all influential for *Cahiers* during this time, while the spectral presence of theorists such as Guy Debord and Theodor W. Adorno can be felt in certain texts, despite their complete absence as explicit points of reference.[40] Rather than amalgamating them into a homogeneous theoretical stew – or the "SLAB" of Bordwell's polemic against the strand of film theory that took inspiration from *Cahiers*[41] – the writers at *Cahiers* unstintingly wrestled with the contradictions and discords produced by the intermingling of these different lines of thinking, many of which were still in a state of organic gestation at the time that they were taken up by the journal. Thus, rather than generating a critical output that conformed to a rigid, pre-established editorial line, this openness to the vacillations of critical theory yielded a turbulent maelstrom of theoretical activity.

Perhaps the most convulsive element within this melting pot comes from an unexpected quarter: André Bazin. It is a cliché of film studies that the *Cahiers* of the Comolli/Narboni era was unambiguously anti-Bazinian – that, so to speak, the journal's spiritual "father" was subject to a violent Œdipal rejection.[42] Against this view,

39. On one occasion this was elicited by *Cahiers*' common work on Soviet montage with the newly founded journal *Change*, edited by the discontented former *Tel Quel* contributor Jean-Pierre Faye. Cf. "Cinema/Ideology/Critique (II): On Criticism at Its Critical Point," infra.

40. The affinities between *Cahiers*' thinking and that of Debord and Adorno are now freely acknowledged by Comolli. Cf. infra, pp. 49-51, 100-102, 107.

41. The acronym stands for Saussure-Lacan-Althusser-Barthes. Cf. David Bordwell, "Historical Poetics of Cinema," Georgia State Literary Studies, no. 3 (1989), pp. 369-398.

42. Alternatively, Dudley Andrew likens the relationship to Brutus turning on Caesar. ("Foreword," in André Bazin, *What Is Cinema?*, vol. II [Berkeley: University of California Press, 2004], p.

we should have no hesitation in declaring that the outlook of the later *Cahiers* was *profoundly determined* by the journal's Bazinian heritage, and that it was this legacy that was the underlying point of distinction between *Cahiers*, on the one hand, and its rivals (such as *Cinéthique*) or epigones (such as *Screen*), on the other hand. A belief in the cinema's fundamental relationship with the real – no matter how overlaid with skepticism toward the ideological uses to which it is put – is what led *Cahiers* to seek out the productive fault lines in their favored works from the auteurist canon, rather than reject them outright as *Cinéthique* did.[43] Furthermore, the contemporary filmmakers they held up as paragons of a "materialist cinema" – Godard, Straub/Huillet, Garrel, Rivette, Jancsó – can themselves be seen as fundamentally Bazinian in their aesthetic convictions.

It is true that the later *Cahiers*' struggles with this theoretical heritage often took the form of a repudiation of Bazin, and particularly his purported "idealism," which at times bordered on hysterical excess.[44] Just as often, however, they opt for a guarded defense of the journal's founder: notably, in his review of *Othon*, "La vicariance du pouvoir," Narboni will claim that Straub/Huillet's practice operates a "displacement" of Bazin's ideas in "Théâtre et cinéma," one that represents "the essential *almost nothing* that separates idealism, in one of its most coherent manifestations, from materialism."[45] Similarly, while Bazin is one of the manifold polemical targets of "Technique and Ideology," Comolli invariably adopts a favorable tone toward his predecessor – certainly to a greater degree than any of his other adversaries – and approvingly quotes Lenin that "intelligent idealism is more intelligent than stupid materialism."[46] In the end, what Serge Daney would, in 1990, define as the *Cahiers* "line" is just as valid for its foundations under Bazin as it is for the journal in its Marxist phase: "that the cinema has a fundamental relationship with the real, and that the real is not what is represented – and that's final."[47] It is telling, moreover,

---

xx). Perhaps a more apt historical parallel would be Marx's repudiation of Hegel. Although Marx spared some his most heated vitriol for Hegel's work (especially in his early writings), few would contest the deeply Hegelian nature of his thinking, a debt which was recognized in more conciliatory terms later in his life.

43. Cf., for instance, Gérard Leblanc, "Bazin, Welles et la RKO," *Cinéthique*, no. 6 (1970), pp. 27-32.

44. Cf., in particular, Pascal Bonitzer and Serge Daney, "L'écran du fantasme," *Cahiers du cinéma*, no. 236-237 (1972), pp. 30-41. This binomial article was given the prefatory heading "Les théories idéalistes du cinéma: André Bazin" in the issue's table of contents.

45. Jean Narboni, "La vicariance du pouvoir," *Cahiers du cinéma*, no. 224 (1970), p. 45. Translated as: "Vicarious Power," trans. Leigh Hafrey, in *Cahiers du cinéma, 1969-1972*, ed. Browne, *op. cit.*, p. 156. Pascal Bonitzer similarly describes Bazin as a "'theorist,' who, although he is an idealist, nonetheless posed problems in such a fashion that it is urgent to re-mark them on a materialist basis" and claims that the beginnings of this work can be found in both Narboni's article and "Technique and Ideology." Cf. "Ciné-Forum," *Cahiers du cinéma*, no. 230 (1971), p. 61.

46. Cf. infra. This citation, taken from Lenin's *Philosophical Notebooks* (where Lenin is speaking with reference to Hegel), would support the analogy between Bazin/the later *Cahiers* and Hegel/Marx proposed in footnote 42.

47. Serge Daney, *L'Exercice a été profitable, monsieur* (Paris: POL, 1993), p. 301.

that virtually all the *Cahiers* writers of this period would later recognize their debt to Bazin, with Comolli himself aptly describing his relationship with Bazin as "an affinity which comes from an opposition, that is what is interesting. In trying to critique Bazin I ended up very close to him."[48]

The Argument of "Technique and Ideology"

The contours of the argument developed by Comolli in the six installments of "Technique and Ideology" must be understood within the context not only of the broader theoretical framework of *Cahiers*, but also with respect to the specific debates into which he intended the series to be an intervention. The primary impetus for the commencement of the series was the publication of a parallel series of articles by Jean-Patrick Lebel under the name of "Cinéma et idéologie" in issues no. 34, 35, 37 and 41 of *La Nouvelle Critique*, which were then collated and swiftly published by Éditions sociales (a PCF-owned publishing house) in May 1971. *Cahiers* perceived Lebel's text – and its heavy promotion within the PCF's cultural organs – as an unequivocal rebuff to itself, *Tel Quel* and *Cinéthique*, lumped together as the "ideological current" of cultural theory.[49] Against an emphasis on the ideological determination of the cinema's "base apparatus" (to use Jean-Louis Baudry's term), Lebel strains to defend its scientific underpinnings: both in terms of the actual machinery involved in the creation of cinematic images, and in the epistemological value of the images produced. It is against this position – seen as belonging to a "technicist discourse" – that Comolli directs his introductory comments, but while at this point (May 1971) he refrains from delving into the deeper political divisions subtending the conceptual antagonism with Lebel, these would come out into the open later in the year.

In its November 1971 issue, *Cahiers* published Pascal Bonitzer's article "Fétichisme de la technique" (part of a series of texts by the writer which can be seen as a valuable companion piece to "Technique and Ideology") and the editorial statement "Cinéma/idéologie/politique: Poretta Terme (2)," both of which explicitly label Lebel's text "revisionist" – the common term used by French Maoists to describe the pur-

48. Cf. Jean-Louis Comolli, "'Yes, we were utopians; in a way, I still am...' (Part 1)", *op. cit.* Needless to say, the complex relationship between Bazin and the later *Cahiers* requires a much more detailed discussion than is possible here.

49. Lebel's work, indeed, seems to have largely gone down in the history of film theory as the straw man for Comolli's argument. One of the few English-language texts to seriously take his ideas into account (or even to have evinced any signs of reading him directly), nonetheless ends up siding with Lebel over Comolli on a number of questions. Cf. James Spellerberg, "Technology and Ideology in the Cinema," *Quarterly Review of Film Studies*, vol. 2 no. 3 (1977), repr. in *Film Theory and Criticism: Introductory Readings*, ed. Gerald Mast and Marshall Cohen, 3rd edition (Oxford: Oxford University Press, 1985), pp. 761-775.

ported political bankruptcy of the PCF.[50] The interim period had been marked by the flashpoint ignited by the prohibition on selling the book *De la Chine* (a glowing account of the cultural revolution written by the Italian journalist Maria-Antonietta Maccocchi) at the PCF's annual *L'Humanité* festival. Enraged, *Tel Quel* used the ban as a pretext to launch its "anti-revisionist" *Mouvement de juin 71*, and by the time of its December 1971-February 1972 issue, *Cahiers* was openly declaring its affiliation to the Maoist strand of Marxism-Leninism.[51]

The most obvious counterpoint to Lebel's book, however, was not a *Cahiers* text, but an interview given by the *Tel Quel* editors Marcelin Pleynet and Jean Thibaudeau to *Cinéthique* no. 3 (dating from April 1969), in which Pleynet unambiguously proclaimed that "the cinematic apparatus is a properly ideological apparatus, it is an apparatus which diffuses bourgeois ideology, even before diffusing anything else," and highlighted the role of *Quattrocento* perspective in the cinema's prevailing representational system to support his case.[52] The comments provoked a rash of theoretical texts on the pages of both *Cinéthique* and *Cahiers*, but it must be stressed that the latter journal *never* unequivocally endorsed the theoretical viewpoint underpinning Pleynet's comments: that the ideological determination of the cinematic apparatus inevitably leads the cinema to regurgitating bourgeois ideology, and that the only viable alternative available to filmmakers, as the *Cinéthique* editors suggested, is to opt for "mutism" or cinematic self-reflexivity. In their October 1969 editorial, Comolli and Narboni uphold a subtly different stance, one more in accord with Althusserian theory. The *Cahiers* editors' emphasis is not on the cinema's role as an ideological apparatus, creating a distorted view of the world in accord with the dominant ideology; rather, they stress that *reality itself* is "entirely ideological," and that it is thus the "vague, unformulated, untheorized, unthought world of the dominant ideology" which cinematic instruments capture.[53] Hence, while the vast majority of films may well "carry forward" ideology "without any gaps or distortions," Comolli and Narboni argue that a key aspect of their critical function will be to highlight those works – whether classical, modernist, avant-garde or militant films – capable of provoking a "discrepancy or a rupture with [the cinema's] ideological function," one which for the

---

50. Pascal Bonitzer, "Fétichisme de la technique: la notion de 'plan'," *Cahiers du cinéma*, no. 233 (1971), pp. 4-10; Pascal Bonitzer, Jean-Louis Comolli and Jean Narboni, "Cinéma/idéologie/politique: Poretta Terme (2)," *Cahiers du cinéma*, no. 233 (1971), pp. 46-47.

51. For the avowal of this political turn, cf. "Politique et lutte idéologique de classes: Intervention 1," *Cahiers du cinéma*, no. 234-235 (1971-72), pp. 4-12.

52. Marcelin Pleynet and Jean Thibaudeau, "Economique-formelle-idéologique," *Cinéthique*, no. 3 (1969), pp. 7-14. The ideological nature of the perspectival code dominant in post-Renaissance Western systems of representation was a major area of theoretical work for the *Cahiers* writers, who were markedly influenced by the work of Pierre Francastel and Jean Louis Schefer on this issue, and is a central preoccupation of "Technique and Ideology."

53. Cf. infra, p. 254.

most part takes place on the level of the signifier, in a film's formal operations, and only secondarily in its explicit content.[54]

Much the same viewpoint is expressed in "Technique and Ideology." In the opening installment of the series, Comolli rejects the basis of Pleynet's argument just as thoroughly as he does that of Lebel, and points out that both writers metonymically substitute the camera for the cinematic apparatus as a whole, thereby occluding other, less openly visible aspects of the cinematic signifying process (such as color grading and sound mixing). Instead, Comolli argues that a "materialist theory of the cinema" must "draw out both the ideological 'heritage' of the camera (as much as its 'scientific heritage,' the two, as we shall see, are not in any way exclusive of each other) [...] and the ideological investments which have been made in the camera."[55] Comolli thus treads a fine line of argumentation: while he can agree with Pleynet that "the code of *perspectiva artificialis* has acted as a repressive system"[56] he will later approvingly quote Kristeva that "to substitute ideology for the signifier is [...] not only a theoretical error, but it also leads to a blockage of the work specific to the cinema, which comes to be replaced by discourses on its ideological function."[57]

What may appear as a contradictory argument can perhaps be clarified with recourse to two Althusserian concepts. The first is the distinction between ideologies in the specific, historically determinate sense, and ideology more generally, as that which "human societies secrete [...] as the very element and atmosphere indispensable to their historical respiration and life."[58] The second is Althusser's concept of overdetermination: that is, the fact that any given situation is "complexly-structurally-unevenly determined" by the structural totality.[59] Reading Comolli in the light of Althusser, then, the cinema is historically *overdetermined* by bourgeois ideology,[60]

54. Idem. This stress on the ability of a film to create discrepancies or ruptures with the dominant ideology – even beyond the intentions of the filmmaker – led to a tacit privileging of the *critical work* done on a film, over any quest to find its ultimate underlying meaning or intended ideological function. Not only did such an outlook sharply differentiate the *Cahiers* writers from their *Cinéthique* counterparts – who largely refrained from critical re-readings of canonical films – it also placed them much more integrally in the journal's own hermeneutic lineage.

55. Cf. infra, p. 153.

56. Cf. infra, p. 165.

57. Cf. infra, p. 186, fn. 44. The quote comes from Julia Kristeva, "Cinéma: pratique analytique, pratique révolutionnaire," *Cinéthique*, no. 9-10 (1971), pp. 71-79. Comolli notes that although the interview was published in *Cinéthique*, Kristeva's comments also seemed to be *aimed* at *Cinéthique*. Similarly, a notice in issue no. 229 of *Cahiers* speaks of the *Cinéthique* issue as a "juxtaposition of irreconcilable texts." Cf. "Cinéthique 9/10," *Cahiers du cinéma*, no. 229 (1971), p. 54.

58. Althusser, "Marxism and Humanism," *op. cit.*, p. 232. In the same text, Althusser ridicules the "utopian idea of a world in which ideology (not just one of its historical forms) would disappear without trace, to be replaced by science," and specifically opposes the notion "that art could merge with knowledge or become 'everyday life'." *Ibid.*

59. Louis Althusser, "On the Materialist Dialectic," in *For Marx*, *op. cit.*, p. 209.

60. Indeed, in a later editorial these are precisely the terms in which the argument of "Technique and Ideology" is presented. Cf. "Politique et lutte idéologique de classes: Intervention 1," *op. cit.*, p. 6.

but this by no means entails that film is by its very nature an idealist phenomenon unwaveringly diffusing this selfsame ideology. As such, his argument can be summarized with the following passage:

> If we are in agreement with Lebel in refusing to brand the cinema with a "natural ideological taint," we do not do so in order to conceal, behind an inconsistent "scientific basis," the fact that it is under the effects of an economic demand – that is, within ideology and as an instrument of ideology – that the cinema is progressively imagined, made and purchased.[61]

From this point on, Comolli will shift the focus of his text from a theoretical discussion of the cinematic apparatus to a historical overview of the evolution of the cinema. Lebel and Pleynet are abandoned as polemical antagonists, to be replaced by the historical writings of Bazin, Mitry, Sadoul and Leblanc. But it is also at this stage that Comolli's text becomes more fragmentary and, at times, disjointed. While it generally maintains an internal coherency, the contours of "Technique and Ideology" are not always smooth: areas of investigation are foreshadowed but never carried through,[62] abrupt swerves in emphasis occur, and, most notably, the entire series fizzles out: after appearing in five out of the six issues between May and December 1971, a nine-month hiatus intervenes before the sixth "episode" is belatedly published, by which time the journal has radically altered its format. Moreover, its new-found preoccupation with forming a "cultural front" with other revolutionary militants had rendered a discussion of technical changes in the early period of film history rather out of place. A "to be continued" caps off the sixth part of the series, but the promised sequel would, until "Cinema against Spectacle," never materialize.[63]

Nonetheless, the discussions included in these segments – the bulk of which are absent from the prevailing version of the text's English translation – are of a rare theoretical perspicacity. Rejecting both the "idealist" account of film history present in Bazin (the notion that the cinema comes to realize an "ancient dream of humanity") and the technicist/empiricist motivations for technological change that prepon-

---

61. Cf. infra, p. 169.

62. Notably, Comolli announces early in the text that he will focus his attention on two technical procedures residing on the "invisible" side of filmmaking – color grading and sound mixing – but this never eventuates. He similarly moots a planned detailed commentary on Metz's film analysis that is never realized.

63. Of the development of the series, Comolli writes: "The 'to be continued' is a sort of personal signature which interrupts the texts while letting the reader know that they have not been finished. Of course, fatigue, political events and the break-up of the group interrupted the series. But it developed in an unplanned, organic fashion. What still remained to be written was doubtless beyond my capacities, and I feel that 'Cinema against Spectacle' resumes and, on more than one point, completes the text left 'to be continued' 40 years earlier. In any case, this was my project." (Private communication, September 2013).

derate in Mitry's *History*, Comolli hues closely to his argument that the transformations of film technique are the result of the intertwining of the economic and ideological requirements of the governing social order (namely, capitalism, and its accompanying systems of representation). In succession, his argument takes in the birth of the cinema, the advent of deep focus photography in Renoir and Welles (a revenant of the depth of field of early cinema), the invention of the close-up and the arrival of sound, before the series is cut short.[64] Memorably, he homes in on the symptomatic obsession of the vast majority of film historians with the phrase "for the first time..." in their discussions of the invention of formal devices in the cinema's early years,[65] and debunks Mitry's explanation of the temporary abandonment of deep-focus photography in the cinema (that it was due to a change from panchromatic to orthochromatic film stock) by convincingly demonstrating that the historian simply shifts the "last instance" of responsibility for technological change from one technicist rationale to another. The reproaches – from this and other quarters – would notably lead Mitry to issue a defense of his work in 1973.[66]

This is not, however, to claim that Comolli's text is flawless. He will later come to admit the shortcomings of his discussions on the persistence of vision, largely due to the piecemeal scientific knowledge at the time,[67] but other question marks remain. While the ideological/economic impetus for the advent of "moving" photographic images is asserted ("to see life as it is" and "to make this a source of profits"), there is no adequate explanation for why these efforts should crystallize – in four different

64. It is interesting to note that Comolli's argument intersects, on a number of points, with Godard's more idiosyncratic account of film history in *Histoire(s) du cinéma* (1988-98) and other associated works. The economic determination of the "birth" of the cinema, as marked by the inaugural paid screening of Lumière films in the Grand Café, is a central theme of *2 x 50 ans du cinéma français* (Godard, 1995), for instance, while the historical simultaneity of the advent of sound with the New Deal in the US and the rise of fascism in Europe is also broached by both figures.

65. Musser's work on the early years of the American cinema has followed in this vein, at the same time as cautioning against an approach that would "seek to forsake starting points entirely [or], as Jean-Louis Comolli has done, to offer the possibility of so many starting points that the notion of a beginning is not only diffused but ultimately avoided." Charles Musser, *The Emergence of Cinema: The American Screen to 1907* (New York: Scribner, 1990), p. 15.

66. Against the accusation of a teleological approach to film history, Mitry here stated that, "Historians *observe* present facts just as they observe facts from the past. They then research, discover and analyze the cause and effect chains that constitute and *shape* the past. But these *continuous* chains do not entail a *linear* development unfolding within a determinist, univocal logic, inevitably leading from a lesser to a higher degree of perfection. [...] There is *progression* but not necessarily '*progress*.' Progress is a value judgement imposed on these historical facts; it is not the historical facts themselves." Jean Mitry, "De quelques problèmes d'histoire et d'esthétique du cinéma," *Cahiers de la Cinémathèque*, no. 10-11 (1973), p. 121. For a discussion of Mitry's response to Comolli, cf. André Gaudreault, *Film and Attraction: From Kinematography to Cinema*, trans. Timothy Barnard (Urbana: University of Illinois Press, 2011), p. 24.

67. Cf. infra, pp. 82-83.

countries simultaneously – in the mid-1890s.[68] Similarly, what is perhaps the overarching ideological/economic determination of the rise of Hollywood *découpage*, with its privilege of the close-up and its "effacement" of depth – namely, the rise of the star system – is touched on by Comolli but not developed systematically. On other occasions, Comolli concretely posits hypotheses for technological change – sound, for instance, is seen as a response by Hollywood to the threat to its global dominance posed by the "film writing" of Soviet montage cinema – which, while being provocatively stimulating, probably do not stand up to sustained historical scrutiny. But limitations such as these do not detract from the article as a whole; indeed, given the prodigious progress made in film historiography since 1971, it would be a surprise if further historical inaccuracies were *not* detected in his text. From the start of his project, Comolli himself openly admitted that his articles – written on a month-to-month basis as part of a polemical exchange – merely constitute "some axes of investigation, to be taken up and developed more systematically later."[69]

As with the status of Engels' *The Origins of the Family, Private Property and the State* for contemporary Marxist anthropologists, the lasting value of "Technique and Ideology" for film theorists and historians thus derives less from the empirical data that it presents, and more from the method that it proposes. In a section inserted near the middle of the text, entitled "For a Materialist History of the Cinema," Comolli stridently opposes a linear historical outlook that would rest on a "system of direct causality." Again and again, he resists the "teleological" temptation to read the cinema's origins from the standpoint of its present existence, as a point of perfection toward which the assortment of early experiments and inventions were inexorably leading, and insists that this teleological outlook is a flaw common to both Bazin and Mitry, in spite of the more overt differences in their accounts of film history. He equally rejects a standpoint that would see the evolution of the cinema in a state of autonomous detachment from surrounding influences, with its only referential framework being its past development and its future promise – a view he once again ascribes to both Bazin and Mitry. It is in this section that Comolli makes the most extensive appeals to Kristeva and Althusser, marshaling the former's understanding of the cinema as a "signifying practice" and the latter's concept of "differential historical temporalities" to argue for the elaboration of a "historical materialist" approach to film history, in which the cinema's autonomy vis-à-vis other signifying practices (photography, theater, painting) and broader historical processes is distinctly relati-

---

68. Considering Comolli's avowed Leninism, it is perhaps surprising that there is no mention in "Technique and Ideology" of the macrostructural transformation of Western capitalism, from a *laissez-faire* system to a monopoly-based imperialism, posited by Lenin as occurring at the end of the 19th century, in almost exact simultaneity with the invention of the cinema. Cf. V.I. Lenin, *Imperialism: The Highest Stage of Capitalism*, in *Collected Works of Lenin*, vol. XXII (Moscow: Progress Publishers, 1976).

69. Cf. infra, p. 145.

vized. While these specific conceptual apparatuses are far from hegemonic in film studies, the anti-teleological thrust of Comolli's argument – as will be discussed at greater length below – has been widely taken up by the "post-Brighton" school of film historians, and his assertion that "it is no longer possible to keep film history and film theory hermetically sealed from one another"[70] represents an ongoing challenge to the disciplinary boundaries of the field as a whole.

Echoes of "Technique and Ideology" in the English-Speaking World

The exposure of Anglophone film culture to "Technique and Ideology" was almost instantaneous: in the Spring 1972 issue of *Screen* (before the series had even concluded), Paul Willemen noted that "Jean-Louis Comolli's account of the moving picture in *Cahiers du cinéma* is extremely relevant,"[71] while Christopher Williams unmistakably channeled Comolli in his claim that an article by Patrick Ogle omitted "two major terms [...] from his considerations on deep focus cinematography. These two terms are Ideology and Economy."[72] Having undertaken its own editorial shift toward Marxist theory, *Screen* had by this time already embarked on a large-scale, BFI-funded project to translate texts from the French journals seen as theoretical role models for its own work, which led to the publication of translations of "Cinema/Ideology/Criticism" (in three parts, from Spring 1971 to Spring 1972), Gérard Leblanc's "Direction" and Jean-Paul Fargier's "Parenthesis or Indirect Route" in Summer 1971, Pleynet's "The 'Left' Front of Art" in Spring 1972 and *Cahiers*' "John Ford's *Young Mr. Lincoln*" in Autumn 1972. Strangely, while "Technique and Ideology" *was* translated by Diana Matias as part of this project,[73] it was never published in *Screen* itself, nor in the 1977 collection of texts (including the aforementioned translated works) *Screen Reader 1*.[74] After a period of informal circulation, Matias' translation was eventually published in the short-lived periodical *Film Reader* in 1977[75] – but here only the first installment of the series was printed. Later anthologies would include some of the

---

70. Cf. infra, p. 197. The direct target of this proclamation is the "scholastic" division between aesthetics and film history in Mitry's work.

71. Paul Willemen, "On Realisms in the Cinema," *Screen*, vol. 13 no. 1 (1972), p. 38.

72. Christopher Williams, "The Deep Focus Question: Some Comments on Patrick Ogle's Article," *Screen*, vol. 13 no. 1 (1972), p. 73.

73. Matias acted as editorial assistant for *Screen* between August 1970 and the Spring of 1972. A note thanking her for her work was printed in the Spring 1972 editorial. Cf. "Editorial," *Screen*, vol. 13 no. 1 (1972), p. 4.

74. Cf. *Screen Reader 1*, ed. Sam Rohdie (London: BFI, 1977).

75. "Technique and Ideology [part I]," *Film Reader*, no. 2 (1977), pp. 128-140. An annual journal affiliated to the Film Division of Northwestern University, *Film Reader* devoted its second number to the "study of narrative structures" and the "issue of industry/technology/ideology."

other parts of the text, but none would resolve the fragmentary state of its availability in English.[76]

This did not prevent Comolli's text, and *Cahiers'* writings more generally, from having a seminal influence on *Screen*, as well as politically radical journals such as *Afterimage* in the UK, *Ciné-Tracts* in Canada, and *Jump Cut* in the US. The work of Stephen Heath, Peter Wollen, Ben Brewster and Colin MacCabe was decisive in the importation and adaptation of the theoretical paradigm associated with *Cahiers* and *Cinéthique*, while figures such as Laura Mulvey and Kaja Silverman used the psychoanalytic approaches of Oudart and Baudry to develop feminist theories of the cinema. But the crossing of the linguistic barrier also entailed a certain reductionist effect: the convulsions of *Cahiers'* writings were smoothed out to a more easily digestible "line," which has since gone by the various names of "apparatus theory," "1970s theory," "*Screen* theory" or (pejoratively) "Grand Theory," and which in some instances tended to exhibit a more Manichaean outlook toward film practice,[77] as well as a certain Calvinist attitude toward concepts such as "visual pleasure" and spectatorial "work."[78]

Moreover, whereas *Cahiers* was avidly read in the period between 1970 and 1972, there was little awareness *outre-Manche* of the subsequent political peripeteia of the journal (culminating in its "return to the mainstream" under Daney and Toubiana). Communication between the French journal and its English-speaking exegetes was a decidedly one-way affair: the only evidence in *Cahiers* of any awareness of its influence abroad was a terse editorial notice in no. 279-280 warning against unauthorized translations of its articles.[79] A major exception to this state of affairs was a confer-

---

76. "Technique and Ideology" gained a wider readership in the mid-1980s with the re-printing of the first installment in *Movies and Methods* and the publication of the third and fourth installments in *Narrative, Apparatus, Ideology*. Cf. "Technique and Ideology," trans. Diana Matias, in *Movies and Methods*, ed. Bill Nichols, 2 vols. (Berkeley: University of California Press, 1985), vol. 2, pp. 40-57; "Technique and Ideology: Camera, Perspective, Depth of Field (Parts 3 and 4)," trans. Diana Matias (with revisions by Marcia Butzel and Philip Rosen), in *Narrative, Apparatus, Ideology: A Film Theory Reader*, ed. Philip Rosen (New York: Columbia University Press, 1986), pp. 421-443. Rosen made emendations and added editorial comments to the segments of the text published in his collection, some of which are cited in the translator's notes in the present volume. The publication of a modified version of Matias' translation of parts I and II followed in 1990. Cf. "Technique and Ideology," *Cahiers du cinéma, 1969-72, op. cit.*, pp. 213-247.

77. A notable example of this tendency occurs in Dayan's exposition of Oudart's notion of suture. Cf. Daniel Dayan, "The Tutor-Code of Classical Cinema," *Film Quarterly*, vol. 28 no. 1 (1974), pp. 22-31.

78. Visual pleasure was rejected outright by many writers at *Screen* and elsewhere, whereas *Cahiers* tended to offer a more nuanced understanding of its function in the cinema. In an interview given to the weekly magazine *Politique Hebdo* (but which ended up being published in *Cahiers*), for instance, they discuss Straub/Huillet's *Othon* in the following terms: "We feel that *Othon* is a very beautiful film, *also* capable of arousing pleasure, but a pleasure which, let us be clear, has nothing to do with the narcissistic identification and hedonism which is almost always the rule in cinematic spectacle." Cf. "Réponses à 'Politique Hebdo'," *Cahiers du cinéma*, no. 229 (1971), p. 62.

79. Cf. "À propos de la traduction plus ou moins pirate des *Cahiers*," *Cahiers du cinéma*, no. 279-280 (1977), p. 2. It is probable that the editors have *Screen* in mind when they write: "Finally, there

ence on "The Cinematic Apparatus" organized by Stephen Heath and Teresa de Lauretis and held in February 1978 in Milwaukee, at which both Comolli and Christian Metz were present.[80] Comolli presented a paper, "Machines of the Visible," which incorporated a series of fragments from "Technique and Ideology" alongside more recent considerations of issues raised by the articles. Here, however, the French critic did not always see eye to eye with his Anglo-American interlocutors: a screening of his film *La Cecilia* met with a largely negative response from the audience,[81] while a discussion of Peter Gidal's film *Condition of Illusion* led to Gidal curtly telling Comolli, "You must be blind," before comparing his comments to "Radek's speech against James Joyce."[82]

The late-1970s also marked the onset of a backlash against the theoretical paradigm established by *Screen*. As early as the winter of 1975/76, members of its editorial board issued a statement in protest at the extravagances of the journal's deployment of psychoanalytic theory, which led to their resignation two issues later.[83] Rival periodical *Movie*, meanwhile, lambasted *Screen* for "avant-garde intellectual 'terrorism',"[84] while even figures associated with the journal began to take their distances from its approach.[85] Over the course of the 1980s and 1990s, many of the former adherents to a Marxist and/or psychoanalytic approach to film theory shifted their concerns to cultural studies, film historiography or Deleuzian/Foucaldian theories of the cinema. At the same time, in a process beginning with Noël Carroll's heated polemic with Stephen Heath in *October*[86] and culminating with Carroll and Bordwell's *Post-Theory*,

---

are those friends across the world, who participate in or put out journals close to *Cahiers*, and who, concerned with familiarizing their readers with its work, have adopted the habit of reproducing certain texts in the name of a real support and what they suppose to be a *de facto* consensus."

80. The proceedings of this conference were published in book form as *The Cinematic Apparatus*, ed. Teresa de Lauretis and Stephen Heath (New York: St. Martin's Press, 1980).

81. For an account of the film's US screening, cf. an interview with Jean-Louis Comolli: "On the Practice of Political Film," *Ciné-Tracts*, vol. 1 no. 4 (1978), p. 44.

82. *The Cinematic Apparatus*, *op. cit.*, pp. 170-171. Gidal, of course, represented a markedly different practico-theoretical tradition to that of *Screen*, let alone *Cahiers*.

83. Cf. Edward Buscombe, Christine Gledhill, Alan Lovell and Christopher Williams, "Statement: Psychoanalysis and Film," *Screen*, vol. 16 no. 4 (1975-76), pp. 119-130, and "Why We Have Resigned from the Board of *Screen*," *Screen*, vol. 17 no. 2 (1976), pp. 106-109.

84. Ian Cameron, "Editorial," *Movie*, no. 26 (1978-79), p. 1. Cf. also Andrew Britton, "The Ideology of Screen," *Movie*, no. 26 (1978/79), pp. 2-28.

85. A shift away from his *Screen* writings can first be detected in Colin MacCabe's *Godard: Images, Sounds, Politics* (London: BFI, 1980). This standpoint will be repeated in "Class of '68: Elements of an Intellectual Autobiography 1967-81" (in MacCabe, *Theoretical Essays: Film, Linguistics, Literature* [Manchester: Manchester University Press, 1985], pp. 1-32); *Godard: Portrait of the Artist at 70* (New York: Farrar, Strauss and Giroux, 2003), pp. 196-197; and "Bazin as Modernist" (in *Opening Bazin*, *op. cit.*), p. 66.

86. This debate represents one of the most vocal and detailed polemics between these two theoretical tendencies, but often descends into petty personal attacks. Cf. Noël Carroll, "Address to the Heathen," *October*, no. 23 (1982), pp. 89-163; Stephen Heath, "Le Père Noël," *October*, no. 26 (1983), pp. 63-115; and Noël Carroll, "A Reply to Heath," *October*, no. 27 (1983), pp. 81-102.

cognitivist and empiricist strands of film theory launched a full-frontal assault on what they saw as a hopelessly incoherent and deeply flawed set of ideas. By this point, few could be found to defend *Screen*'s legacy, with even those sympathetic to its theoretical heritage, such as Rodowick, accepting that "political modernism" had entered a stage of crisis, and seeking to draw out the contradictions and shortcomings of the original theories, while hoping to salvage a kernel of theoretical validity from amidst the conceptual wreckage.

Although members of the Anglophone academy were the main target for these strictures, it was inevitable that *Cahiers* – seen on both sides of the debate as the intellectual birthplace of "1970s theory" – would find itself in their crosshairs. While accepting the value of Comolli's "emphasis upon the lag between technological possibility and extended use" and his "non-teleological model of change," Bordwell, for instance, would criticize "Technique and Ideology" as "sweepingly reductive," arguing that it made "the concept of 'ideology' do too much work," and that it assumed "that 'bourgeois ideology' rests in place for three centuries, from Caravaggio to *Citizen Kane*," before proceeding to reiterate Sartre's critique of "'lazy' Marxists who replace 'real, perfectly defined groups' by vague collectivities such as 'bourgeois ideology.'"[87] Richard Allen, meanwhile, would devote a monograph to an attempted logical dismantling of many of the precepts operative in *Cahiers*' theoretical arsenal.[88]

One area of film studies, however, in which the reputation of "Technique and Ideology" did not suffer such a decline has been in what has come to be known as the "new film history" movement, pioneered by, among others, Tom Gunning, Charles Musser and André Gaudreault. While the 1978 FIAF congress at Brighton is traditionally seen as the inauguration site of this movement, its project of revisiting and reevaluating the accounts of early cinema provided by the earlier generation of historians (Sadoul, Mitry and Jacobs in particular) can also trace its provenance to Comolli's work. This, at any rate, is the view taken by Gaudreault, who, in *Film and Attraction*, unabashedly asserts that "Comolli's articles were one of the rare studies to give a thrashing to 'official history' at such an early date and in such a systematic and forceful manner," and that his "acerbic critique of empirical historians" formed "a user's manual for the scholars who were soon about to express an interest in the early days of cinema."[89] Gaudreault even goes so far as to call the movement "post-

87. David Bordwell, Janet Staiger and Kristin Thompson, *The Classical Hollywood Cinema: Film Style and Mode of Production to 1960* (New York: Columbia University Press, 1985), pp. 247, 249-250. Ironically, this volume commits some of the same "technicist" errors that were critiqued by Comolli. For instance, the development of film narrative is seen to be determined by the standardization of the 1000-foot film reel. Cf. *ibid.*, pp. 126-127. This tendency will only be exacerbated in Bordwell and Thompson's later work.

88. Cf. Richard Allen, *Projecting Illusion: Film Spectatorship and the Impression of Reality* (Cambridge: Cambridge University Press, 1995). The philosophical apparatus Allen uses to challenge "apparatus theory" is generally Wittgensteinian in nature.

89. Gaudreault, *op. cit.*, pp. 11, 16.

Comolli criticism," avowing that its members "borrowed, consciously or not, from Comolli's shaking up of official history."[90] This esteem for the groundbreaking character of Comolli's work was no doubt a major motivation for Gaudreault to co-organize the "Impact of Technological Innovations on the Historiography and Theory of Cinema" conference in Montreal in 2011, which notably brought together many of the "original combatants" of the "technique and ideology" debates to return to the issues raised 40 years earlier.[91]

"Technique and Ideology" and Comolli's Later Work

The exciting work carried out in this area notwithstanding, it would thus be an injustice – and a seeming reiteration of the "hermetically sealed" division between film theory and film history that he rejects – if the ongoing value of Comolli's text were to be limited to its influence on the "new film historians." Rather, his work has yielded a range of theoretical and practical legacies which are exhausted neither by its take-up by "1970s film theory" nor by its later ramifications for research into the history of early cinema, and one of the most fertile of these legacies has been the impact the text has had on Comolli's own later work, in both film theory and filmmaking.

Many of the details of Comolli's activity after leaving *Cahiers* in 1973 are discussed in greater depth in his recent interview with *Senses of Cinema*, so only a quick summary need be given here. After an initial foray into documentary filmmaking in 1968, with *Les Deux Marseillaises* (an exploration of the June 1968 legislative elections, co-directed with André S. Labarthe), Comolli would make his feature debut with *La Cecilia*, released in 1975 after more than a year of work on the film. Centering on a 19th-century colony of Italian anarchists in Brazil, under the tutelage of Giovanni Rossi, Comolli's analysis of group dynamics within a utopian collectivist project totally detached from the surrounding society was an unmistakable parable for his experience at *Cahiers*, and was interpreted as such in the journal's reviews of the film.[92] Some have criticized *La Cecilia* for being more formally conservative than would have been suggested by the theories developed by *Cahiers*,[93] but the film works on a more subtle level; its challenge to dominant film practice operates above all in its conditions of production. As Straub/Huillet have also sought to do, Comolli

90. *Ibid.*, pp. 12, 16.

91. Comolli gave a video presentation at this conference, while Gérard Leblanc and Jean-Patrick Lebel were also in attendance. Cf. Daniel Fairfax, "Conference Report: The Impact of Technological Innovations on the Historiography and Theory of Cinema," *Cinema Journal*, vol. 52 no. 1 (2012), pp. 127-131.

92. Cf. Serge Toubiana, "Les Arpenteurs," *Cahiers du cinéma*, no. 264 (1976), pp. 41-43; Serge Daney, "Chantez le code!," *Cahiers du cinéma*, no. 264 (1976), pp. 52-54; Pascal Kané, "Le detour par l'enfance," *Cahiers du cinéma*, no. 265 (1976), pp. 19-22.

93. Cf., in particular, Alison Smith, "Jean-Louis Comolli and *La Cecilia*: Theory into Practice," *French Cultural Studies*, vol. 2 no. 4 (1991), pp. 13-33.

attempted to break down the traditional hierarchies prevailing on film shoots, and he concomitantly developed a filming practice based on spontaneity and improvisation among actors and technicians alike.

La Cecilia was notably followed, in 1981, by *L'Ombre rouge*, a political thriller set during the Spanish Civil War. The increased budget and presence of star actors restricted the possibility for a repeat of the shooting style of his earlier film, and the end result duly suffers for it. Comolli himself recognized *L'Ombre rouge* as something of an aesthetic dead-end, and, while it was not to be his last work of fiction, his filmmaking efforts since then have overwhelmingly been focused on documentary works, for the most part made for French public television. While these projects have tackled a wide range of issues, a particular point of attention has been the quotidian reality of electoral politics in France. With *Tous pour un!* (1988), Comolli would repeat the gesture of *Les Deux Marseillaises* by filming grassroots party activists in the Parisian *banlieue* during the lead-up to a presidential ballot, before his geographical focus shifted to Marseilles with 1989's *Marseille: de père en fils*, in collaboration with journalist Michel Samson. Over the course of the next 13 years, Comolli would return to the port city a further six times, charting each election campaign during a period marked by disorientation on the left and the rise of Jean-Marie Le Pen's Front national on the right.

For a time, filmmaking supplanted theorizing about the cinema in Comolli's praxis. With the exception of a few scattered articles published in *Cahiers* in the late 1970s,[94] Comolli refrained from writing about the cinema almost entirely. This reticence began to change in the late 1980s, when he was led back to a preoccupation with film theory after a period of writing on jazz (which has always been Comolli's second great passion).[95] Comolli's various writings since then – whether as journal articles, interviews, seminars or personal notes – have been collected in two major volumes, *Voir et pouvoir* (2004) and *Corps et cadre* (2012), and much of this corpus revolves around a theoretical interrogation of documentary filmmaking practice. Despite totaling approximately 1200 pages of material, only a handful of these pieces have found publication in English.[96]

94. These would include "Le passé filmé" (*Cahiers*, no. 277 [1977], pp. 5-14), "Un corps en trop," (*Cahiers*, no. 278 [1977], pp. 5-16; translated as "Historical Fiction – A Body Too Much," trans. Ben Brewster, *Screen*, vol. 19 no. 2 [1978], pp. 41-54), and a series of articles co-authored with François Géré. All were composed independently of the *Cahiers* editorial committee, and a footnoted comment in "Un corps en trop" received a stinging rebuke from Pascal Bonitzer ("Note sur une note de Comolli et sur un cinéma tordu," *Cahiers du cinéma*, no. 279-280 [1977], pp. 94-97), the tone of which would have been unthinkable while Comolli was still centrally involved with the journal.

95. Notably, in 1971 – contemporaneous with the publication of "Technique and Ideology" – Comolli co-authored the book *Free Jazz/Black Power* with Philippe Carles (Paris: Champs Libre, 1971; repr. Paris: Folio, 2001). He was also integrally involved in the mammoth project *Dictionnaire du jazz* (Paris: Laffont, 1989).

96. Cf. the bibliography, infra, for more details on Comolli's writings.

As Comolli himself recognizes, the traces of "Technique and Ideology," and his time at *Cahiers* more generally, can be felt throughout his more recent writings.[97] It was not surprising, therefore, that he should elect to revisit the original text in 2009. He did so in propitious circumstances: the 40th anniversary of May '68 the previous year had unleashed a flurry of retrospective interest in the period's *gauchisme*, while the heritage of Althusser – long cast to a state of purgatory within critical theory after the scandals of his later career – has been subject to reevaluation with the increased interest in his former acolytes Rancière, Badiou and Balibar, which itself has led to a revival in the philosophical fortunes of radical militancy.[98] The long period of disavowal of the French far left, stretching from the rise of the *nouveaux philosophes* to the "end of history" discourse after the collapse of the USSR, has, it seems, definitively receded.

Accordingly, the pride with which Comolli looks back on the "technique and ideology period"[99] is in no way mixed with embarrassment. But this does not mean that he stubbornly persists in seeing matters through the singular prism of his earlier text. The theoretical framework for his more recent writing has become more pluralist in nature, and has widened to include Debord, Rancière, Nancy, Virilio, Didi-Huberman, Adorno, Deleuze, Bergson and Stiegler among others. Notably, Comolli declares that "the holy alliance of the spectacle and the commodity, foreseen and analyzed by Guy Debord from 1967 onwards, has now been realized."[100] The combination of mechanically reproduced images and sounds is thus, in his view, the "ultimate weapon" for the domination of capital. Moreover, in Comolli's analysis the structural hierarchy of the capitalist social formation has been reversed: the spectacle, he submits, has become the "supreme form of the commodity," to which the base economic functioning of contemporary capitalism is subordinate.[101]

The result is, on the one hand, that many of the precepts governing *Cahiers*' work in the post-1968 period still obtain – or, if anything, they have even gained in validity. The struggle against the spectacle takes place, above all, on the level of forms, of the signifier. Theory must still interrogate the place of the viewer, who, in order to be "emancipated" is in need of being transformed into a "critical spectator."[102] On the

---

97. This was further reinforced when, in interviews with his former colleagues, he revisited the period for the 2011 film *À voir absolument (si possible). 1963-1973: Dix années aux Cahiers du cinéma*, co-directed with Jean Narboni and Ginette Lavigne.

98. In particular, all of these figures have been key participants in a broad project to resuscitate the philosophical validity of the notion of "communism," which has been reflected in conferences in London, Berlin, Paris and New York since 2009. Cf. *The Idea of Communism*, ed. Costas Douzinas and Slavoj Žižek, 2 vols. (London: Verso, 2010-2013).

99. This is the term Bonitzer used to describe the 1969-1973 period at *Cahiers*. Cf. "Nos années non-légendaires," *op. cit.*, p. 148.

100. Cf. infra, p. 49.

101. Cf. infra, p. 50.

102. Comolli here makes a direct reference to Rancière's *The Emancipated Spectator*, trans. Gregory Elliott (London: Verso, 2011).

other hand, while the cinema prepared the way for the later, more pervasive forms of the spectacle (television, advertising, the Internet), its continued existence can only be as "an anti-spectacle, capable of dis-alienating us from the dominant spectacular alienation."[103] Moreover, the fragmentary montage of Vertov and Godard (the "jump-cut" – Comolli uses the English term) has now become the generalized mode of functioning for the audiovisual wing of the culture industry, such that television, in particular, has become nothing more than a frenzied accumulation of redundant imagery. Whereas during their *années rouges* the *Cahiers* writers sought to critique the cinema's "impression of reality," and valued those films which deconstructed the system of representation based on cinematic realism (including through the use of montage-based fragmentation), Comolli now demands that the cinema "incite an infiltration of something of the real into the images and sounds of its representations,"[104] and he finds examples of this cinema in the distinctly neo-Bazinian work of Abbas Kiarostami, Jia Zhangke and Pedro Costa, as well as in the documentary practice which he has so amply theorized over the last two decades.

These are only some of the contours of a rich text that mingles autobiography with theoretical reflection, ruminations on film history with commentary on contemporary media practice, and indefatigable optimism about the future of cinema with unbridled rage at the present global political order. "Technique and Ideology" waited nearly four decades for the promise of its final "to be continued" to be fulfilled, and with "Cinema against Spectacle" Comolli rises to the challenge posed by his earlier text.

Translating "Technique and Ideology"

A final word, then, needs to be said on the issue of translating "Technique and Ideology." Re-issuing a previously translated text inevitably calls for a justification based on the deficiencies of its earlier rendering, and, in this case, such drawbacks are not restricted merely to the piecemeal nature of the text's publication in English. Thankfully, unlike Susan Bennett's translation of "Cinema/Ideology/Criticism" (the deep flaws of which are discussed in a translator's note at the beginning of this volume's appendix), Diana Matias' rendition does not manifestly distort the underlying meaning of Comolli's article. A degree of imprecision, however, is present on two levels.

Firstly, there is a certain terminological vagueness, above all with regard to the theoretical vocabulary (of Marxist, psychoanalytic and structuralist origins) frequently deployed by Comolli. The translator's evident lack of familiarity with many of the lexical vagaries of critical theory is compounded by the fact that, at the time the translation was composed (the early 1970s), many of the terms that were com-

103. Cf. infra, p. 136.
104. Idem.

mon currency in French theory had yet to make their way into the English language.[105] Fortunately, this situation has since been immeasurably improved, and numerous French terms now have widely accepted equivalents in English. To put it bluntly: the task of the translator may have become easier in the intervening four decades due to the fact that English academic discourse in the humanities has become decidedly more "French." Not all of these issues have been resolved, however: many words which, at first glance, seem to have an unambiguous meaning in everyday usage (such as *lieu*, *travail*, *écriture*, etc.), in fact carry important, theoretically specific overtones. It is imperative that these connotations be maintained as much as possible in translation, but this carries the associated risk of a stilted, awkward language. Moreover, debate still rages with respect to certain terms (the renderings of *dispositif* and *appareil*, most notably), while some expressions, both those specific to film discourse and those used more generally, have no suitable English equivalents. In a few instances (*découpage*, *hors-champ*, *jouissance*) the decision has been made to maintain the French original. In all cases, the governing principle has been to strive, where possible, for precision in meaning and consistency in usage. To aid the reader, a glossary of theoretical and technical terms is included at the end of this volume. Guidance, here, is necessary even at the level of the title – "*technique*" in French can mean both "technique" and "technology," and Comolli frequently uses it in both senses of the word.

The second issue posed by the text, and one where the present translator's philosophy patently differs from the earlier version, concerns Comolli's writing style. Whereas "Cinema against Spectacle" is written in a limpid, compelling manner, "Technique and Ideology" presents a number of stylistic challenges for accurate and faithful translation. Above all, the text is marked by labyrinthine, almost Proustian syntactical constructions. Gargantuan sentences are woven from a multiplicity of parenthetical remarks and dependent clauses, such that the original thrust of a sentence is often lost sight of, if not abandoned altogether for a markedly different line of thought. The text, indeed, was written at the high point of the journal's reputation for "illegibility," a charge which the writers frequently had to confront. In the May 1971 issue, for instance (the same issue in which the first installment of "Technique and Ideology" appeared), *Cahiers* printed a letter from a sympathetic reader who, while applauding their general project, admitted that he "subscribes to the rumor circulating that finds *Cahiers* to be unreadable; alongside articles that are complex but quite well written, the result of a clarity of thought, one can find others whose

105. This situation was to a certain degree ameliorated by the modifications carried out by Rosen and Browne in their re-publications of the text. The downside to this process, however, is that passages from the same text now exist in several different variants, a phenomenon compounded by the fact that the "Machines of the Visible" article published in *The Cinematic Apparatus*, containing a number of extracts from "Technique and Ideology," was translated without reference to Matias' work.

muddled, recondite aspect is such that it is difficult to read past the first column."[106] The response from the editors was at times almost apologetic, but they were also resolute in maintaining that "reading *Cahiers* requires work." In response to a similar question from an interview with the magazine *Politique-Hebdo* printed in the same issue of *Cahiers*, they were even more adamant:

> Firstly, there is no question of us ceding to the bourgeois conception of a reading that could be done *without work*. Reading is work. The accusations of "hermeticism," "illegibility," "jargon," and so on have always been the weapons of obscurantist reaction when confronted with productive theoretical work. [...] Without losing sight of the specificity of each signifying practice, it is possible to think the problem of a *general materialist writing* capable of articulating these practices and reflecting on their interpenetration, their interdependence.[107]

The mode of writing of their own texts was thus a matter of capital importance for the writers at *Cahiers*, and was a conscious component of their attempts to break with the dominant systems of representation, even if this carried the risk of the journal becoming unreadable. Moreover, it should be recalled that texts such as Comolli's were not composed within the sedate conditions of academic research, with its rigorous peer review process, but were mostly written at a hurried tempo, with the publication deadlines of a monthly periodical constantly looming, and at the same time as he had to concern himself with the various administrative tasks of the journal. An extra round of editing may well have smoothed out the rougher edges of these texts, but in their published state they stand as symptomatic testimonies to the frenetic, headlong nature of their composition. Little of this quality, however, comes through in Matias' translation, which overwhelmingly tends to break down Comolli's serpentine passages into acceptably bite-sized sentences, and concomitantly has frequent recourse to loose paraphrasing rather than the direct translation of the original. Any gain in "legibility" is thus more than offset by a substantial loss in the stylistic flavor and, more importantly, conceptual logic and flow of Comolli's work.

This is not to pretend that tackling the translation of this text does not generate a wide range of thorny questions, and a cavalier attitude toward the issue of legibility is certainly not advisable. But it should be maintained that "Technique and Ideology" *is*, at its base, an eminently comprehensible work, and in striving to reproduce the text in the English language, every effort has been made to replicate the forms and structures of the original, while ensuring that it remains accessible to English readers, and without falling into pedantry or a slavish adoption of French syntactical norms. It is for the reader to judge the success of this approach.

---

106. Christian Oddos, "Lettre de Lecteur," *Cahiers du cinéma*, no. 229 (1971), pp. 54-55.
107. "Réponses à 'Politique-Hebdo'," *op. cit.*, p. 64.

Some Notes on the Translation

In general, I have maintained Comolli's original references for French texts as much as possible, and offered English translations in square brackets where they exist. This practice has been extended to works that Comolli cites in their French translation, where this information is judged to be of value to the reader. For those passages which have reputable English translations, these have been used in the present volume, with the occasional modification necessary when the detail is pertinent to Comolli's argument. Quotes from Bazin are derived from Barnard's 2009 translation of *What Is Cinema?*, which in general more faithfully reproduces the original than Gray's earlier effort.

In addition to Comolli's own footnotes, translator's notes have been provided for the purposes of furnishing the English reader with contextual information. Comolli's notes are given in Arabic numerals, while translator's notes are given in Roman numerals, and appended to the end of the volume. Occasional additional information has been given in square brackets within the text itself. When Comolli himself has made interpolated comments in his citation of other authors, these are italicized and marked with the initials "JLC."

"Technique and Ideology" was reproduced without any amendments in *Cinéma contre spectacle*, but Comolli did allow himself to intervene into the text on one level: by providing extra commentary in the image captions. His more recent comments are provided within square brackets, below the original captions.

Cinema against Spectacle

Introduction

The six installments of "Technique and Ideology" which conclude this book were published by *Cahiers du cinéma* between the spring of 1971 and, 15 months later, the autumn of 1972 – that is, amidst the highs and lows of a crucial period for the team behind the magazine. Coming out of the struggle to keep Henri Langlois as head of the Cinémathèque française (in April 1968) – a battle led from the front line by *Cahiers*, which was victorious, in the sense that Langlois and Mary Meerson returned to their posts at the Chaillot cinema, taking back their offices and their wondrous machines on the Rue de Messine – we entered the events of May with the same spirit, participating in the proceedings of the "*États généraux du cinéma*" in the École Louis Lumière, on the Rue de Vaugirard.[i] After May came June. The "return to order" provoked a more aggressive, more fervent form of political engagement. The magazine swung to the left. Soon, the "editor in chief" was abolished – I mean the title and not the function – and in our opposition to the spectacle we even went as far as banishing photographs and frame enlargements from our pages. This occurred just before the appearance of the sixth installment of "Technique and Ideology," and today it is not absurd to see this circumstance as being linked to the fact that a "to be continued" does not cease to leave this final section unclosed, incapable of being spared from our new iconoclasm.

Why publish this sequel today? It is true that the text had only been available in libraries. But this reason is not enough. What commenced in the impassioned setting of the far left in France opened, more than we could have imagined, onto what was going to become of the world and of ourselves. Something worse. Having promised to blossom and bear fruit, these gardens of concern[ii] quickly became fallow and barren. In this book, however, I will restrict myself to returning to the question of the politicization of the field of the cinema, in which we had our part to play. The holy alliance of the spectacle and the commodity, foreseen and analyzed by Guy Debord from 1967 onwards, has now been realized. It governs our world. From pole to pole, across the tropics, capital in its current guise has found the ultimate weapon for its domination: images and sounds combined. Nothing has changed in the wake of the pitiful debacle of the stock exchanges, banks, profiteers and functionaries. The major media outlets have changed the lyrics to their jingles, but not the video clips accompanying them. The same preachers are still standing at their pulpits. Everything is transpiring as if capital's self-manducation had not struck it at its core: its gospel is preserved, its orthodoxies are maintained, its formal models are as untouchable as ever, and its love of profit is as immoderate as ever, even when there are no more profits to be had. The show must go on![iii] The same screens show, on loop, the same audiovisual standards, the same commodified buttresses for the need to see and hear, the same forms and the same formulae. There is no before, there is no after. Time is suspended, history frozen. The communion in the cult of the market is provided on a permanent basis, as if there were no other task to be relentlessly undertaken than to produce the poor, in order, consequently, to devour them. Thus capital represents itself to itself as ensnared in a cycle, wherein resurrection follows crisis and construction follows destruction, in a sort of life beyond death, like an epilogue after the end. Or like a film on loop?

The omnipresence of the market is, above all, audiovisual in nature. Never have our eyes and ears been awash with so many artificial effects. Never in history have so many machines given so many people so many images and sounds to see and hear. And never have these images and sounds so massively tended toward uniformity. Since these images and sounds penetrate into all houses and all minds, since they cross all spaces and all times, how could this not have the most extreme consequences? Alienation, as revealed by Marx, is no longer merely what sweetens the bitter pill of misery; it is no longer at hand for the sole purpose of rendering service to capital, capable at any moment of making its dominance accepted, desired and maybe even loved. The overwhelming *flux* of audiovisual entertainment has become, in the last hundred years of the cinema, the fixed form of the opium of the people. That is to say, it is the most promising market, precisely because this spectacular flux remains, as Marx notes with regard to religion, the consolation of those teeming masses who have nothing else with which to console themselves. The television series is more powerful than the cabaret, the music hall, the ditty, the *show*. In 1929, 1930 and the years following, in the depths of the "crisis," Broadway was quickly overtaken by Hollywood in providing consolation to the masses. It is true that the bankers of that time leapt out the window more willingly than they do today, and that, in all their desperation, the films of that era showed themselves to be more lively. Luc Besson is not Busby Berkeley.

But perhaps this unremitting torrent of alienation has become pleasure itself. Perhaps these spectacles, these images and sounds pervade our lives for the overarching goal of making us *love alienation* itself? Is the spectacle content with serving the commodity? What if it had become the supreme form of the commodity? More glistening than the commodity, more flexible, more seductive – more necessary? The sparkle is there in order to hide the horror. The mask is pleasing. This domination of the spectacle, I fear, has gone far beyond what Debord was able to predict and announce.[1] Reason beyond reason. The entire world shows itself off as a single great

1. Guy Debord, *Œuvres* (Paris: Gallimard, coll. "Quarto," 2006).

spectacle. Moreover, this complete inversion in the function of the spectacle seeks to – and often manages to – turn us into *complicit* spectators, not "alienated" by the imaginary representations of a "life" which would be the mendacious version of "real life," but quite simply alienated from what gives us pleasure, what we like, what seduces us; alienated, that is (if this term is still necessary) from our own desire for alienation.[2] I am speaking about us, about those of us who were *cinephiles*; and I am speaking about myself, because I still think of myself as one. The membrane of appearances is unyielding.[iv] Whoever rubs up against it suffers. Capital crumbles while the spectacle hardens.

This is what we have to understand: we have entered a new age. The cinema has been its mentor, agent, actor and star.[3] But what the cinema did in its first 60 years is nothing compared to what television – the principal weapon of the mass media – will have done in the following 60 years. The will for power of the generalized spectacle is totalitarian. Nothing escapes from its hegemony, there is no margin, no outside – apart from death. And yet, the spectacle must be combated in its very omnipotence. To struggle against the domination of the spectacle is to lead a vital combat to salvage and preserve something of man's human dimension. *This struggle must be carried out against the very forms that the spectacle employs in order to maintain its domination.* The struggle of forms lurks in most forms of struggle.[4] Defeating or overcoming the existing order of things requires the invention of forms that are different to those serving to repress our consciousness and our movements. The unstinting battles and wars of the exploited against their masters can be led astray and lose their power if they reaffirm the same forms through which the domination of capital is exercised, whether this occurs in information technology, advertising, the media or the spectacle. Too often, in our everyday struggles, we speak the language of the enemy. But we will only create another way of speaking about the world, and about our hopes, if it is within the ambit of a common language, and we must liberate this beautiful captive from those who corrupt her. At the same time that utopia must be reignited, the word itself must be reclaimed – arise, utopians! It is incumbent upon

---

2. Jacques Rancière, *Le Spectateur emancipé* (Paris: La Fabrique, 2008) [*The Emancipated Spectator*, trans. Gregory Elliott (London: Verso, 2011)].

3. "[The cinema] is not the same as the other arts, which aim rather at something unreal through the world, but make the world itself something unreal or a tale [*récit*]. With the cinema, it is the world which becomes its own image, and not an image which becomes the world." Gilles Deleuze, *L'image-mouvement* (Paris: Minuit, 1983), p. 84 [*Cinema 1: The Movement-Image*, trans. Hugh Tomlinson and Barbara Habberjam (London: Athlone Press, 1986), p. 57].

4. In August 2008, in the "*États généraux du documentaire*" at Lussas, I participated, with Marie-José Mondzain and Patrick Leboutte, in a seminar entitled: "Forms of Struggle and Struggle of Forms." Our departure point was the following quote from Guy Debord: "We never really contest an organization of existence without contesting all the forms of language belonging to this organization." The phrase comes from the 1959 film *Sur le passage de quelques personnes à travers une assez courte unité de temps* (Guy Debord, *Œuvres cinématographiques complètes*, Gaumont DVD, Paris, 2005).

us, both spectators and filmmakers, to break up the domination of the spectacle from within, chain by chain, and to pull it apart in order to push it out of synch, to pierce it with off-screen space [*hors-champ*], to chip away at it with intervals. Cameras and microphones are everywhere, screens are everywhere, and we are impelled to be in their midst: so let us turn them around! Since Narcissus there have always been mirrors between us and our own selves. Turning our enemies' weapons against them does not involve the conquest (!) of the central organs of alienation (the boards of TV networks, the White Houses, Disneyland, etc.) as much as it involves the denunciation and corrosive destitution of the dominant forms, the majoritarian modes of showing, the fashions in which the spectator is fashioned, treated with contempt, turned into a mere *commodity*. It is incumbent upon us to change these methods, to replace them with different ones. Throughout its history, the cinema has more than once been in a position to conceive of and construct a spectator worthy of the name, one who is capable not only of seeing and hearing (and even this can not be presupposed) but of *seeing and hearing the limits of seeing and hearing*. That is, a critical spectator. One who the spectacle wishes would disappear. One who some of us claim not to have ceased to be. An *emancipated spectator*, which I prefer to call a *critical spectator*.[5]

Either the spectators of today set themselves up against the spectacle, or they will disappear as such. This amounts to saying that if you are no longer an "emancipated" or "critical" spectator, you will no longer be a spectator at all. There is no "simple spectator." The spectator is an agent of representation by dint of perceptually and imaginarily participating in representation – unless this representation accomplishes everything for him, simply assigning him to a place of exteriority, imposing meanings and sensations on him, and formatting him through commentary and the administration of blocking effects. The freedom of the spectator is nothing but the freedom of forms and significations. At the end of the chain, the formatting of audiovisual works culminates in the formatting of seeing and hearing, of feeling and dreaming. There is a certain amount of discipline operative in this formatting. These fettered and imposed forms are programmed reductions in the ability to think. Like the holy man in the desert, the future spectator, if he eventuates, will be tempted by the maddening saraband of spectacular effects occupying the immeasurably vast and numerous screens. He will have to protect himself from it, to accept that his appetite for seeing will be frustrated, to subdue and to fend off his longing to be blinded by the flickering lights, and to be engorged by the accumulation of visual and acoustic effects. The cinema is endlessly constructed and reconstructed by confronting the spectacular aspect that inaugurated it and made it succeed. In an unresolved skirmish, the logic of the *always-more visible* confronts its opposite: its dark side, what is not shown, the *hors-champ*, the hidden, the not-yet-visible and possibly the never-

5. Rancière, *op. cit.*

visible. At its very origins, the *graphein* designated in the term *cinématographe* links what we now call the cinema with a logic of the written trace, which is also a logic of effacement, of covering over, of the palimpsest, the lacuna, the lack.

Today, yesterday: this book is thus composed of two parts. The first, "Cinema against Spectacle," reprises and develops some of the motifs which were familiar to us at the beginning of the 1970s – while nonetheless placing them in the context of a crisis of gazes, screens and situations which is our present condition.[6]

The second is composed of the six articles which appeared under the title "Technique and Ideology" in *Cahiers du cinéma*.[7] These articles are reproduced without any re-touches or corrections. The original illustrations are also reproduced, with the exception of a few which, unable to be found, have been replaced.

I believe that the questions addressed in this series are still active today, 37 years later. They are all the more active for having been so successfully repressed, for belonging to a grey zone which we do not want to know about, for disturbing us more than seducing us, for having fallen under a contemporary malediction, along with the very idea that a "theory" of the cinema can be useful and practicable. It is true that the spectacle, given over to entertainment, abhors "thought," and even revels in expelling all forms of thought from its temple. To a much greater extent than in Marx's or Debord's time, the spectacle in progress pulls together all sorts of "passages to the act" (channel-hopping, "interactivity," games, and so on) whose primary effect – if not their very goal – is the *suspension* of the possibility of the slightest passage to thought. Let us say that the *passage to the act of purchasing* now programs the absence of thought. And let us also say that global consumerism is structured by the desire-not-to-have-to-think.

Much has changed, therefore, between one era and the other: the degradation of the political dimension, the rise in the power of the media, the intertwining of the spectacle, information and the commodity, the prostitution of public television, the place of the cinema and the place of the spectator... But what is strange is that these *modifications* almost all head in the same direction, as if the path were inexorable and we had no other choice but to keep going further and further down it. Far down

6. The term "theater against spectacle" was devised and discussed in the correspondence which has taken place between Jean-Luc Nancy and Philippe Lacoue-Labarthe since the 1970s, in response to the question, "Is the scene primal?" Cf. Denis Guénon, *Livraison et délivrance* (Paris: Belin, 2009), pp. 337-351. As for the term "cinema against spectacle," its development can be located in the course I gave to the Department of Audiovisual Studies at the Université de Paris-VIII between 1997 and 2004, then in the seminar held at the Ateliers Varan in 2001-2002 and at the École de Beaux-Arts in Geneva in 2006 and 2007.

7. Nos. 229, May-June 1971; 230, July 1971; 231, September 1971; 233, November 1971; 234-235, December 1971/January-February 1972; 241, September-October 1972. These six articles were translated into English (*Screen*, 1974 [*sic*]; *Film Reader*, 1977) and were also collected in a volume for an Italian publication: *Tecnica e Ideologia*, trans. Sandra Lischi and Anita Piemonti (Parma: Pratiche Editrice, 1982). [For more information on the text's translation history, see the translator's introduction to the present volume].

indeed: the suppression – relatively speaking – of advertising on French public television networks has in no way changed the nature of their programming, even if it has altered some of their scheduling patterns.[v] The same priorities of production and broadcasting are held to the fore: comforting entertainment comes first.[8] The subject matter can be frivolous or serious, but the command to entertain is applied above all to the forms, which are meticulously formatted in order not to divide audiences. The watchword of all television networks is to exclude any program which could be "divisive." TV-films produced by public television (for example, the numerous adaptations of classic novels) are not among these objects that are *difficult to take in*. The rule is always that they should be comforting, even at the risk of becoming dreary or boring. The "subjects" addressed can be hotly contentious – for the media, at least – but their formal application must in no way be *unsettling*. The television viewer – the client – must be *content*. Public television sees itself torn between the wish to shift toward the authorized and vaguely degrading perversity of reality television (receive confession from Mireille Dumas![vi]) and the no less perverse desire to promote a pacified society, capable of treating, through the good old formal recipes, the good old *bad treatments*. Pacification, repletion and perversion – this is the liberal market. By countering the satisfaction of the "need" to see, to see an ever greater amount, "ever more," by countering optical voracity and all this anxiety to accumulate an abundance of the visual, the cinema of the *hors-champ* does not speak to us about our present: it hurls us into it, rushes us into it. How? By summoning us from the place of the *unsatisfied spectator*, the spectator who is unsatisfied above all, I take it, by his own place, a place of worry, trouble and lack. The spectator today has a sharpened consciousness, and he is aware of being engaged in a global combat where images and sounds do not die or live without him – without us.

---

8. A dose of the absurd remains: bereft of advertisements (and hence bereft of market share), the public television networks stubbornly insist on referring to the ratings provided by Médiamétrie. This form of delirium can only be explained by the very simple fact that in the post-advertising era, the same administrators run their networks in the same way they always have done, as if they knew of no other way. This is less a formatting of films or television, and more a formatting of the modes of thought of those in charge of public television's ethos and finances. In the end it was advertising that changed television, and not television that changed advertising. Cf. Bernard Stiegler, *La Télécratie contre la démocratie* (Paris: Flammarion, 2006).

Cinema against Spectacle

Great mutations are linked, not to solemn historical events, but to what we could call discursive ruptures, that is, what are commonly known as Renaissances: there is a general mutation in the system of values, and writing is captured in this conversion because these new values require a new regime of production and diffusion. The refinement of 'Gothic' writing and its generalization across Europe correspond to the Renaissance of the 12th century; the passage from the manuscript to the book corresponds to the great Renaissance (of the 15th century); meanwhile, today, at a time of undisputed crisis in humanist values, a new writing is being sought and worked on: a writing of images and sounds.

– Carlo Ossola, "Variations sur l'écriture," preface to Roland Barthes, *Le Plaisir du texte* (Paris: Seuil, 2000), pp. 36-37.

I. Opening the Window?

If the beginning of history never took place, if identities did not possess any dates of birth, and if our roots were ahead of us, then only identity-fluxes would exist, which could only be grasped in the movement of lines crossing time and space, and which could only be learnt at certain privileged moments of their journey, at certain peaks of their circulation. These privileged moments could be determined by pressing against the window, like a train passenger, in order to locate the precise levels of the trajectory when, converging at great speed, several rails merge, constitute a configuration of lines and then separate again.

– Elias Sanbar[1]

[Film's] illusory nature is that of the second degree, the result of cutting. That is to say, *in the film studio the mechanical equipment has penetrated so deeply into reality that its pure aspect freed from the foreign substance of equipment is the result of a special procedure, namely, the shooting by the specially adjusted camera and the mounting of the shot together with other similar ones.* The equipment-free aspect of reality here has become the height of artifice; the sight of immediate reality has become an orchid in the land of technology.

– Walter Benjamin[2]

One. – Appearing in *Cahiers* in 1972, the sixth episode of "Technique and Ideology" promised that it would "be continued." This follow-up remained a promise, as the series was left unfinished. It is tempting, and at the same time absurd, to pick up the thread broken 37 years ago... Broken? These six articles from 1971-1972 have not ceased to shape my work, through the course of several hundred pages published since 1988 in a range of journals and anthologies, as well numerous interventions in

1. Elias Sanbar, *Figures du Palestinien: identité des origines, identité de devenir* (Paris: Gallimard, 2004), p. 14.

2. Walter Benjamin, "L'Œuvre d'art à l'époque de sa reproductibilité technique," 1939 version, translated [into French] by Maurice de Gandillac, Rainer Rochlitz and Pierre Rusch, *Œuvres vol. III* (Paris: Gallimard, coll. "Folio essais," 2000), p. 299 ["The Work of Art in the Age of Mechanical Reproduction," trans. Harry Zohn, in Benjamin, *Illuminations*, ed. Hannah Arendt (New York: Schocken, 1968), p. 233].

cinemas, schools and festivals.[3] Re-reading them today, I discover (in the fullest sense of term: I had not read them since their original publication) certain motifs maintained throughout the technological, economic and mediatic vicissitudes which have affected the place of the cinema in our societies and which, to a certain degree, have drowned it in the bath of the so-called "audiovisual" flux – a development which could barely be discerned at the beginning of the 1970s. Included among them are: the will to (re)think the cinema through the relationship between man and machine; the hypothesis, formulated and re-formulated, that the forms and figures produced by the interplay of instruments and techniques bear semantic implications, independently of the will or knowledge of the authors; the conceptual inversion that sees the "place of the spectator" as not being external to the represented scene and as being the actual object of the *mise en scène*; the constant reference to André Bazin...

Two. – Nothing is ever written outside of one's own era. And, above all, what I can read in "Technique and Ideology" is the echo of an era, an earlier era, the era of *Cahiers*. For me, it was the real era. The night and the moment.[i] It is not for me to "revive" this epoch, those tremendous years (1965-1973),[4] not least because they still haunt me, because this era is not dead, because I am caught in it like a rat in a trap, and would risk lacking the undeniably necessary elastic distance between who I thought I was then and who I think I am now.

The era I am speaking about began at the moment when the yellow-covered *Cahiers* became polychromatic, and when Jacques Rivette left his role as *éminence grise* in order to replace Éric Rohmer as editor. It is the moment when, with Jean-André Fieschi and then Jean Narboni, we found ourselves – the "young ones" at his side – breaking free of the influence of Rohmer and Douchet. Their influence on me, however, was important, and it is still at work today – at the price, no doubt, of a major gap between us.[5] It may be that I was not the only one to be so divided. We admired Rohmer and his writing style, as much as Douchet and his critical pertinence. But we also admired the rarer texts written by Rivette, we felt ourselves engaged by the manner in which he thought about the cinema, and the sides he took in the issues of the time. And from my modest position as editorial secretary, I could not avoid see-

3. The lion's share of what I wrote between 1988 and 2003 has been collected in *Voir et pouvoir* (Lagrasse: Verdier, 2004).

4. The history of this period, the history of *Cahiers*, remains to be written. Antoine de Baecque's book leaves me unconvinced, as, I fear, it is guided by certain partisan considerations.

5. As much as his films (and particularly his later films), I love the writings of Éric Rohmer (who started out life as Maurice Schérer). See: *L'Organisation de l'espace dans le Faust de Murnau* (Paris: Cahiers du cinéma, 1977); and *Le Goût de la beauté*, texts collected and presented by Jean Narboni (Paris: Cahiers du cinéma, 1984) [*The Taste for Beauty*, trans. Carol Volk (Cambridge: Cambridge University Press, 1989)]. I can also recommend reading *Éric Rohmer* by Pascal Bonitzer (Paris: Cahiers du cinéma, 1999). As for Jean Douchet, I will restrict myself to citing his *Art d'aimer* (Paris: Cahiers du cinéma, 1987), the quintessential text of the great art of interpretation.

ing how detached the yellow-covered *Cahiers* were from global movements. There were wars: Korea, Indochina, Algeria,[6] the colonial wars and decolonization struggles in Africa and Cuba; Vietnam was not far off... And Auschwitz and Hiroshima were not far in the past. Politics was thumping at the gates of the cinema. Godard had just shot *Le Petit Soldat* (1960), still banned in 1962, the year I joined *Cahiers*. And we regularly saw Cécile Decugis, editor for Godard and Rohmer, who had just been released from prison, after being sentenced for her active support for the FLN. How could all this pass unnoticed?

At the same time, cinephilia could also be used (and understood) as a means of repression. The cinema speaks of the world by filming it, of course, and it is, in any case, for this reason that we went to see so many films, from all countries and all eras. But only up to a certain point. The cinema enveloped the world, defined it, rendered it perceptible and intelligible, absolutely. And yet we felt that it ought to come out of this embrace unscathed. Thus, the yellow-covered *Cahiers* was and was not – wanted to be and did not want to be – on the margins of history. The cinema would have enough resilience, we hoped, to hold itself aloft from political contingencies. This gave it the ability to claim the status of an art form (a question which was still very contentious at the time). Our Champs-Elysées office was thus an excellent observation post, all the more so given that engaging the cinema in the battles of the day was out of the question.

Three. – This marvelous distance was, however, in the midst of being diminished. *Cahiers* – Bazin, Rohmer, Rivette, Truffaut – had welcomed Italian neo-realism, beginning with Rossellini, as a major event, precisely because the cinema had been torn to pieces by the war, led through the streets, exposed to the dangers of the time. *Paisà, Germania Anno Zero* and even *Europa 51* (all three by Roberto Rossellini, 1946, 1947, 1951) are not films outside of history; they speak of the violence of the present.[7] We encountered these films turned out toward the world. But was there a need for widening the field, for embracing history? We refused to see the extent to which the entire cinema was implicated in the evolution of our world.

Maybe this fatal entanglement was still not very perceptible? It could soon be verified that it was only very slowly becoming an object of thought for cinephiles.[8] There was, among us, as well as among our elders, a sort of resistance, possibly out of

6. In 1960, the Manifesto of the 121 was signed by three of the magazine's editors: Jacques Doniol-Valcroze, Pierre Kast and François Truffaut.

7. But some years earlier, in the US, some of our most important filmmakers, Chaplin, Capra, Lubitsch, Lang, Hawks, Hitchcock, Fuller, among others, had made politically engaged films for Hollywood. The cinema had not been waiting for neo-realism to venture into present-tense history. This present-tense history was nonetheless still recorded in the studios.

8. Cf., for example (and to widen the circle): *Le Cinéma américain: analyses de films*, ed. Raymond Bellour, 2 vols. (Paris: Flammarion, 1980), a collection of texts from the 1970s.

a concern to protect the magic circle of the cinema, or to be protected by it, a reluctance to accept that the cinema was a stake in the economic and ideological battles shaking the world. War and propaganda yielded films. When we loved them, it was for the cinematic intensity that they brought to the screen. We wrote about *Steel Helmet, Pick-up on South Street*[9] and *Verboten!* (Samuel Fuller, 1951, 1953, 1959) without placing too much emphasis on the ideology of these films, without analyzing their conditions of production – that is, the complex economic contradictions of the American system – and without reflecting on the "context," on the possibly divergent effects that they could induce.[10] In short: of the economic and ideological determination of film technique – which would become the motif of my papers in 1971 – I saw nothing...

Four. – No matter how blinded we were by our cinephilia, we nonetheless ended up knowing that when we visited *chez* Langlois, when we took our seats in the front row, it was to cross over to *the other side of the mirror*, to enter the world by means of films, to enter into the films in order to cross over to life. Initiations do not only have a ritual basis: they give forms a function, they imprint signifiers on the skin of the subject who submits to the procedure. The screenings at the Rue d'Ulm left traces, they branded us. Was it not, for the cinephile that I was, a means of feeling the pressure of the world as an *aesthetic pressure*? It seems to me that this is still the case today, and that, as far as I am concerned, I can only envisage a relationship to the world if it is mediated through artistic practice. It is true that I see this practice starting from the place of the spectator, and that, to my mind, cinephiles, assiduous spectators – those who we used to call *amateurs*[ii] – are artistic operators (even if they make no claim to any status as artists) to the extent that they enter into a real practice (watching films), and acquire an experience which is not so much a matter of culture (erudition, mastery of reference points) as it is a matter of *jouissance* (or a loss of bearings). Criticism is the entrance hall of art. The cinémathèque was burning.

The cinema, for us, was not to be detached from the world, to evade it, to disconnect from it; on the contrary, it was to be burdened by the world, to be mixed up in it. A cinema which is not only "impure" according to Bazin's famous definition, but sullied, infused with flesh and blood, dissected with calipers. Unclean, somber and

---

9. A film which, as we knew, had been transformed to suit the demands of global distribution, with communism having given way to drug trafficking at the center of the plot.

10. With our work on *Young Mr. Lincoln* (John Ford, 1939), *La vie est à nous* (Jean Renoir, 1936) and *Kuhle Wampe* (Bertolt Brecht/Slatan Dudow, 1932), as well as *Z* and *L'Aveu* (Costa-Gavras, 1968, 1969), one of our chosen tasks would involve drawing out the network of divergences or inconsistencies between the explicit program of a propaganda film and the ideological effects that it could arouse, which were often at odds with the sermon thrust to the fore. We would soon become convinced that the cinema was not reducible to its ideological statements, that it was necessary to search further, on two sides: that of the textual writing of these films, of their signifying network; and on the side of the base apparatus, and the ways in which it is governed by ideology.

dark – this is why we could not love Wyler, why we had to prefer Ford, and particularly the Ford of *Grapes of Wrath*. We were quick to understand this, thanks, among others, to John Garfield in *Force of Evil* (Polonsky), Welles in *Touch of Evil*, Widmark in *Pick-up on South Street* (Fuller), Mitchum in *Out of the Past* (Tourneur). In short, while admiring Lang and Walsh (more so than Preminger and Losey), I never felt that I was a "*macmahonien*" (as we called them at the time).[11]

Five. – I did not believe that there had to be, as a categorical imperative, a *transparent mise en scène*. Re-reading "Technique and Ideology" today, this is the motif which stands out. The screen is not a window, and if the cinema shows, it also hides. It opens and shuts. It inscribes a dissemblance within resemblance, and this is why it constitutes a lure. The screen is ambiguous. Outside-inside. Front-back. Bright-dark. Surface-depth. The cinema shares with painting the fact that everything passes over a *surface*, in the two dimensions of the screen. The third dimension, the impression of depth, the depth of field, constitutes the first and principal articulation of the cinematic lure: the surface seen as depth.

The cinematic gesture displaces us. Gushing forth from the powerful beam of light which comes at us from the rear, a trace rests on the white screen like the outline of a shadow, a brush works the light to turn it into a darkened blot hanging over the world. At the speed of light, a shower of abrasions spreads out across the two dimensions of the screen, carving an imaginary depth into it. It bathes our transfixed bodies in a glimmering projection of photochemical matter, a patchwork of palpably material audiovisual vibrations, more corporeal than ghostly. This matter, and these vibrations, are separated from the body of the actor, and return to the body of the spectator via machines. These machines are not immaterial; they filter what they convey. Does the exaltation of transparency involve a denial of the role of man in the machinery, or an effacement of the material incidence of projection, of the screen, the frame, the machine? Maybe. Filming (and projecting) gives support to a gesture of mediation or intercession, through which, no doubt, the image and the world are conjugated, but on the basis of their differentiation rather than their fusion. The intervention of the cinema alters the world, skews it, transposes it, makes it pass through a new level of opacity, considers it insufficient, incomplete, not yet appropriated. When filmed, the world goes missing: from now on, the cinema takes its place, by representing it – in both senses of the word. "The represented is not the real," as Roland Barthes said. Nor is representation. Representation signals the vacancy, the lacuna and the malfunction which makes it possible and maybe even

11. The four filmmakers in question: Fritz Lang, Raoul Walsh, Otto Preminger and Joseph Losey, constituted the "four aces" for the cinephiles who named themselves after the MacMahon cinema in Paris, which they attended regularly. Curiously, they insisted, at the time, on the motif of the transparency of *mise en scène*, or "invisible" *mise en scène*, which is not overly characteristic of the style of these filmmakers, with the exception of some of Walsh's films.

necessary; it notes the lack as real; it joins the edges up, it sutures the cut: it creates matches. Thus, the cinema is above all the art of the match, of montage; and montage is first of all composition, articulation. Whereas the world allows its cuts, interruptions, breaches, fractures, jerks, jolts and elisions to be seen, the cinema intervenes to keep the machinery fastened and secure. This is why the world invented by the cinema is more cyclical than the world of our daily experience. It starts over with every film, every screening. There is a beginning and an end. In the cinema, we are taken into this repetitive temporality, which is to say that we are far from the eternity of Paradise. So let us here leave all transparency behind.

Six. – Bazin's "window opened onto the world" comes from Alberti.[12] Alberti writes that everything in painting occurs as if the surface of the canvas were "made of glass or a translucent material," an "open window."[13] Open, yes, but open onto what? The "story," as Alberti clarifies.[14] This *historia* (or *istoria*) is, therefore, not at all the same as Bazin's "world." It can be translated as "scene" or as "tale." Let me quote Jean Louis Schefer:

> We have here one of the major concepts in *De Pictura*. Neither the term "history," nor "anecdote," nor "subject" are totally fitting. The *historia* is the very object of painting, which results from an invention (the subject, which can be the object of a narration or a description) and a completed composition (arrangement of forms, parts, bodies). We can not, however exclude this simple meaning: Alberti's 'realist' program demands that painting show and relate. In its most formal definition, the *historia* is an arrangement of parts (bodies, characters, things) bestowed with meaning.[15]

Both the scene and the tale, then, are artifice, they have more to do with mediating, composing and producing than with capturing. The scene only exists through the combination of the painter's gestures; the tale engenders the world onto which it "opens."

As for Bazin's window, it seems that it does not depend on an artifice, does not proceed from a fiction, does not interfere in the things it receives, but that it allows

---

12. Leon Battista Alberti's *De la peinture – De pictura* (1435) exists in two French translations, by Danielle Sonnier (Paris: Allia, 2007) and Jean Louis Schefer (Paris: Macula, 1992) [For a recent English translation of this work, cf. Leon Battista Alberti, *On Painting: A New Translation and Critical Edition*, trans. Rocco Sinisgalli (Cambridge: Cambridge University Press, 2011)]. See also: Gérard Wajcman, *Fenêtre, Chroniques du regard et de l'intime* (Lagrasse: Verdier, 2004).

13. Alberti, *De Pictura*, trans. Jean Louis Schefer, *op. cit.*, Book I, §12, p. 101.

14. "First I trace on the surface to be painted a quadrilateral of the size that I want, made of right-angles, which is for me an open window through which one can see the story, and there I determine the size that I want to give to the men in my painting." (Alberti, *op. cit.*, Book I, p. 115).

15. Alberti, *op. cit.*, Book I, note on p. 115.

the world to come through and imprint itself on the sensitive surface of the celluloid. Its transparency claims to be neutral, and thus assumes that the world is already there, already created, already composed, offering itself to be viewed, to be filmed. It opens onto a given world, whereas Alberti's window opens onto a becoming, a to-be-constructed. For Alberti, the open window is precisely the lure constructed by the painter. The surface of the painter's canvas or the wall of a fresco is not made of glass, but it functions *as if it were*. The lure functions on the principle of painting itself. The window is an effect of belief.

But by wanting to master this artificial depth, by wanting to construct the scene on which the window opens, the painter, following Alberti's advice, interposes a transparent veil between the world and the eye. By doing this, he veils as much he unveils. This veil is divided by a dense set of threads organized in regular squares. These threads cut (the word is Alberti's, who names the veil the "intersector") the rays of light composing the famous "visual pyramid" linking the eye and the object. The visible is thus submitted to a rational program redesigning it; the visual pyramid adds its lines of force to the world's spectacle; the vanishing point proceeds from a calculation and gives rise to an entire series; the veil is interposed between the mind and the world in order to regulate the visible.

The *historia* constructed with the aid of the intersector is cut off and separated, by this same intersector, from the creative gesture: the scene is on one side of the veil, the artist is on the other.[16] The veil is, of course, transparent; its transparency, however, is not immaterial. It thus evokes a *screen*, so much so that that the scene which is visible on it resembles a mental projection, without the projection ceasing to be a material *dispositif*. The veil serves to distance us from the world. There is a distancing, a gap in the creative gesture. This is the meaning of Dürer's etchings. Such a *mise en perspective* can be given the name "*mise en scène*." The practical and moral distance which is interposed between the desire of the artist and the object of this desire appears as the condition of the very possibility of the artistic gesture.

There is therefore a leap between Alberti and Bazin. The window seems the same, but it does not open onto the same vista. For Alberti, as for Bazin, four centuries later, the world was a divine creation. Alberti nonetheless presents painters as using art to become "almost the equal of a God."[17] This is a contradiction, but an active one: the world is already there, already created. Absolutely. But the painter renders it in its truth and beauty, he recreates it. There is resemblance, but there is also reconstruction. As far as I can understand, the window, for Bazin, opens onto a world which imposes itself of its own accord – without any condition other than that the

16. On this theme of *separation*, cf. Marie-José Mondzain's book: *Homo spectator* (Paris: Bayard, 2007).

17. Alberti, *op. cit.*, Book II, §25, p. 133.

window should be open. The human input is minimal. As opposed to what happens in Alberti's view, the artist is not supposed to rival the divine creator.

Seven. – Let us return to Bazin and seek to understand how a (more or less direct) "dialogue" can be established between the world and the window – in this case, the window of the camera. We have a glimpse of it in *La Région centrale* (1970-1971) by Michael Snow. The principle of this film is well-known: a camera mounted on an articulated robotic arm capable of moving in any direction – up, down, right, left and in every combination of these directions – films a desolate landscape in northern Quebec.

> I wanted to make a film which would utilize the perfectly circular movement of a camera on all the planes of a hypothetical sphere, and not only the habitual horizontal movements and very rare vertical movements. Pierre Abbeloos (a film technician from Montreal) and myself constructed an apparatus capable of allowing a camera to make the oblique movements that I dreamt up, without photographing itself or the camera operators. No existing film equipment allowed such an operation.[18]

There is no longer any doubt – since we have come to be observed day and night by a multitude of surveillance cameras – that the machine-camera has no need of a human eye's framing in order to film what the visible world presents to it. The "takes" recorded can correspond to no human look. What is it, then, that allows this footage to subsequently be visible for a spectator? It is the fact that it is governed (through the use of short focal lengths) by the optical and perspectival "laws" accompanying it, that it is linked to a thought (whether clear or not) based on a centering of the world through the powers of the eye, or of the eye as the central power. I can see Michael Snow's film projected on a screen because the camera which filmed it was ordered, from the beginning, by the coordinates of binocular human vision as imitated by the cinema. And in spite of the inhuman contortions of the machine, the lure is primal, the visual rendering of its activity resembles what an eye gifted with extraordinary motor capacities could perceive. This, then, is the cinema's anthropomorphic center of gravity.

When the machine is "alone" before the world, man has already passed through it. On the one hand, the lenses of the automatic camera have been devised in the manner I just described; on the other hand, there enters into play the temporal object which every strip of images and sounds unspooling through a projector or video player becomes. This is what "humanizes" the camera's automatism. *La Région cen-*

---

18. Michael Snow (www.medienkunstnetz.de). The movements of Snow's machine are a constant challenge to the human body's role as an axis governing the look.

trale lasts 196 minutes. Camera surveillance footage, in contrast, has an unlimited duration (and does not constitute a work). Watching a film or video demands, however, that the same duration, whether pre-determined or not, is shared between the machine – in this case, the projector – and the spectator. On its own, this "synchronization" (to use Bernard Stiegler's term) ensures the role of man in an affair which seems to exclude him. The face-to-face between film and the world, as desired by Bazin, is always mediated, both by the combination of technology and science developed since the Renaissance, and by the place of the spectator, which is defined by a shared duration. We share time with machines, and these durations govern our relationship to the world, which translates them so that they become our own. The camera measures time: it is a *clock* which turns at 24 or 25 images a second. And it is only in this ordered time that the camera records a discontinuous succession of fragments, of varying lengths, of the visible "scene." Let us agree that this involves a *reduction* and *abstraction* of the world, precipitated and condensed in the system of the machine and in no way given over to us "such as it is, in and of itself." And let us remember that the first film in history, *Sortie d'usine* (Louis Lumière, 1895) was shot three times, giving rise to three different versions (with or without hats, bicycles, carts, dogs). The factory gate, a great opened "window," let a flood of workers exit the factory, but it was also appropriate that it could be closed again before the end of the film reel (57 seconds). The first film is therefore at one and the same time a documentary (real workers) and a fiction (three takes with changes in performance and costume).[19] This is possibly the moment to recall Christian Metz's abridged formulation: "Every film is a fiction film."

Eight. – In these years – 1963, maybe – I remember a debate between Jean Rouch and Roberto Rossellini, in the UNESCO building, under the aegis of their common friend Enrico Fulchignoni. The discussion concerned the glorious term "*cinéma-vérité*," which Jean Rouch reprised from Dziga Vertov. Rossellini issued forth the slogan: "Things are there, why manipulate them?"[iii] It was a fatal turn of phrase. I must confess my admiring disarray, at the time, upon hearing this powerful formula. For a long time, I told myself: this is what defines *mise en scène*, as I can dream of practicing it, later; and as I already appreciate it, as a spectator, happy not to feel that I am being manipulated. For it is not that "things" risk being "manipulated" in the cinema;[20] rather, it is the spectator, carried away by the *mise en scène*. For the cinephiles of the time, every "manipulation" – that is, every crude dissimulation, every form of propaganda, every brand which is supported, underlined, reinforced, every narrative stratagem quickly given away; in short, every form of advertising rhetoric – seemed

19. Cf. Harun Farocki, *Arbeiter verlassen die Fabrik* (1995).
20. In any case, they are always manipulated: you always have to install the equipment, the sets, the bodies; you always have to switch on the power.

to bear witness to the greatest indignity, and were only useful for maintaining a certain contempt for the spectator, considered a feeble, immature and impressionable creature. Thirty years later, this is where we have seen the most frightening changes occur: almost nothing that is shown on television screens (private and public) is free of a redundant, perfectly banal descriptive commentary. Everything – what we must see and what we must think about what we see, or rather, what we are told we "see" – is said over and over again. It is truly remarkable that this tiresomely didactic mode has been adopted by all the world's television networks – including Arte, which congratulates itself for regurgitating this lesson to its despairing viewers.[iv]

Later, much later, resuming my work on Rossellini's films, watching them again while filming *La Dernière Utopie*,[21] I returned to this fascination. Coming from the mouth of the director of *Stromboli* (1949), *Viaggio in Italia* (1953) and *Amore* (1947), films which strike us due to the manipulation to which their actresses (Ingrid Bergman and Anna Magnani) are subjected, the fatal turn of phrase appeared to me as the imprint of a wondrous duplicity. Rossellini is also the director of *Francesco, giullare di Dio* (1950) and *India matri bhumi* (1957), two sublime films on innocence. Like Rossellini, I had dreamed of intervening to the least degree possible in what I would film (for example, *La Cecilia*, 1976). Later on (with *On ne va pas se quitter comme ça*, 1981), I made the most of the form of *auto-mise en scène* favored by documentary filmmaking. The term "documentary" – which is not the name of a stable category – describes, to my mind, nothing other than *a certain relationship with fiction*:[22] whereas, when the film reaches the screen, the differences between "fiction" and "documentary" are only conventions, and appear, during the screening, almost totally muddied (both forms have narratives, stories, characters and fictional drives, and both forms have filmed bodies), this is much less the case when it comes to the cinematic gesture, that is to say, the genesis of the film. To put it briefly, in order for a film to be called a "cinematic fiction," the actor (whether professional or not) acts *as if he is not being filmed*. As if the camera had become *transparent*, invisible. (We will come back to this.) This is the essence of fiction in the cinema: to lie, from the outset, about the conditions of production. In the documentary film, this pious dissimulation is impossible. Not trained, not educated, not captured within a system of

21. Jean-Louis Comolli, *La Dernière Utopie* (*la télévision selon Rossellini*), 90', INA-Vivo Film, 2006.

22. "Every film is a fiction film which re-elaborates certain unconscious contents. The fact that this dreaming occurs in a wakened state obliges to structure its contents, to subordinate them to an impression of reality, but it does not destroy them. The spectator lets himself go to the film in the gaps in his consciousness. He can experience a different object relationship, a different eroticism, a different love relationship. The censorship is not his own, but that of the film. Here, there is an irreducible obscenity." Christian Metz, *Le Signifiant imaginaire* (Paris: Union générale d'éditions, 10/18, 1977) [*The Imaginary Signifier: Psychoanalysis and the Cinema*, trans. Celia Britton et al. (Bloomington: Indiana University Press, 1982)]. I shall take this occasion to remind the reader of the great debt I owe to Christian Metz and, in particular, his analysis of the place of the spectator.

conventions, the woman or the man who plays "herself" or "himself" does not have the same requirement to *pretend not to be filmed.* Quite the contrary: what happens to him is precisely that he is filmed, he participates in the event (an occurrence which is much rarer in his existence than in the existence of the professional actor), he throws the dice of the "all or nothing," of the "once and for all," and has his spirits lifted, his life revitalized in the process. Why should he hide this? Any man or woman, engaged in a documentary experience, takes *pleasure* in it, and, whatever we wish to know about it, this is not all that *transparent.*

As for *auto-mise en scène,* it can take a wider meaning than the original anthropological definition.[23] I would describe it as the interaction between the filmed body and the filming machine. Inevitable in the practice of "documentary" filmmaking, this interaction can be understood as the phantasm of a subjective relationship with a machine, first the camera, then the sound recording equipment, above and beyond the technicians who serve them. These machines are imagined to have a place in the exchange, in the name of the unknown and absent spectator that they represent at the moment of the filming, but that they do not stand in for. Far from it: they can neither mime nor evoke this absent spectator, who is thus *projected* by the filmed subject. This returns us to the point that the filmed subject lends vision and hearing to the machines, and assumes that these machines have an attentiveness, an interest, even a desire for him. This is something that is unthought, from which the unconscious is not excluded. Let us say that it is the cinematic machine itself which functions as a *mirror,* and not the screen, nor the "window" of the camera.[v] I lend the machine the feelings which spill out of me, which it makes spill out of me. There is something of a slight delirium, a sweet madness, in the relationship that develops between the filming machine and the filmed body, at least when this body has not yet been domesticated by the cinema.

But how can we not also know that any posture of withdrawal from the fact that a film shoot inevitably involves performance is a trap, that the effacement of the filmmaker is an artifice, possibly even more powerful than the most visible marks of a personal style or will, that any strategy of camouflage or stepping into the background is just as artificial, involves just as much artifice, as a more obscene manipulation, and that it only lets itself be glimpsed when masked, when daubed with innocence and discretion? Rivette, the Rossellinian *par excellence,* considered the director to be a vampire, and one whose activity is not restricted to the night.

For the mere entry of a camera into a given place changes it into a studio, a scene. This is the inevitable artificiality that Rossellini's formula wants to deny. It would not be so astonishing to also find here the Christian postulation of Bazin's works: the world is given to us once and for all. "End of the construction site," as Rouch ironi-

---

23. Cf. Claudine de France, *Cinéma et Anthropologie* (Paris: Maison des sciences de l'homme, 1982), p. 367.

cally filmed at the end of *Moi, un Noir* (1959). But in his first film, the superb *Fantasia sottomarina* (1936), Rossellini does not hesitate to include the most naïvely exquisite of manipulations. The squids and fish which play out this brief story of love and fear in an aquarium are moved by strings held by the young Rossellini himself. And these strings are perfectly visible, much like those pulling the puppets played by Totò, Ninetto and Laura Betti in *Che cosà sono le nuovole* (Pier Paolo Pasolini, 1968). It is assumed that the world is given in an absolutely natural manner, but that the spectator can not see very clearly, or is supposed to "forget," that is, be in *denial* about the strings and special effects. The same can be said for the special effects of the cinema of the past, before the digital era. Most often done crudely, they remained visible and denounced themselves as a concentration of artifice. And yet, we "believed" in them. I knew very well that they could be seen, but I would act as if they remained imperceptible.

The world, for Rossellini, is there, undoubtedly, but the cinema does not leave it in tranquility. The disturbance of the world is, in any case, a Rossellinian obsession. He is one of those who sees the cinema as a spoilsport. "I do not demonstrate," as he was fond of saying, "I show."[24] Now, as "anti-demonstrative" as Rossellini can claim to be, "showing" involves extracting the thing shown from its "life" outside of the film, from its non-cinematic context, in order to import it into another living ensemble, to furnish it with another context. Showing immediately involves highlighting, and therefore questioning, doubting. Or, on the other hand, a belief that all one is doing is showing presupposes an implicit recourse to a prerequisite disposition for believing, much like a religious person believes, when given the sacramental bread and wine, that "this is my flesh, this is my blood." It is there, and it is not there. Even the least interventionist cinema still reverses the polarity of the world, and every process of capturing images makes the filmed scene pass – without punning on the laboratory terms – from the positive to the negative. This is what reunites Rossellini with Rouch's endless construction site – in spite of the controversy between them. Maybe the cinema actually made by Rossellini differs from what he would have liked to make? It seems to me that, here, destruction results from construction, rather than the opposite (as in Maoist dialectics).[vi] The world is no longer there such as it is, in and of itself. Yesterday, it seemed to us to be a given. To believe in this would be to stop believing in the cinema. If the cinema, as a force of destruction, can nonetheless *save* something from the world, this is because the latter has already lost so much of its force, and maybe even its substance. The spotlights have chased the shadows from the garden of Eden. The cinema thus celebrates itself as a trace of death – the death

24. According to Claudio Bondi's eyewitness account in *La Dernière Utopie*, *op. cit.* [Rossellini here plays on the likeness between the words "demonstrate" (*demonstrare*) and "show" (*monstrare*) in Italian, a likeness also present in Comolli's French (*démontrer* and *montrer*).]

of the cinema, but also the death of the world which underpinned this cinema. For example: *Sunset Boulevard* (Billy Wilder, 1950).

It is left to us to admit that all this – whether a ruse or not, a manipulation more or less explicit, more or less visible – is only a matter, precisely, of *style*. Or, to put it differently: a system of marking and unmarking which places the artistic gesture in a *critical* (*historical*) sphere where the divine gesture, as far as we know, has no role. The epiphany is above all suspicion. The real, non-hypostasized practice remains imprinted with clumsiness, failure, deficiency, contradiction, perspiration and desecration, all of which make it unique and singular just as surely as the "miracle" of an encounter removed from any mediation would. If we imagine that machines can have "relationships," it is quite fortunate that such relationships can be with our bodies, mixing together our conscious and unconscious selves. Do we not know that many machines, if not the majority of them, are devised and designed to extend the life of the human body? They are prostheses (cf. André Leroi-Gourhan, Gilbert Simondon, Bernard Stiegler). But the camera both prolongs and limits the eye at one and the same time. The frame delimits our look by exercising a non-symbolic violence on it. For, in the cinema, the frame is always there, whether it is perceived or not, whether we pay attention to it or not. It is always there, waiting to be discovered as such, as what limits the portion of the visible that is accessible to the cinema. Now, this frame is discovered from the moment that it *moves*, whether in a pan, a tracking shot or a zoom. In the cinema, movement is the non-actual, non-actualizable power of the frame. Evidently, this is not the case in photography. And in a further difference with photography, the frame in the cinema is no longer defined only in terms of space or surface, but in terms of duration, time. The frame is a duration. This duration ensures that the framed and non-framed elements come (or are able to come) to *play* with the edges of the frame and inscribe them with a fragility, a precariousness, and even a spitefulness for the visible. This is not because I see the frame with my own two eyes (in principle), it is not because this frame is immediately inscribed in my ordinary visual field, in the *norm* of seeing, or because my gaze in the cinema is not framed. It is because my gaze is bounded by the limits of the frame and duration. This double limitation is the constraint which ushers in the advent of cinematic form.

If the "window" is to be understood, then it must be according to Bazin's great precept that "the frame is a mask [*cache*]."[vii] Framing involves eliminating everything outside of the frame from view. The frame as a mask does not only conceal a more or less important portion of what the visible world lets us see (the visual field), but forbids us from seeing what is not yet within the frame, or what is no longer within the frame. In other words, framing involves masking a succession of past and future temporal actions one behind the other, or one beside the other. The hypothesis of the open window is invalidated by the power of the frame as a mask, as an *active form*, sometimes invisible and sometimes visible, sometimes perceptible and sometimes not. The frame is an oscillation between an awareness of the contour and an awareness of the content. This *to-and-fro* situates the spectator in an ambivalent in-between [*entre-deux*] position. In the cinema, we see differently to how we see in real life. We see with a single eye, from an assigned position, with consented immobility, through accepted blinkers. The mask is more oppressive than the window. It opens onto the drama that has come to the visible, the passage of time, the entries to and exits from the field. From the very start, this withdrawal affects every "positive" definition of the will to show. The will to show is the will to dissemble. The game of the mask ties in with the hide-and-seek game of the principles of narration: do not tell all, do not reveal all, defer the resolutions, allow ambiguities to simmer. The cinematic frame-mask is, in its own way, a narrative condensation. *It is what is not there that allows it to continue.*

There is another meaning to the phrase "to show is to hide." What is shown takes the place of what is not shown. What is currently visible is replaced by another visible, is buried underneath it, rendered obsolete. What is not there, having previously been there, haunts what is there. At the heart of the visible, within its realm, there is the non-visible. Under the image there is the screen. Under the screen, the wall.[25] This is another meaning of the term "mask": the mask is a screen, the screen is a mask. There is another nuance: at the center of the frame, what do we see? Not much, perhaps? The cinema makes us doubt our own ability to see. There is nothing more cinematic than the tale of "The Purloined Letter," borrowed from Edgar Allan Poe by Jacques Lacan: whatever must not be seen is brightly exposed at the center of the image.[26] It is for this reason that "seeing" in the cinema does not suffice, and, in a way, is missing from its place. It is a matter of wanting to see, or of believing in seeing, of carving out the visible, of doubting it, or perhaps even of turning away from it in order to begin to see.[27] The exemplary story recounted by Harun Farocki in *Bilder der Welt und Einschrift des Krieges* (1988), a modern fable, is well-known. An American miniseries about the camps, *Holocaust* (1978), gave the impetus for a CIA functionary to comb the vaults of the US Air Force, and confirm that American bombers had indeed flown over Auschwitz in 1944-1945 and photographed it. These aerial photographs were seen, but they were not read. All the details of industrialized death were there, were photographed. But the eye was not there: the crematories of Birkenau were not seen, only industrial installations in Auschwitz-Monowitz. We had to

25. Wajcman, *op. cit.*

26. Jacques Lacan, "Le séminaire sur *La Lettre volée*," in Lacan, *Écrits* (Paris: Seuil, 1966), pp. 11-61 ["Seminar on *The Purloined Letter*," *Écrits*, trans. Bruce Fink (New York: W.W. Norton, 2006), pp. 6-50]. Some films have staged (in their own fashion) this proximity between blindness and hypervisibility. For example: the opening sequence of *Snake Eyes* (Brian De Palma, 1997).

27. Both now and in the past, cinematic practitioners such as John Ford, Jean-Luc Godard, Danièle Huillet/Jean-Marie Straub and Abbas Kiarostami partly base their approach to *mise en scène* on the *doubt* that it is enough to "show" in order to make us see (or hear). In other words: the spectator begins by experiencing the fact that he can not see, that he can not hear (or at least not very well). The film is there to teach him how to see and hear better.

wait for 33 years and the shock of a televised fiction for these images to finally be seen for what they were, the photos of an active death camp.

In one word, the cinema allows for vision and hearing to be exercised – that is to say, to be *re-educated*. It reveals the deficiencies of these faculties by bringing them into play, and it points to their limit: the blindness that is at the center of sight, the deafness that is at the center of hearing.

Nine. – The whole quarrel surrounding the "base apparatus" and its ideological determinations, of which "Technique and Ideology" was a sort of partisan overview, could thus be rewritten today, from a distance, as the confrontation of two aesthetic conceptions. The first (which can be called classical) assumes the effacement of the traces of the elaboration of the work, of the process of creation, of work itself. The gesture which creates the work presents itself as "pure," untainted by any effort, above and beyond any performance, miraculously untouched by the materiality which supports it. It is the magic of *mise en scène*: transparency.

Perhaps we need to wedge the circus into the genealogical tree of the cinema. In the circus, too, there are machines and bodies, humans and animals, lights and spectators. And then there is this magnificent phrase from Alexis Grüss (I am quoting from memory) when responding to anyone who speaks to him about "his art": "*art is work effaced by work.*"[viii] Can we use this formula in relation to the cinema? I think not, precisely to the extent that the cinema relies on machines. In the cinema, recording and projection, analysis and synthesis come in pairs. Each "image," each frame only appears fugitively by effacing its predecessor, before it in turn is effaced by its successor. Appearance and disappearance, inscription and effacement are one and the same thing. What is effaced is what is inscribed as a trace. This effacement leaves behind traces, and these are the traces of the non-effacement of work.

The other conception, opposed to the first, allows something of the conditions of production – the contradictory phases of the process of production of the work – to be seen, or even just glimpsed. The cinematic machine shows itself, is perceived in action, even when it is not explicitly filmed – let us say that, when it is off-screen [*hors-champ*], it is not outside of the scene [*hors-scène*].[28] And when it is filmed, as in *Man with a Movie Camera* (Dziga Vertov, 1929), this *mise en abyme* can be read as a certain duplicity. On the one hand, it allows us to see the material and technical procedures which produce the film. But on the other hand, this unveiling of the lure does not prevent the unspooling of the film in the projector, that is, the synthesis which allows us to "see" how this analysis functions. On the screen, the movement is fixed, and a frame lasts longer than the fraction of a second which is reserved for it.

---

28. I note in passing that this *mise en abyme* (the cinema in the cinema) has become a generalized condition, and that it has lost its didactic dimension (Brecht). Could it now be the case that there are cameras everywhere in our lives, except in films?

The film has stopped but the projection continues. It is through the effect of a very Brechtian paradox that the rupture of the illusion effect does not put an end to the scene, nor to the play, nor to the theatrical *dispositif*, but instead revives the desire for illusion. The suspension of illusion is the desire or the promise of the illusion still to come. Such is the *fictional fatality* of the cinema, which reduces the distance between what is called "documentary" and what is called "fiction," which re-situates them within the act of a gentle caress. One does not work without the other. Stimulus, unease, vertigo (Kiarostami). When the machines make themselves forgotten, we leap to the fictional side of the cinema; when they return to the surface (looks to the camera, acts of *auto-mise en scène*, on-screen cameras), we return with them to the documentary side of the cinema (Brian De Palma's *Redacted* is a fiction which mimes the "documentary" reality-effects produced by the cameras of today: home cameras, press cameras, surveillance cameras, webcams, etc.). It will be granted that this back-and-forth game is indeed what moves the cogs of the cinematic mechanism; that it is what makes the place of the (cinema) spectator an endless tourniquet where "true" and "false," nature and artifice, spontaneity and preparation, freedom and work are brought together without ceasing to be opposed to each other. The spectator *does not know* what is going on with this manipulation. Films even teach him *not to know, to accept not being able to know*. This is why it is quite likely that doubt and belief are one and the same thing in the cinema (and not just in the cinema). Let me go back to Rouch: "*cinéma vérité*" is a necessary paradox. We just have to *believe in it*: a rather strange definition of truth.

In the cinema of the past as much as in the cinema of the present, I enjoyed a taste of both conceptions: one where the framework was visible, and one where it was invisible. Where did this eclecticism come from (an eclecticism which was not yet considered to be an ideological vice)? On the one hand, I loved the cinema when it embraced the world, when it made the world regurgitate its contents while appearing to barely even lay a finger on it (Mizoguchi, for example). On the other hand, the sharp edge of the gesture (in Oshima's films, for example), its glimmer, astounded me. I wanted both darkness and the brightest light possible from the cinema. I was yet to understand that opposites can complement and support each other, that they can turn around one another like the two sides of a Möbius strip, that the attraction of opposites is particularly applicable to the cinema; that, as in the potter's workshop, it is the random possibility of defects which is what makes for the cinema's beauty; and that, as in the paintings of Caravaggio, it is the "brightest light" which casts the darkest shadow. Neither Mizoguchi nor Oshima, in any case, feared the Brechtian dualities: spinelessness and courage, shame and nobility, ignominy and grace...

Both were necessary: the code, shared by the greater number, including, for example, the code of transparent *mise en scène*; and what breaks the code, or what escapes from it, the singularity of a disconcerting act of writing.

This dialectical step forward was yet to be taken. When it was taken, it happened in a collective movement. In 1965, Rivette handed over the reins. We (Narboni and myself) would maintain the magazine on the basis he had set down: an openness to contemporary thought (Barthes, Lévi-Strauss, Foucault, Metz, then Deleuze, Legendre, Schefer, Virilio, Baudrillard...); an appropriation of the theoretical tools of Lacanian psychoanalysis and Althusserian Marxism; a re-evaluation of the "classics"; a consideration of the ideological and political dimensions of the history of the cinema ("Cinema/Ideology/Criticism," with Jean Narboni in 1969); an interest in the documentary cinema (first Rouch, then Perrault; with Louis Marcorelles and "Le détour par le direct," also in 1969); and, perhaps most importantly, a critical recognition of and active support for the "new cinemas" around the world: the first films of Jean-Marie Straub and Danièle Huillet; those of Jerzy Skolimowski, Glauber Rocha, Miklós Jancsó, Jean-Pierre Lefebvre and Gilles Groulx, Bernardo Bertolucci and Marco Bellochio, Ousmane Sembene, Otar Iosseliani; and the new American cinema, John Cassavetes, Robert Kramer, Shirley Clarke... We thus felt capable of holding the two ends together: on the one hand, the politicization of the cinema and the critique of the "left-wing fiction" (Daney)[ix]; on the other hand, re-tracing the history of the cinema, revisiting Hollywood, and, at the same time, focusing on the latest films.

This was the beginning of a collective intellectual adventure, not without its detours and fixations, where we first found ourselves under the patronage of Daniel Filipacchi and Jean-Louis Ginibre, before flying with our own wings. On board: Jean Narboni, Jean-André Fieschi for a while, Jacques Bontemps, then Pascal Bonitzer, Sylvie Pierre and Jacques Aumont, Bernard Eisenschitz, Jean-Pierre Oudart and Serge Daney, Pascal Kané, Jean-Claude Biette, Pierre Baudry and Michel Delahaye (who came from the earlier team and who we broke with). Serge Toubiana, Alain Bergala, Serge Le Péron, Philippe Pakradouni joined us later. There were agreements and disagreements, both cordial and otherwise. I remember it as a kind of melting pot where mergers and splits would take off or come to a halt without warning, following the most taxing of alternative regimes. In short, it was what is called a "group": both torn apart from the world and tearing itself apart, like every group. What were these years around 1968 for us at *Cahiers*? They were the years of a surprising conjunction. The *nouvelle vague* preceded May '68 by almost ten years, but by the same token it foreshadowed it and colored it. Since that time, I look back on those years as being both carried forward and shattered into pieces by the spirit of May. Narboni has written about this time in much more precise terms than what I have said about it here.[29]

Ten. – Beyond the aesthetic quarrel and its ideological stakes (masking or unmasking the traces of the work), this question broaches the *very functioning of the base appa-*

29. I invite the reader to consult: Jean Narboni, "Les futurs antérieurs," in *Les Années pop: cinéma et politique, 1956-1970*, by Jean-Louis Comolli, Gérard Leblanc and Jean Narboni (Paris: BPI/Centre Pompidou, 2001). On this period more broadly (1965 to 1975), cf. Jacques Rancière's postface to *La Parole ouvrière* (Paris: 10/18, 1976; repr. Paris: La Fabrique, 2007) and *L'Arrogance du présent* by Jean-Claude Milner (Paris: Grasset, 2008).

ratus. My hypothesis is that, quite simply, the traces of the work can not be effaced by the cinema (even if they could be effaced by other artistic practices). Why? Because the cinema is, essentially, the *work of machines*, which have not been calculated to disappear in what they produce, but, rather, which leave all kinds of marks (regularity, for example, or duration). These lead, as we have noted, to visible and recordable reactions on the part of the bodies they encounter. On the part of the spectator, we know, the cinema is a *cosa mentale*.[30] But on the part of the *mise en scène* and production, it is *mechanical*. And unless we assume that the spectators *would not like to see*, a dolly shot (whether forward, backward or sideward, and no matter how much it has been infused with the grace of a Max Ophüls or the delicate touch of an Alain Resnais) or a crane shot (no matter how much breath it takes in to escape its own weight, as in Mizoguchi) remain visible movements in and of themselves, and can not fail to be noticed and to be received as a decision to make a machine move in relation to one or more bodies within a specific setting.

Mobilizing and deploying machines, cinematic *mise en scène* becomes visible as such. The movements of the camera apparatus link, or, indeed, are linked to, the movements of filmed bodies; and, at times, they separate, or are separated from, these bodies. But in all cases the camera "speaks" these movements – both its own and those of the bodies or objects in the scene – and it speaks them without becoming conflated with them. Camera movements, variations in focal length, shadows, lights, everything which creates an effect, even if almost imperceptibly, designates the artifice at work, the distancing from nature. The historical approach of differentiating the values of shots, from the most distant to the closest (I am thinking, for example, of the work of Jean Mitry,[31] a major point of reference for "Technique and Ideology"), thus yields the hypothesis of an implicit visibility of the filming machine, and even of its "autonomy." In order to be able to speak of a close-up, a medium shot, a long shot, or a tracking shot, it is first necessary to imagine that the filming machine can be mobile, that it can be shifted or carried around. *Man with a Movie Camera* opens up the range of these possibilities, to the extent that it makes an animated character out of the camera on its tripod, which, alone on the screen, dances, bends over and skips about, thanks to the simple magic of stop-motion photography. In one of the strongest cases of *mise en abyme* in the history of the cinema, the machine itself becomes an entity, an isolated being, parodying the human body, reserving its graces for the other machine, the one filming it.

---

30. The example of the shot/reverse shot has been analyzed as a match that is more mental than material in nature. This is the meaning of the notion of suture reworked by Jean-Pierre Oudart (*Cahiers du cinéma*, no. 211 [April 1969], and no. 212 [May 1969]) ["Cinema and Suture," trans. Kari Hanet, *Screen*, vol. 18 no. 4 (1977-78), pp. 35-47].

31. Jean Mitry, *Histoire du cinéma*, vol. I and II (Paris: Éditions universitaires, 1967-1969, repr. 1995).

Eleven. – One of Lumière's most famous cameramen, Alexandre Promio, reputedly invented the first tracking shot in the history of the cinema. When in Venice, Promio had placed the camera on a boat and filmed the palaces fronting onto the Grand Canal as they passed by. Sending his minute-long film to Lyons, he confessed his doubts: would the spectator (who was also totally new to the cinema) put up with this new type of movement, which was so "unnatural"? Was it the palaces which moved, all by themselves, along the river? Would the audience be frightened by these masses of stone appearing to come toward them? Had these immobile buildings suddenly become mobile? We know the extent to which fear is a recurrent motif in the early years of the *cinématographe*. Spectators were astonished at having taken fright, as much as they admired the representations capable of making them take fright. But what Promio feared and what the first spectators were afraid of was not entirely of the same order. For the locomotive projected onto the screen of the Indian salon at the *Grand Café* in Paris, which advanced toward the camera (and thus to us, the spectators), there is the recognition of a relatively banal phenomenon in a railway station, which becomes surprising in the salon of a Parisian café. There is displacement and *estrangement* (in Carlo Ginzburg's use of the term). At the same time, there is the apparently natural quality of the fixed shot, which gave the dual effect of transparency and reassurance. It is not the filming machine which is moving, but the other machine, the filmed locomotive.

If the spectator does not notice the frame, it is above all because, remaining fixed, it does not bring attention to itself. In the case of the palace on the Grand Canal, the movement is real: the frame moves at the whim of the boat which carries the camera; but Promio was worried: would this movement be perceived as such (as an innovation: a mobile *cinématographe*), or would it first be perceived (as was the case for all the other films on view at the time) as a *non-movement*: a *fixed frame* accommodating the movement of buildings, in exactly the same way that the fixed frame accommodated the movement of a locomotive some months earlier. There was thus the risk of seeing something strange and disturbing: the buildings gliding along the water and *moving across the image*! Promio feared that the spectators would confuse the perception of movement within the frame with that of the movement of the frame itself. Immobilized in their seats, the cinema's first spectators likely had difficulty in imagining that they were being carried by the movement of the camera. In any case, the question was posed. The movement in the frame appears *more real* than the movement of the frame.

We know that the optical experiments put forth by *Gestalttheorie* make us alternate between seeing the ground and seeing the figures of a drawing.[32] According to

32. "Everyone now knows these autostereograms which have appeared in recent years, made of a single image, in which the eye, at first, does not recognize a figure, but only a more or less repetitive ensemble of colored motifs. By looking at it from a certain distance, and making a certain effort, one's vision can be situated not on the plane of the stereogram, but on a virtual horizon point,

this principle of alternation, I assume that the frame is not perceptible in and of itself at first. Its static immobility is perceptible, but the rectangle of light framed by darkness is not. To tell the truth, the frame is not made to be seen. And yet, it is indeed there, as a cause and condition of the image, as the homothety of the screen. It imposes itself, and the spectator's gaze submits to it. Now, everything happens as if it were the gaze of the spectator onto the screen which was framed and not the screen itself. And if this is the case, then we have one of the first acts of violence carried out by the cinematic gesture – the gesture which makes us notice the frame. But because the image is surrounded by darkness, because we see it as simply a luminous rectangle cut out of the screen, the frame can in a certain manner remain "invisible," "latent." An effort at accommodating it is needed to distinguish it, and not keep to what it "contains," to what it shows. We could understand Bazin's leitmotiv in this light: when the window is opened, we can forget the reality of the frame and see the world grace us with its movements within the window frame, with the result that the latter is lost from our view, and only the former occupies our thoughts. However, the perceptual denial of the frame fully participates in the *naturalization* of this cinematic operation. "The train is above all a place where the immobile traveler is seated and watches a framed 'spectacle' pass by."[33] Here, the homologous relationship between window and frame is underlined, much as it will be by the car windows so often filmed by Abbas Kiarostami.

Fixed frame/moving world, as opposed to moving frame/fixed world? The question is no longer even posed. Everything takes place as if we had accepted movement being inverted in the same way we can turn a glove inside out: the real movement of the camera now leads to a synchronous imaginary movement in the spectator. Those inverse sensations at the beginning, those illusions in the illusion, were corrected,

---

located behind this plane; the flat image is then transformed into a frame opening onto a little three-dimensional scene, staggered across several depth levels, and populated with perfectly identifiable forms. In sum, we have here a case of 'perceptual ambiguity': the same graphic support is the basis for two radically different perceptions. Some may compare the image at the beginning to a confused sensation, and the following three-dimensional scene to true perception, taking over the preceding perception as well as its material basis. The *Gestalt* theorists will, by contrast, state that it is simply a matter of two distinct perceptions, where two organizations of the material – each one linked to a different attitude taken by the subject – are expressed. A third, more analytical, attitude can be added to these two, according to which the observer is able, by playing with his memory, to identify common graphic elements in the two organizations. But this does not mean that the first image – even if it is, in a sense, less satisfying – should be considered as the simple material, or even as a stage in the construction of the second organization (which would bring the elements back together in order to assemble forms and create the impression of depth). There is indeed – if expressing it in this manner is insisted upon – a common material for all these perceptual operations: but it lies beyond these two images, and neither of them makes itself 'seen' better than the other." Victor Rosenthal and Yves-Marie Visetti, "Sens et temps de la *Gestalt*," *Intellectica*, no. 28 (1999), pp. 147-227.

33. Jean-Louis Leutrat, "Les chemins de fer," in Leutrat, *Le Cinéma en perspective: une histoire* (Paris: Nathan, 1992). This relationship is developed by Raymond Bellour in *Le Corps cinéma* (Paris: P.O.L., 2009), pp. 72-82.

then forgotten and repressed. The imaginary displacement linked to the movements of the apparatus opens up, on the side of the spectator-body, to an enjoyment of virtualization, ubiquity and simultaneity. I am magically transported from place to place (the flying carpet of the screen), everywhere, throughout all ages. Instructed by this school – the cinema, that is – the spectator reconstructs a coherence between his ordinary sensations (I am mobile in a fixed world) and what he feels in the cinema (it is the camera moving, not the setting). Once again, there is a naturalization of the scene. Permit me to leave Promio's question open. What if it was the world which really had moved in the frame? What if the historical advent of the cinema had arrived just in time to highlight this tipping point, this moment when the world itself began to vacillate?

Twelve. – Let us give yet another example of this abstraction of the real frame. In *Kid Auto Races at Venice* (1914), which is accepted as the first film where Chaplin appears with all his accoutrements, there is a *mise en scène* – the term is apt – of the ambivalent relationship between a man (Charlie the tramp) and a machine (the camera, mounted on a stand and operated by a cameraman and his assistant). The tramp can not prevent himself from entering into the field of the camera while it films the race. He is shooed away by the assistant, the cameraman, a policeman, etc., sometimes with civility, at other times – more often – brutally. But the man preventing the camera from shooting in the round returns to position himself inside what he guesses – with precise intuition – to be the *frame*. But what frame?

The description of what takes place in this little film can not avoid being twisted around: it is one of the first systematic cases of *mise en abyme*. A camera films a camera which films a spectacle, or, more often, as is the case here, a body. As a general rule, we see the filmed camera and not the filming camera, although the decisive role of the latter can not be denied: there is a film, there is an image of a camera in this film. If there is a film, then there is a camera filming the (fictional) camera in the process of filming. The filming camera is invisible, but logically present. It is precisely the *impossibility* of the filmed camera.

Now, Charlie visibly embarks on an amorous relationship with the filmed camera (let us designate it Camera #1, and the other one, the filming camera, Camera #2). He can not get away from it, he gapes at his reflection in the lens, he takes shape within its frame. We see all of this rigmarole. And what we see of it evidently passes through the frame of Camera #2, a true object of instant love for Charlie. Camera #1 is the apparent cause of this love, while #2 is the real cause. The relationship, as I said, is thwarted: the men who are filming with Camera #1 are striving to eject Charlie from its frame, as they only want images of the race, without this *excess body* [*corps en trop*]. Of course, the repeated efforts to chase the intruder are evidently filmed by Camera #2. If Charlie is supposed to be expelled from the frame of Camera #1, he remains within the frame of Camera #2, which films the entire action, including Camera #1. Let us repeat: when Charlie is chased away from one frame, he is not chased away from the other. We are therefore led to *imagine* the frame from which he is excluded, because he does not cease to be included in the frame that we do see, that of Camera #2. We do not see what the operator of Camera #1 sees, because we see him seeing, we see him turning the hand crank, and we see him not turning it so that he can shove the impertinent tramp out of his way. We can thus speak of an *imaginary field.*

Having exited from the frame, the tramp (with admirable simpering, seduction and self-seduction) is still framed. Repelled from the imputed field of Camera #1, and at the very moment when he is supposed to have been chased away from it, he is still inside the frame of Camera #2. The latter constructs a frame which acts as the *hors-champ* of Camera #1. Which amounts to asking: where is the *hors-champ* if it has become the field [*champ*]?

Let us pursue this thought. A 180-degree match cut makes us see that *we only see what is taking place at the expense of the repression of the real circumstances which permit this view.* This time, Camera #1 and its servants are no longer filmed by Camera #2 from the back, but from the front. The indefatigable Charlie now places himself between them and us, between this camera and our look, he leaves and returns, occupying a space which can only be the very space framed by Camera #1.

But... what can this camera that we now see from front-on frame, if not, at the same time as Charlie, Camera #2, which is in the process of filming the scene? The "real" camera? The two cameras are face to face. An immemorial memory makes us know what "face to face" means: a situation of reciprocity, an exchange of looks. But nothing of the kind is produced. Camera #1 only films Charlie's swaying hips. *As if all that were there were Charlie, as if there were no other camera in front of it.* Fiction. The spectator is thus led to mentally block out the camera filming in order to only see the filmed camera, even though the latter, even if it was filming, could only film, behind Charlie's body, the camera in front of it. We could call this figure an *imaginary reverse shot* [*contrechamp*].

This short film is exemplary: it disassembles the logic of our blindness, such that the frame that we see is not that inside which the action is actually taking place (the game with Charlie and the edges of the frame of the filmed camera), but its supplement: Charlie's game with the frame of the filming camera. The real frame (Camera #2) remains *invisible as such, that is to say, as a mask.* The imaginary frame (Camera #1) *phagocytizes and absorbs the real frame.* The spectator is vampirized. What we see does not exist for the camera that is supposed to be filming it. And the camera which actually does film the situation (Camera #2) becomes co-extensive with the unlimited, unframed, *natural* human field of vision. *As if the frame that it determines did not exist as itself, as if it had no reality.* Thus, extraordinarily, Charlie does not leave the frame even when he is chased from the frame. His body relentlessly stays within the frame, it relentlessly acts as an obstacle to the view of the cameraman, and occupies the spectator's field, precisely as if it were the extension of our own gaze, its supporting framework, and the only thing it was aimed at. Charlie plays with the frame, enchants the edges of the frame, places his body at the center of all that is visible. Right from the beginning, the charm of the cinema has been divined. It is a charm that will not wear thin.

Thirteen. – Supposing the existence of a *mise en scène* without manipulation would be a contradiction in terms. Rather, the question lies within the respective logics of different modes of filmmaking (which are, as we know, forms of thought). In sum, it is even necessary to examine and interrogate the modes of manipulation, their means and ends, their moral and political perspectives. *Mise en scène* as manipulation thus designates itself on the cinema screen by letting itself be seen, by making us, I dare say, see how it films while it is filming. This self-interrogation [*auto-mise en cause*] is of the same order as advertising's manipulation of opinions in the age of the mass media. In order to manipulate public opinion, the media must publish (or program, broadcast, etc.) the manipulative information. At once, they print and archive the traces of manipulation by themselves. The influence of the mass media, linked to their real or supposed audience, predisposes them to manipulation, whether they are manipulating or being manipulated. What they can not dissemble is the information made public for the purposes of this manipulation. Neither news broadcasts nor the "paper" press disappear once their task is accomplished (or their dues paid) – they are classified, analyzed, conserved by archivists.

I became aware of the political aspect of archiving while working with a researcher (Marie-José Gaudin) for the preparation and filming of *Jeux de rôles à Carpentras* (1998). In this age of short-term memory, where we are told that the flux of information repeatedly passes without leaving any traces in our minds, these traces nonetheless exist, in archives, libraries, cinémathèques, (and, for example, at the Institut national de l'audiovisuel, where 60 years of public television have been digitally stored). What we were able to see without seeing, read without reading, hear without hearing, everything in our history which is written in the present and manufactures the ignorance of the past, all this is saved and lies in wait for the work of a filmmaker and editor to return before our eyes and beneath our ears, and to make us finally realize that understanding the present moment involves, precisely, creating a work of montage.

And thus the memory of the act accompanies the act. And if it were necessary to come back to "transparency," it would be in this new sense: that the traces will always shine through and can not be effaced, no matter how much care is taken to do so. Through the mechanical regulation of distances, durations, focal lengths, movements, the camera imprints its presence on the sensitive surface. With varying degrees of ostentation, of course. Transparency is what leaves the trace to be seen, not what effaces it. That which weaves this supposed "transparency" from reality is indeed artifice.

Fourteen. – How can one not see, without expressly willing not to, that a cinematic frame is a *torn fragment* from the "seamless fabric of reality" (Bazin)?[x] How can one not see, moreover, that we can never speak of "*an* image" in the cinema, that the image is never "alone," except in books (such as this one) which contain isolated frame enlargements? There is no "cinematic image" in the singular. They are not orphans, nor are they single. Each "image," since this term persists, is only an "image" when captured, transferred and worked on by the succession of other images which comprise the film. Whirlwind. Tapestry. Montage. Each point of the image is taken into an embroidery where numerous other images (and sounds) make a network with it, connect with it, foreshadow it, pull at it, frame it, enter into a montage with it.

Thus the visible part of the world imprinted in this isolated image is nothing, and this image itself is nothing, without a collaboration with the images surrounding it, preceding images which have already been seen and have disappeared, and images not yet visible, not yet present, which will follow it. They all traverse it with their non-presence, give it a consistency, a truthfulness, a meaning that it could not have by itself. The invention of the *cinématographe* is that of the *image-series*, the still image only has meaning when it is multiplied and potentially linked to the other still images of the series – namely, the film.

In this sense, the cinematic "window" diverges from Alberti's window. Only what is visible on the surface of the earth, Alberti writes, is a matter for painting. The painter is only concerned with what is on offer to his view. It is impossible to say the same for the filmmaker. What is exposed and imprinted in the fraction of a second that it passes in front of the window (of the camera) is *nothing* without everything that came before, and everything that will come after. In the same way that pressing on the trigger of Étienne-Jules Marey's chronophotographic rifle for one second yielded a series of 12 snapshots, starting the motor of a modern camera records several still images in succession (filming "image by image" requires a specific setting). The material, or the object, of the filmmaker is less Alberti's "surface" than it is duration. Space is *turned into time.*

In the cinema, *units of time* are units of form and meaning. Each cinematic shot is defined primarily by a duration (whether linked to the original take, or resulting from an editing process) which imposes itself on the spectator as coming from the work, no matter how this imposed duration will be felt by him. There is a subjectivity in the perception of objective durations (the timecodes in the camera and the projector) which imaginarily makes them vary, and gives them a mental rhythm proper to each singular subject during each singular screening.

Fifteen. – Even before the first experience of an *edit* in the history of the cinema was attested, *montage* was potentially present in the very first film, even though, as we know, it was filmed in a single shot. Between each of the still images which comprise this series of around 50 seconds, there is a *gap* and a *match*, and thus a premonition of what we will end up calling *montage*. Montage is prepared by the succession of still images, and it is a logical deduction and material consequence thereof. Because two still images are always separated from each other by the tiny interval of the *interimage*, they participate in a discontinuity, and the *impression of continuity* which emanates from the fact that their projection gives them movement can now only be a supplementary degree of the lure. Separated, distant, slightly dissimilar even within their resemblance, they appear to "match" (by being consistent with each other) according to a continuity effect equivalent to the "match cut" produced between two shots edited together.

We know that two contiguous still images (which only the slim interval of the *interimage* separates) are *different* even if they represent the same thing. They are "the same." Or almost. The entire functioning of the cinema is inscribed within this *almost*. Why? Because from one to the other there is a gap in time (a minimal one, lasting a fraction of a second) which can also be a minimal leap in space if the subject of the take moves (the locomotive, the workers), or if it is the camera apparatus itself which moves. Without this leap between a still image and each of its immediate neighbors, all of them desperately static, there is no movement. From one still image to the next, this *almost nothing* nonetheless derives a lot of meaning.

Sixteen. – Adriano Aprà tells us that Roberto Rossellini was fascinated by the coincidence between the structures of stars and atoms... In his unfinished film on science,[34] he dreams of a correspondence between the infinitely large and the infinitely small, from the "macro" to the "micro." Following his example we propose to resituate a reduced model of montage in any given succession of still images. This contiguity, while being purely mechanical, already brings a range of conjunctions and disjunctions, proximities and distances, into play. Repetition and variation, identity and difference.

From every still image to every other one, as I have just emphasized, there is at one and the same time an *ellipsis* (of a slight fraction of space and time) and a *match* (that is, a soldering together of two discontinuities). The very functioning of the cinematic machine functions on two levels: 1. a discontinuous capturing of the world – an affirmation, and thus an admission, that the "seamless fabric" hypostasized by Bazin is torn by the take, and 2. a sewing together of these fragments or shards. In order for the cinema to arise, it is hence necessary that 1. the apparent sensorial continuity of the world should be segmented, divided, broken down [*découpé*] (that is, altered) and then 2. these tiny but indisputable rifts should be stitched together, sutured, in order to produce an *impression of reality* which, as I said, is also an *impression of continuity*.

34. Cf. the presentation that Adriano Aprà makes on this matter in *La Dernière Utopie, op. cit.*

Negation, transcendence, reconstruction. There is, and this is my hypothesis, a solidarity between the organic functioning of the cinema and a conception of the world organized dialectically. During the cinematic operation, the world of sensory appearances, the primary world, is negated by its transformation into still images, the impression of temporal and spatial continuity is contradicted by the process of cinematic segmentation. The analysis of movement is thus precisely what negates movement, suspends it, breaks it up, fastens it. From this negation arises affirmation, from this deconstruction arises the possibility of a reconstruction: with the synthesis of movement which occurs through the use of the projector, the impression of continuity returns, the world depicted recovers its movement, its "life." But this "life" now returns as a *lure*. The *sublation* [*relève*][xi] of the negative presents itself at the same time as a lure.[35]

Here I would like to correct one of the points tackled in "Technique and Ideology": at the time, the term "retinal persistence" was used to explain the synthesis of movement caused by the fusion of images quickly following one another. It is now accepted that something else is taking place.

> It was known that a rapid succession of static images can create the impression of unity in movement, and this principle is at the foundation of the cinema. But the consequences remained to be drawn. Wertheimer was able to do so by studying very simplified versions of this phenomenon: in essence, he projected a rapid succession of discs or luminous segments, while varying the durations, distances, exposure intervals, as well as the intensities and colors. The *gestalt* psychologists discovered, in these stroboscopic phenomena, the crucial fact which was decisive for their theory's later development. Here they found an original perception, which is neither a summation nor a synthesis of preliminary, isolated local sensations, nor an interpretation of sensations by means of belief. They saw in this a striking confirmation of the theses that they had begun to develop: perception makes local processes interact with each other, although they may not necessarily be synchronized, it integrates them on a permanent basis, at a distance and on a temporal level, and this is how the perceptual field is constructed, such as it is lived in the present. And as it is a matter, here, of movement, time and space are equally involved. [...] It is therefore, if you will, the global identity of the figures which is decisive for the identification of all the specific points, across the movement which animates them. Worse yet, certain conditions of presentation provoke the perception of a strange category of movement, a movement without a perceptible mobile object, a sort of "pure transition," which Wertheimer gave the

35. In *La Ressemblance informe ou le gai savoir visuel selon Georges Bataille* (Paris: Macula, 2003), p. 268ff., Georges Didi-Huberman analyzes the "dialectic of forms" such as Bataille puts it to work in the texts and photo-montages of the journal *Documents* (1929-1930).

name "phi phenomenon." [...] A conclusion imposes itself: time, space and movement are contained in a single organization, they are phenomena of the structure imposed by the totality of the field. Everyone is prepared to admit that our experience depends on what precedes it. But what is more surprising is that it is also determined by what is experienced afterwards. If, therefore, trajectories are sometimes gestalts constructed on the basis of their extremities, it is because *time itself is organized.* The present is not a pure isolated moment, but rather a window which opens and slides along the passage of time; it does not only retain the effective participation of the past, but also integrates our immediate future.[36]

The window returns, but this time it is temporal and mobile – is it the cinema?

Projected on a screen, the world seems to recover its fluid and continuous passage. It was disarticulated, now it is re-articulated. But this re-composition is not the return to a prior state. The disarticulation which can no longer be seen is still there, imprinted in a succession of stills; the analysis of images is embedded in the photogrammatic skeleton of the film. It only provisionally "disappears," during the time of the projection, for it comes back, and it is all that is left when the filmstrip comes to a rest. Effaced by the synthesized movement of the projection, analysis has not ceased to play a role. Without it, there is no synthesis; without the static quality of the still images, there is no movement. The synthesis of movement realized by the projection is thus a lure which, under the cover of the impression of reality, dissembles the profound unreality of the cinematic process. This is the resolution (or reconciliation) of opposites in the transcendence of their division and opposition, which nonetheless maintains an inexorable gap from them. The same concern for *continuity* is constantly encountered in sound-mixing procedures, which *mix* various sounds, of various origins – voices, noises, music – in an ensemble which gives a sentiment of unity, where the ruptures and fissures only act as *concerted audio effects*. Much like the color-grading process which consists, on the one hand, of *correcting* the chromatic and luminescent qualities of the images, and, on the other hand, of attenuating or extinguishing any shock of contrast or luminosity between two successive shots, and thus of softening the transition and smoothing out the impression of continuity, sound-mixing is both a workshop repairing faulty sounds and an insistence on their accomplishment as parts of an integral whole.

36. Victor Rosenthal and Yves-Marie Visetti, *op. cit.* In the final remark we can locate an echo of the Augustinian formula on the "three presents," the present of the present, the present of the past and the present of the future. Cf. Paul Ricœur, *Temps et récit*, vol. I (Paris: Seuil, Essais, 1983), p. 32 [*Time and Narrative*, vol. I, trans. Kathleen McLaughlin and David Pellauer (Chicago: University of Chicago Press, 1984), p. 15].

Ontologically – to come back to Bazin – the cinema transcends negation (analysis) by dissimulating it in the lure of synthesis. The world that it casts doubt on by negating its primary sensorial qualities is once again proffered in a movement of affirmation, a movement which is still a lure: synthesis negates the negation on which it rests, which permits it, which supports it as an affirmation. The negation of the negation retains a part of what was negated, as the *remains.*

Seventeen. – By being subtly opposed to ordinary human perception, the cinema proffers a view of the world different to that of the spectator in the darkened room. The cinema presents us with a world which is the lure of the world of our senses, a reconstructed world, whose new presence – whose resurrection – passes through the negation of its old qualities, their transcendence. The cinema removes itself from the world of ordinary sensations in order to proffer another mode and another world of sensations to us. The ideological factor in such a program – playing with division in order to suspend it, playing with difference in order to reserve it, playing with contradiction in order to overcome it – affects all films as their *unthought.* The succession of cinematic images provides an *analogon* of visible reality. As true to life as it may be, this *analogon* is a tangled knot of contradictions. According to St. Augustine, it is because a representation resembles the "true" that it is "false." Let me quote him: "Surely something the eyes see is not called false unless it has some likeness to something true. For instance, a man that we see in a dream is not a true man but a false one, for the very fact that he has a likeness to the true."[37] The tracing is pushed back, unveiling is a form of covering over. In the darkened room, a trap is laid for the naïve

37. St. Augustine, *Soliloques*, Book II, trans. [into French] Denis Marianelli (Paris: Migne, 1999), p. 77 [*Soliloquies*, Book II, trans. Gerard Watson (Warminster: Aris & Phillips, 1990), p. 83]. A few pages later, St. Augustine, in his dialogue with Reason, discusses the paradoxes of the *true* and the *false*. Permit me this lengthy quote: "*Reason*: It is one thing to wish to be false and it is another not to be able to be true. [...] For a painted man, even though he is trying to look like a man, can not be as true as what is written in the books of writers of comedy. Pictures, images, etc., do not wish to be false and are not false because of any desire of their own, but because of a certain necessity, to the extent that they follow on aims of the maker. But on the stage Roscius was by his own will a false Hecuba, but by nature a true man. By that same will he was a true tragic-actor, by the very fact that he was carrying out what he intended to do, and a false Priam, because he made himself like Priam, but was not Priam. There follows from that something extraordinary, but undeniably true. – *Augustine*: What's that? – *Reason*: This: the source of what is true in some things is identical with the source of what is false. The only thing which helps to their being true is that in another respect they are false. So they can in no way achieve what they wish to be or what they ought to be if they avoid being false. For how could Roscius whom I have just mentioned be a true tragic-actor if he were unwilling to be a false Hector, a false Andromache, a false Hercules and countless others? Or how would the picture be true, if the horse were not false? Or how could the image of the man in the mirror be true, if it were not a false man? Well then, if it is of help to some things to be something false in order that they might be something true, why are we so greatly afraid of falsities and why do we seek after truth as after some great good?" [p. 95] This final question exceeds the scope of the cinema, while everything which precedes it is a commentary anticipating the ambiguous effects of the cinematic lure.

gaze. Behind the life of the screen, death is woven into the strip which whirls inside the projector.

A still image is indeed a splinter detached from life and preserved in an emulsion, a *fall* from life into death. But a still is just a still: it does not lie about its reality, that of a determined fragment, an avowedly isolated particle. Only an illusion can pass off that which it shows, that of which it is the frame/mask, as the object itself in its visual totality. Here we are at the heart of the cinematic paradox. The cinema as a machine at work always shows itself in the midst of functioning. We must *want to not see it at work.*

So what can be so astonishing about the fact that the majority of films spin tales around dualities such as "life/death," "appearance/disappearance," "true/false," "nature/synthesis"? These are only so many declensions of an "ontology of the cinematic image." Ideology and technique go hand in hand, no matter what the film, from the moment that the cinema machine (camera + projector) is put to work. It is not only the works which are historical, and not only the circumstances of their production, the *doxa* which cradle their conception; not only the techniques, as they appear to us, and as they are perfected into given historical moments under specific ideological and economic pressures. It is the base apparatus, its minimum degree of functioning, which is historical, linked to a certain moment of Western history – the "history of the eye" and the thematic recurrence of life passing away... The weaving together of still images makes us perceive something of the mythical, religious and philosophical ruminations which led to the invention of the *cinématographe*. From the Italian Renaissance to the industrialization of photographic procedures, over the course of three centuries, an incredible fever propelled scientists and dabblers, artisans, technicians and inventors to play around with images, resulting in both hope and despair. If, as Alberti claimed, Narcissus is at the origin of painting, something of his reflection, or his shadow, is still floating around in the modern machines of the visible: the image, desire, defiance and death are all there, entwined in a fatal dance.

II. Inventing the Cinema?

> I had to look through thousands of meters of film before hitting on the sequence of the Soviet army crossing Lake Sivash; and it stunned me. I had never come across anything like it. As a rule one was faced with poor quality films, or short snippets recording day to day life in the army, or else show pieces, which smacked too much of planning and very little of the truth. [...] Suddenly – quite unheard of for a newsreel – here was a record of one of the most dramatic moments in the history of the Soviet advance of 1943. It was a unique piece; I could hardly believe that such an enormous footage of film should have been spent on recording one single event continuously observed.
>
> – Andrei Tarkovsky[1]

One. – We now know just about everything that can be known about this invention, thanks (among others) to Laurent Mannoni's work *Le Grand Art de la lumière et de l'ombre: archéologie du cinéma.*[2] Here, I would like only to draw out some threads woven into the tapestry. The cinema came at a given moment in history, and this moment is not arbitrary. But there is a not-yet-invented cinema which came before its invention. Well before the Lumière brothers, images of all kinds were made to move; pictures, drawings, sketches, paintings, inkblots and photos were all animated. For example, Émile Reynaud – with his optical theater, projecting a series of drawings which were painted on glass and appeared to move – devised a *dispositif* (including a darkened room, a projector and a translucent strip) which was not very far away from cinematic projection... Photography proceeds from lifelike imagery, photography, projection and the screen come from magic lanterns, and the darkened room, of course, comes from the theater. The cinema was ready for a long time, it had been dreamed too many times for it not to exist in a thousand different varieties. A whole series of inventors, tinkerers, sideshow exhibitionists and experimenters went to work at making images, including photographic images, move. The Lumière brothers represent a point of condensation within an infinitely more complex fabric.

---

1. Andrei Tarkovsky, *Sculpting in Time*, trans. Kitty Hunter-Blair (Austin: University of Texas Press, 1989), p. 130.

2. Laurent Mannoni, *Le Grand Art de la lumière et de l'ombre: archéologie du cinéma* (Paris: Nathan Université, 1995) [*The Great Art of Light and Shadow: Archaeology of the Cinema*, trans. Richard Crangle (Exeter: University of Exeter Press, 2000)]. In 1971, we were bereft of this work.

The man of the late 19th century was an avid fan of machines. This period witnessed the parallel development of the ideologico-economic project of world conquest (the colonies) and the scientific fantasy of an ever-progressing mastery over nature (Jules Verne, engineering schools, aeronautics, the grand structures of dams, highways and railways...). It is both the era of heavy industry – mines, steelworks, weapons manufacturing, arsenals – and the triumph of automated labor (Taylorism: 1880) which assures capital's domination over the worker's time. The mad saraband of images which makes us dream and makes us afraid accompanies this violence.[3] Dispossessed of himself, his time, his gestures, the worker is also going to be dispossessed of his dreams by the nascent industry of the spectacle. People frequented fairground stalls so they could "show off." The visual, and acoustic, phantasmagoria which magnetized the era gave the laboring classes the chance to be entertained, to be "diverted" in the literal sense of the term: distracted from the worries of everyday life. The cinema appears at this fulcrum between the alienation and reconstitution of labor power.

Two. – The Lumière brothers, Auguste and Louis, were part of this new industrial bourgeoisie. Their father, Antoine, was the director of an important factory producing photographic plates. The inventive spirit of the two brothers allowed the family business to pass from an artisanal stage to an industrial stage. The Lumière family made their fortune with the "blue label" plates manufactured on the production line by hundreds of workers, who appear in their first film, *Sortie d'usine*. The "blue labels" were sold everywhere. Their advantage was to be rapid, allowing for very short poses (with an exposure time of one 250th of a second). A photograph (taken by Louis Lumière) showed Auguste jumping with both legs over a chair, seized in the necessarily brief moment when his two feet are in the air.[4] A "snapshot." The race for ever greater speed began.

More important still, to my mind, the fundamental parameters of the cinematic recording of shots are put into place from the earliest films, and will be reiterated up until our own day. In the entire cinema which does not involve animation or synthetic imagery, that is, in the entire cinema which confronts a body (whether human or not) and a machine, and functioning with the impression of reality, the following five dualities are still just as pertinent as they were in the first static shots: shadow/light, frame/mask, near/far, stasis/movement, slow/fast. Montage and the advent of

---

3. Do we have to reiterate that the upsurge of industrial capital responds to the crushing of the Paris Commune, the massacre of the masses, the collapse of a non-authoritarian, non-hierarchical political hypothesis? At the same time that it gave birth to the proletariat as a concept and a problematic reality, a proletariat in struggle, in becoming, the Commune died from persisting in being what it was, a fertile laboratory of individual initiatives, of revolutionary desire and subjectivity ("faults" which will all be corrected later).

4. Reproduced in: *Les Images des Lumière* by Bernard Chardère (Paris: Gallimard, 1995), chap. II.

sound films will enter into the mix at a second stage. We know that the absence of sound haunted the so-called "silent" image: the world is active in the first films by the Lumières, trains bellow smoke, the leaves of the trees move, children laugh, cats mew. All these inaudible sounds are nonetheless filmed at their source. The image of the sound is recorded, but not the sound itself. From the very first moment, the term "sound-image" should thus be used. In the same way that montage is inscribed in the succession of still images, sound is inscribed in the succession of images, that is to say, sound is silently figured by the moment of the beings and objects recorded by the cinema.

At the same time that machines are regulated, bodies, too, are regulated. *Discipline and Punish* by Michel Foucault[5] ought to be re-read, with a focus on the captivating nature of the repressive foundation he depicts: this is the backdrop for the fantasies of the charlatans who peddled phantasmagoric spectacles. The optical fever of the era speaks, in its own manner, of the dream or the hope of an upsetting of coordinates, of a vacillation of appearances, as if everything which appeared certain, solid, stable, could disappear in a single breath, then return at will. Slow-motion, acceleration. Separation, combination. *Fort/da.*[6] The effect of the disappearance of images, their fading, is already present in the magic lantern projections, and the world, perhaps, begins to be seen as a succession of dissolves. Projections did not restrict themselves to "representing" the world by repainting it with the colors of the lantern's plates. Instead, they superimposed themselves on it in order to recompose it. The meaning of these arts and techniques is rather poorly understood if it is not admitted that there is too often an underestimation of the grip that visible forms (sculpture, painting, engraving, photography, cinema) exert on the mind, and not only on the modes of seeing, but also on the modes of feeling and thinking.[7] Technology, whether mechanized or not, proffers models, "templates," which spread through society and end up not so much "representing" it as presenting themselves before it, giving it their style, branding it. Toward the mid-point of the 19th century, for example, the static projections of the magic lanterns began to stir from their repose. It is not just images that are wanted, but motion, sequences. This, therefore, is the moment that

5. Michel Foucault, *Surveiller et punir* (Paris: Gallimard, 1975) [*Discipline and Punish: The Birth of the Prison*, trans. Alan Sheridan (London: Allen Lane, 1977)].

6. Sigmund Freud, *Beyond the Pleasure Principle* (1920). "Freud's observation is succinct: one of his grandsons had the habit of hurling little objects at hand away from himself while pronouncing the prolonged sound *o-o-o-o* which constituted an attempt at the word "*fort*" ("forth" in German). Freud equally observed in the same child a more complete game: holding a thread attached to a reel in his hand, the child threw it around in his cradle while pronouncing the same *o-o-o-o* sound, then brought it back to himself while exclaiming "*Da!*" [here]. Freud links this game to the situation of the child in this period: a period where his mother is absent for long parts of the day. The game thus symbolizes the disappearance and re-appearance of the mother." (Stéphane Barbery, www.barbery.net).

7. On this question, see the hypotheses worked on by Gérard Wajcman in *L'Objet du siècle* (Lagrasse: Verdier, 1998).

machines themselves begin to move: it is utterly appropriate that the locomotive is the first mobile machine to be filmed. As for machines for showing or projecting images, they all, more or less, became machines for and in movement: the lanterns moved back and forth on rails, the glass plates were able to slide, the strips spun around, the perforations jumped up and down. The world is shaken by a great trembling.

At the same time, Western civilization ("the" civilization) embarks on its triumphant march. Science and technology, philosophy and ethics frame the colonial expeditions in Algeria and the rest of Africa. Let us recall that the cinema is quick to play a role in the symbolic appropriation of the colonies. There is a cinematic conquest of the exotic world (the term appears in 1860). The other, the distant, the foreign was visited, photographed, filmed, exposed, projected.[8] "Making the natives sweat" was not enough, they also had to be filmed. After photography, and in tandem with it, the cinema constructed the image of "the Other" which was undoubtedly needed by the West: ferocious, but not too much, and able to be *framed*. The cinema became a machine for taming the wild.

At the same time – and I mean at almost the same moment, or at most a few years later – worrying signs of a series of "discoveries" appear and converge, discoveries which threaten contemporary rationalism and humanism. Charcot displays his hysteric subjects on a stage in La Salpêtrière,[i] and has them photographed and filmed;[9] Freud publishes *The Interpretation of Dreams* (1900), Proust arrives on the scene with his involuntary memory (*In Search of Lost Time* appears between 1908 and 1922), Einstein publishes his *Theory of Special Relativity* in 1905, and in 1900, Max Planck develops the first outlines of *quantum theory*.

Whether as cause or effect, the cinema becomes associated with the shattering of certainties in a world until then presented as solidly positive. The vicissitudes of the subject, plunged into the unconscious, the implication of the observer in the observation, or of the analyst in the transference, the random state of particles, all these phenomena seem to lead to a weakening of common sense, a relativization of "objective" facts, a crisis of the frontiers between "inside" and outside," and the drifting of the Cartesian subject... The stories of the world tip over into the virtual, the multiple, the reversible, the spectral.

8. First the Lumière cameramen, then their counterparts from Albert Kahn's company, crisscrossed the world, ceaselessly filming it. Closer to our time, there is the famous sequence with the postcards in *Les Carabiniers* (Jean-Luc Godard, 1962)

9. Cf. Georges Didi-Huberman, *Invention de l'hysterie: Charcot et l'iconographie photographique de la Salpêtrière* (Paris: Macula, 1982) [*The Invention of Hysteria: Charcot and the Photographic Iconography of the Salpêtrière*, trans. Alisa Hartz, (Cambridge, MA: MIT Press, 2003)].

At the same time, and contradictorily, the cinema is praised *for what it is not*. It is admired[10] for being capable, by itself, of showing the world "such as it is" (the Rossellinian approach to showing [*monstration*]). It is also said to do so "objectively." Of all the arts of the visible, it is that which most actively implicates the subjectivity of the spectator, and passes itself off as (and sells itself as) a *mechanical reflection of an objective given*. It is the modest triumph of the lure – the *impression of reality* – to not at all be detected as such, and to pass unnoticed. It is understood that it is the *machine*, with its technical connotations, which guarantees the "objective" rendering which the cinema is supposed to have brought about. The machine is praised for validating our familiar and reassuring perception of a continuity and fluidity of movement in the world.

At the same time, it is accepted that first the photographic, then the cinematographic instrument extends the eye, provides it with a power which is in some way supernatural – that is, mechanical. Even the *daguerreotype* was able to simultaneously astonish and reassure through its capacity to "objectivate" the world. Daguerre's plates were admired because they gave a version of the visible more perfect than what the best human eye could claim: "details invisible to the naked eye" were engraved onto the plates, as if the chamber itself was also working.[11] This is also the theme of *Man with a Movie Camera*. The acceleration of shots immediately induces a mutation in the human perception of the world. No human look has decomposed or analyzed movement. In order to expand the bounds of human perception, there is a need for a machine, for the sciences (optics, chemistry, physics). Eadweard Muybridge and Étienne-Jules Marey literally photograph what *is not seen*, what can not be seen. Rapid-exposure photography gives access to a reality which is not visible to the naked eye, a sort of invisible, or poorly visible, world. The first consequence: *everything is not visible, but everything can become so*. The extraordinary proliferation of representational machines, the visual practices and fads throughout the course of the century, questions once more the ancient division of the world into two parts (two kingdoms): that which is visible, and that which is not. What escapes from sight is soon condemned to being seen. The field of the visible includes a reserve which one day or another will be conquered, and even ghosts will leave a trace on the film stock. Everything had to be seen, including what concealed itself from sight. And so it became urgent to invent tools in order to see what can not be seen. The eye, the look, glasses, the *camera obscura*, the photographic camera claimed to unify the world by

10. Cf. the remarkable collection of articles and texts of the era in *Le Cinéma: naissance d'un art 1895-1920*, ed. Daniel Banda and José Moure (Paris: Flammarion, coll. "Champs arts," 2008). Reading this work supports the claim that at its birth the cinema was interpreted by its contemporaries as being, at one and the same time, both "life itself" and a defiance of death.

11. Cf. Jean-Louis Comolli, *Voir et pouvoir*, *op. cit.*, p. 229. On the *daguerreotype*, cf. *Le Daguerréotype français: un objet photographique*, ed. Quentin Bajac and Dominique Planchon de Font-Réaulx, exhibition catalogue (Paris: Musée d'Orsay, 2003).

changing it into images. A new *conquest* of the world excited minds, mobilized capital: a conquest of the territory of the Visible, ceaselessly augmented, in order to always see *more, further, larger, smaller, more alive.*

Here there is a double game. The eye is beaten by the machine but takes revenge thanks to its rival. On the one hand, the cinema allows to "see better," to "see what can not be seen with the naked eye." Of movement, for example, it gives a version considered to be of an authentically documentary quality precisely because it does not depend on the "natural" capacities of the human eye. On the other hand, we admire that the images it produces remain in conformity with the norms of human vision, that they "resemble" the world such as we see it in everyday life. Extraordinary, ordinary. The fanciful and the realistic.

Three. – Right away, we learn, commentators and promoters saw the cinema as a means for transmitting images of living beings to future generations. That is to say: images of living beings who had died. Echoing *Genesis* as well as Alberti, Giovanni Papini wrote this astonishing commentary in 1907:

> When contemplating these ephemeral luminous images of ourselves, we almost feel like gods contemplating their own creations, made in their image to resemble them. Involuntarily, it occurs to us to think that there is *someone* watching us, just as we watch the figures of the *cinématographes*, and before whom we – we who deem ourselves to be concrete, real, eternal – would only be colored images running rapidly towards our death for the pleasure of his eyes.[12]

Now, what does the cinema provide us with if not an imitation of life which does not go right up to death? Perhaps the actors playing Christ in the numerous filmed Passions (at the beginning of the 1900s) are nailed to the cross, but they can come down from it and go back up again. The spectators all know it: the Passion can only be replayed, reconstituted (*La Ricotta*, Pier Paolo Pasolini, 1963). The false death of the actor, the fiction of death, replays the true false death of Christ, resuscitated from among the dead. For, in representation, we live several times – death is now held at bay, played, replayed, unplayed. If death can be repeated, then life, in its representations, is stronger. Man exchanges the reality of death against a *figure of death* (*Der müde Tod*, Fritz Lang, 1921). We gain from this exchange. In the cinema, the screening is repeated. When death is filmed it returns, departs and returns again. Death in the cinema is episodic. There is a *jouissance* involved in repeating it.

We are witness to a virtualization of bodies, of situations, of everything which in real life is constrained, blocked, weighed down; we are witness to the desire and necessity to break free from ourselves, the desire to go everywhere, the desire for

12. In *Le Cinéma: naissance d'un art*, ed. Banda and Moure, *op. cit.*, p. 138.

ubiquity, for transformation, disguise, the carnival. When the cinema appears, all this is behind it. The first spectators, actors, subjects and filmed bodies knew, with an unconscious understanding, that they had realized this mysterious partition of humanity's mechanical dream, this dream which brought them to go to a darkened room to see and celebrate, as their fright dictated, the separated power of a representation of the world "like life itself" without actually being life itself.

Four. – Let us still keep in mind that the still images which decompose movement, action or gestures do not proceed from a perceptive human process, but from an act of *mechanical hothousing*. The analysis of movement is strictly the act of a machine, the machine commands human perceptions. Meanwhile, synthesis, a mental process, is the act of the spectator, although aided, it is true, by a machine. This is the reason why a new type of "convulsive beauty" surges from the series of snapshots taken by Eadweard Muybridge: the body bent and folded over by the machine. The dancing couple, the kiss, the soldier running with his rifle, the woman in a nightgown, as well as the horse and the dog, are there to witness a new adventure of the body. The body is delivered to the photograph which will transform it, cut it up, immobilize it, twist it, seize it in such moments of disequilibrium that even Pontormo had not dared to depict. Let us consider the series of static images "taken" by Étienne-Jules Marey[13] with his "chronophotographic rifle": when gazing upon these images today, we are arrested by the *disfiguration of the visible* which takes place. Phosphorescent strips were attached to the bodies of the photographed athletes, and they were like bones shining in the night of the studio, skeletons fixed in their movements. The fragility of the appearance of the human body was underlined when it was stripped back to the these white, luminous lines. A *corporal machine* takes shape, the puppet or the doll replaces the volumes of flesh and blood. Marey scrutinized the bodies he filmed, but he did so at cross-purposes to all forms of naturalism, reducing people and birds alike to abstractions, contours, sketch outlines. I imagine that the scientist in him clung to this *plastic* or pictorial dimension as much as he did to the resemblance of movement. Here, science and technology are active on a different terrain,[14] they batter the

---

13. Apart from Laurent Mannoni's book (*op. cit.*), the reader may consult the following works: *E.-J. Marey, la passion de la trace* by François Dagognet (Paris: Hazan, 1987) [*Etienne-Jules Marey: A Passion for the Trace*, trans. Robert Galeta and Jeanine Herman (New York: Zone Books, 1992)]; *Mouvements de l'air – Étienne-Jules Marey* by Laurent Mannoni and Georges Didi-Huberman (Paris: Gallimard, 2004); and *E.-J. Marey, actes du colloque du centenaire*, ed. Dominique de Font-Réaulx, Thierry Lefebvre and Laurent Mannoni (Paris: Arcadia, 2006). A film should also be cited: *Scènes de chasse au sanglier* (Claudio Pazienza, 2007), which ironically puts Marey's chronophotographic rifle to use and reinvents the analysis of movement in order to turn the photographic trace into the trace of the very absence of every real living body, even that of a wild bore.

14. Cf. the films of Jean Painlevé which continue and disrupt Marey's work. Under the watchful eye of science, once again, "reality" is, on the one hand, discovered "objectively," and, on the other hand, in the same movement, covered over with a fantastic mask. *Documents*, the periodical put out by Georges Bataille and Michel Leiris, published two "close-ups" excerpted from Painlevé films.

figurative codes, they require an *estrangement* of the look: bodies are no longer entirely bodies, gestures are at one and the same time divided and multiplied. Marey, therefore, is not only an "inventor" of serialized snapshot photography on a photosensitive strip of film: he initiates the *transformation of the visible world by machines used for filming*. In his "views" can be seen the hidden truth of the cinema, which is none other than this: the analysis of movement is entirely anti-naturalist, it fixes poses into so many contorted anthropomorphic grimaces, it disfigures appearances. When synthesis will come to reconfigure these suspended gestures, the prior disfiguration will not be abolished, but only repressed.

Like the trajectory of an arrow, all movement is decomposable into an infinite number of "freeze-frames." In order to divide it into 10 million poses, all that is needed is ultra-rapid film stock, an enormous magnum, a shooting speed of 10,000 frames per second, and none of this is inconceivable on the condition of finding a little bit of space, for, extended in time, a simple gesture will extend itself into space to occupy a surface incommensurable with its initial amplitude. We do see a relation between the representation and the object represented, but this relationship is falsified, anamorphosed. Multiplied, the image becomes the deformation of the object, and possibly its negation as an altered object. From Marey onwards, the analogical representations of the objects and creatures of this world can be thought to pass directly from the other side of the mirror of the fantastic, in an unexpected affinity with the deformations of bodies and time that we encounter when reading Lewis Carroll's *Alice*.

Five. – We now arrive at the first screening of Lumière's *cinématographe*. The illusion was far from perfect. The noisy camera-projector was in the hall, the chairs were taken from a salon. The screen was quite different to the ones we are familiar with now: the images were in black and white, with very high contrast levels, the projection was jumpy yet scintillating... The impression of reality which resulted could only be very approximate. Nonetheless, the illusion worked. The spectators believed in the moving bodies of the workers freed from their factory. They believed in the rustling leaves of the tree behind the baby Lumière. They believed in the locomotive pulling into a railway platform. These spectators loved the power of illusion so much that they repressed it from their consciousness, an awareness that they could not fail to have of the material conditions of the screening. This palpably recalls the famous "Baltimore soldier" recounted by Stendhal (*Racine et Shakespeare*, 1823) and cited by Antoine Compagnon:

> Last year (August 1822), the soldier who was on guard duty inside the Baltimore theater, seeing Othello on the verge of killing Desdemona during the fifth act of the tragedy of the same name, cried out: "It will never be said that a damned negro killed a white woman in my presence." At the same moment, the soldier fired his gun, hitting the arm of the actor playing Othello.

Compagnon adds: "This is a very rich story, which Roland Barthes, from whom I discovered it, greatly liked. I only recently found its source. It interested Stendhal in the context of a reflection on illusion, and to his eyes it was illustrative of the 'perfect illusion'." For Barthes, this story was witness to what realism had to be in order to be really realist."[15] And Bernard Stiegler comments in his turn that:

> Art presupposes belief, but also, just as much, distance, that which Proust speaks of with regards to La Berma interpreting *Phèdre*, which he can not find, and which is the dimension opened by belief, where the latter is able to *distinguish* art *as such*, that is, as *another plane of reality* to that which quite simply exists, this is what I see in the anecdote that Stendhal evokes in *Racine et Shakespeare*, the story of the Baltimore soldier.[16]

The question is posed differently for the cinema than for the theater, I believe: here, might not *distance* be the reverse side of belief? Not what contradicts it, but what permits it? The first screening thus pushes down on the spring of the film spectator's foundational denegation: *I know very well* that I am at the cinema, in a darkened room, that I paid for my ticket, that there is a projector, a screen, and so on, that I am in the most conspicuous artifice possible, *but all the same*, I am going to believe that what I see on the screen is life such as it is, captured in its natural surrounds, without artifice. The two contradictory principles, illusion and reality, are paradoxically linked. It is not the case that one destroys the other, rather they give an impetus to each other. In the cinema, and, I fear, only there, belief and doubt turn around each other in a tourniquet. In the past, in 1895, doubt and belief, in the tiniest moment of hesitation, were one and the same thing. To doubt for a split-second, for example, the ability of the locomotive to enter the *Grand Café*, was to believe in it.

If fear there was, and stupefaction, it was a fear of the vacillation of conscience in a flash produced by the omnipotence of the illusion that struck each of the spectators. It is not the real rediscovered on the screen which was so striking, but the power of representation all of a sudden condensed there, on a sheet hung up in a boulevard café.

Six. – This omnipotence of the nascent cinema is accompanied, or rather, passes through, a denial of the form, which is not seen, as if it were cancelled out by the object represented. Let us return to Bazin's example of the frame/mask. We see, or we believe we see, what there is in the frame, we do not see that it is a mask and therefore not a frame at all, and yet... The question of the *hors-champ* is all the more

15. Antoine Compagnon, "La notion de genre, introduction: forme, style et genre littéraire," lecture given on February 17, 2001 (www.college-de-france.fr)

16. Unpublished text.

operative in the nascent cinema due to the static shots being striated by a crowd of moving figures, the bodies of passers-by, carts, stagecoaches and carriages of various kinds, animals, children... The edges of the frame are assailed with activity, and this very tension should enable them to be perceived for what they are. What could be more vibrant, more materialized than these two pairs of vertical and horizontal lines, which have the confounding power to separate the visible from the non-visible? But no. Through a form of blindness, the spectator is subjected to the *hors-champ*, but does not see that this is precisely what skirts the image, what surrounds the screen. The mask is active, but it is not conscious. And yet, the experience of these spectators should soon teach them that the *hors-champ* is not just an expanse of concealed space, but that it is also temporal, that absence, here, is only the imminence of a presence, its promise and its threat, its expectation and its regret. Maybe the film, itself a temporal object (incidentally, the duration of films increases very rapidly, exceeds a half-hour, then an hour), arouses on the part of the spectator an imaginary occupation of time more than space?

Let us give another example of the systematic torsion of "vision" at work in the cinematic operation. To the naked eye, we are, as we know, held for the majority of the time in an illusion of continuity and fluidity. But when this continuity or this fluidity of the movements of the world are filmed, the opposite surges up. Every movement is dislocated, discontinuous, a succession of freeze-frames, a succession of jumps. This discontinuity is materialized by the stunted back-and-forth of the sewing machine's presser foot, this surrealist accessory which thanks to Louis Lumière came to the aid of the cinema. The succession of fixed points fabricated by the shooting of footage (at 16, 18 or 24 images per second) becomes the matrix of the restoration of movement. Discontinuity gives rise to continuity. The filmstrip turns: analysis. It turns again: synthesis. The magic of machines.

We know that, all proportions guarded, the film projector functions on the same principle as the camera: the same loop of film, the same clamps, the same system of threading, the same type of lenses. The essential difference is that the lamp is behind the image, while in a camera the light is evidently outside the window through which the film passes. It is therefore the same stop-start mechanism which, immobilizing the film in a succession of arrested moments, fabricates the still images that provide the analysis, and which, bringing the strip back into movement, renders synthesis possible. Here there is a logical curiosity which induces us to dream. Life and death on the same ribbon, according to the direction in which it moves, and whether the source of light is behind or in front of the window! From the start, it is a throw of the dice: the Lumière brothers' camera served successively as a developing bath and a projector, in a condensation which allowed for the rapid, immediate success of the *cinématographe*. In the space of a single day, the Lumière cameramen could film an event, develop the film and project it that same evening to the individuals who had taken part in the event, and who, a little later, saw themselves on the screen. Through this acceleration of the time of representation, audiovisual journalism was invented at the same time as the cinema. There was a primacy of presence within representation. Living beings saw other living beings in an almost synchronous moment. At the same time, the bodies were duplicated, the spectator's actual body was doubled by a spectral body.

This is, of course, what analogue – and then digital – video brought to fruition, and what the cinema could only promise. Which leads us to ask if the film on celluloid and the film on magnetic tape (or a hard drive) belong to the same world, that of the cinema? My response has always been yes, absolutely: the undeniable differences, the contradictions between the formats nonetheless leave the fundamental parameters of the cinematic image intact. What remains of the cinema's basic skeletal fabric in the transition to the electronic, or digital, image? It took only a few years for the electronic image to docilely conform to the cinematic model and align itself with the latter's lexicon: we took to speaking about "images" even though there were no more still frames to individualize them. Beyond this, the process of magnetic recording is itself carried out through a series of traces and effacements (which may even have a more material existence than they do in the cinema): the information transmitted on the monitor screen by the magnetic tape is effaced by its successors, so that they, in turn, can appear. The smooth tape moves in a continuous manner, but the recording and reading operations put discontinuity back into this continuum. Traces are chiseled into the smooth surface. Scanning, as it is aptly known as. And, when screened "live," the electronic decomposition (analysis) of light and color intensities, and their re-elaboration into a "signal" which, in turn, is recomposed (synthesized) by a "receiver," functions as a series of *calculated ephemeral reductions*, effaced as soon as they are formed: traces which abolish themselves the moment they pass.

On the other hand, the electronic shutter of mini DV cameras can be set to film at 2, 4, 6, 8, etc. frames per second. A stop-start system of jerks which, in its turn, designates the cinematic skeleton (see *Disneyland, mon vieux pays natal*, Arnaud Des Pallières, 2000). So there are points of contact. Perhaps the only radical divergence – apart from the "quality" of the image – remains the access to the loop of immediacy: a video camera films live an action seen at the same moment by those who are being filmed. This immediacy would have a tendency to abolish all sense of distance, to enclose the subject in a self-fascinated specularity, if video shoots did not re-establish some of the cinema's protocols and rituals. It is always possible to add a delay to video's instantaneity.

Seven. – The movement of images is not, therefore, in the images themselves. This movement comes from the machine, the camera, the projector. The machine gives movement back to what was recorded as "dead," so that it can "live" once more. If the *reproduction of life* passes through the machine, this means that life on the screen is not really "the same" as life in real life. Here, perhaps, we should postulate an *absence* which changes everything. I have underlined how much filmed realities, bodies, movements, were partially wiped out by the process of filming. Tiny fragments of space, matter, light, time, disappear forever from the recording which is supposed to capture them. Their absence, by contrast, is recorded. And in this case, synthesis will not remake what analysis has unmade. It as if the infamous window were armed with a grid, or a prism, which lets a part of the luminous intensities pass through, while blocking the rest. This missing part is recorded as a lack, an absence. Free of any self-interest, the machine imposes a relationship between us and the world which is partial and fragmentary, uneven and aleatory. But *we do not see it* during the film screening. Taken into the lure, the spectator *sees the opposite of the very thing that makes him see.*

Eight. – The film spectator is defined above all by the fact that he can not stop or even slow down the mechanical scrolling of the film in the projector. This is why the (new) mastery of the DVD spectator (for example) poses a problem: zapping through a film confers the spectator's capacity for analysis – and consciousness – with a power that had been withdrawn from him in cinema screenings. In the cinema, the spectator is carried away by the film, he does not dominate it. He is impotent before the unspooling of the film projected before his eyes, and more impotent still before the mental effects it induces. It does not stop effacing itself. It goes too quickly (synthesis is speed) to be perceived or even known by the spectator. There is a spilling over. The film spectator is at the same time in a state of belief and a state of lack of control. Who recognizes themselves today in these two qualities?

III. Filming the Disaster?

> It is scandalous not to recognize what is demanded and what is at stake in this movement [May 1968]: the will to escape, by any means necessary, from an order which is alienated, but so powerfully structured and integrated that even its contestation still risks being used by it. And it is scandalous not to understand that the violence that certain forms of this movement is reproached with is a response to the immense violence under the cover of which most contemporary societies are preserved, and of which police brutality is merely an open manifestation.
>
> – Leaflet for the Writers and Students Action Committee, 8 May, 1968.[1]

One. – In the cinema after the Second World War, how could it be ignored that everything was breaking apart at the seams? Certainly, the history of the cinema had never been a paradise. It had been marked by patent wars, corporate wars, film wars. Its history was a sepulcher containing a never-ending series of involuntary sacrifices. Films censored, projects unrealized, directors thwarted, and sometimes even driven to suicide... A subterranean history, a negative history, needs to be written. A history of what was not possible, what was eliminated, could reveal the real dimension of what did take place. Shadows are a part of the picture. How can we not keep in our memories the tribulations of Eisenstein inside and outside the USSR, or those of Welles in Hollywood, or the fate of Stroheim's *Greed* (1924)? The cinema is (just about) contemporary to us, we are implicated in it as spectators, witnesses, chroniclers, analysts... as actors, too, shining beacons of dreams and downfalls. This is why we must demand that historians give us a *non-pacified* history of the cinema, a history which takes into account the violent creative torsion by means of which arise works that were neither wanted nor desired by their contemporaries (and less still by those in control of the commodity circuits).[2]

---

1. Maurice Blanchot, *Écrits politiques, 1953-1993*, texts selected and annotated by Éric Hoppenot (Paris: Gallimard, 2008), p. 142.

2. Let us dream of a history of the evolution of cinematic forms and the variations in their use over the course of (certainly brief) phases which periodize "the century of the cinema," following the pattern of Erich Auerbach's *Mimesis* (Berne: C.A. Francke, 1946), and its "representation of reality in Western literature." As far as photography is concerned, see: *La Naissance de l'idée de photographie*, by François Brunet (Paris: PUF, 2000); for painting, sculpture and architecture, see *L'Invention de la liberté* by Jean Starobinski (Paris: Gallimard, 2006, reprint, with *Les Emblèmes de la Raison*, of the Skira edition, Geneva, 1964) [*The Invention of Liberty: 1700-1789*, trans. Bernard C. Swift (Geneva:

Two. – The cinema is a battleground, absolutely. But the battle has become global; it affects everything which is shown in the world and is carried to a high level of intensity by the new power of the mass media. Social control and ideological programming are linked today more than in the past to the occupation of the field of visibilities by the objects of the audiovisual industry:

> At the same time, audiovisual media have, as we know and with the consent of every protagonist in the great post-modern display of self-exhibition, become the major instruments of an ideology that is as pornographic as it is puritanical. All over the world, reality television, in which everyone is forced to put their private life on show, functions as the new asylum of modern times. [...] It is a vast zoological garden that is organized like a realm of never-ending surveillance in which time has been suspended.[3]

My hypothesis is that this power, this harmfulness, is due, above all, to *forms*. It is through forms – the use of images, sounds, montage, narration, the conversion of bodies and words into forms, the regulation of duration – that these audiovisual objects serve to fashion our reception, to mould our perception. The spread of formal norms, their alignment with the desire to see and hear, is today a major fact, foreshadowed and feared by T.W. Adorno – but not imagined on this scale, with these consequences.[4] What is new is the *overlapping patchwork* of these alienations: the cults of profit, performance and success; communion in business, fervor in the market, the engulfing vortex of mass culture; powerlessness before the media... Everywhere, words and forms are used to promote the regulation of practices and the "values" of submission, as well as being used to make norms accepted and circulated, to such an extent that amateur practice is downgraded to the practice of consumption.

Skira, 1964)]. As for the cinema, we can refer to the recent study by Antoine de Baecque, *La Caméra-histoire* (Paris: Gallimard, 2009) [*Camera Historica: The Century in Cinema* (New York: Columbia University Press, 2012)], and to some other works as well, which, while presenting themselves as monographs, nonetheless have the ambition to chronicle both the work and the world which it traverses. To restrict ourselves only to the most recent examples, there are: *Que viva Eisenstein!* (Barthélemy Amengual, Lausanne: L'Âge d'homme, 1990); *Roman américain: les vies de Nicholas Ray* (Bernard Eisenschitz and Christian Bourgois, Paris: Cahiers du cinéma, 1990) [*Nicholas Ray: An American Journey*, trans. Tom Milne (London: Faber and Faber, 1993)]; *Luis Buñuel y los nuevos caminos de las vanguardias* (Mercè Ibarz, Valencia: IVAM, 1999); *Orson Welles, une caméra visible* (Youssef Ishaghpour, Paris: La Différence, 2001); *Mikio Naruse, les temps incertains* (Jean Narboni, Paris: Cahiers du cinéma, 2006); *The Adventures of Roberto Rossellini: His Life and Films* (Tag Gallagher, New York: Da Capo, 1998); *Nuit et brouillard, un film dans l'histoire* (Sylvie Lindeperg, Paris: Odile Jacob, 2007).

3. Élisabeth Roudinesco, *La Part obscure de nous-mêmes: une histoire des pervers* (Paris: Albin Michel, 2007), p. 197 [*Our Dark Side: A History of Perversion*, trans. David Macey (Cambridge, MA.: Polity, 2009), p. 137].

4. Theodor W. Adorno, *Minima Moralia: Reflections from Damaged Life*, trans. E.F.N. Jephcott (London: NLB, 1974).

This formatting through forms is an insufficiently analyzed phenomenon, quite simply because it reaches into *our alienation*, into the exquisite heart of the pain of today. Our alienation, this ever-present companion, takes advantage of our individualist and vaguely libertarian credo by subtly suggesting we adopt the products and current fashions of the market, presented and vaunted as being "our choice," "our taste," "our desires," etc. And yet, what we buy, and then try out, is the money which has produced the object which reproduces the money. It is impossible not to notice an affinity between this fake diversity reigning over the market of images and sounds and the *pseudo-alternation* between twin political formulations that characterizes what we consent to call "Western democracies."[5]

Three. – In the age of the mass media, capitalism is characterized – for the first time in modern history – by the constitution of mega-conglomerates in the sphere of "communications" (telephony, media outlets, the Internet) whose social object – and source of profit – is the redefinition and appropriation of the register of *relations between individuals* – or what we used to pompously call "communications." From chatrooms to the various "instant messenger" websites to social media sites, not to mention blogs, YouTube, etc., the "relationship market" is in an expansive mode. No more need for the cinema (one-to-one) in order to do a "one-by-one-all-at-once (peer to peer). In fact, what is happening is that consumers are put to work by making them hand over to the market, of their own free will, the state of their "exploitable" relationships. Once again, consumption is linked with the "passage to the act." Exploitation on the one side, surveillance on the other, as these relationships, noted down and priced accordingly, leave behind traces. These new capitalist enterprises are hence grappling with the contradiction between mass production, which requires standardization and the uniformity of procedures and formats (that is, a minimum-cost economy), on the one hand, and the atomization of subjectivities and the pulverization of "tastes" on the other hand. Both are indispensable for the renewal of the passage to the act of purchasing. In short, this would entail a tailor-made economy, which, if it was actually followed, if it was real rather than imaginary, would make costs explode and render any mass-scale operation impossible.

On the one side, there is the standardization of products; on the other side, there is the exaltation of the "personality" of the purchaser. On the side of the products (as normalized as possible), an accompanying message foregrounds their "difference," more imaginary than real. On the side of the clients, there is the triumph of the ideology of the individual, which, I would say, is prudent and measured, just enough so as not to spill over into a socially and economically irrecuperable margin. The exaltation of the individual does not extend to marking out their singularity (which

5. Cf. Jean-Luc Nancy, *Vérité de la démocratie* (Paris: Galilée, 2008); and Alain Brossat, *Le Sacre de la démocratie* (Paris: Anabet, 2007).

exists as an exception to the rule); rather, it makes an ephemeral effect of this singularity glimmer, without breaking with the order of normality (the differences between each individual do not disturb the desire of everyone to conform to the norm, even while being "different"). The implicit normalization of individuals, concealed by the cult of small differences inflated to a state of pseudo-originality, echoes the constant and repetitive model of mass production, livened up with fantastic wrappings (new styles, new credit sequences, video clips, ads, etc.) which alter very little of the base object. In other words, *the clients are, in the long term, made to conform to the products.* The dominant audiovisual forms end up *modeling* tastes, critical capacities, expectations and satisfactions.

Today there is therefore a mass spirit toward an even greater degree of alienation than the commodity fetishism described by Marx. The voluntary submission to the "values" of the market has become one of the privileged signs of the conditioning of the human race, claimed by some of us as a distinction. Materially and mentally domesticated by money, man is in the process of becoming an animal capable of individually consuming that of which he has no need, other than having been massively induced. Is commerce the ultimate way to "be together"? Let us dare to paint the following scene: the masters of the world at the steering wheel, the masses pushing the cogs, constrained to pay with their bodies in order to propel the whole contraption into motion. All alienation begins by being content with itself, content with the pleasures it draws from that which possesses it. But it only makes sense when it is a matter for everyone. It is, first of all, that which is shared. It ties up that which has to do with the intimacy of the subject ("my choice") with that which confirms the individual's belonging to the multiple, the reassuring recognition that each person finds in the group which provides them with norms. Since Adorno, the question has been turned inside out in every direction. It is both fascinating and inexhaustible.

Jacques Rancière is right to point out that the critique of alienation has itself become mechanical, that we should hear the solitary voices down below or off to one side which, no matter how "alienated" they may be, utter a speech in the margins, a speech in struggle.[6] Do we still need to ask what the language is in which this strug-

6. Jacques Rancière, *La Parole ouvrière, op. cit.*, as well as *La Nuit des prolétaires: archives du rêve ouvrier* (Paris: Fayard, 1981, repr. Paris: Hachette, coll. "Pluriel," 1997) [*The Nights of Labor: The Workers' Dream in Nineteenth-Century France*, trans. John Drury (Philadelphia: Temple University Press, 1989)], and, more recently, *Le Spectateur émancipé, op. cit.* Focusing on artisans and laborers from the middle of the 19th century, Rancière shows, through ample quotations from them, how workers borrow the words of their masters in order not only to answer back to them, but also to affirm their dignity when face to face with them. It is indeed "from within" alienation and, I dare say, using its own terms that a struggle is possible. Just as, in the same manner, theater spectators can not be considered to be totally captured by the alienation of illusion... This demonstrates, conversely, that alienation, even if it is not entirely omnipotent, is powerful enough to be seductive. Such a viewpoint can be seen in the works of Serge Daney (a precursor), Slavoj Žižek, Luc Boltanski, Naomi Klein, etc. Numerous thinkers have tried to flush out this contemporary monster, so at ease in our midst. The familiar form of alienation makes us tolerate (and almost like) our own hothousing by

gle is spoken, what the acceptance of dominant forms is in which it formulates a contrary statement? In *The Emancipated Spectator*, Rancière discusses the supposed alienation of theater spectators, the "illusion" in which they like to bask. The cinema is not the theater, in the sense, first of all, that the cinematic lure is not the same as dramatic illusion. In the theater, the three dimensions of space are tangible. In the cinema, as we know, one dimension is missing: the third dimension. This implies a very different work of disavowal for the cinema spectator. The filmed scene no doubt "resembles" the world to a greater degree than the theatrical scene can possibly dream of achieving. But the more a film resembles the world, the more it differs from it. In the theater, the spectator's body is confronted with actor-bodies in a body-to-body which is not virtual, even if the stage is symbolically partitioned from the auditorium. In the cinema, the effects of bodies demand to be embodied, and this capturing of bodies is always problematic, aleatory, miraculous. The spectator's body, relatively disembodied by the conditions of viewing during the screening, is projected onto a screen which sends back its own projection.[7] In short, I readily believe that the supposition of an emancipation of the theater spectator is perhaps more logical than the supposition of his blindness. In the cinema, in contrast, the power of the lure, its complex mechanics, results in the spectator feeling a great deal of *jouissance* in not severing himself from the illusion, in playing with it, in twisting around the tourniquet of the "true" and the "false." It seems to me that this is not the case in the theater: the artifice is not subject to debate, has no statute of limitations (which is demonstrated by the episode with the Baltimore soldier). The place of the theater spectator, for these reasons, at least, is not ruled by the disavowal of the "I know very well, but all the same." It is therefore necessary to specify the different forms of alienation.

Four. – As cinephiles avidly gulping down the milk of our maternal cinémathèque, we were not predisposed to despise an "alienation" that we shared with many others. We applied the Leninist precept in vogue at the time: don't throw the baby out with the bathwater. An awareness of the mass of alienations peddled by Hollywood cinema, whether we liked it or not, did not prevent us from loving films infused with the ideology of the good law and the just cause (*Band of Angels*, Raoul Walsh, 1957), exemplary success stories (*Young Mr. Lincoln*, John Ford, 1939; *An American Romance*, King Vidor, 1944), films containing grand allegories (Morality, Justice, Faith, etc.) as well as films containing their guilty reverse side (*Written on the Wind*, Douglas Sirk, 1956)... All this cinema was propelled by a major principle: the *right to*

---

capital. Bernard Stiegler's work over the last 15 years is also central to this discussion, in particular: *La Technique et le temps* (Paris: Galilée, 1994-2001) [*Technics and Time*, trans. Richard Beardsworth and George Collins (Stanford, CA: Stanford University Press, 1998-2011)] and *Mécréance et discrédit* (Paris: Galilée, 2004-2006).

7. Cf. Metz, *Le Signifiant imaginaire*, *op. cit.*

assume responsibility for the story of the world. Origins, conquest, the division between Good and Evil, civilization… The imperialism of American cinema is above all an imperialism of the narrative.

We critiqued it, but at the same time we partook of its cinematic fruits. The task was – and for me it still is – to *save* the cinema from the ever-present threat of being shipwrecked in the ideology which surrounds it and spills over into it. The reduction of a film – provided it is at least a little dense, a complex network of signifiers, a node of tensions and contradictions – to its ideological statements [*énoncés*], whether explicit or not, appeared rather moronic to us. It was our manner, maybe even our mania, to go forth and contest the militant discourse, in this area where forms and signification were articulated differently to meanings and statements. Back then, this took place in the framework of the collective work on *Young Mr. Lincoln* (*Cahiers*, no. 223 [January 1970]). More recently, I have been known to screen the first 20 minutes of *Triumph of the Will* (Leni Riefenstahl, 1934), where certain gaps open up between the operation of propaganda at the service of the Nazi cause and the manner in which the mechanism of the cinematic operation undoes this program through a filtering process. For example, the sequence showing the Führer's triumphal march through the streets of Nuremburg can be turned against itself, it seems to me, due to its repetitive insistence on the same shots of the delirious crowd, a repetition not only of the images, axes, dolly movements, but also of the ambient sounds, which duly trot out an identical cry of "Heil Hitler!" (live, synchronous sound could only be recorded in the studio, or, as occurs later in the film, when rally orators speak into the microphone). The filmmaker is subtle enough that, in the rest of the film, she plays on the equivocation between the singularity of bodies, faces, voices (which the cinema is unable to lie about) and the desired uniformity of the individuals in the group (cinema as a mass art). But during the live filming of Hitler's speech, the 10 or 20 cameras mobilized all take practically the same images, the microphones record the same sounds, and this recurrence is more funereal than festive. The unanimity of the German people celebrating their master becomes the unanimity of forms themselves, the sadness of signs. As for the Führer, the gesture he makes with a gently tensed arm, due to its repetition, shows the filmed body as a puppet, as Lubitsch (*To Be or Not to Be*, 1941) and Chaplin (*The Great Dictator*, 1940) saw all too well. In the end, when Leni Riefenstahl places one of her cameras *behind Hitler's back* (the shot occurs twice), the strange quality of the angle comes to trouble us: the master is seen from behind. Is this the point of view of his bodyguard? A minion? A secret admirer?[8]

Five. – In short, the question of alienation was a *truly* political question for the *Cahiers* group in the 1970s. There was even the risk of renouncing what had made us love

8. Cf., in Bernard Eisenschitz's excellent *Le Cinéma allemand*, the pages dedicated to Leni Riefenstahl (Paris: Nathan, 1999, pp. 60-61).

the cinema, the fact that it was a *popular art*, that that is what it had been, and that that is what it wanted to be again. We had to say why that is no longer what it is, at least not in the same manner. Here, too, this history is yet to be written. To touch on a few reference points: the rise to power of television, usurping some of the cinema's capacity for seduction; the infamous "market segmentation," which carved up theaters, film genres and, of course, the families of the viewers; the increase in the price of tickets – that is to say, commerce's eager grab for the circulation of films, puffing them up and stuffing them full; the multiplexes, producing consumers, the only idea they could possibly have of the "popular"; the expanded role of marketing, advertising, merchandise tie-ins... All this marks the cinema's entrance into the supermarket, even if it is "cultural" in nature.

Television, in contrast, has not ceased to embrace all kinds of "publics," of varying sizes. I understand the choice I made in the middle of 1980s to work for public television (INA, France 3, La Sept, Arte) as the persistence of the same political concern, in two senses: 1. to show on the small screen (as much as possible) formal systems which diverge from the dominant ones (the series *Marseille contre Marseille*, for example, with Michel Samson, and its attempted re-conquering of the political body and political speech); 2. to reach viewers who have not already been strictly classified within the cultural segments of the market: owing to their numbers – more than a million even for lesser-watched programs – television viewers constitute a random sample of the public, which only rarely occurs in the specialized circuits of art-house cinema. In other words, my goal has been to maintain the principle of a political and artistic *public sphere*.

The popular dimension accorded to the cinema, whether or not it was a fantasy, overlapped exactly with the popular dimension of mass alienation. To have condemned it out of hand would have been to renounce the possibility that the cinema can play a role in the historical and political arc of the world we live in. At *Cahiers*, we were more ambitious. We did not want the cinema to be stowed away in a cultural pigeonhole marked out to receive it. We were against the kind of culture which manufactures "values," or "cultural wealth," on the basis of artistic experiences cut off from the world, detached from the social body. In this sense, in spite of all our differences, we were very close to the Situationists. Moreover, due to the effect of May 68 on our small group, we were implicitly (and sometimes explicitly) forbidden from *appearing to be in agreement or complicity with the society we were combating*, by, for example, publishing books. Daney was the first to break this taboo with *La Rampe*, a collection of his texts from the period 1970-1982, and when he did so I told myself that he had made the right decision. I owe the essence of what I think about the cinema's place in today's world to these texts, and notably the earlier ones ("Sur Salador"), elaborated in the *Cahiers* office, against and at odds with the rest of the world. The book appeared in 1983, and already the post-1968 years were disappearing from the horizon, repressed by an abject political and cultural *qualunquismo*[i] – it suddenly became urgent to stake out how one had been able to think during those years, and how, in the new climate, one could attempt to use them to keep on thinking. This is what made *La Rampe* necessary.[9]

I recall that during the famous month of May, when we were gathered together in a permanent mass meeting at the École Louis Lumière, for the *États généraux du cinéma*, even there we forbade ourselves from filming the movement in progress. And we kept to this prohibition: we waited until the sinister month of June, with André S. Labarthe, to film *Les Deux Marseillaises*. To explain this abstention, I will cite Blanchot: "Hence, we will never write about what took place and what did not take place in May: not out of respect, nor even out of a concern to not restrict the event by circumscribing it. We admit that this refusal is one of the points where writing and the decision for rupture join each other: both are always imminent and always unforeseeable."[10] If it is true that today, some 40 years later, such an abstention can be regretted, or misunderstood, it is also true that May does not stop in May, and that many of its echoes have definitively been filmed.[11]

All this was true before '68, and even more true afterwards. We did not want an "art cut off from the people." This is why we obstinately defended the American cinema, and our auteurs, even in Hollywood, well before this became fashionable, when the cinema was one of the principal vectors of the ideology whose most resolute adversaries we wanted to be.

This is what explains, at least from this belated retrospective overview I am now undertaking, why it was difficult for me to *truly* love what was known as the New York experimental cinema. I could admire it, yes, I understood the battle it was waging, but from a distance, from the outside. As astonishing and subversive as they could be, these films left no place for me other than that of the *non-dupe*. I needed to believe, to be taken into the illusion and overtaken by it, a spectator like all the rest, no better or worse, abused and amused, like in the yo-yo game with the spectator (Freud's *fort/da*) pushed to the limit by *To Be or Not to Be*. The deconstruction of the lure *without the lure*, without the construction of the lure, quickly bored me. In the same way, the "avant-garde" cinema, films made by artists, seemed to me to have aged too quickly, to have grown up too quickly, no longer taking the effort to delight the *lost child* with the lure, this lost child which forever marks the place of the spectator. What should we make of the renewed strength of the "artist film" in the present day? Often these films seem to be addressed to spectators who are supposed to be, or become, "connoisseurs," if not buyers, and they are surrounded by expert commentaries, where the work is dissected by authorized voices before even being exposed to view. But what has happened, in these works, to the *mise en scène* of the spectator?

---

9. Serge Daney, *La Rampe* (Paris: Cahiers du cinéma-Gallimard, 1983; repr. Paris: Cahiers du cinéma, coll. "Petite bibliothèque," 1996).

10. Blanchot, *Écrits politiques*, *op. cit.*, p. 156.

11. Cf. *Le Cinéma de mai 68*, vol. 1 and 2, DVD box sets released by Éditions Montparnasse in the collection "Le Geste documentaire," supervised by Patrick Leboutte and Vianney Delourme, 2008.

The spectators of a Fritz Lang or Ernst Lubitsch film were supposed, in one way or another, to *believe in it,* to not be placed above the fable, above the lure, they were supposed to be plunged into the illusion, even if the cards were turned over at the crucial moment. Is it not this entire dialectical play with the spectator desired as a complicit confidante, or even as consenting victim – that is to say, a definitively naïve and credulous spectator – which is precisely what is not sold in contemporary art galleries? The reply will be: but the spectator of the past no longer exists. But it is this ideological slippage (which is also, possibly, an anthropological vacillation) which is precisely what troubles me, what I feel the need to interrogate. What sort of spectator do we travel with in our lives? And what type of spectator is waiting to catch us out?

Is this one of the reasons which made me balk at Guy Debord's theses (in *La Société du spectacle,* 1967), and which still prevent me from adhering to them unconditionally? In my view, he did not hesitate for a single moment to throw all cinema and all art overboard, granting no importance to the internal battles sundering all artistic fields, and most notably the cinema. Writing "Technique and Ideology," I was conscious of trying to resist this brutal liquidation, in one fell swoop, of all 20th-century art forms, unworthy of the slightest consideration because they were the vassals of capital. It seemed to me – as an effect of the period – that, perhaps, in these powerful analyses which hit the vastest targets in the right spot, the finesse required to take into account the primary and secondary aspects of the primary and secondary contradictions was lacking... For me, the great Maoist casuistry did not contradict Debord, it completed him against his will. "Technique and Ideology" also recounts this: the idea that, with regards to narrative and illusion, it was not all over and done with; that the impression of reality analyzed by Bazin is indeed the basis of the lure, of course, but that this lure is not reducible to the harm attributed to the powers of illusion; that there is a positive aspect to cinematic ambiguity, which deceives in order to undeceive more than the other way around; that the lure has a history, and that it therefore has meaning, that it is a tool allowing us to deconstruct some of our everyday forms of blindness and deafness. In sum, turning alienation against itself, we used the (historically defined) cinema in order to critique the (ideologically predominant) cinema. The cinematic lure, as a support and a mechanism for spectacular alienation, functioned as a reduced model of the functioning of belief in our political societies. And given that we believed in the people, that the people believed, and that like the people we, too, believed (in all kinds of things), we journeyed across the cinema as the playing field where the *forms of belief* are mobilized by political power relations. This is still my position. *The cinema is political because it is founded on a system of lures which induces the belief of the spectator to play a role.* And, if we understand the cinema as a battlefield, it seems to me that it is the domination of the spectacle denounced by Debord which enters into crisis, and that it is from within this field, with the theoretical tools forged in the analysis of films, that we can better understand and combat the holy alliance of capital and the spectacle.

Six. – Flashback: 1945-1950. Europe is in ruins. This is what Rossellini films in *Germania Anno Zero*. What do we make of these ruins? How much more sacrifice, in a time of peace, will wash away the crimes of war? And, therefore: how do we reconstruct it? This history is recounted by the most innovative films. Alain Robbe-Grillet is correct to underline (in a series of radio interviews) that this omnipresence of ruins was above all a sign of urgency: a Renaissance was desired.[12] The death camps, all that we did not know or did not want to know about the extermination of Europe's Jews, the cities razed by Allied bombings, the atrocities of all kinds, the atomic bombs on Hiroshima and Nagasaki, the millions of dead, even the episodes of civil and military resistance against the Nazi order and its accomplices, all this ushered in a new era. The cinema coming out of the war carried this messianic expectation (*Stromboli*, *Europa 51*, Roberto Rossellini, 1949 and 1951). The world was in the process of changing and this could only be carried out by the invention of new languages. In the tone of Robbe-Grillet's voice, I can hear a kind of joyous rage. Disperse the already ruined rhetoric. Raze the ruins of a European humanism of which Nazism was both the culmination and the annihilation. Refuse the notion that the children of Europe should be obsessed by the specters of the Old World, the very ones which led to the catastrophe (this is the fable at the heart of *Germania Anno Zero*). There is an urgent need to rebuild in a different manner, to film in a different manner. This took place in Italy. The rise of neo-realism swept away Mussolini's Cinecittà. There was a belief that the times had changed. Indeed they did change, once the cinema, leaving behind the "Sleeping Beauty" studios, filmed the Italian populace where it was, where it lived and where it fought – in the streets.

This era did not last. In 1960, 1965, 1968, we knew only too well that the hostilities of the Cold War had liquidated the hopes of the Resistance-Renaissance. We knew that, between 1947 and 1953, a vehement "witch-hunt" led by Senator McCarthy had purged the American administration, its education system, as well as Hollywood and Broadway, of those who were suspected of being or ever having been "reds." Nor could we ignore the procession of wars: Korea, Indochina, Algeria, Vietnam... The ghosts of fascism and Nazism, which we were rid of for good, or so we had thought, returned to haunt our consciences and, more frightening still, to re-occupy the real from which they had been chased away. Germany stopped de-Nazifying, instead, ex-Nazis were being protected; the same was happening in Italy with the Mussolinian elites; and from these two U-turns a left would be born in both countries which would eventually turn to "armed struggle." As for France, both the people and practices of Vichy were being maintained. We knew that Papon started out as the secretary-general of the Bordeaux prefecture under Vichy, and as such was responsible for the Service of Jewish Affairs; that he would subsequently go to Morocco (repressing the nationalist forces), and then Algeria (ordering torture and repression in the Con-

---

12. *Préface à une vie d'écrivain*, 25 radio programs on France Culture, Summer 2003.

stantine department); that, upon returning to France, he participated in the Gaullist plot and, in October 1961, as Paris police prefect, commanded the bloody repression of a demonstration of French Algerians (resulting in several hundred deaths). The same Papon, the following year, 1962, also gave the order for the massacre at Charonne.[ii] What a pretty pastoral scene, this; what an exemplary itinerary. He was right under our eyes. It was enough to sober us up.

Seven. – When the camps were opened, the slow, very slow process of becoming aware of the extermination of Europe's Jews began (and it must be said again and again that this was carried out by Europeans – the Nazis were European, after all – in the name of "European" ideals, with the complicity and, more or less, the tacit accord of many other Europeans, including the Allies themselves...).[13] The immediate future of the cinema was going to be affected by this fact, still not spoken about openly, but partially known, with the questions surrounding it brooded over, not given answers. As different as their methods may be, first Rossellini (*Germania Anno Zero*, then *Europa 51*), then Resnais (*Hiroshima mon amour*, 1958) and Antonioni (*L'Avventura*, 1960), inscribed their films with an embarrassment, a "suspicion," a "bad conscience," if not an appeal without response, which all function as much, if not more so, in the writing processes of these films as in their explicit "messages."

The world had changed, yes, of that there is no doubt. And with it the cinema.[14] Changed? Was it not necessary to assume a link, albeit a tenuous, obscure one, between this civilization responsible for the "abomination" and the cinema historically linked to it since the very first film (*Sortie d'usine*: itself a symbol of this link) and which has accompanied it so faithfully since then? As I have said, it was difficult for this cinema loved by us to mask the active role it had taken in the massification of the world, in both the West and the East[15] – its complicity with "mass culture" which

---

13. See, not only *Shoah* (Claude Lanzmann, 1985), which is both patient and incisive; but also a fragment detached from the series *Un vivant qui passe* (1997), where Maurice Rossel, a young delegate for the CICR in Berlin during the war, tells of his visits to Auschwitz and then Theresienstadt, not without evincing, on occasion, the sort of everyday anti-Semitism that affected the European elites in the 1930s and 1940s. (Cf. Jean-Louis Comolli, "Ceux qui se perdent," *Voir et pouvoir, op. cit.*, pp. 414-424.)

14. Cf. Jean-Louis Comolli, "Fatal rendez-vous," in *Le Cinéma et la Shoah*, ed. Jean-Michel Frodon (Paris: Cahiers du cinéma, 2007), pp. 69-84 ["Fatal Rendezvous," trans. Anna Harrison and Tom Mes, in *Cinema and the Shoah: An Art Confronts the Tragedy of the Twentieth Century*, ed. Jean-Michel Frodon (Albany: State University of New York Press, 2010)]. Antoine de Baecque has returned to the question of the cinema's changes after World War II in *L'Histoire-caméra, op. cit.*, pp. 55-103 [*Camera Historica*, pp. 31-77].

15. In "L'Œuvre d'art à l'époque de sa reproductibilité technique," Walter Benjamin stresses that "Mass reproduction is aided especially by the reproduction of masses. In big parades and monster rallies, in sports events, and in war, all of which nowadays are captured by camera and sound recording, the masses are brought face to face with themselves." (1939 version, *op. cit.*, p. 313, note 21 ["The Work of Art," *op. cit.*, p. 251]).

also produced fascism, Nazism and Stalinism. I recall the opposition proposed by Benjamin between the "aestheticization of politics" (fascism) and the "politicization of aesthetics" (communism).[16] Up until the war, up until the Hollywood films engaged in the fight against Nazism, up until the series *Why We Fight*,[17] the cinema (with very few exceptions) had done the impossible: idealizing social relations, propagating a spirit of submission, returning the world to a state of virginity, taming violence, domesticating alterity, corrupting savagery. In short, "humanizing" all forms of exploitation, whether of the proletariat or of the colonies, and civilizing all forms of otherness. As Daney, following on from Bazin, would say: sharing a shot, or a film, was seen as a renunciation of savagery, and was proof that manifest alterity was not so radical that it could not be filmed. Put in charge of the high command of the *civilizing mission of the West*, the cinema became a central stake in the totalitarian ambitions of the ideologies which fought for the control of the world.[18]

---

16. *Ibid.*, p. 316 [p. 242].

17. *Why We Fight* was a series of seven documentary films, under the stewardship of Frank Capra, 1942-1945. André Bazin wrote of it in the following terms: "The shots used in these films are in a way straight historical facts. We spontaneously believe in facts, but modern criticism has sufficiently established that in the end they have only the meaning that the human mind gives to them. Up to the discovery of photography, the 'historical fact' was reconstituted from written documents, the mind and human language came into play twice in such reconstructions: in the reconstruction of the event and in the historical thesis it was adduced to support. With film we can refer to the facts in flesh and blood, so to speak. Could they bear witness to something else other than themselves? To something else other than the narrative of which they form a part? I think that, far from moving the historical sciences toward more objectivity, the cinema paradoxically gives them the additional power of illusion by its very realism. The invisible commentator, whom the viewer forgets while watching Capra's marvelously edited films, is tomorrow's historian of the masses, the ventriloquist of this extraordinary prosopopoeia that is being prepared in all the film archives of the world and that wills the men and the events of another time back to life." André Bazin, "À propos de *Pourquoi nous combattons*," *Esprit*, no. 123 (1946), pp. 1022-1026 ["On *Why We Fight*," trans. Alain Piette and Bert Cardullo, in *Bazin at Work: Major Essays and Reviews from the Forties and Fifties*, ed. Bert Cardullo (New York: Routledge, 1997), pp. 187-192]. As for the anti-Nazi Hollywood films, cf. Eisenschitz, *Le Cinéma allemand*, *op. cit.*, p. 75-77.

18. Let us recall the refusal of Fritz Lang to become the "official filmmaker" of the Third Reich and his flight to the USA in 1933. In his "autobiography" published in Lotte Eisner's *Fritz Lang*, the filmmaker writes: "Since I now made films in Germany, I acquired German citizenship, of which I was deprived in 1933 by the Hitler regime. After the Nazis had come to power, my anti-Nazi film, *Der Testament des Dr. Mabuse*, in which I put Nazi slogans into the mouth of a pathological criminal, was banned, of course. I was called to see Goebbels, not, as I had feared, in order to be called to account for the film but to be told by the Reichspropagandaminister to my surprise, that Hitler had instructed him to offer me the leading post in the German film industry. 'The Führer saw your film *Metropolis* and announced, "That's the man to make national-socialist film!" I left Germany the same evening." Lotte H. Eisner, *Fritz Lang*, trans. Gertrud Mander (New York: Da Capo, 1976), pp. 14-15.

Eight. – It could be that the SS were fully knowledgeable of the reasons why they forbade themselves from filming the inner functioning of the death camps.[19] There was, of course, the will to efface all traces of the crime, and thus not to imprint them on film. But there was something else. The cinema was made to subjugate the masses, not to record (that is, to reveal and diffuse) the spectacle of mass death – of real, final, non-virtual death, a death which is not followed by the ritual "resurrection" of fiction cinema, a death without a "second take."[20] This mass death was the unfilmable horror, without fiction, without a story. These SS-men knew perfectly well that nobody would reawaken from the death they suffered in the gas chambers, that no redemptive water would ever gush out of these showerheads. They also knew (*The Triumph of the Will* shows this in 1934) that the cinema was made to film the masses in movement – disciplined, militarized and choreographed as much as possible, but *living* – and not these dead masses, these piles of dead bodies.

If the cinema came to be loved throughout the world, if it came to be indispensable, it is because it also films people *one by one*, because it individualizes them even when they are in massive political or religious gatherings. It is not enough for Leni Riefenstahl to film groups of Hitler Youth fanatically roused by the figure of the Führer; she still gives each one of them a singular body, a name, an origin, in short, she makes them individuals (at first, in the series of scenes where these young people get ready, play, laugh, they are adolescents united in the healthy camaraderie of what seems to be a bland version of the boy scouts; they then introduce themselves and remain, in spite of their individualization – surname, first name, province, etc. – in conformity with the model, and even reinforce it with their physical differences).

Meanwhile, the masses led to their deaths in the extermination camps had been rendered anonymous, the convoys of men and women were stripped of their names, torn from their social and familial history.[21] Since its birth, the cinema had persevered in doing exactly the opposite: giving its characters a name, a subjectivity, a family, a group, a destiny, and giving these to those chosen few from among the immense crowd of unknowns.

---

19. On this question, cf. Annette Wieviorka, *L'Ère du témoin* (Paris: Hachette, coll. "Pluriel," 2002) [*The Era of the Witness*, trans. Jared Stark (Ithaca, NY: Cornell University Press, 2006)]; *Déportation et génocide: entre la mémoire et l'oubli*, (Paris: Hachette, coll. "Pluriel," 2003); *Auschwitz, la mémoire d'un lieu* (Paris: Hachette, coll. "Pluriel," 2005). Cf. also the works of Georges-Didi Huberman: *L'Image survivante* (Paris: Minuit, 2005); *Images malgré tout* (Paris: Minuit, 2004) [*Images in Spite of All: Four Photographs from Auschwitz*, trans. Shane B. Lillis (Chicago: University of Chicago Press, 2008)]; and Gérard Wajcman, *L'Objet du siècle, op. cit.*; Sylvie Lindeperg, *Clio de 5 à 7* (Paris: CNRS, 2000); *Nuit et brouillard, un film dans l'histoire, op. cit.*

20. Cf. J.-L. Comolli, "L'absente de tout miroir," *Voir et pouvoir, op. cit.*, p. 459.

21. Cf. Pierre Legendre, "Analecta: l'attaque nazi contre le principe de filiation," in Alexandra Papageorgiu-Legendre, *Filiation: Leçons 4, suite 2* (Paris: Fayard, 1990), pp. 205-209.

Nine. – The Nazi interdict takes on, then, an unexpected meaning: to remind us that one of the roles of the cinema is to *lie to the masses about death*. All the lure can do is lure. When the Nazis, however, were losing the war and beating a retreat on all fronts, the Allied armed forces penetrated the camps (which were still not identified as death camps), bringing with them the cinema. As if to respond to the Nazi interdict (at that point just as unknown as the extermination itself), it became an obligation to film the liberated camps. But it is not that simple. The debilitation of cinematic recording before the reality of mass death immediately became apparent to the cameramen. Before telling us anything else, the images taken at Falkenau and Bergen-Belsen betray the disarray and anguish of those who filmed them. A doubt arises (unprecedented on this scale in the history of the cinema): What if the spectators of these images *did not believe in them*? What if they came to think that they were impossible to realize *without special effects*?

This is the violent introduction of the motif of mistrust in the cinematic relationship. To restore some confidence in the cinema, it becomes necessary to deploy montage, and a rhetoric of images. Sidney Bernstein, who conceived and produced *Memory of the Camps*, made an appeal to his friend Alfred Hitchcock.[22] The idea was to incorporate *mise en scène* into the document, and thus into the shoot, in order to revive the possibility of belief. This *mise en scène* is a *mise en fiction*: filming the surrounds of the camps, everyday life alongside mass death; filming the German spectators forcibly brought before the collective graves, filming their look at death as a mediation and a relay of the spectator's look. The cinema demands of itself that it validate – render lifelike – the images of unrepresentable death.[23]

My hypothesis is that the dream factory – which was metonymically used to represent (and format) the entirety of world cinema – suffered grave failures directly after the war. The chorus of "the show must go on" was over. Nothing could keep on continuing "just like before." The prohibition of images of mass death filmed in the camps doubtless contributed to saving the cinema from an odious infamy. Kept at bay by the SS, and thus less directly compromised, but promoted, in contrast, by the Allies (including the Soviets), the cinema was able to maintain itself as a central

22. Cf. Comolli, "Fatal rendez-vous," *Le Cinéma et la Shoah, op. cit. Memory of the Camps* was shot in 1945, primarily at Bergen-Belsen, edited in London (with Hitchcock supervising), and immediately shelved: de-Nazification was suspended due to the Cold War. Forty years later, in 1985, the American public television show *Frontline* recuperated the reels, restored them, added a commentary by Trevor Howard and broadcast the film.

23. Of course, I understand that real deaths have really been filmed thousands if not millions of times. My argument is that these deaths lose their reality when they become images, when they are framed, cut and edited together. Without being able to fictionalize it when it is real, the cinema virtualizes death. But mass death, and the death of the masses, puts an end to this movement. Between a documentary death and a fictional death, it is neither the image nor the depiction that changes, but the credence of the spectators. We understand the extreme importance of *context* which alone allows to know if we are dealing with a fiction film or with newsreel footage. The belief of the spectator is thus partly a mental projection.

laboratory of *likeable* and *desirable* alienation. And yet, a fissure opened up. The liberation of the camps by the Allies (*Falkenau*, 1945, and *The Big Red One*, 1980, both by Samuel Fuller), the horrors, therefore, which were filmed *post mortem*, the confrontation of the former "cinematic innocence" with this new gift that I have just evoked, the rise of an incredulous and distrustful spectator,[24] all these factors have an effect on Hollywood's Grand Narrative. The failure and death – the loss, the madness and the return of the repressed – that is precisely at the heart of Western conquest (see Joseph Conrad) comes back to insistently haunt us. The cunning of desire, the overturning of good intentions and the perversion of the righteous (recurrent themes in Lang and Hitchcock) suggest that the conscience and will-to-power of the American hero come up against a limit which exceeds him, which is no longer linked to his own strengths or qualities. This is the meaning behind Welles' entire œuvre. *Citizen Kane* (1941) is a prescient film. Fritz Lang on the one side, Hitchcock on the other? Even if it is unaware of it, the cinema watches over us. It vibrates with the tension of electric currents. It is a surface resonating with what obscurely announces itself.

24. This new spectator is thus also a spectator of newsreel films made for propaganda purposes, and is the fruit, on the one hand, of everything which tends to instrumentalize cinematic images, and, on the other hand, of everything which, in these documentary images, gives the cinema a *truth effect* that fiction can no longer provide so simply. It is probably the immense gap that separates the images brought back from Bergen-Belsen by the English cameramen from World War II newsreel footage that was screened during the war, oriented as it was toward propagandistic ends, which makes us doubt the authenticity of the former. This gap was understood both as a rupture (we have never seen this before) and an exaggeration (they must have manipulated the images).

IV. Cutting the Figure?

> But it is not enough to cut out, it is necessary to sew the pieces together.
>
> – Henri Bergson[1]

> It is not a good idea to interrupt the narrative too often, since storytelling works by lulling the reader or listener into a dreamlike state in which the time and space of the real world fade away, superseded by the time and space of the fiction. Breaking into the dream draws attention to the constructedness of the story, and plays havoc with the realist illusion.
>
> – J.M. Coetzee[2]

One. – In 2007, on the occasion of the *États généraux du documentaire* at Lussas, together with Marie-Pierre Duhamel-Muller, I interrogated the evolution of montage practices in the last few years. Now, technologies have their own logic. Changes in the way of doing things have consequences which always exceed the statements proffered in a film and adopted by an author. I was therefore interested in a form of editing known as the "jump-cut," which is currently very widespread. I choose to define the jump-cut as an edit which visibly provokes a jump in the continuity of a shot, in the singularity of a take. An ellipsis arises where there is not supposed to be one: within the continuity of a situation, itself filmed in continuity. And so, there is a jump. And it is perceived as a tear, as a rip. Cutting within a single shot, a single take, makes a greater or lesser portion of the frames (or "images," as they are known as in video) disappear. At the same time as the image, the sound, too, is cut. The two fragments thus created from within a spatio-temporal continuum (the filmstrip) are placed end to end, a more or less awkward linkage which allows a feeling of catastrophe to set in.

In the "documentary" cinema and in the products of audiovisual information (reportages, magazine shows) the use of the jump-cut first appears as a response to a constraint. How to cut within the scene, in the filmed body and speech, in order to

1. Henri Bergson, *Matière et Mémoire*, 7th edition (Paris: PUF, 1939), p. 37 [*Matter and Memory*, trans. Nancy Margaret Paul and W. Scott Palmer (New York: Macmillan, 1913), p. 33].
2. J.M. Coetzee, *Elizabeth Costello: Eight Lessons* (London: Secker & Warburg, 2003), p. 16.

control the duration and the meaning, if nothing in the filming process has arranged for the possibility of these cuts? In the "fiction" cinema, the possibility of shooting a scene or a take multiple times, of making bodies conform to the constraints of the frame and the lighting, without forgetting the role of the script girl (who anticipates the editing during the shoot) means that the recourse to a jump-cut during the editing is not a practical "necessity," a forced, more or less catastrophic, choice, but an artistic decision, a *style*, the formal system of a sequence. For example: the scene in the car with Jean Seberg in *À bout de souffle* (Jean-Luc Godard, 1960). The convertible drives around, the nape of Jean Seberg's neck is always there, while a series of cuts matches herself to herself – but, surrounding her, the background "jumps." From the same driving sequence (unity of the scene) various fragments are edited together, in a tension between *identity* (Jean Seberg's position) and *difference* (the portions of space linked together, which are nonetheless taken from the same referential space: the Champs-Élysées). The result is an effect of acceleration and fragmentation, a motif of *playfulness*, evoking torn-up paper and collages. This pictorialization is, at the same time, a rhythmic montage of space, a raging gesture by the one who cuts without seeing the object of the cut disappear into it. On the contrary, Jean Seberg's head comes back again and again, unaltered, on both sides of the edit. Cutting on a face is aggressive. This gesture was liberating. Today, in clips, ads, magazines, it is the stereotypical marker of an opportune "modernity." In the end it is merely a rhetorical effect. This is what needs to be interrogated. From *Man with a Movie Camera* (Dziga Vertov, 1929) to *Bowling for Columbine* (Michael Moore, 2002) the meaning of fragmentation has changed.

Two. – Every cut is a *cut in time*.[3] There is a temporality in film, a temporality of consciousness (the active sum of perceptions, sensations and attentions of the subject). The two temporalities are opposed to and composed with each other. We can ask why it was so early in the cinema's history, from Griffith onwards, that the challenge of the match has generally been to attenuate or mask the (relative) violence of the cut? (A violence which is due, among other things, to the ruptures in proportions, because a medium shot is joined to a close-up, or shots at more or less perpendicular axes are joined together, as are gestures, looks, speeds, etc.). Cuts become transitions more than interruptions, matches are not so much jumps as stepping stones from one point to another in space and time, by eliminating the flagrant aspect of the rupture. The match-cut is thus an act of stitching together. And montage (a set or

3. I refer the reader here to Gilles Deleuze's two *Cinéma* books: *L'Image-mouvement* and *L'image-temps* (Paris: Minuit, 1983/1985 [*Cinema 1: The Movement Image*, trans. Hugh Tomlinson and Barbara Habberjam, and *Cinema 2: The Time-Image*, trans. Hugh Tomlinson and Robert Galeta (London: Athlone Press, 1986/1989)] which have inspired some of the lines of thought developed here – albeit with more of a focus, in my case, on *documentary practice*.

system of match-cuts) tries to annul the fragmentation *that it can not avoid being* by making it pass for a series of impulses, a dynamic fluidity.

This is the success of the illusion of the cinema. The match-cut principally wants to be an *invisible* stitching which links up two pieces of material and disappears in the join. It must be noticed because it claims to assure an impression of continuity, of completion, which represses both the discontinuity of time and the world (which we prefer to remain unaware of) and the discontinuity (which we are unaware of) of the photogrammatic skeleton. Rhythm, respiration; montage is supposed to be ductile, conductive. It cradles, supports, bends and unbends without breaking (apart from some notable exceptions, from Stroheim to Eisenstein, and then Welles, etc.). The time taken up by the film takes on the allure of a homogenous continuum, of the same order as the temporal flux in which we imagine ourselves to be immersed. The scene is naturalized. The artifice is disguised as being natural. But this smoothing out of all fractures, this filling in of all breaches, is simply the effect of an important act of repression: one concerning death, the rupture instigated by death. *Analysis is on the side of death*, as I have stressed, while *synthesis is on the side of life*. This is exactly what the invention of the cinema will repeat, it is this *topos* which it will enduringly install into systems of thought. Analysis divides, synthesis unifies. Representations tend to be more synthetic than analytic. And as the cinema relates this synthesis to "life," by miming its movement, discontinuity is not welcome, because it brings *rupture into the living* (see, for instance, the fractured, jerky image in *Sauve qui peut (la vie)*, Godard, 1980). The jerkiness in the time-image seems to cite the jerky movements of the *danse macabre*, this major figure of the Western imaginary which propagates the theme of a "victory of death." By means of the discontinuous, the jerk, the non-linked, it is the death throes of the skeleton, and even death itself, which makes a comeback.

And yet the jump-cut seems to work against the mimetic cinema of the "temporal flux," and thus against transparency. As a resolutely "modern" brushstroke, it is deemed to undo illusion by opening us up to an awareness of fragmentation. Unfortunately, the opposite happens. The principle of tearing images and sounds to shreds functions, in fact, as a form of *diversion* – that is, as a denial of the very destruction of which it is the agent. Inasmuch as the fragment makes itself act, it does not provide us with the means to grasp it. Fragmentation prevents an awareness of fragmentation; it only authorizes an awareness which is itself fragmented, a broken consciousness, incapable of inhabiting its own dream. The film which splashes over us is no longer a projected surface. It no longer leads us toward a more or less labyrinthine interiority, it no longer initiates us to the dangers of the world (*Die Nibelungen*, Fritz Lang, 1923; *Wind across the Everglades*, Nicholas Ray, 1958). In short, this undone time is decidedly no longer that of an experimental subjectivity. It is the time of the control over time, that is, over short periods of time, easier to control than long ones, in the duration of which an unforeseen and undesired event can take place.

Three. – Jump-cut editing is editing which *designates itself.* The cut is no longer masked by the match. It is abandoned to the illusion of continuity and plenitude constructed by the cinematic lure. However tiny the leap between two fragments of the same shot may be, it will remain visible. The join between two edges underlines this rift instead of overcoming it. The cut is stripped bare. The tear replaces the match. This should lend support to everything I wrote earlier against transparency. But no, that is not the case. Let us try to understand why.

With the generalization of rapid montage, television implanted an *aesthetic of abbreviation* in the 1970s. The triumph of audience ratings is the triumph of an impatient world (impatient to win, to dominate), a world with a spirit of dogged competition (market share). Time is money, the impatient television audience is the prey, and they must be captured with the first harpoon blow, to be locked up in a flickering of appearances capable of barring the way to any subjective projection. Hence, the frenetically agitated scopic drive in a kaleidoscope of visual effects. The world is too slow, too heavy, it must be leavened, emptied, robbed of substance.

The "real" time of an action (classic examples: opening a gate, ascending a staircase, crossing a street, traveling, etc.) is (almost always) shortened in the cinema. "Filming work," for example, always involves spectacularizing it, that is, accelerating and eliding it. The potter needs hours and hours to mould and bake pottery, as does the cobbler to fashion a boot, and neither the film nor the spectator are in a position to wait that long. Narrative involves abridgement.[4] But, as a rule, this abbreviation must – apart from the caricatured accelerations of a Tex Avery – stay within the bounds of verisimilitude, of *the experience of duration possessed by every spectator.* I know – *we* know – how much time is required to ascend a staircase, cross a street, run through the Louvre (as in *Bande à part,* Godard, 1964). (This is not to speak of learning a language, grieving the death of a loved one, or being pregnant... all these times are – still – incompressible, and only representable in the cinema by abbreviated forms.) Even when it deceives us, it still makes a reference to a realist temporality possible. *Real time* in the cinema can only be a realistic truncation. And rare indeed are the films which attempt to impart, in real time, an action represented in continuity: *Berlin 10/90* (Robert Kramer, 1990), or *Empire* (Andy Warhol, 1964).

It is thus accepted as convention that the represented durations are only so many synecdoches or metaphors of real duration. This is the rhetoric of ellipsis, or, to put it differently: representations of duration can be passed off as being "correct" when they are condensed and combined through a process of montage. This conformity to common sense returns these abbreviated forms to the real experience of each spectator. By saving the temporal and spatial coherence of the scene, the "invisible" edit leaves the spectator free to imagine that "behind the representation," "behind the curtain," a reality is being profiled, with its temporality not determined by the narra-

4. Cf. Comolli, *Voir et pouvoir, op. cit.*, p. 338.

tive, with its autonomy intact. The illusion leads to a "reality," to a world of liberty for the spectator, opened from the very interior of the filmic forms that are imposed on him. Outside/inside. Lived time is a ghost which haunts spectacular time.

It happens, as I have noted, that the invention of the cinema carries this promise of virtualization within itself. Alleviating the world by making an image of it. Mastering durations by abridging the real temporalities of nature, of objects, of living beings. Precipitating and eliding physiological processes, long apprenticeships, maturations, decompositions. Dematerializing in order to accelerate.[5]

It would nonetheless be an error to see the birth of the cinema as the accomplishment of this dream alone. The cinema appears, throughout its history, to be torn between a propensity to virtualize the world, and the fact that it can not fail to inscribe itself with a material trace of this same world: the chemical vibrations, waves, tints, pigments and shades, and above all the slowness, the heaviness of time (24 images a second can also be very slow). There is a tenacious persistence of a duration as endurance. The "Lumière minute" can last a long time.

The virtualization of matter, bodies and spaces, which renders them at once recognizable and manipulable, identifiable and transformable, was, therefore, only *one* of the dimensions of the cinematic operation – the most playful one, it is true. There was also, however, "the impression of reality" (Bazin). The spectacle was accelerated, and the world as spectacle was too. The wall demolished in one of the Lumières' first films rose up again, with spectacular magic.[6] But when the leaves on the trees moved it was a much bigger miracle. Up until then, no magician had been able to make the leaves of painted or photographed trees move. The Lumière brothers' *cinématographe* did not triumph over its competitors through its spectacular phantasmagoria, but through its *mimetic power*. The spectators preferred the duplication of the world over its transformation (in the magic lanterns). They wanted *realism*.[7] In the cinema, the object and the image of the object resemble each other all the more when they are in motion. It is this resemblance that the *ballast of the real*[i] which founds the illusion holds onto. Before inventing worlds, cinematic analogy demonstrates its power at the primary level: that of the *familiar*, of the *common*. There is a realist fatality of the cinema, a fact which implies a *realism of durations*.

5. I call attention to two important books by Paul Virilio: *Vitesse et politique: essai de dromologie* (Paris: Galilée, 1977) and *La Machine de vision: essai sur les nouvelles techniques de représentation* (Paris: Galilée, 1988) [*The Vision Machine*, trans. Julie Rose (Bloomington: Indiana University Press, 1994)].

6. *Démolition d'un mur*, Louis Lumière, 1895.

7. The realism in question is of the first degree: the resemblance between life and the images of life, a resemblance which is entirely assumed, as we have underlined here on several occasions. Later, with narrative technique becoming more complex, this base realism will evidently no longer be enough to constitute the realism of a film or a scene. Nonetheless, ever present, it is the unperceived basis for successive realist constructions.

On one side: impatience and feverishness, an appetite for seeing, the "see it with your own eyes" of the gawker at the fairground and its sideshow attractions... On the other side: the plunge into a fascinated gaze, an absorbing image, a penetrating duration, a figure which gives itself the time to incarnate the filmed world. There is a need for the history of the cinema to be written as a struggle between the frustration and the satisfaction of the desire to see, between *writing* and *spectacle*.

Four. – Now, this is a matter concerning the human figure.[8] The body, the face, the countenance: the cinema is the figurative art *par excellence*. The face has never been celebrated in quite the same way that it has been in the cinema; the close-up is a fulfillment of the promises of the portrait in painting. It can be played with (deformations, transformations, disfigurations, masks, make-up, effects), but resemblance remains the basis for the impression of reality and realistic representation in the cinema.

The effect, however, of these gestures of abbreviation – cutting, ellipsis, elision, shortening, acceleration and so on – is to exile the human figure to a "new world," one that is dematerialized, de-realized, abstracted. Has the commodity taken hold of our forms, our figures, our faces? The soul is pursued by the model. Photography and cinema are the weapons of this advertising-driven interception. Typecasting has become the norm. Typecasting abridges, simplifies, classifies, indexes, reduces the real ambiguity of every face. The cinema has long worked with the ambiguity of the bodies and faces that it filmed. Cary Grant? James Stewart?[9] They possess an indeterminate, floating ambiguity, one that is neither assignable nor calculable. This ambiguity is reduplicated, in a fashion, by the intrinsic ambiguity of cinematic images. The resemblance is seized upon, indeed, but in a duration which both confirms and undoes it, by submitting it to the usurious passage of time, modification and alteration. The *same* in the cinema is always-already in the midst of changing. The most static of shots is not static at all: time circulates within it. This time which passes through the shot is translated by the barely perceptible difference (and *différance*) of a still image with its immediate neighbors. A cinematic shot is always a process of transformation into an act.

My conclusion is that there is, in every cinematic scene, a *realist tension* linked to its analogical force. We can understand this tension as the difficulty filmed bodies have in letting themselves be totally virtualized by the cinema. I have claimed that the body has its own temporalities: its own weight, its own connections and disconnections, its own singularity. It carries its freedom around with it. Fragmenting or cutting on the figured body is an act of violence carried out against it. The classic

---

8. Cf. Jacques Aumont, "Figurable, figuratif, figural," in Aumont, *À quoi pensent les films?* (Paris: Séguier, 1996).

9. Cf. Luc Moullet, *Politique des acteurs: Gary Cooper, John Wayne, Cary Grant, James Stewart* (Paris: Cahiers du cinéma, 1993).

match-cut also has this function: it stitches together pieces of bodies which have been disconnected by the take and the cut, and which need to be re-connected to give the illusion that the body is still maintained in its entirety, not mutilated. This concern did not affect painting or sculpture. Is Picasso's *Demoiselles d'Avignon* (1907) conceivable in the cinema? I am not so sure. It remains to be seen. Guaranteed by the machine that produces it, analogy is a jealous force. The filmed body is bound to resemble a body, the body of the spectator – all differences are suspended in the resemblance, the recognition of the species' forms. With regards to Picasso, Georges Bataille wrote:

> If the forms brought together by the painter on a canvas had no repercussion, for example, since the talk was of voracity – even on an intellectual level – then those horrible shadows which collide into each other's heads and those jaws with hideous teeth would never have sallied forth from Picasso's brain to instill fear into those who still furrow their brow in honest contemplation, and painting would at the very most be good for distracting people from their rage, much like bars or American movies. But why hesitate to write that, when Picasso paints, the dislocation of forms leads to a dislocation of thought?[10]

The work of Bataille, along with Didi-Huberman's commentary on him, revolves around the question of the centrality of the "human figure,"[11] of the gaps which are hollowed out in it or on the basis of it, of the logic of *resemblance* which crosses it, however much *disfiguration* it is led to endure. The gap, precisely, which separates painting from cinema is entirely due to the analogical power the latter inherits from photography: the recording of the passage of time, and the destruction caused by this passage. If, in the cinema, analogy is *a fatality, a destiny*, it is because it produces time, constructs phases, because it is not satisfied with a single glance, but places itself in a quivering duration of the infinitesimal or the infra-visible, and actuates the endless processes of resemblance across all possible forms of dissemblance.

The *cut*, the *mutilation* of the body or the face through framing and montage as much as through the action represented (such as the slicing of the eye in *Un Chien andalou*), can not avoid returning to the cinematic sovereignty of Bataille's "human figure," even if only by doing it harm. The grimaces, masks and make-up, the special effects and digital deformations which chew up the human face like a soft paste (another of Bataille's terms) remain exposed to this reference, or condemned to be turned toward it, even when these bad treatments affront the spectator's face, the human face watching in the shadows. I'm thinking of the "digital faces" of the characters in Avi Mograbi's *Z 32*: the ill-ease is not that great, we know roughly what is

---

10. Georges Bataille, "Le 'Jeu lugubre'," *Documents*, no. 7 (1929), p. 369 (cited by Didi-Huberman, *La ressemblance informe, ou le gai savoir visuel selon Georges Bataille*, *op. cit.*)

going on, it is more a case of *disturbance*. The disfiguration of the represented face doubtless arrives at the imaginary, idealized dimension of the spectator's own face. But through this projection the face is also reached as a real, reverberative surface, sensitive to what corroborates one's own configuration, only able to find itself visually "pierced" by the traits that it can *recognize as close to itself, as its own*. The synthetic monsters created through special effects do not attain the tremendous power of the monsters in *Freaks* (Todd Browning, 1932), precisely because they lack any remains of *humanity*, of *human presence*, of the *unformed remains of the human form*, which assures the cinematic relationship between the filmed body and the body of the spectator.

On this delicate point – the analogical resemblance following the canons of anthropomorphism (at once confusing and disturbing) – it is perhaps less fitting to refer to the Picasso of the 1930s than to Jeff Wall's more recent photographs arranged and shown on illuminated containers (for example, *After "Invisible Man" by Ralph Ellison, the Prologue*, 1999-2000, or *In Front of a Nightclub*, 2006) where everything is *lifelike*, where the represented bodies incontestably attest to the salience of the "human figure," but where a light, a pose, a set, or an arrested gesture appear to be displaced from their natural place. The photographs are both true and false at one and the same time. They are desperately adjusted, and yet no manipulation can be observed. In all this mimed, acted but affirmed resemblance, I see the effect of a strange alteration, which has drawn little attention but which is nonetheless manifest, which is close, to my mind, to what already occurred at the origins of the cinema, in the Lumière films, and which perhaps has not ceased to be produced since then, albeit discreetly, subtly: the world, the body, the figure, are all there, it is true, but they are slightly corroded by their very depiction. This is a form of usury, but it is also a new rejuvenation.[11]

Five. – On the other hand, filming the human body often amounts to giving it a situation, a context, implicating it in a *hors-champ*. The human figure is in the middle. The body is not only a form but a center, a radiating point. The filmed body is never alone, even when it is isolated on the screen. It enters in conjunction with all the other filmed and absent bodies, with the filming bodies and the bodies of spectators. The form of the figure thus imposes the concern for a dignity in the relationship with other figures. But it is not as simple as that. The documentary experience often encounters a reticence in those who have already given their willing agreement. This goes without saying, because nothing is signed, nothing is contractual, nothing states that this agreement can be invoked at any moment: entering into the game of the film, therefore, signifies neither submission nor alienation. The difficulty is more on the level of freedom: the shoot can be understood as a system of constraints. Now,

11. Cf. the magisterial *Jeff Wall* by Jean-François Chevrier (Paris: Hazan, 2006).

this dimension of freedom is already present in the filmed body itself. When filmed, something inside the body is revealed to the take. No body is totally capable of being framed. There is a spilling over, a de-framing. Only the duration of the take authorizes the extraneous performance [*jeu hors jeu*] of the filmed body, its plasticity, its own movement, its indiscipline. Rapid cutting cuts out this freedom of the filmed body to not be completely in the take, in the shot. The duration of the shot induces fantasies about the disorderliness of the filmed body.[12] We see the relationship of forces. The body, when filmed, is transformed, framed, reduced, augmented, made disproportionate, re-temporalized; in sum, it is re-written. But not without impediments, not without resistance. It is the bumps and scrapes recorded by the machine that give the take its value as a true inscription, such that no take is identical to any other.

What we see in the cinema still comes within the scope of *true inscription*, in the sense that there has genuinely been a simultaneous presence of body and machine, and the cinematic take has recorded this co-presence as a *relationship*. What matters, therefore, is the truthfulness of this relationship. This question is impossible to avoid, without making the switch to synthetically generated imagery. The filmed relationship is a *cinematic fact*. The impression of reality attests to it, and likewise, in a circular fashion, it is validated by it. From the basis of this true inscription arises the belief in a situation, characters, and so on.

When we make a cut in the *scene* of this relationship, the site where bodies and machines are conjugated, then one of two things happens. Either this cut does not act as a rupture, but as a stitching, which masks discontinuity by creating a *match* (there is – and this is an important nuance – a rupture, but not a rupture effect), or, by contrast, the cut leads to a perceptible rupture (even if the intention is to minimize this effect). In the latter case, the scene appears to be undone (or easy to undo), with little resistance, and little consistency. Nothing about it will have been strong enough to prevent it from appearing to be custom-made, capable of being altered on demand. The cinematic fact is attenuated (and this is possibly the hidden logic of the operation: to disqualify the cinema by providing the viewer with a true inscription of the relationship of a body and a machine). "I cut, I affirm myself by cutting... and you, filmed body, you are not sovereign, you are at my disposition." There is indeed an unveiling of the cinematic artificiality of the filmed situation, but at the same time its recuperation by an authoritarian gesture which at once denies the autonomous power of the cinematic operation. The artifice designated as such makes this manipulation (carried out by the filmmaker, or the editor) appear legitimate, and the will to control appear "normal." This turns the spectator into a witness, a judge, and no

12. Cf. Yves in *Le Moindre Geste*, Fernand Deligny and Jean-Pierre Daniel, 1958-1968. But also Buster Keaton and other slapstick performers.

longer a character imaginarily implicated in the scene. The spectator oscillates between a place of implication (illusion) and a place of control (signature).

The filmed body is on the side of the accident. The body is contradiction, subversion. The cinema has to domesticate it. But there is always something left behind by this training. There is a tension, a deterioration, a spilling over. And the primary form of this spilling over – which is an *autonomy* of the filmed body with regards to its framing regulated by the machine – prompts the constitution of an area of play, a deployment which would be proper to it. To receive the freedom of the body, the requisite duration is needed.

Six. – Autonomy means that the gestures and speech of the character seem to obey its free arbiter, its fantasy, its unconsciousness. The intervention of a *cutter* who makes the image, and the body in the image, jump, is thus immediately legible as violence, or even violation. A part of the spontaneous positioning of a space-time and a speech-form, proper to this filmed body, is destroyed by the gesture of the cut, which marks the potency of an exterior will acting on the interior of the scene. The jump-cut affirms that there is a will superior to the will of the filmed body, or to what remains of its independent will, to its order and its disorder. The jump-cut frames meaning. It orients, selects, chooses, guides. It does this to the spectator, of course, but also, in the last instance, to the filmed body itself, barely "controlled" during the shoot, but taken back under control during the editing. Montage as revenge.

But, of course, the most serious detriment occurs with the *editing of filmed speech*. Even before the jump-cut was generalized, recorded speech was savagely cut and chopped up on television, to reduce it, control it, guide it, sometimes, even, to make it say something different. But also: to accustom us, by means of the cuts in sound and in speech, to an auditory world made of chaos: non-articulated fragments, bursts of speech without any outtakes, phrases interrupted. (How many times have we heard the phrase: "clean up the sound"?) In short, a remodeling of speech – and, as a consequence, of the *logos* – which is also a massacre of speech, and which can only lead to contempt for both the speaker and the listener. With this intrusive surgery practiced on the living world, the era of "sound bites" has been ushered in, an era which is far from being over, and which has given political discourse the form of an advertising slogan.

On the one hand, what is cut out is almost always what is considered to be "surplus to requirements": the signifying elements which inscribe something other than the obvious meaning, that is, which retain something of the time, the duration, the accidents and the reality of the enunciation. What is left is the statement, that is, unified signification. On the other hand, as soon as I perceive that edited speech has been sifted out from the flux of filmed speech, that certain passages have been selected from it, while others have been censored, and that the editing lets me know this, it is no longer possible to believe in the fiction of an autonomous speaker – that is to say, in his dimension as a *character*. The mysterious charm linked to the chaining of words to words and sentences to sentences – what psychology, following on from poetry, has dubbed *free association* (again, freedom) – vanishes in an instant. Either the represented (edited) speech gives me the effect of only being governed by the free and unconscious arbiter of the character, or it makes me know that it is externally controlled by an editor who has left behind the traces of his work. This is not the same thing. In the first case, there is a lie. But a fertile lie, which, granted, does deceive, but which by the same token deftly handles an illusion of spontaneity and freedom, which we play with, which we can feign to have been taken in by ("I know very well, but all the same"). Is this not what we expect from actors in cinematic fictions: that they should make us believe that they are inventing their dialogue, gestures and movements on the spot? In the second case, there is a sterile truth which utters the *deed*, but not the *doing*. When I behold the edited film, it is signified to me, without any prevarication, that *everything is performed*. In the first case, this is not said to me. And even if, inevitably, it is true that everything functions at the moment that I am beholding the film, the power of the cinema is to return what was past, what was already done, to the present of an *in the midst of being done*, an *in the midst of happening*.

It is understood that cuts and matches do not entirely have the same meaning in their fictional and documentary versions. There is a summoning of the real world, of the referent, in the documentary gesture, an implication, a direct address which exceeds what takes place in its fictional counterpart. The real bodies and referential identities continue to exist outside of the films. The individual destinies, however much they have been able to be transcended or exalted by the cinematic operation, persist in unfurling in the "real" world. This world is characterized (as it has long been) by the fact that, in it, penalties, wounds and death are not virtual. Here, the cinema's virtuality finds a sort of anchoring in "earthly reality," to echo the term Auerbach used when writing on Dante.

Seven. – The extent to which cinematic forms, and, for example, montage types, are historically inscribed must be reiterated, both in terms of what determines them, as well as what, in their turn, they determine. Let us return to the signal example of *Man with a Movie Camera*. Dziga Vertov and his wife and editor Elizaveta Svilova create a work, for one of the first times in the history of the cinema, based on the principle of rapid, and sometimes very rapid, montage. If ever there has been fragmentation, this was it. Many of the shots last for less than a second. Together, they have the effect of a vision that is disarticulated, hacked up, rattled, struck with vertigo. Of course, there is a coherence to it. The film is a "history of the eye" – what is more, of a mechanical eye. This bulging eye is insatiable, gluttonous, ready to swallow everything. It is, therefore, not absurd that the fragmentation of vision should become exasperated. At times, even the very limits of the visible are attained and even breached. In a crazed dance, the images of the streets of Odessa, buses, trams, pedestrians, people asleep, policemen, crowds are all mixed, superimposed, doubled up; they run into each other, and break apart into two or three pieces, and nothing about all this is metaphorical, because these effects literally happen on the screen. Above and beyond this, however, fragmentation reigns. It happens that this "history of the eye" is, in reality, a story of the weaknesses of the human eye, which is supplanted by the camera. The spectator's eye is barred by the mechanical eye. At one point, toward the end of the film, we return to the theater shown at the beginning, and there both the spectators in their seats and we ourselves see nothing on the screen but a series of black and white streaks: a pulsing beat, if I dare say, in its raw state, vacillating, trembling, palpitating, flickering, dazzling, blinding – could we not be led to believe that this is a depiction of the scopic drive itself, the absolute desire to see everything, the will-to-power of the perfected eye? Vertov must affirm the force of the cinema, he must bring into play all of its functions and all of its magic, with the aim of forming a new man with a new eye, a *kinok*.

I read this as the *political birth-act* of the cinema, to the extent that this film shows how the cinema is capable of changing the world – by filming it. This ambition has never been repeated. It is inscribed in a precise, limited, critical historical juncture. For Vertov, the factory of the new man of socialism went together with the utopia of a cinema capable of bringing people closer together. The Vertovian project explicitly has the cinema at its center, with an editing room toward which everything converges, and from which everything departs, a social and political central nervous system. It is a fact that the cinema has always borne this mad hope. What was once dreamt of accompanies those who come afterwards, or, rather, receives them. But the Vertovian dream could only be a total one, it required all the enthusiasm of an entire society. We are far from it now. Even Vertov was far from it back then.

It is true that a certain number of masterpieces in the history of the cinema, after Vertov, deploy a great virtuosity in rapid montage, and even without going down the path of avant-garde formalism – without reaching the extremes attained by Eisenstein – hyper-fragmentation has on occasion been a system of writing. Let us cite, among the classics, some sequences from *Man of Aran* (Robert Flaherty, 1934), for example, the shark hunt. Or more recent examples: the semi-imaginary boxing match, the swimming trip and the bar sequences of *Moi, un Noir* (Jean, Rouch, 1959). But we still have to place these works of rapid montage in historical perspective. If forms have meaning, if they act, as I believe, in the thinking of time, then it will be necessary to interrogate them in their relationships with cinematic methods (which, themselves, are forms of thought) in the other works and, furthermore, in the other fields of the general artistic production of the era. Rapid editing "Vertov-style" triumphed, in the 1970s, in video clips and ads, before becoming the standard of all audiovisual production. We must ask why, for what? And against what?

In the blinded world of the spectacle which is our own, the principle of fragmentation has switched sides in the battle. The dissemination of slivers of shots, frames, durations and effects, which once signified the nascent omnipotence of the alliance between man and machine, somewhat in the vein of a solidarity of desire, a sharing of vertigo, has today, alas, taken on an entirely different meaning. The market has torn the world to shreds, broken up relationships of solidarity, wrenched neighbors apart from each other without bringing others closer together, shattered memories by delocalizing them, and dispersed those who used to love gathering together in front of a screen. It is through entirely different formal means that the cinema today hopes to resurrect the vitality of Vertov's utopia: through protracted durations, through documentary materialities opposed to the dominance of the virtual, through articulated montages, and through words which are more than a psychological supplement but carry the weight of a common history, of a community at once possible and impossible. These are all antidotes, it seems to me, to the contemporary disaster of pointless imagery and redundant speech, of frenetic, impatient, egotistical accelerations and precipitations, which may appear to our successors as the irrefutable inscription of the death drive that has carried us off into its spectacular excess.

Eight. – And this is why a masterpiece of complexity in the representation of the human figure accomplished by the cinema (let us be specific: Jules Berry in *Le Crime de Monsieur Lange*, Jean Renoir, 1935) has now become fastidious, cumbersome. The time required for its incarnation is now judged to be *too long*, too slow. The level of attentiveness it requires is too elevated. The fundamental ambiguity of the cinematic image (analogy/duration) is too slow, is deferred for too long, to give us any hope of pleasure; its doubting, unfocused, fitful, perplexed and even suspenseful qualities demand too much viewing time. The mode of reading of journalistic information – rapid, clear, objective – has been imposed. The commodity needs action.

I see a certain spectatorial fatigue arise when confronted with the representation of the human figure in its ambiguity, in its resistance to conform itself to the norm – a fatigue before a non-promotional cinema, which has nothing to sell because its desire is elsewhere. This fatigue is translated – in the media, in TV game shows and advertisements – by an impatience, by a haste to treat the figure badly, to disfigure it. The human figure has become the object of the rage of images. We know all too well that these wounded, tortured, murdered bodies are common currency for the images diffused by the media. To the affront that the filmed figure is subjected to is added the affront of figurative destruction. In *Documents*, Bataille appealed to the ability of shock, collision and the montage of contrasts and ecstasies to confront the comforting anthropomorphism of "normal" Western vision. This insurrection of images is now captive to the profusion of advertisements and photographs that make up the commodified image, and by the most invasive clips and "visuals" imaginable. Certainly, the sliced-up eyeball has yet to be plastered up on Decaux billboards.[iii] But images which stir up the heart for the purposes of a facile "scandal" are no longer so rare. Should we conclude that, in the end, we are no longer in the same era as *Documents*?

Nine. – The ways in which images are cut and assembled are not, therefore, ahistorical. Montage becomes more restricted at the very moment that so-called "democratic" societies, organized for the benefit of globalized capital, more and more overtly enter the *era of control.*[iv] There is a strange synchrony between the generalization of control procedures and the exile which pushes the spectator outside of his place of implication, putting him in the place of a "controller," from which he can judge from an *external* vantage point and not find himself in the position of *being judged.*[13] This exile is linked with the reduction of representation to being nothing but its *spectacular* dimension, which presupposes that nothing other than the *scopic drive* is implicated – nothing, for example, of a possible projective elaboration in the imaginary.

Ten. – Let us be clear: all montage is control (as is the case with all *mise en scène*, all artifice, all filming, including "documentary" shoots). Well may the classical system of matching mask the cut that it sutures, but it can not prevent this cut from being the mark of the choice that has been operated, and of the rejection of some part or other of the signifying elements. The choice has been made, but the operation is veiled by a match. This is why classical match-cutting does not give responsibility for the intentions behind a film *to the cut*. Rather, it shifts these intentions back to the earlier decisions of *mise en scène* made during the shoot, as if montage were less decisive. The cut does not cut, rupture does not rupture, and so on. But there is illusion. Let us examine this a little.

If I see a film that constructs the possibility of my belief in an *hors-champ*, an off-screen scene [*hors-scène*], and an off-screen time [*hors-temps*]; that makes me feel an opening up of things, a floating of significations; that makes me share a certain wandering – I can recognize that I have been deceived, of course, but with consent, and not blindly, for I well know that these apparent margins are, in reality, determined by a signifying logic, which is controlled by a narrative strategy. This does not, however, prevent me from enjoying the wondrous illusion that there is liberty in the pathways traveled by spectator.

By contrast, the jump-cut – juxtaposition without illusion – forcibly tells us that a gesture, a succession of phrases, a moment of presence of the filmed body or a duration have been chosen *for me, in place of my intentions*, with the clearly avowed goal of making me know that I am only being shown "the best" of whatever has been filmed, that, consequently, I am being spared what an author, a supervisor, a control-

13. On the "place of the spectator" in classical representation and political morality in the 17th and 18th centuries, cf. Luc Boltanski, *La Souffrance à distance* (Paris: Gallimard, coll. "Folio Essais," 2007), pp. 75-110. The "moral spectator" analyzed by the author through the works of Adam Smith is the townsman observing his peers, whose suffering he views, and chooses whether or not to share. A century later, in the cinema, this question of "sharing" can no longer be posited in the same terms. A "*dispositif*" relieves the "spectator" of his "impartiality."

ler have judged not to be of interest to me... This modus presents me as having to be "framed" to myself (I have had this chosen for me), as not having responsibility (the selection has already been made), and, above all, as not desiring to take the risk of an error in the path marked out for me (the work is made in order to satisfy).

Eleven. – From its origins, the cinema has been presented as a sort of divided, torn-up monster, where the *will to control* and the *demand for liberty* have confronted each other. The powers (on all levels, beginning with the power of the filmmaker) take care to control the audience, their expectations and their affective or symbolic prerogatives. There is social marketing within the spectacle industry, which evidently culminates in the ratings-driven programming of television. But the spectator has difficulty with being controlled. He is like the undisciplined child who refuses to be called to order. Owing to its very duration, the film screening remains a forest of *paths that lead nowhere.*[v] To travel down one or another of these paths is to move forward while groping about in the dark, proceeding through *trial and error,* in a peculiar gait, with each step going further off the beaten track. The freedom of the cinema spectator requires forms which act without enclosing, forms overflowing their frames, durations of slow dissolution, windows, absolutely, but windows through which blows the wind of the real, and absences where the spectators dream about what is no longer on the screen.

The cut in the shot, showing no gentleness toward the filmed bodies, threatens the utopia of an all-encompassing time which would welcome us (and possibly bury us). With the jump-cut, time is flaunted as an *adjustable variable.* We have the advantage over it. There is less fear, less of the unknown, more science fiction. This evidently makes a greater or lesser amount of the will-to-power enter into the montage. But the powers of the will are such that it also knows how to not always show itself.

Twelve. – In the hope of making us conform to them, of rendering them "natural," of making them the air that we breathe, television, therefore, broadcasts *forms.* These forms are, above all, *durational norms.* They constitute, as we know all too well, *accountable time.* Television programs have fixed durations, regardless of the stakes, as if works could not breathe for themselves, as if they needed a lumbar brace to be able to stand up. These programs are timed with minute precision, and, in parallel, the shots are ever more brief, for time is money, and if you can show in 3 seconds what would have taken 10 or 20 seconds in another economy of writing and production, then you can profit from the difference. But what does a shot lasting 2 or 3 seconds teach me? Nothing, apart from an aptitude in reflex vision, in the hunter's passing glance. Can this even be considered "seeing"? It is doubtful. In rapid montage, the shot hurries away from me before I have even had the time to catch up with it. It passes before me, ever onwards, closed off from its surrounds. A shot which endures, by contrast, first weighs on me like a constraint, and because it endures, it then opens up to my presence and lets me inhabit it with my fantasy (which can also be to evade it). And if the sequence is cut up [*découpée*] into matched shots, the illusion of continuity given by these matches still leaves me with a certain margin to err, to wander within a determined form.

There is nothing astonishing about the fact that *the other of the markets* (of business, of the media) should be *unaccountable time*. The slow time of metamorphosis (the digital effect of *morphing* is always accelerated), of ripening, of rotting, organic time as a whole is not "manageable," whether by the spectacle (fast-motion, dissolves...), by commodity exchange ("just-in-time" production strategies, stock rotation, etc.), or by the event-focused media. Subjective time – the time of organs, neuronal circuits, dreams – also eludes the measuring gauges. So many floating, elastic temporalities, often with an extreme slowness, come up against the regulated time of the markets.[14]

There is always a trace, a phantom of referential temporality in representations (which are themselves temporalized). The time of the film leads back to the time of the spectator, which, in turn, leads back to the time experienced outside of the movie theater. The regime of durations furnishes models and formulates forms, it moulds the manners in which we apprehend the world. This is why the question of durations is directly political. Time is war.

14. Cf. Pierre Sansot, *Du bon usage de la lenteur* (Paris: Payot, 1998).

V. Changing the Spectator?

The detour is right at the source of every literary work. The literary work which does not give itself over to the detour is nothing but a literal report of the real. And even in the era when it was considered that literature's aim was to reproduce the real as closely as possible, even in this absolute mimesis, it always went further.

– Édouard Glissant.[1]

And as we are made up of all those of with whom, day after day, we have coexisted, that their pain, their perplexity, their harm is our own, we are never done with balancing the accounts.

– Pierre Bergounioux.[2]

The majority of commercially distributed cinema, to the extent that it is a 'development' of pre-existing material, increasingly comes within the sphere of the aesthetics of advertising, and invents the themes and preoccupations (the growing 'awareness' in the twin/rival forms of propaganda and advertising) that this aesthetic implies.

– Serge Daney[3]

One. – The jump-cut is only one of the modalities of the general fragmentation that is the governing principle of industry standards (whether in the cinema or television, fiction or documentary). *Channel-hopping* occurs less between "programs" broadcast by different television channels than it does within the programs themselves – and it thus becomes a programming of vision. The disintegration of durations and shots scatters the spectator's mind, forbids any form of concentration, dooms him to the compulsive repetition of the cut and the jump. Would we not have the right to

---

1. Édouard Glissant, *Les Entretiens de Baton Rouge*, with Alexandre Leupin (Paris: Gallimard, 2008), p. 107.

2. Pierre Bergounioux, *Où est le passé?* (Paris: Éditions de l'Olivier, 2007) (interviews with Michel Gribinski).

3. Daney, "Sur Salador," in *La Rampe, op. cit.* [An English translation of this article was printed as "On Salador," trans. Diana Matias, in *Cahiers du cinéma, 1969-1972: The Politics of Representation*, ed. Nick Browne (London: Routledge, 1990), pp. 115-123.]

assume that an entire sector of the industry of the audiovisual spectacle is dedicated to soberly calculating how to make the spectator an *addict* of visual effects? How is it that we know this? The television producer's handbook in France imposes a minimum number of shots in a TV-film: no less than 1200 shots, I am told, for a 90-minute film, or an average duration of little more than 4 seconds![4] What precision! What anguish! Let us simply note that this stroboscopic flashing bars the very possibility of a gaze. It is the triumph of pulsation: all that remains is a rhythmic hammering.

Two. – On the other hand, the present world is obsessed with a concern for *ringing true*, perhaps because this present world is filled to the brim with screens, ads, simulacra and "virtual realities"? Is it the case that our societies, having renounced the creation of collectivities, have nothing in common apart from "images"? Does it not seem that the spread of the "visual" ends up weakening it and turning it into a sort of catch-all which hews closely to the world? But where is the world? Behind the images?

The jump-cut tears apart the screen illusion which postulates the conformity of the representation to an increasingly absent "real." For the spectators of the Lumière films, it was, on the contrary, the power of appearance of the represented world that led to their popularity, and established a belief in the power of representation. The screen was the surface of the efficacy of the "real." Times have changed. The match-cut, as a denial of the cut (the illusory match) belongs to a historical moment where, for the spectator, the cinema was entirely an encounter, in effect, with illusion, bringing belief into play. Today, there is still illusion, still belief, but the statements of the audiovisual sphere (above all) and the cinema (all the same) are more racked now than they were in the past by an *obsession with the real*, an *appeal to reality*, as if there were a need to validate cine-belief[i] with a manifest, explicit reference denoted and indexed to the "real." Illusion can now only function on the condition of being strongly guaranteed by a non-simulated reality. We have lost count of the films which, since *Close-up*, followed by *Life and Nothing More* (both by Abbas Kiarostami, 1990 and 1991), up until *Still Life* and *24 City* (Jia Zhangke, 2006 and 2008) have needed to film documentary traces of the world, precisely to show something of its collapse (the collapse of the old world, yes, but is there any other kind?). In the face of this, the fictions based on old systems (the fable, the novel, theater, cinema) appear rather weakened, to the extent that they should demand a reinforcement of credibility from the document, the documentary, news footage. But were there not already newsreels and journalists in *Citizen Kane*? The real ruins of Berlin in *Germania Anno Zero*? Are we only, perhaps, witnessing the recent amplification of an old

4. This information is given to me by a director who regularly works on feature films made for public television. The standards in question are universally respected. How many films in the cinema, today, refrain from competing with this frenetic accumulation of chopped up images?

postulate, that, in the cinema, fiction and documentary are two sides of the one coin, and inevitably meet and intersect with each other? Has it not seemed preferable, in the past as well as the present, to administer a dose of filmed reality to a fictional story in order for us to keep on believing in it? Does the earthquake in *Life and Nothing More* not simply continue on from the tuna-fishing sequence in *Stromboli*? Why? Because, by filming the world, the cinema *de-realizes* it, because it produces an altered version or translation of it in the sense of an added virtuality, because the world thus filmed tends to substitute itself for the non-filmed world, because the non-filmed world disappears more and more each day behind the filmed world, because "fictions" need a minimum basis in reality (the reality of situations and of bodies), so as not to end up in the sinister "filmed cinema" made fun of by Daney. We still need to observe that this demand for a *surplus reality* (often given the predicate "documentary") which bolsters those fictions de-realized by the dominance of generalized spectacle in no way prevents numerous films from the US, Asia, Europe and elsewhere from rushing headlong into the countless "de-realities" (whether parascientific, mystical or magical) that provide such an enticing stomping ground for cinematic fiction. Between, on the one hand, those fictions that interrogate the zones where spectacle and the world overlap, and, on the other hand, those fictions that are gigantic machines (costing enormous sums of money – or, in other words, greatly coveted by the industry) whose phantasmatic or mystico-mythic narratives speculate on bouts of panic induced by the emergence of techno-humanity, how can we not see the effects of one and the same anguish concerning the deracination of our present-day realities? Against the totalitarian and totalizing spectacle, the cinema, or what is left of it, claims at the very least to guarantee the continued existence of a certain layer of the world, and of real experience, in what insists on enduring as our history. The term "documentary" thus presupposes that *there is something real to document*: some corner of the world, the reality of a relationship, the singularity of a subject; whatever is still obscure, rough and hoarse in the world... The documentary has an interest in the war of facts and narratives as something real, something which takes place in our world and in our lives. Documented facts are *neither reversible nor virtual*. Let us say that there is a conflict, in the functioning of the cinema, between the side of the document and the side of the spectacle. As opposed to what happens in the spectacle's logic of omnipotence, the documentary gesture bears in mind that *not everything is possible* in films, that *not everything is filmable* (for example, making a "documentary" on Neanderthals by using actors to play them). The freedom of creation that we demand is limited from the start by that part of the world which refuses or escapes from being turned into spectacle. Documentary practice is a sort of ascesis where one accepts being constrained by the resistance of facts, objects, bodies, situations, men and women who are not at our service, not at our beck and call, who can be neither mobilized nor modulated at our will. Those who enter into our films will not be blurred out.

It is fortunate that these limitations still obtain: they assure us that the world has not entirely submitted to the control of the spectacle. We do not have the means, or even the desire, to "reconstruct" in the extraordinary world of the studios what has been destroyed in the ordinary world. The documentary must register what has disappeared, what is no longer there. The cinema that we love (to make) will not lie about disappearance, degradation, ruins. Look at Rossellini: the ruins of Berlin in *Germania Anno Zero*, the diggings at Pompeii in *Viaggio in Italia*. "Docu-fictions" want to know nothing about this loss, this dereliction. But what if, to see the world such as it is, it is better to start off with what does not let itself be seen? For what is missing from the visible today is not missing by chance. The gas chambers and the crematoriums at Auschwitz were destroyed by the Nazis, desperate not to leave behind any traces of their mass crime. There is nothing left but ruins. To *reconstitute what has been razed* (using digitally synthesized images) would be a spectacular ignominy. To show that not everything can be shown puts the spectator in a real position in relation to the Spectacle's illusion of totality. Against the spectacle, the cinema must show that the world is not totally visible, that seeing is seeing beyond the frame, seeing that there is an *hors-champ* which can not be framed. The *hors-champ* is not only what the frame hides by showing, it is everything that remains outside the possibility of being seen, outside the place of the spectator, it is what does not make the image (and thus what does not make the spectacle). It is *the hors-champ of every image*.

As such – and this is its greatness – documentary cinema poses a *buttress of the real* against the desire to be in command of everything, to reinvent everything. We do not have access to the "whole" story. What do we make of death, for instance? A fiction? A fable? An allegory? But no. In documentary cinema, death, when filmed, can not be reversed, repeated or replayed. There is no "second take." The diseased, the wounded, the dead are so forever, even after the camera has stopped filming. This *hors-film* is another name for the real. Well may the tribunal be filmed, but the sentences are carried out in the real world.

Three. – How, then, should we understand the recent mania for covering the fence palings of public parks, the façades of buildings, even the walls surrounding the Assemblée nationale with photographs? These "images" start out by hiding the places over which they are plastered. What sense is there in making a piece of the visible disappear by putting another one in its stead? Is it in order to say that, beforehand, there was "nothing to see here"? What need was there to adorn the Jardin du Luxembourg with giant photographs hung over its palings? Was this not done in order to deny its status as a public park – that is, a public space outside the market? Having become an open-air gallery, it provides a display window for the photography market, formats the gazes of passers-by in directing them to see *what they are being shown*, and participates, by the same token, in the generalization of the spectacle's superiority over the non-spectacular world.

This upping of the stakes discreetly leaves us behind. In the long term, seeing so many "images" blinds us. (I here put "image" in quotation marks because it is perhaps still possible to save the image from its present aggravated collusion with the commodity and propaganda. Moreover, in the refusal of the cinema to let itself be totally devoured by the spectacle, a pitched battle for the reconquest of the image by means of images is being played out on the brink of the abyss.[5]) There is a glut of images, a nausea of the visual-virtual.

What we call "the real" will continue to increasingly hide itself away from our gaze, from our consciousness. As a result, there is an appeal to the *reality effects* which are intended to provide us with the guarantee that there is something like a reality (and one which we would be a part of). For example, voluntary scratches on the film would not take on the meaning of interposing the veil of a distancing effect between the object and its image, nor would they represent an emphasis on the mechanical fabrication of this image... They would, rather, be witness to the exact opposite trend, the authenticity of the take, of the accident which is not effaced as a trace of this missing real.[6] The "real" is indeed what has neither a place nor a name, what hides away, flees and surges forth without any warning; it is indeed what has always been missing. And yet, everything occurs *as if* the generalization of the spectacle induced a certain consciousness of this lack... It is the "return of the real," at least in the form of an obsession.

I do not know if all this is enough to account for the vertiginous proliferation of "documentary" films across the entire world.[7] Everywhere, the suspicion of an effacement of the real is floating about, and because it seems urgent and crucial to try to retain something of the real before its total disappearance, it is the cinema, paradoxically, to which we turn – this same cinema which, as we know, was one of the vectors of this effacement (it is true that it is more the documentary part of the equation which is called upon here – but we know that "documentary" and "fiction" are merely the two names of the cinema, its two permanently enmeshed faces). The paradox is only apparent. At the same time that it contributed to transforming the world into spectacle, as I have outlined above, the cinema gathered together the forces opposed

5. This is one of the themes powerfully treated by Marie-José Mondzain, in *Le Commerce des regards* (Paris: Seuil, 2003); and: *L'Image naturelle* (Paris: Le Nouveau Commerce, 1995).

6. But they would recall, to my mind, the jabs to the elbow Luc Moullet, in one of his first films (*Terres noires*, 1961), would give to his cameraman in order to shake up the shot, not out of malice, but, I presume, with the idea of momentarily unsettling the cinema machine with a provoked accident as an effect of the real.

7. Some 4000 documentary films, a majority of which are feature-length, were made and produced in France last year, I am told. In 2008, more than 800 French documentaries were presented in the "Incertain regard" program of the *États Généraux* of Lussas, Gérald Collas tells me. The most astonishing fact is that the majority of these films were made without any support from public television, which, as we know, can not tolerate anything other than the formats that they themselves have imposed (in a social case of auto-immune deficiency syndrome).

to the spectacle. These are, above all, forces of writing: rigorous *mise en scène*, the role of the *hors-champ*, the work on duration, precise formal games, the principle of frustrating the satisfaction of urges, the logic of ambiguity... everything that leads to the implication of the spectator and the restitution of his imaginary projections. The cinematographic operation posits that there is still a reality to take the side of – that there is still *reality* in the relationship of the spectator to the film.

If the cinema ever had been the motor agent of the virtualization of the world (or, as Baudrillard writes, its "disappearance"[8]), it is not anymore. Through a surprise shift in the battlelines at the end of the century just past (the 20th century), it now manifests itself as a modest, but still the most important, obstacle to the total domination of the commodified spectacle. Everything, or almost everything, now appears on screens that are not those of the cinema, but rather, those of the media, and the spectacular cinema of the major commercial chains runs on totally different lines to the cinema of the 1940s and 1950s. Spectators are shaped by the commodity system, which, with the support of advertising and the media (and a great deal of money), has managed to make films profitable before they are even seen. The screening, as a result, is presented as a sort of "test," where we can play at verifying what public chatter has already divulged. Of course, here I am describing the Orwellian dream of a total administration of the film market.

We are not at that point yet; there will always be rebellious and restive spectators to contradict this picture and set me straight. All the better. If what we call "the cinema" must persist, it will be as an *anti-spectacle*, capable of dis-alienating us from the dominant spectacular alienation. I demand that the cinema of today call for and incite an infiltration of something of the real into the images and sounds of its representations; and that it thus attest, I dare say, to the reality of the real. In a world positively governed by the spectacle, filled to the brim with images, crammed with the visible, drowned in light, the cinema (or what I call the cinema) will take on responsibility for the dark side, the *hors-champ*, the non-visible, an image which is lacunary, imperfect, fragile and, in short, "not everything."

Four. – Throughout the course of the last century, the film industry has carried out the ideological project of naturalizing the cinema effect: the transition from the "silent" to the "talkie"; from black and white to color; from 1.33:1 to 1.66:1, then Cinemascope; from mono to stereo sound, then to Dolby... But this perfecting of the lure withdraws us – through its very perfection – from the possibility of perceiving anything about it. Now, to be lured is not to be blinded. But "technical progress" has only

8. From *L'Échange symbolique et la mort* (Paris: Gallimard, 1976) [*Symbolic Exchange and Death*, trans. Iain Hamilton Grant (London: Sage Publications, 1993)] and *Le Système des objets* (Paris: Gallimard, 1978) [*The System of Objects*, trans. James Benedict (London: Verso, 1996)] up to *Pourquoi tout n'a-t-il pas disparu?* (Paris: L'Herne, 2007) [*Why Hasn't Everything Already Disappeared?*, trans. Chris Turner (London: Seagull, 2009)].

made the vision of what takes place on the screen closer to what takes place in the life outside of the darkened rooms of the cinema. And, in parallel, the filmed version of the world proposed (imposed) by the great cinematic spectacle is less and less detached from the manner in which this world presents itself as a spectacle outside the movie theaters. Dazzling lights, deafening sounds, garish colors, the incessant appeals made by advertising... The great cinematic spectacle resembles the great commodity spectacle like a brother. (Once again, the summits of capitalist cannibalism which have recently been scaled change nothing about this fact, on the contrary: this, perhaps final, moment of devouring is precisely the moment when we hear, from all sides, fabulous cries of "The show must go on!").

The lure is thus now constructed on the basis of a *denial of the denial*: we are no longer "in the cinema," but "in the spectacle," immersed in images and sounds, "in" a virtual reality which resembles real reality and can be confused with it, when it does not outrageously exaggerate it. Now, the greater the impression of reality, the less active is this disavowal. The *all the same* of belief no longer has to struggle so much against the unreality of the effects of the earlier cinema, it no longer has to imaginarily make up for the failings of resemblance. Let us agree that it is difficult to perfect the lure any further.[9] It is still more difficult to suppose a spectator opened to the game of doubt and belief, as the old spectator was. The market of images and sounds demands an agile, channel-hopping spectator: a kind of *Little Lord Fauntleroy* taking pleasure in the crumbs of power that the real lords leave him, amused at this minuscule control, imagining himself to be at their level. These real lords, however, do not zap at figures, but at beings. The control of representations is key to the exercise of power.

Are we witnessing the exhaustion of the desire to be lured, a desire which was the foundation of the cinema? What should we make of the new model of spectator, honed by the formatting and advertising of television? Is the model now that of a "client," informed, active, if not hyperactive? The television viewer is caught in a compulsive series of "passages to the act" which may be tiny, but all the same, drinking a beer, making a phone call, voting for "your" candidate, are all mini-transgressions of the cinema spectator's site of ritual impotence. This new spectator is no longer overwhelmed by the film, he is no longer dealing with a film stronger than him, he is no longer caught in a tangle of belief and doubt. With him, we see the extension of the reign of the *little know-it-alls*, the heroes of everyday cynicism, who can not be fooled by anything. Capitalism has supposedly won across the board, and

9. There is, of course, "the myth of total cinema" (Bazin). But the various attempts at 3D cinema have come up against the fact that the imaginary depth given to the flat screen by the spectator (the lure of depth) is – for the moment – more magical than a depth simulated by machines. The new attempts launched by Hollywood perhaps perform better in this regard, and if this is the case it would be a new amputation of the *cosa mentale* that the cinema was. Would the result be a screen without belief?

it is necessary not just to accommodate oneself to it, but to play to its song sheet. Ideologies are dead, and believing is now out of the question – except when it comes to religion, of course!

The illusion that we no longer have any illusions is the worst illusion of them all. It deceives by feigning to undeceive. It creates a blind and barbaric cynicism – the opposite of what happens in the cinema, where what we take pleasure in is precisely the fragility of illusion, the vacillation which allows us to perceive the role of desire as a desire to be deceived. This is why the cinema spectator only rarely becomes the follower of a fanatical sect.[ii]

Five. – When I drift over the threshold of dreams and project myself into the filmed figures, when I see them doing everything that I can no longer do during the screening, when they walk, talk, run, jump, love, fall and injure themselves, when my constrained body finds itself taken away by the exaltation of the filmed bodies, when I imaginarily project myself into the scene and mingle with what I am watching, where is the true, and where is the false, the fictive, the imaginary? If I go to the cinema, it is indeed to try out the powers of illusion and my willingness to cede to them. And, as a consequence, whatever the fascinations of the "realist" spectacle may be, the spectator that I am is never completely fooled, because he knows that he is in the cinema. My hypothesis is that the cinematic system prevents the spectator from completely tipping over into a belief without respite. He believes, yes, but only while doubting his belief.[10]

The place of the spectator is the place of play. It is not a matter of knowing, *it is a matter of not knowing* – as in Rohmer's *Triple Agent* (2004). In the world, our world, where the lures are invisible even though they are active everywhere, we are increasingly asked to "choose." Let's not fool ourselves, we are the ones who have been "chosen" – by the market, class, education, our relations, our heritage, everything. It would thus be a matter of liberty, in this society, to be able to withdraw oneself from the imperative of "choice" for even a single moment. Let us remember Bartleby's "I would prefer not to." Not choosing any side, deferring the act: the film screening maintains the act of disavowal and allows, during the time it is experienced, for a suspension of the principal of non-contradiction which organizes the practical world. I can take pleasure in a certain state of indecision without being crushed by a truck, or by my colleagues and superiors. To prefer not to, this is what distances us from the pressure of the world for a moment. Disavowal is akin to an authorization for a change of logic. In the time protected from representation, the spectators are not supposed to pass to the act: it is up to the characters to do it for them.

Everything artificial, false, fabricated, untruthful and illusory in the functioning of information, in the credo of the media, in the ideological propaganda of business, not

---

10. Cf. Metz, *Le Signifiant imaginaire, op. cit.*

only is not avowed but is not even avowable. The powers that blind us certainly do not leave us the means to think about our place in *their* game – this possibility, and this thought, must be wrested away from them through struggle.

Is this infamous *transparency*, a favored slogan in our society, none other than *the lure which does not let itself be seen*? Reading *Society and the Spectacle*, the insistent link made between "spectacle" and "secrecy" is striking. I believe that this is the situation we face today, far more than was the case in the 1960s. So maniacal is the driveling obsession with "celebrity worship" – of royalty, politicians, businessmen, mafiosi – that the visible (spectacular) part of the political activity of the leaders of our "democracies" gradually takes on a forced allure, like the painted faces of farces, carnival masks or marionette puppets: at one and the same time *resemblance* and *dissemblance*. Thousands of magazines, thousands of screens protruding from the televisual hydra, put on their covers (and take cover from) the same faces, with the same gangsterish features we find in a Scorsese film. All this harping on about *transparency* has not finished ringing in our ears quite simply because this secrecy is the most well-known thing in the world: is it because we can no longer shake off our own shame? It is true that the recent scandals and fraudulent activities revealed since the "crisis," as it has so desperately been baptized (although it is really the normal progress of globalized capital), and the gesture of revealing the cards hidden under the table, lurking in complicit shadows, would like to convince us that all this (banking) secrecy has been "relaxed." Another entry in the media's newspeak vocabulary. But with facts and practices obstinately constituting a hostile testimony, the words "justice" and "morality" – having come from a distant past and referring to old, now incomprehensible "values" – must be salvaged by the media.

Six. – So: technique and ideology. The history of the cinema is *the history of the meaning that the cinema allows us to read into the world*, thanks to the articulation that this history realizes between technical evolution and variations of meaning. It was not due to the random luck of inventors that this new technology appeared, became widespread, and then withdrew itself, but as the result of the convergences of identifiable interests. It is (almost always) a matter of developing the market by conjointly working on the perfection of the lure and the amplification of the spectacle. The stubbornness of filmmakers (Rouch and Brault) was needed to push a manufacturer of cameras used for scientific purposes (Coutant) to refine the 16mm portable camera so that it had the capacity to be synchronized with a tape recorder. The packaged unit – synchronized image and sound, with 10-minute magazines – permitted, for the first time in history, *anybody* speaking, *anywhere, at any time*, to be filmed. In *Chronique d'un été* (Rouch and Morin, 1960), our friend Marceline Loridan walks, while speaking, through the Place de la Concorde in Paris, then into the Baltard pavilions in what used to be Les Halles.[iii] As she does so, she is filmed with a handheld camera, resulting in an exterior tracking shot with live sound.[11]

Hollywood (or Boulogne-Billancourt, Babelsberg, Mosfilm, Cinecittà...) had more than sufficient means to refine the use of synchronized sound in location shooting. The only thing that was lacking was the reason to do so. As long as streets and plazas were reconstituted in studios in order to be filmed on 35mm, with lighting, actors, extras, what the devil was the use of investing in a different technology, and a "low-end" technology at that? As the work of artisans, the *direct cinema* inaugurated a revolution, and not just on the technical level: everyone can now be filmed in their own settings and with their own speech.[12] On the one hand, this goes hand in hand with the barely resistible spectacularization of societies: everyone is filming, will film, will be filmed; with 16mm and Super-8, and then video, mini-DV, mobile phones... But on the other hand, this opens up the cinematic scene to everyone, ordinary men and women: for the first time in history, the people are filmed where they are, in their own bodies, in their own places, with their own gestures, with their kin, their speech, their stories, their internal worlds. The fact is that the people have passed onto the screen, and the old caste divisions have been smashed. The historians of the future will give a more just account of this transformation than we can. At each moment in its history, a particular conjunction of techniques and forms (in the shooting process and in the editing process) enables the cinema to play the role of a seismograph capable of recording the tensions coursing through the world-as-spectacle. The technico-ideological history of the cinema is an analysis of the particular states of the desire to see and be seen, of the need for reality or virtuality. The cinema explores our time, which is, above all, the time of the cinema.

---

11. "In the documentary [direct cinema] will bury the dictatorship of commentary from above, these expert voices always speaking in the place of others, until then too often dealt almost physical blows, but from this moment having to cede their place to the multitude of filmed bodies expressing themselves freely, in their own workplaces or living environments," Patric Leboutte, presentation given at the seminar "Formes de lutte et lutte des formes," *États généraux du documentaire*, Lussas, 2008.

12. Cf. Jean-Louis Comolli, "L'Âge des aiguilles," *Voir et pouvoir, op. cit.*, p. 685.

Technique and Ideology: Camera, Perspective, Depth of Field

Introduction

Today, it is just about admitted by the majority of film critics (as the certain effect of a certain amount of pressure) that every film is an ideological product, that it is made in and diffuses an ideology, and that by dint of this fact, however "artistic" it may claim to be, it has something to do with politics. Two symptoms of this recognition of the ideological status of the cinema can be seen in: 1. the increasing number of special issues dedicated to "political cinema" or "politics and cinema" in magazines and journals which until now have had a predominantly cinephilic orientation; and 2. the inflated number of films in the cinema market with an explicitly political theme.

But there is still a point of blockage, where the strongest resistance to a critical analysis of the ideological inscription of the cinema manifests itself, and this point, curiously enough, is not the demand for an autonomy of aesthetic processes; rather, it is the insistent demand for an autonomy of technical processes. A certain number of critics, filmmakers, and, of course, the majority of technicians themselves, energetically *forbid* everything that participates in the domain of film technique – its instruments, procedures, norms and conventions – from any ideological implication whatsoever. They are (more or less) happy to grant that films entertain some relationship with ideology on the level of their themes, their production (their economy), their diffusion (the ways in which they are read), and even on the level of their realization (the director as subject) – but none of them are ever willing to see the practical techniques and apparatuses that, bit by bit, *make* the film, in the same way. They demand that film technique be given a place off to one side, sheltered from ideology, outside of history, social procedures and signification processes. Film technique, they tell us, is precisely a *neutral* technique, capable of being used to say anything and everything, not saying anything in and of itself, and only saying what it is made to say (whether by the filmmaker or the technician). It is a vehicle, an instrument, something that conveys a message, and, to this end, it effaces itself in this conveyance. Indeed, there is no lack of common sense examples showing us that cameras have been indifferently used to make both fascist and communist films, or that the close-up intervenes in Hollywood films just as often as it does in the films of Eisenstein, and so forth.

Let us acknowledge this *demand* for a "place off to one side" for film technique, and let us question precisely this place. Whence comes the fact that the widespread, persistent discourse of the technicians (which is often reiterated by filmmakers and critics, especially at present, when the question has become more urgent) endeavors, by protecting the field of technical and instrumental practices from any ideological attack and/or impact, to keep technique behind the scenes as a self-evident fact, and not on the stage, where meaning is played out? After all, placing technique off to one side, keeping it in reserve, also entails making it take up a specific position, and making it fill in a specific slot in the ideological discourse of the technicians – that is, in technical and/or technicist ideology. In order for this discourse to be maintained, a certain conception (a certain *image*) of film technique must first be constituted – one which in turn constitutes this discourse – and it will subsequently have the function of confirming and perpetuating this same discourse.

Because it has the merit of formulating the implications of this discourse-of-the-technicians, the long study by Jean-Patrick Lebel, "Cinéma et idéologie,"[1] will here serve me as a principal point of reference (only with regard, of course, to the questions of concern to us in this text; many other points raised by Lebel call for other discussions). Lebel writes:

> The cinema is indeed a scientific invention and not a product of ideology, since it rests on a genuine knowledge of the properties of matter that it brings into play; the proof is that it works, and that, employing certain material (various instruments + properties of light + persistence of vision) in order to film a material object, it obtains a material image of this object.[2]

And:

> It is not the filmmaker, but the camera, a passive recording apparatus, which reproduces the filmed object(s), in the form of a reflection-image constructed according to the laws of the rectilinear propagation of light rays; and these laws, indeed, define the effect known as perspective. This phenomenon can be explained in a perfectly scientific manner, and has nothing ideological about it.[3]

These fragments are very clearly inscribed with the presuppositions that lie at the basis of Lebel's text and that give focus to the discourse-of-the-technicians targeted here (a discourse which can be heard and read in film schools and universities where film technique is taught, and in the manuals which profess it, etc.):

1. Jean-Patrick Lebel, "Cinéma et idéologie," initially appearing in *La Nouvelle Critique*, nos. 34, 35, 37 and 41, then, under the same title, supplemented by previously unpublished passages, released by Éditions sociales in 1971. Needless to say, it is necessary to refer to all of this study, but here I only discuss certain theses from the first part of the text (appearing in no. 34 of *La Nouvelle Critique*).
2. Lebel, "Cinéma et idéologie," *La Nouvelle Critique*, no. 34, p. 70.
3. *Ibid.*, p. 71.

1. *The fact that film technique somehow has a scientific heritage.* (We will interrogate the importance and legitimacy of this heritage later. For now, we will maintain it as a given principal.)
2. From this point, it is concluded that technique inherits, as an added extra, the scientificity[i] of this science, or, in this case, the twin virtues of precision and neutrality.

Before examining, therefore, the ideological avatars of a particular technical procedure – namely, cinematic depth of field, chosen for its exemplary status – I will have to pass through some questions pertaining to the phenomenon which has taken on the mythical name of the *invention of the cinema*, that is, to the ideology, and even the mythology, invested in the relationship of film *technique* (in its origins) with its "foundational *sciences*." (It goes without saying that I will here only be able to indicate some axes of investigation, to be taken up and developed more systematically later, as the complexity of this problematic – as yet little explored – demands that we return to it more than once, and from more than one angle.)

I. On a Dual Origin

The ideological place of the "base apparatus"

Here we must immediately specify that, in writing "Cinéma et idéologie," Lebel intervenes in the debate opened by Marcelin Pleynet in *Cinéthique* and developed both by that journal and *Cahiers*.[1] What did Pleynet say?

> Have you noticed that all the discourses that can be held on a film, or on the cinema (and large quantities of them have been held), start off from the *a priori* non-signifying existence of an apparatus producing images, which can then be used indifferently for this or that purpose, on the right or on the left? Does it not seem to you that before interrogating themselves on their "militant function," filmmakers ought to interrogate themselves on the ideology produced by the apparatus (the camera) that determines the cinema? The cinematic apparatus is a properly ideological apparatus, it is an apparatus which diffuses bourgeois ideology, even before diffusing anything else. [...] To wit: it is a camera producing a

1. Cf. *Cinéthique*, no. 3, "Économie, idéologique, formel," interview with Marcelin Pleynet and Jean Thibaudeau ["Economic-Ideological-Formal," trans. Elias Noujaim, in Sylvia Harvey, *May '68 and Film Culture* (London: BFI, 1978), pp. 149-164]; a number of articles in *Cinéthique*, notably: no. 5, "Direction" (Gérard Leblanc) ["Direction," trans. Susan Bennett, *Screen*, vol. 12 no. 2 (1971), pp. 121-130], "La parenthèse et le détour" (Jean-Paul Fargier) ["Parenthesis or Indirect Route," trans. Susan Bennett, *Screen*, vol. 12 no. 2, pp. 131-144]; no. 7-8, "Notes sur l'appareil de base" (Jean-Louis Baudry), pp. 1-8 ["Ideological Effects of the Basic Cinematographic Apparatus," trans. Alan Williams, in *Narrative, Apparatus, Ideology: A Film Theory Reader*, ed. Philip Rosen (New York: Columbia University Press), pp. 286-298], as well as the long collective text appearing in no. 9, pp. 51-59. Cf. also *Cahiers du cinéma*: "Cinéma/idéologie/critique" 1 and 2 (nos. 216 and 217); "Travail, lecture, jouissance" (Serge Daney and Jean-Pierre Oudart, no. 222) ["Work, Reading, Pleasure," trans. Diana Matias, in *Cahiers du cinéma, 1969-1972: The Politics of Representation*, ed. Nick Browne (London: Routledge, 1990), pp. 115-136]; "Film/politique" (Pascal Bonitzer, no. 222); "La vicariance du pouvoir" (Jean Narboni, no. 224) ["Vicarious Power," trans. Leigh Hafrey, in *Cahiers du cinéma, 1969-1972, op. cit.*, pp. 150-162]; "La Suture" (Jean-Pierre Oudart, nos. 211 and 212) ["Cinema and Suture," trans. Kari Hanet, *Screen*, vol. 18 no. 4 (1977-78), pp. 35-47]; "Le concept de montage" (Jacques Aumont, no. 211); "Montage" (Jean Narboni, Sylvie Pierre and Jacques Rivette, no. 210) ["Montage," trans. Tom Milne, in *Cahiers du cinéma, 1969-1972, op. cit.*, pp. 21-44]; "Le détour par le direct" (Jean-Louis Comolli, nos. 209 and 211); and "L'effet de réel" (Jean-Pierre Oudart, no. 228) ["The Reality Effect," trans. Annwyl Williams, in *Cahiers du cinéma, 1969-1972, op. cit.*, pp. 189-202].

> perspectival code directly inherited from and constructed on the *quattrocento* model of scientific perspective. It would be necessary [...] to show how the camera is meticulously constructed to "rectify" all perspectival anomalies, to reproduce in its authority the specular code of vision such as it is defined by Renaissance humanism... It is not without interest to note that it is precisely at the moment that Hegel brings the history of painting to a close, at the moment that painting begins to become aware that the scientific perspective that determined its relationship to the figure contains a precise cultural structure... It is not without interest to observe that it is at this very moment that Niépce invents photography (Niépce, 1765-1833, was a contemporary of Hegel, 1770-1831), summoned to reinforce the Hegelian closure, to produce the ideology, normality and censures of the perspectival code in a mechanical fashion. In my opinion, it is only when a phenomenon such as this is thought through – that is, it is only when the determinations of the apparatus (the camera) which structures the reality of its inscription are thought through – that the cinema will be able to objectively envisage its relationship to ideology.[2]

Let us inscribe the questions posed by this text as the basis of our work. They are:

1. The relationship between the photographic (and then cinematic) image and the pictorial representation of space such as it is regulated by the *quattrocento* perspectival code, which dominates Western painting for five centuries, although not without exceptions (see, on this point, the work of Francastel, who mentions the plural coexistence of several figurative systems).[3] This relationship functions on the level of ideologies and cultural representations.
2. The relationship between the invention of photography and the invention of the cinema, between photography and the cinema, in both their common points and their differences. That is, the question of the technological birth of the cinema.
3. The determining role of the "camera" apparatus in reflections on the ideology of film technique. I shall begin with this final point.

When Pleynet, at first, and then, following on from him, the editors of *Cinéthique* and Jean-Louis Baudry,[4] put forward the problematic of the inscription of the birth of cinema in a given socio-historical moment (the latter half of the 19th century), and within the ideology which is then dominant, we can observe, without taking into consideration the entire gamut of film technique, that they are directly targeting the *camera*, as the "apparatus which structures the reality of its inscription (that of the cinema)."

---

2. Pleynet and Thibaudeau, "Économie, idéologique, formel," *Cinéthique*, no. 3, *op. cit.*, p. 10.
3. Cf., notably, Pierre Francastel, *Peinture et Société* (Paris: Gallimard, coll. "Idées-arts," 1965).
4. Jean-Louis Baudry, "Notes sur l'appareil de base," *Cinéthique*, no. 7-8, *op. cit.*

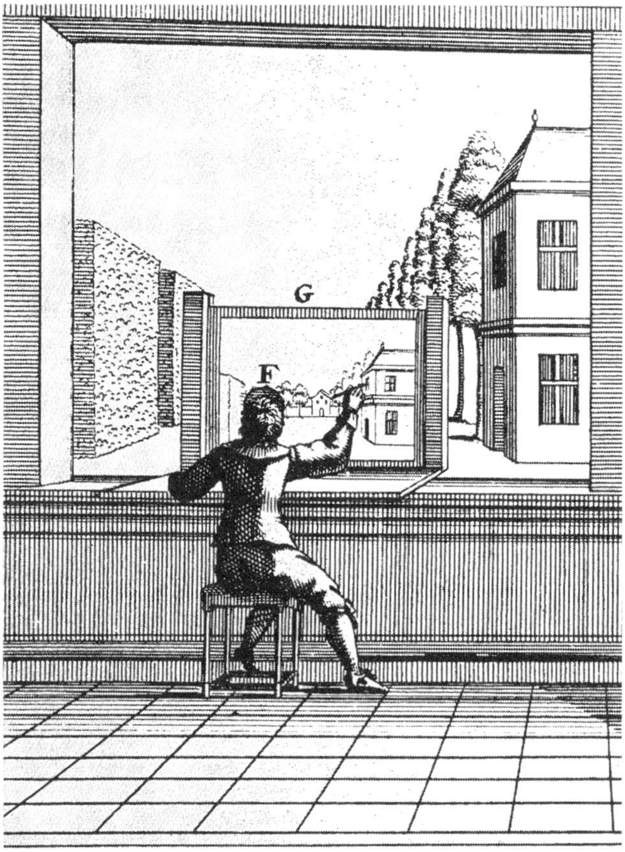

Fig. 1: Jean Dubreuil, *La Perspective pratique* (1642).

[Pictures showing pictures are inevitably a form of *mise en abyme*. These drawings and engravings thus illustrate the modalities of perspectival representation or the practice of the *camera obscura* and the pinhole camera (see the following pages): images within the image, frames within the frame, etc. It is remarkable that the drawn or engraved depiction of these modes of obtaining "faithful" or "objective" images is presented with a distancing effect which denotes the artificiality of the representation. The use of *mise en abyme* designates the image as an artificial fabrication, contingent on its conditions of production. *Mise en abyme* avows and signals the power of the artist over the image.]

The notion of a "base apparatus" (Baudry) is posited as follows: since the camera is the apparatus which produces the *visible* according to the system of monocular perspective contemporaneously governing the representation of space, it is from this angle that we must explore, for cinematic material as a whole, the perpetuation of this representative code and the ideology which it nourishes (or replenishes). Once the key element of filmmaking (the camera) falls under the sway of this ideology, one struggles to see how the cinema can claim to escape from it.

And yet, when Lebel critiques the positions of Pleynet, *Cinéthique* and ourselves, setting himself the task of dismantling the "accusation" that the cinema has an "ideological nature," I find it striking that he also chooses, as the object and prevailing figure of his demonstration, none other than the camera. Certainly, since it was a matter of responding to his adversaries on their own terrain, and since we had put ideology "into" the camera, he, too, had to banish ideology from it, providing it, instead, with the guarantee of a kinship with science. Once again, the camera *alone* is the subject of discussion, and once again it occupies the difficult position of both *representing* all film technique, and transferring its "perfectly scientific" reality onto film technique – in opposition to the theses stating that it is "purely ideological."

It is true that one of Lebel's first remarks seems to indicate a certain embarrassment, as if it were symptomatic of the abuse implicated in making the camera the focal point of the debate. He writes:

> Let us note that the word camera here (as well as in the rest of the argument that follows)[5] does not merely designate this customarily black object known by the name of the "camera," but the entire technical process which, from filming to projection, engenders the mechanical reproduction of reality in a form that is "imaginary" (in the precise sense of the word). This is what the ideological current in question here sometimes calls "the camera effect." In other words, the term camera should not be understood in the restrictive sense of the object itself, but as encompassing an entire technical process, developed through a series of technical operations (all based on the same scientific principles conforming to the laws of the propagation of light) which characterize the cinema as a means of reproduction.[6]

Lebel provides a good explanation – without criticizing it – of the *hypostasis of the camera* effectuated by the "ideological current" that he critiques, but the rest of his text never shows the reader that he prevents himself from doing the same. Quite the contrary, the cornerstone of his discourse consists precisely in the scientificity of the camera:

> The camera is not an ideological apparatus in itself. It does not produce any specific ideology, nor does its structure fatally condemn it to reflect the dominant ideology. It is an instrument which is ideologically neutral precisely inasmuch as it is an instrument, an apparatus, a machine. It rests on a scientific basis and is

5. Where Lebel critiques the positions of Pleynet, *Cinéthique* and ourselves.
6. Lebel, *op. cit.*, p. 68.

> not constructed *according to* an ideology of representation (in the speculative sense of the term), but on this scientific basis.[7]

The camera, then.

For it is here, in this *camera-site*, that these two discourses confront each other: one ascribing film technique to ideology, the other ascribing it to science. Let us observe that whether it is claimed that the essence of the technical equipment used to make films finds its founding origin in an assortment of scientific discoveries, or whether it is claimed that this equipment is governed by the ideological representations and demands dominant at the time that it is perfected, in both the former case (discourse-of-the-technicians) and the latter case (attempts to elaborate a materialist theory of the cinema), the example perpetually given is that which is used to produce the cinematic *image, by itself,* and purely from the standpoint of *optics* (indeed, at first Pleynet's attention is willfully focused on a *single* one of the constitutive elements of the camera – the *lens*; whereas for Lebel, who cites the phenomenon of "persistence of vision," the Science referred to and constantly invoked is *geometrical optics*: the "laws of the propagation of light").

We are therefore faced with a certain image of the camera: it is the metonymic *representation* of all film technique, *the part standing in for the whole.* It is *put forward* as the *visible* part for the *whole of technique.* This symptomatic *displacement* must be questioned in the very manner in which the articulation of the duality technique/ideology is posed.

To elect the camera as the representative, the "deputy" of the whole cinematic apparatus not only falls under the category of the synecdoche (the part for the whole), it is above all a reductive operation (from the whole to the part), and ought to be discussed due to the fact that, *on the theoretical plane,* it reproduces and confirms the *cleavage that does not cease to mark itself out in the technical practice of the cinema* (in the practice of filmmakers and technicians; in the spontaneous ideology of this practice; but also in the "idea," the ideological representation of film production made by spectators, focusing on the shoot and the set, overlooking the editing table and the lab), *between the visible part* of film practice (the camera, the filming, the crew, the lighting, the screen) and its *"invisible" part* (the black space between the frames, chemistry, developing baths, laboratory work, negative copies, the cuts and "matches" of the editing process, the soundtrack, the projector, etc.), with the latter *repressed* by the former, and generally relegated to the unthought, "unconscious" side of the cinema. It is, for example, symptomatic that Lebel, so careful to affirm the scientific calibration of the cinema, thinks only of deducing it from geometrical optics. He only once mentions persistence of vision, which nonetheless makes what marks the specific difference between cinema and photography function – that is,

7. *Ibid.*, p. 72.

the synthesis of movement (and the scientific work which has allowed us to produce it, see below), and he squarely forgets the other patron science of the cinema and photography: photochemistry, without which the camera would be no more than a *camera obscura*. As for Pleynet's remarks, they are equally valid for the *camera obscura* of the *quattrocento* as they are for the magic lantern of the 17th century, and the assorted projection devices which were the antecedents of the *cinématographe* and the photographic apparatus. It is obviously in their interest to brand these various perspective machines with a kinship with the camera, but this comes at the risk of not seeing precisely what the camera hides (it does not hide its lens): film stock (and the devices feeding it through the camera), emulsion, and the black space between the frames, which in the end are, above and beyond the lens, essential to the cinema, and without which there would be no cinema.

It is, therefore, not a given that what is currently produced in practice must be reproduced in theory. The reduction of the hidden part of technique to its visible part runs the risk of promulgating this dominance of the visible, this *ideology of the visible* (and what it implies: the masking and effacement of labor) as Serge Daney has defined it:

> [The cinema] postulated that from the "real" to the visual, and from the visual to its filmed reproduction, the same truth was *reflected* infinitely, with neither distortion nor loss. And it may be supposed that in a world where one readily says "I see" for "I understand," such a dream did not come about by chance, for the dominant ideology, which sets up the "real = visible" equation, has every interest in encouraging it. [...] But why not trace the issue further back still, and challenge that which is both served by the camera and precedes it? Going back further, why not interrogate what serves the camera and precedes it: the quite blind trust in the visible, the gradually acquired hegemony of the eye over the other senses, a society's taste and need for seeing itself reflected, etc.? [...] The cinema is therefore connected to the Western metaphysical tradition, a tradition of seeing and sight for which it fulfils the photological vocation. What is photology and what indeed might the discourse of light be? A teleological discourse, undoubtedly, if it is true that teleology "consists of neutralizing duration and force to the profit of *the illusion* of simultaneity and form" (Derrida).[8]

And yet, undeniably, it was this "hegemony of the eye," this specularization, this ideology of the visible linked to Western logocentrism that Pleynet was in fact targeting when he underscored the importance of the perspectival code of the *quattrocento* for the base apparatus: the image produced by the camera can not fail to confirm and

8. Serge Daney, "Sur Salador," in: "Travail, lecture, jouissance," *Cahiers du cinéma*, no. 222 (1970) [Repr. in Daney, *La Rampe* (Paris: Cahiers du cinéma, coll. "Petite Bibliothèque," 1996), pp. 16-28].

reinforce "the specular code of vision such as it is defined by Renaissance humanism." That is: a code with the human eye at the center of its system of representation, and with this centrality at once excluding all other representative systems, assuring the domination of the eye over all other sensory organs, and placing the eye (the subject) in a truly divine position (this is the humanist critique of Christianity).

A situation of *theoretical paradox* thus arises: it is by focusing on the domination of the camera (the visible) over the whole of film technique which it is supposed to represent, inform and program (through its function as a *model*), that one intends to denounce the submission of this camera, in its conception and construction, to the dominant ideology of the visible.

If the gesture privileging the camera, as the basis for the ideological chain in which the cinema is inscribed, is theoretically founded by everything that is implicated in this apparatus – through the determinant, principal role of the camera in the production of a film – then this gesture, itself incapable of being prolonged, would remain caught in the same chain.

We must therefore change our perspective – that is, we must take into account what this gesture designating the camera thrusts aside in its movement – in order to prevent this (necessary and productive) emphasis on the camera from being re-inscribed into the ideology on which it is focused.

A materialist theory of the cinema must (it seems to me) draw out both the ideological "heritage" of the camera (as much as its "scientific heritage," the two, as we shall see, are not in any way exclusive of each other, contrary to what Lebel seems to say) and the ideological investments which have been made in the camera, given that it is not solely the camera that is under question, whether in the making of films or in the history of the invention of the cinema. If those aspects of technology, science and/or ideology which are put into play do indeed turn out to be determinant factors, it is only in relation to other determinant elements. These can, of course, be secondary in relation to it, but then we must interrogate this *secondary quality*; that is, the status and function of that which is covered over by the camera.

To underline once more the risk that there is in theoretically making the entire cinema function on the *reduced model* of the camera (the risk is that of being blinded, with the camera acting as an ideological screen in the very discourses which assign it this ideological place), it suffices to point out the near-total lack of theoretical work dedicated to the soundtrack, for example, or indeed, to laboratory processes (as if seeing the light – geometrical optics – had barred the ability to see its work: photochemistry), and this bias can only be explained by the dominance of the visible within both film practice and theoretical reflection on the cinema.

Is it not time, for example, to *shed light* on the ideological function of two techniques (equipment + procedures + knowledges + practice – combined and fused in view of the realization of a goal, an objective which thenceforth constitutes, founds and authorizes this technique), both of which reside within cinema's hidden, uncon-

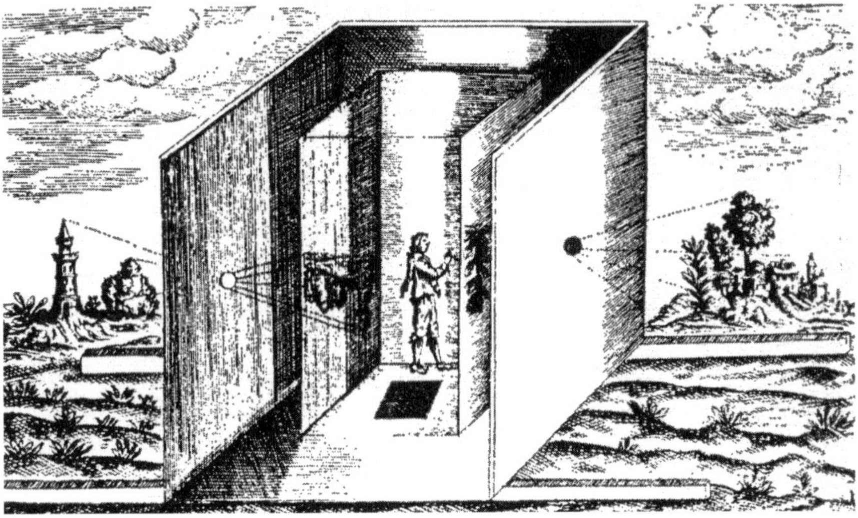

Fig. 2: Athanasius Kircher, *Ars magna lucis et umbrae* (1646): A *camera obscura.*

scious realm (with the very rare exception of filmmakers such as Godard, Rivette, Straub...): *color grading* and *sound mixing*? This is what we will attempt.

Birth = deferral: The invention of the cinema[i]

Because it has been at one and the same time widely studied but poorly understood,[9] and because it accumulates often unlinked events, which appear more or less accidental, haphazard, or even contradictory, and which in any case can barely be read as the reassuring course of "progress," the long gestation period of the cinema (with no lack of "inexplicable" blanks or gaps, including practically all of the 19th century), and the period of its birth, is the site where the majority of phantasms and myths about the cinema are anchored and reinforced. In their quest for its foundations, film theorists and historians seem motivated by the same desire felt by André Bazin: "An art's origins provide us with a glimpse of its essence..."[10] And yet it should not be a surprise that this elusive "essence" be never more elusive than in the very realm in which it is sought, a realm which is already that of mythology.

9. As a matter of fact, volume I of the *Histoire comparée du cinéma* by Jacques Deslandes (Brussels: Casterman, 1966), which covers the period 1826-1896, completes (and sometimes corrects) the work carried out by Georges Sadoul. This publication has the merit, notably, of citing the declarations of inventors, the texts of patent applications, etc., thereby sketching out an interesting *ideological tableau.*

10. André Bazin, "Le mythe du cinéma total," in *Qu'est-ce que le cinéma?*, vol. I (Paris: Cerf, 1958), p. 25 ["The Myth of Total Cinema," trans. Timothy Barnard, in Bazin, *What Is Cinema?*, ed. Timothy Barnard (Montreal: Caboose, 2009), p. 17].

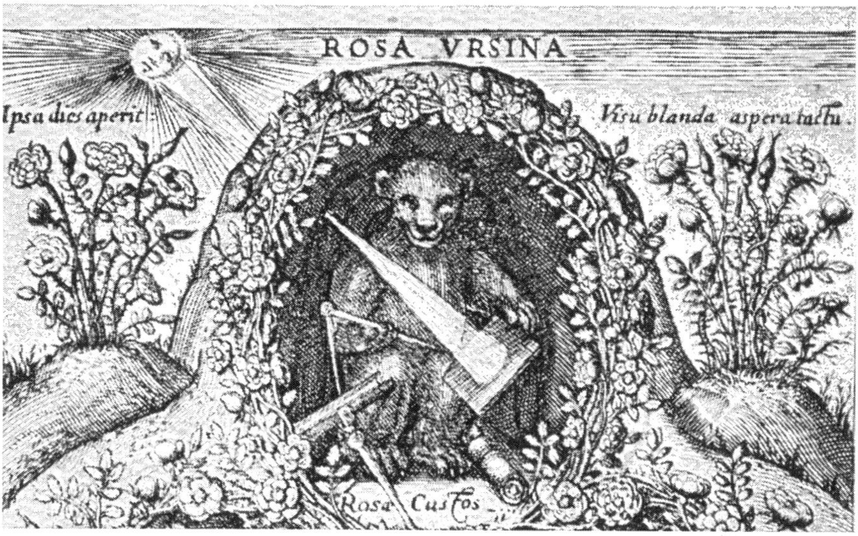

Fig. 3: Christoph Scheiner, *Rosa ursina sive Sol* (1626-1630): A *camera obscura* inspired by Plato's cave.

Nor should it be a surprise that the decisive intervention of science in this realm be less decisive than Lebel would have us believe.

None other than Bazin – who can often be a useful point of reference on these questions, given the extent to which the interpretations he proposes, due to their very idealism and humanism, focus on the ideological foundation of the invention of the cinema, re-mark it, and thus constitute a revelatory and extremely precious tool – emphasizes, before the historian Jacques Deslandes and pre-empting his theses, the "artisanal" character of the discoveries which led up to the cinema, in order, we suspect, to gaze in wonder at it all the more, and in order to re-inscribe the invention of this machine in the oneiric and mythological space of man, to literally *humanize* it by demonstrating the insignificant role of technology, machines and the sciences, and the constant delays they experienced, in comparison to the force of the ancient and properly mythical dream of capturing images of life, of *representing* the living world.[11]

> George Sadoul's admirable new book[12] on the origins of cinema leaves us with the paradoxical sense that the relationship between economic and technological de-

---

11. We will note elsewhere that in his "Ontologie de l'image cinématographique" [*sic*] (*Qu'est-ce que le cinema?*, vol. I ["Ontology of the Photographic Image," trans. Timothy Barnard, in *What Is Cinema?*, *op. cit.*, pp. 3-12]), Bazin couples representation with death, and in particular the Egyptian practice of embalming. Jean Louis Schefer's current research is similarly posed on this axis, albeit on entirely different theoretical presuppositions.

12. Georges Sadoul, *L'Invention du cinéma (1832-1897)* (Paris: Denoël, 1946).

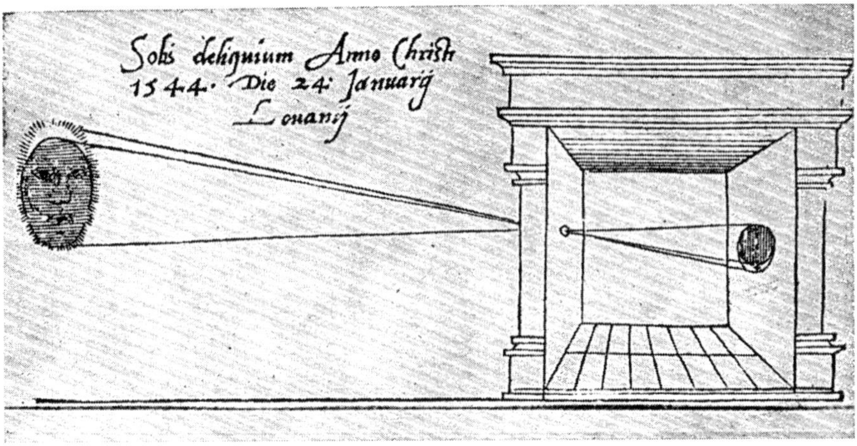

Fig. 4: Athanasias Kircher, *Ars magna lucis et umbrae* (1646): Graphic demonstration of the "pinhole camera."

> velopments on the one hand and the imagination of cinema's inventors on the other has been inverted, despite the author's Marxist beliefs. It seems to me that in this instance we need to reverse historical causality, which proceeds from the economic infrastructure to the ideological superstructure, and view fundamental technological discoveries as fortunate and propitious accidents essentially secondary to the initial conceptions of cinema's inventors. Cinema is an idealist phenomenon; men's idea of it existed fully equipped in their brains, as in Plato's higher world, and the tenacious resistance of matter to the idea is more striking than technology's prompting of the inventor's imagination. Cinema, moreover, owes practically nothing to the scientific mind. Its inventors were not at all scientists (with the exception of Marey, and he was interested in analyzing movement and not in the inverse process of recreating it). Even Edison, in the end, was nothing more than a brilliant Jack-of-all-trades, a giant of the Concours Lépine. Niépce, Muybridge, Leroy, Joly, Demenÿ and Louis Lumière himself were obsessive eccentrics, handymen or, at best, clever industrialists. [...] Basing ourselves on the technological discoveries that made cinema possible gives us a very poor account indeed of its discovery.[13]

Note how much Bazin wheels out all the arguments, casts out all the lines: the primacy of the "dream" over science, carefully positioned within the idealist project underscored by Bazin himself, could not but be read by *Cinéthique* as additional "proof" of the "natural ideological inclination of the cinema": "Bazin always emphasized the idealism presiding over the invention of the camera, the artisanal, unscien-

13. Bazin, "Le mythe du cinéma total," *op. cit.*, pp. 21-22 [pp. 13-14, translation modified].

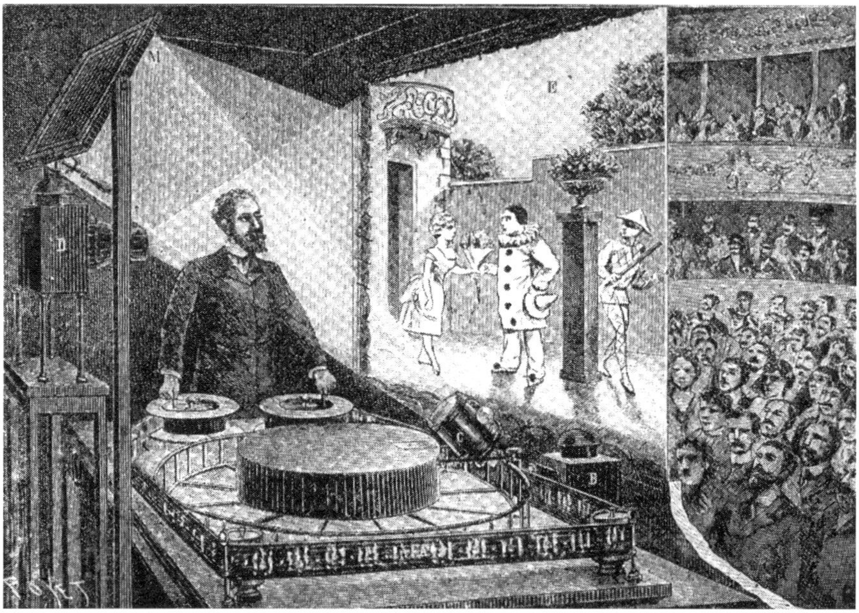

Fig. 5: Émile Reynaud's "*Théatre optique*" (1888).

tific character of its construction. The camera realized man's ancestral dream: to reproduce reality, and thus to reproduce himself."[14]

Lebel opposes his discourse on the scientificity of the cinema to this text (and, through this text, to Bazin's text quoted above). But given that, as it happens, not only *Cinéthique* and Bazin, but also the vast majority of historians – including the works of both Sadoul and Deslandes (who corrects his predecessor on more than one point, but who can not avoid heading in the same direction) – resist recognizing any determinant role for science in the matter, Lebel manifests a certain embarrassment, as can be witnessed in both of the two arguments he makes.

1. He correctly points out that prior to the industrial stage of the development of society all technico-scientific inventions could only be carried out in artisanal conditions: "[This] conflates the type of production (craftwork/industry) with scientific research in the proper sense of the term. As if, from a scientific point of view, craftwork was tainted. As if all the great discoverers and researchers in the history of humanity up until the 20th century had not *all* been artisans."[15] We are utterly in agreement, the question is not whether the "inventors" of the cinema were artisans or not (they were, more or less inevitably), but to what extent, despite or because of this artisanal status, their preoccupations and their research can also claim a scienti-

14. Gérard Leblanc, "Welles, Bazin et la RKO," *Cinéthique*, no. 6 (1970), p. 30. We will further critique some of the positions of this article.

15. Lebel, *op. cit.*, p. 71.

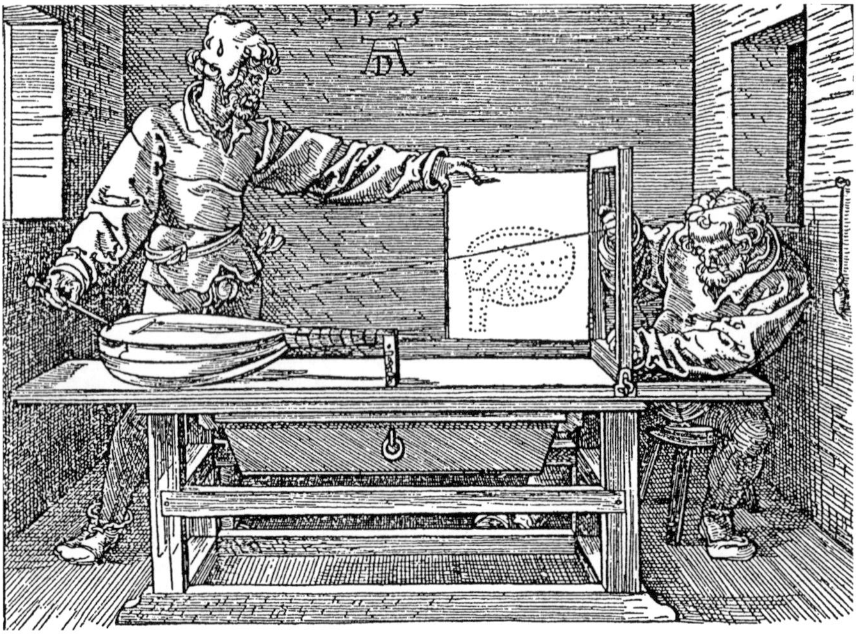

Fig. 6: Albrecht Dürer, *Man Drawing a Lute* (1525).

fic status. This, in the end, is the only question that should be posed, but it is precisely this question that eludes Lebel.

2. The inconsistency of Lebel's other argument is even more striking:

> When this allusion to the artisanal character of the invention of photography and the cinema, made in order to disqualify its scientific aspect, relies on the fact that the cinema concretizes an old "dream" of humanity whose ideological aspect is obvious (and [*but – JLC*] historically determined), this only leads us further astray. It is as if the airplane – itself invented in artisanal conditions – were resented for concretizing an old dream of humanity whose ideological content is no less obvious (and just as historically determined). And thus, in order to struggle against the ideological effect of the Icarus myth, the producers of socialist (or materialist) airplanes were instructed to denounce the ideology that the airplane produces by "deconstructing" it, to the extent that, short of systematically making it crash, they would at least assure its passengers a level of discomfort sufficient to break them from their fascination with the sky, and to constantly remind each traveler that they are not actually flying, but are only in the air thanks to and by means of an apparatus, and that, as a consequence, their concrete relationship to the real world has not been altered.[16]

16. *Ibid.*, p. 71.

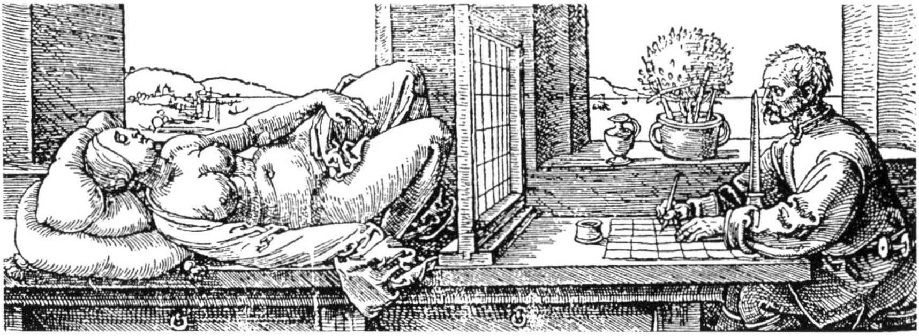

Fig. 7: Albrecht Dürer, *Man Drawing a Reclining Woman* (1525).

Certainly, Lebel is careful to add: "Of course, this is a caricature..." But the excesses of his comparison are barely attenuated: for, quite blinded by his concern to make the cinema (or the camera) a *scientific object*, a pure technical system, he does not see that comparing it to another technical system such as the airplane quite simply excludes the cinema from the area where it has a role (and where the airplane has no role, even if it is a means of "communication"...): that of signifying processes, and even of ideology itself. It is indeed because the cinema is (whether it is a scientific object or not) a signifying practice, because it produces meaning and ideology, that the fact that it realizes an "ancient dream of humanity" is important, that this debate matters to us, and that Lebel thought it a good idea to intervene into it...

First of all, we must point out the symptomatic fact that all film historians (even Deslandes, to whom we shall now make reference) are embarrassed at having to choose an *anterior limit* to their research: only utterly arbitrary decisions make them designate an event, a date or an invention as the inaugural moment of their work. Strictly speaking, the prehistory of the cinema is lost in the dark night of ancient times and myths: the cinema has not only realized an "ancient dream of humanity," but has also prolonged a series of "ancient" empirical realities and representation techniques.

Deslandes, for example, chooses 1826 and the invention of photography (or rather, in point of fact, of the photographic plate sensitive to light) by Niépce and Daguerre, but this privileges only one of the cinema's constitutive technologies, and precisely one which can be historically dated. As for the others (the camera, the decomposition and synthesis of movement) he is inevitably constrained to reach further and further into the past, as a result of their ancient, charged history. With regard to optics, we know that the camera is nothing but the barely refined adaptation of the *quattrocento*'s *camera obscura*. But this darkened box was known in pharaonic Egypt (347 BC), as well as in 9th-century Arab science, and, in their *Dictionnaire du cinéma et de la télévision*,[17] Bessy and Chardans detail its appearances and refinements since Bacon (1260).

17. Maurice Bessy and Jean-Louis Chardans, *Dictionnaire du cinéma et de la télévision* (Paris: Jean-Jacques Pauvert, 1965-1971).

With such an ancient lineage, the *camera obscura* was an instrument which was not only known, but also handled, used and studied by scientists and artists from century to century, right across history, and well before the question was raised of understanding the whys and wherefores of the tiny, obscure, inverted image which was revealed at its base.

But the issue becomes rather more troubling: matters are no different when it comes to the phenomenon which constitutes the other major axis of the cinema's technical specificity: that which, since the 19th century, has been termed "persistence of vision," but which was long known and studied, at least since the Arab astronomer Alhazen (965-1038), author of *The Book of Optics* (where he also mentions the *camera obscura*), who not only provides a critique of the then dominant theory of vision, according to which the eye emitted "light rays," by signaling the persistence of impressions of light after the closure of the eyelids, but who also offers a perfect description of the continuous circle the eye perceives when a hot poker is rapidly twirled in front of it.

Thus, the principle themes of the invention of cinema – the production of an *image* of the world and the *illusion* of continuity produced by the movement of objects – were constituted several centuries before the perfection of light-sensitive plates and the photograph. The role played by science in and of itself in this invention must hence already be considerably relativized, since: 1. the two phenomena in question come within the category of empirical observation ("optical illusions," whose status we will look at later), and 2. they were noted down, commented on, "explained" in each century according to those philosophies that were (ideologically) dominant at the time, even if it was in the name of science that these systems of explanation were baptized (it was necessary to wait for "epistemological breaks" such as the *camera obscura*, the slow and chaotic constitution of geometrical optics in the 17th century, and the persistence of vision in 19th-century psycho-physiology).

Moreover, coming closer to the formal date of the invention of the cinema in no way leads to very different observations.

Firstly, as Bazin notes, there is the relatively modest role played by the sciences and scientists as such in the gestation of this instrument. We have already seen that the *camera obscura*, in making the rectilinear propagation of light rays apparent (without yet being its experimental verification), was conceived of and improved upon practically outside of all constituted scientific knowledge about light and optics: the only scientific practice with which it had a real relationship was, in fact, the system of laws governing *perspectiva artificialis*.[18]

---

18. This was so much so that the word *prospectiva* or *perspectiva* designated, in Medieval Latin, optical science itself (cf. the treatise on optics titled *Perspectiva* by John Peckham, who died in 1292). The painters and theorists of the *quattrocento* and *cinquecento*, following on from the work of Alberti, who mathematically and geometrically founded the laws of perspective, distinguished between *perspectiva* (or *prospectiva*) *communis* or *naturalis*, which seems to have designated both the science

This is not, therefore, where the decisive gesture comes from. The perfection of the photographic plate shows this even more: here there is a leap forward, triggered, certainly, by Niépce's researches on lithograph processing and the means of copying engravings by a chemical procedure. Yet this leap was brought about without the aid of any scientific hypothesis, whether with regards to the exact nature of light or of photochemistry. To be convinced of this, we only need to quote Niépce himself: "To find in the emanations of the luminous fluid an agent susceptible to imprinting, in an exact and durable manner, the images transmitted by optical processes, and to imprint them, not, I stress, with the splendor of their diverse colors, but with all the gradations of black and white shading."[19] As for Daguerre, we know that the *trompe-l'œil* spectacles of the *Diorama* (in which, from 1822 onwards, "lights and sounds of all manners competed to give the spectator 'the perfect illusion of reality'," to great popular success) led him to seek to "capture, through a new medium, without recourse to an illustrator, the views offered by nature."[20] Finally, it should be added that it was only a century after these innovations (1940-1945) that the action of light on a sensitive surface was theoretically explained.[21]

The importance of scientific research is most notable with respect to "persistence of vision": in 1824, the English mathematician Roget published a series of experiments on what he dubbed "a curious optical illusion," the stroboscopic effect. Some years later (1830), and practically at the same time, the physicians Faraday, in England, and especially Plateau, in Belgium, published the results of their experiments on the spinning of cogged wheels in the same or in opposite directions. Plateau immediately drew on these experiments for his *phenakistoscope* or *fantascope* (1833), a scientific curiosity which became a fashionable toy, and at the same moment (once again), Stampfer, professor of Applied Geometry at the University of Vienna, distributed his "stroboscopic discs," perfectly identical to Plateau's plates, and constructed the *zoetrope*.

Deslandes attributes this abrupt *condensation* of research and invention to a "renewal of interest within scientific circles in the problems posed by the mechanics of vision." Bazin also finds it astonishing:

---

of vision and the act of vision itself ("perceiving things from a point of view," in Schefer's words) and *perspectiva artificialis*, which, "in contrast, is based on Alberti's angular perspective and permits correct constructions" (Schefer [*Scénographie d'un tableau*, Paris: Seuil, 1969, p. 76]).

19. Cited by André Vigneau in *Une brève histoire de l'art de Niépce à nos jours* (Paris: Robert Laffont, 1963), p. 63.

20. Cited by Deslandes, *op. cit.*, pp. 63, 65.

21. On the "belatedness" of photochemistry and the theory of the physics of light in relation to photographic practice, see *La Science de la photographie* by Gérard de Vaucouleurs (Paris: Elzévir, 1947): "We had to wait until recent years to see the appearance of a coherent theoretical explanation of the subtle and mysterious mechanism by which light acted on a sensitive surface, an explanation which was sought after, in vain, for more than a century. This mechanism involves complex phenomena, with interventions by the most elementary particles of nature: ions, electrons, photons, such that only the most modern theories of matter and light enable them to be interpreted."

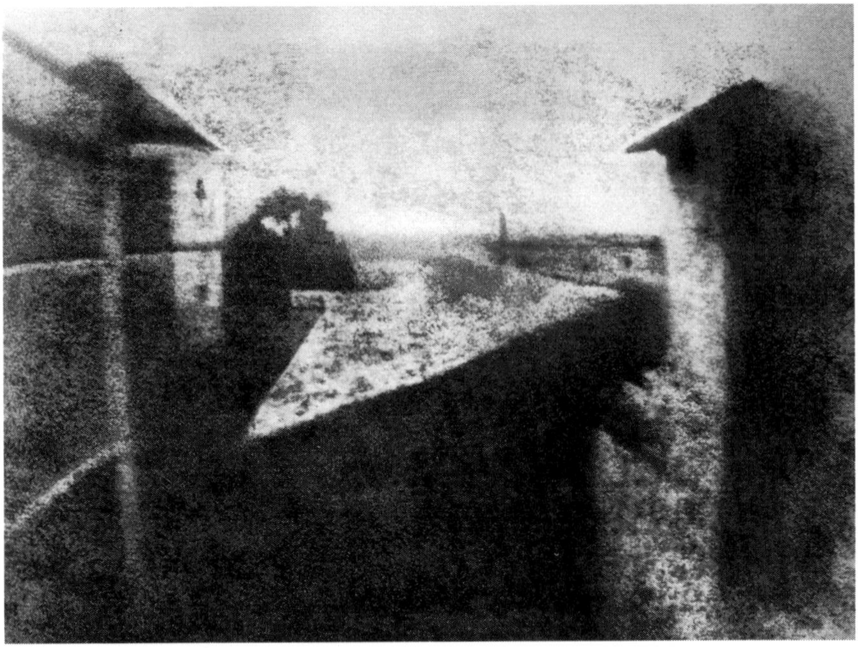

Fig. 8: The "first photograph" by Nicéphore Niépce, taken from his bedroom, at Le Gras (1826).

> It may not be irrelevant to note that, despite the lack of any scientific connection between them, Plateau's work was more or less contemporaneous with Niépce's. It as if, for centuries, inventors had waited for chemistry, quite independently of optics, to take an interest in the automatic fixing of an image before themselves becoming interested in the synthesis of movement.[ii]

The causes of this "delay" – or of the contemporaneous research on photography and movement – need to be taken into account. It seems, in all likelihood, that it is not appropriate to look for them in the respective states of the relevant sciences... But rather in the rift opened up by photography in the figurative representations of the world, in the fresh questions it provoked – by duplicating it and by having the tendency to replace it, as its perfected version, as its privileged representative – on the central role of the human eye, its solar position, its intimate relationship with the world (an intimacy between the subject and life, now mediated and disturbed by a machine). We must look for them, therefore, in the sphere of ideology.

We will put forward the position (in the form of a hypothesis, and in order to rewrite Bazin's comments) that it is at the precise moment that the invention of photography (the light-sensitive plate) refines the *camera obscura* and thereby accomplishes what generations of painters had demanded from the technique of *perspectiva artificialis* (allowing the most faithful copy of nature: "the most excellent manner of painting is that which imitates the best, which renders the painting most similar to

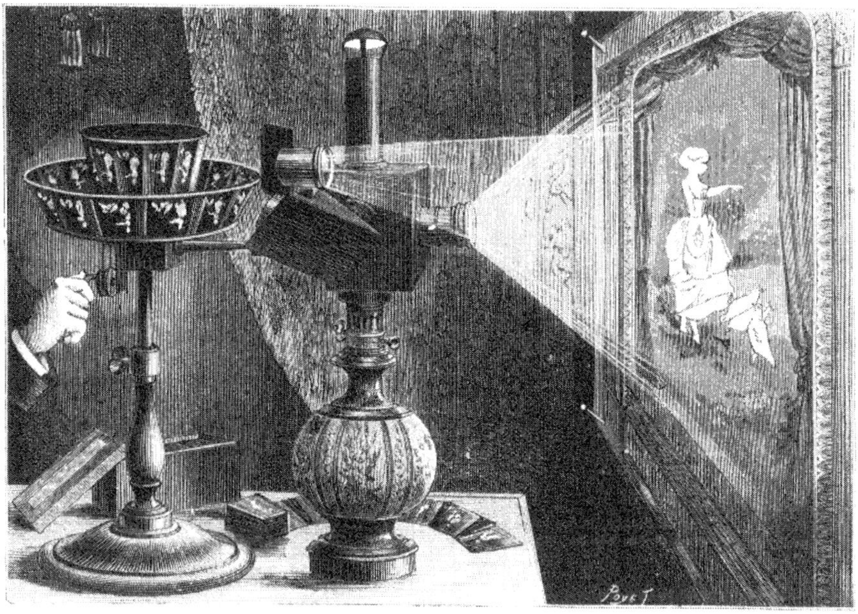

Fig. 9: Émile Reynaud's *praxinoscope* during a projection.

the natural object that it represents," writes da Vinci) – the first photograph, as we know, shows a perspective of rooftops – and at the precise moment that the triumph of monocular perspective as a system of representation, where the eye of the spectator (or the painter, or the subject) occupies the center, directs the vanishing lines and governs the divergence and convergence of light rays, seems to be assured, it is at this very moment that the eye abruptly appears as neither entirely unique, nor entirely irreplaceable, nor particularly perfect (the "lens" [*lentille*] in the *camera obscura* – identical, as da Vinci already noted, to the crystalline sphere of the eye– becomes the "lens" [*objectif*] of the camera). The camera duplicates the eye, perpetuates its principles of representing the world, its codes of normality, and at the same time undermines its hegemony, outstrips it.

This double movement of confirmation and relativization has, as its probable effects, a reinforcement of trust in the analogical, perspectival representation of the world (the photographic image can not be doubted, it manifests the truth of the real world) and a crisis of confidence in the organ of vision which had, up until then, controlled (scientifically, through the "laws of scientific perspective") all representation, by constituting itself as an official yardstick (we are reminded of da Vinci's advice: "For the first tree, you will take a solidly fixed pane of glass, and you will likewise fix the position of your eye, and draw this first tree on the glass by tracing its contours; then move the glass laterally, until the contours of the real tree and the drawn tree touch each either; then color your drawing in such a fashion that, with

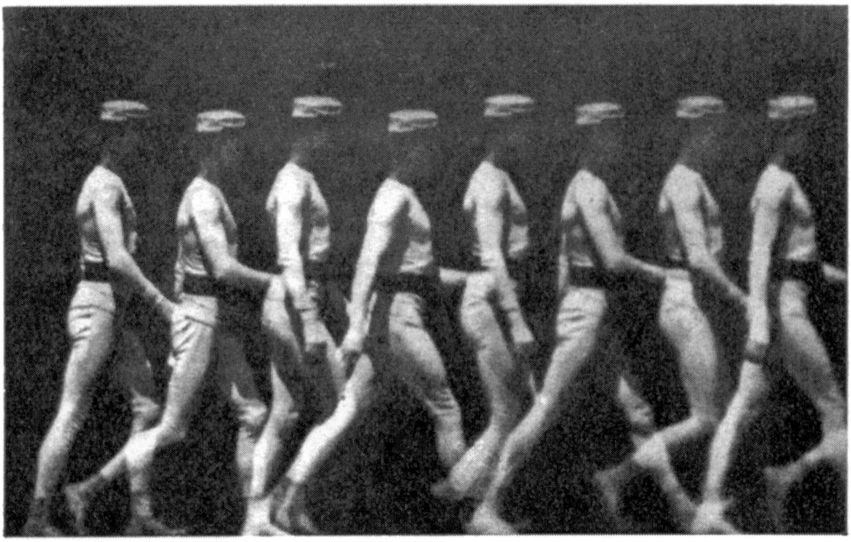

Fig. 10: Partial chronophotographies by Marey (circa 1885).

regards to the colors as well as the shape, they resemble each other, and such that, if you close one eye, both appear painted on the glass at an equal distance.")[22]

The sudden scientific interest in "optical illusions"[23] may represent a symptom of this crisis of confidence; devalorized, *decentered* by the eye of the camera, the human eye can once again become an object of scientific research and experimentation. Aberrations make a return within and against the ideology of the normality of the eye, legislated by the laws of perspective. We have noted that it is not at all the case that these "illusions" had not been known for a long time, to the extent that, for numerous scientists and philosophers, they had undermined all blind faith in the human eye. But this doubt on the level of science called, to a certain degree, for being compensated, being filled in on the level of ideology, such that the inscription of doubt and lack was systematically covered over by the inscription of normality

22. Leonardo da Vinci, *La Peinture*, texts collected and translated [into French] by André Chastel (Paris: Hermann, coll. "Miroirs de l'art," 1964), p. 172. For da Vinci even more than for Alberti, the eye of the observer is the truth criterion of what is represented: it is well-known that da Vinci was led to critique Alberti's linear perspective for the reason that the spectator's eye, when faced with a painting composed according to perspectival laws, could only see this flat surface without any deformation at a certain imposed distance, with a deformation of the lateral parts of the canvas being produced when the eyes draw close to its center.

23. See, as quoted by Deslandes (*op. cit.*, p. 247), the program of a conference given in London in 1881: "The propagation of light; light waves; concave and convex mirrors; Darker's kaleidoscope; refraction; the light spectrum; mirages; diffraction; interferences; Newton's rings; the iridescence of pearls, feathers and soap bubbles; chromatic and monochromatic light; the persistence of light on the retina; the *thaumatrope*; the *kalotrope*; the *photodrome*; Bayle's *choreutoscope*."

and the centrality of the eye. It is in this sense, too, that we can agree with Marcelin Pleynet that the code of *perspectiva artificialis* has acted as a repressive system.

If it is necessary, after all this, to supply yet another piece of evidence for the fact that the invention of the cinema was only constituted as the response to an ideological demand, it will be found in the total contradiction apparent between the projects, intentions and declarations of the majority of the cinema's series of inventors, and the stance of one of their ilk, the physiologist Marey, who without doubt came closest to reaching the final apparatus, but who, from a scientific viewpoint, saw no benefit in it. At a time when what Deslandes has called "the search for the absolute," and what Bazin has called "the myth of total cinema," was dominant, and when, from all quarters, the aim was for the perfect and complete reproduction of life – the photographic image + depth + movement + colors + sound (as a journalist for *Le Temps* very naïvely put it: "It is thus that, bit by bit, science, with its giant leaps forward, will succeed in ridding us of death, its only obstacle and its only enemy…") – Marey perfected the *chronophotographe*, which is distinguished from the camera by the fact that it used photographic paper rather than film, except that, as Deslandes notes:

> A gulf separates the *chronophotographe* from the cinema camera, and it is not only on the level of technical specificity […] but with regards to the very destination of the device. The essential goal of the cinema camera is to obtain a long ribbon of images which, when later threaded through a projector, will create the illusion of movement. The only function of the *chronophotographe*, by contrast, is to record movement and immobilize it.[24]

The physiologist Marey is interested above all in the decomposition and analysis of movement, and even though he studied the possibility of projecting his images, and worked on several models for a *chronophotographic projector*, it was only to observe the recorded movement several times in quick succession. This is why he did not envisage working with a film, but contented himself with an *endless loop*:

> In order to properly capture the nature of a movement, it is advantageous to reproduce it a number of times. This can be naturally obtained with an apparatus containing a rotating disc. But given that, in order to produce images, we must use a strip of film, it needs to be closed in on itself in order to continuously rotate, repeatedly passing the series of images in front of the lens.[25]

These same preoccupations led Marey to condemn the cinema:

24. Deslandes, *op. cit.*, p. 141.
25. Cited by Deslandes, *ibid.*, p. 143.

> Animated photographs have permanently fixed movements which are essentially fleeting... but, in the end, they show what the eye could see directly; they have added nothing to our powers of sight, divested them of none of their illusions. Whereas the true character of a scientific method is to supplement the insufficiency of our senses and correct their errors.[26]

As Deslandes states: "He saw no interest in projecting 'life as it is' on the screen."[27] To which we should add that in the very field of his research on the physiology of movement, Marey quickly felt the realism of the photographic image to be an *impediment*, and was led to denaturalize its setting, through the use of black backdrops, white clothing, even covering one leg of a subject in black in order to prevent it from blurring the outline of the other leg, and finally placing reflective strips on arms and legs, recorded discretely, in order to attain a purely graphic quality: "Animated images have been immobilized, and turned into geometric figures: the sensory illusion has vanished, but it has made way for the satisfaction of the mind."[28]

Even a moderately attentive reading of the history of the invention of the cinema can detect the abuse involved in exaggerating, for the needs of the objectivist cause, the role played by science, both theoretically and practically, in this invention. Nor, however, for want of science occupying this role, should this history – of which I have only raised certain questions here – refrain from indicating *economics* as a principal determination in the constitution of film technique, as well as *ideology*, in a twofold process of determination, with the two linked to each other in the form of a social demand/response mechanism.

In effect, the birth of the cinema, in all the "histories" dedicated to it, can be read as a multiple and fragmentary phenomenon: disseminated, shattered, started over with each new "instrument" perfected, with each new supplementary detail, with

26. Cited by Deslandes, *ibid.*, p. 144.

27. *Ibid.*, p. 130.

28. *Ibid.*, p. 144. Let us note, once more, that another scientist, Albert Londe, put in command of the medical photography laboratory at La Salpêtrière by Charcot, worked on chronophotographic instruments, but, like Marey, declared that the *cinématographe* was without interest from a scientific point of view – "cinematographic representation puts the observer in exactly the same situation as before the model himself." Nonetheless, Londe emphasizes that it is a different matter when the *cinématographe* is sped up or slowed down: "By slowing down the speed of the synthesizing apparatus, movements which normally escape the eye can be made visible. [...] Conversely, certain movements escape the eye due to their extreme slowness, such as the growth of plants and animals, for example. By taking a series of photographs at suitable, but remote, intervals, they could be made to rapidly pass before our eyes and instantly reproduce the phenomenon in its entirety." One of the great axes of the development of scientific cinema is foreseen here, and it is worth pointing out that it is in the use of a "special effect," in other words, in the transgression of the impression of reality, that this axis is first inscribed. It is not enough, as Lebel says, to "hook up a camera to a microscope [...] so as to film what happens between the slides" in order to make a scientific cinema such that "the result obtained has nothing 'ideological' about it"; it is still pertinent, when filming microscopic images, to break with the normality of "realist" proportions.

each new patent, and, at the same time, deferred, delayed due to the lack, in one after another of these instruments, of some technical detail, with a new solution for each new problem – to the extent that what changes from one instrument to another is often infinitesimal, as is what is found to be lacking. With the "new" invention of the Lumière brothers – prefigured a thousand times over – the dual game of the "advance" and "delay" of technical progress is terminated abruptly, but not miraculously. It is a qualitative leap, but at what price?

Bazin and Sadoul both point out that "since Antiquity there had been no obstacle to the invention of a *phenakistiscope* or a *zoetrope*";[29] and we could add that "almost nothing" had prevented the advent of photography since the moment (1550, it seems) that a lens was affixed to the *camera obscura*, in the same way that *almost* nothing separates Émile Reynaud's *praxinoscope* from the Lumières' *cinématographe* – except for the fact that, despite photography having long become widespread by that stage, the images are drawn rather than filmed.

We find ourselves faced with chains of investigation (on the production of the image, its freezing and reproduction, and on the synthesis of movement) which were more or less parallel, independent, disordered, with often simultaneous and independent inventions (large swathes of the various histories of the cinema are dedicated to patent disputes) developed on the common foundation of ancient empirical observations, which only converge and become complete at a very late stage: a half-century after the experiments of Faraday, Plateau and Stampfer on the persistence of vision and the stroboscopic effect, a half-century, too, after the invention of the photographic plate. By contrast, in the final years of the 19th century, we bear witness to a mad dash for patents, and a simultaneous eruption onto the market of several, practically identical, recording-projecting devices. The competitors reach the finish line together.

Bazin interprets this series of deferrals and delays as proof of the "resistance of matter," and even as the belatedness of technology and science in relation to the idea and the myth, since the majority of inventors had a very clear idea of the goal and the significance of their efforts: the production of a faithful and total representation of life, "realizing the ancient dream of humanity." But, according to Bazin, the very reason for this delay can not be ascribed to an inevitable discrepancy between the "dream" and its "realization." On the one hand, it is more due to the fact that, if the "scientific" conditions of the definitive production of the camera were brought together more than 50 years before its development, the scientists themselves were barely preoccupied, as we saw, with overcoming the technical and practical difficulties of creating such a device, because they were barely interested in creating it in the first place. On the other hand, from the moment that the production of the camera

29. Cf. Bazin, "Le mythe du cinéma total," *op. cit.*, p. 22 [p. 14 – Bazin is paraphrasing Sadoul in this citation].

came to be inscribed within a social demand and an economic reality, matters were hastened, and efforts were greatly escalated.

Deslandes, whose outlook is by no means Marxist, points out:

> The importance of Edison's *kinetoscope* (1892-1893) is not of a technical nature, but of an economic and commercial nature. It would, indeed, be a vain pursuit to seek to demonstrate that such or such an instrument from 1895 or 1896, destined to project moving images, derives more or less directly from the principle and the mechanism patented by Edison. [...] There is no merit in reviving the disputes concerning which of the technical particularities of the first instruments of projection or cinematic recording came first. The guiding thread can not be found here. The essential deed, the point of departure which finally led to the practical realization of moving projection, was the nickel that the American spectator slipped into the slot of Edison's *kinetoscope*. [...] This is what explains the birth of the cinema spectacle in France, England, Germany and the United States during the year 1895. Moving photographs were not only a laboratory experiment, a scientific curiosity, they could now be considered a profitable form of spectacle. There is no need to seek the origins of the Lumières' *cinématographe*, Robert William Paul's *theatrograph* or Skladanowsky's *bioskope* in technical descriptions and earlier patents, but in the columns of numbers in the account book of Raff and Gammon's Kinetoscope Company, charged with the commercial exploitation of the Edison instruments [*more than $48,000 in less than one year – JLC*]. [...] The men who, in 1895, developed instruments designed to allow the public projection of moving photographs for commercial ends were not disinterested researchers pursuing a vague Promethean dream. They were practical minds.[30]

The English historian Brian Coe had already made this point:

> The appearance of the *kinetoscope* and its commercial exploitation among the broader public marks the decisive turning point in the history of the *cinématographe*; not only was it henceforth proven that moving images could now be obtained in a practical manner – which had been surmised for a long time – but it was above all demonstrated that they could make money.[31]

The cinema thus owes its existence to the reciprocal reinforcement of an ideological demand ("to see life as it is") and an economic demand (to make it a source of profits). It is no different to the majority of technologies, which tend toward the

---

30. Deslandes, *op. cit.*, pp. 213-214.

31. Cited by Deslandes, *ibid.*, p. 213 [The quote from Brian Coe is taken from "William Friese Greene and the Origins of Kinematography," *The Photographic Journal* (March-April 1962), p. 16].

realization of an objective assigned by and constituted in both of these two demands. And this, it seems to me, is what it is important to establish – and not lose sight of – in the case of the cinema, for if we are in agreement with Lebel in refusing to brand the cinema with a "natural ideological taint," we do not do so in order to conceal, behind an inconsistent "scientific basis," the fact that it is under the effects of an economic demand – that is, within ideology and as an instrument of ideology – that the cinema is progressively imagined, made and purchased.

II. Depth of Field: The Double Scene

If our intention is to illustrate, by way of example, the function of the technique/ ideology duality in the field of the cinema, and to mark the contradictions and forms of resistance to which all discourse on the autonomy of technique is now constrained, then why should we examine depth of field, when it is merely one technical effect among many others? It is certainly an effect upon which, since its use by Welles in *Citizen Kane*, all number of theorists and critics have conferred the status of a stylistic procedure, and which their responses have invested with a certain number of interpretations. But this alone does not motivate our choice, for we could be told, in response, that what takes place with respect to depth of field, from the moment that a filmmaker (or a film) implicates it in a signifying process, also takes place with respect to the close-up, or camera movement, which are "neutral forms" charged by a text, made meaningful by an utterance, and inhabited by an ideology. Even more so, given that it is worth noting, precisely, that the theoretical discourses triggered by the pretext of depth of field have not burdened themselves with a concern for respecting any kind of fundamental neutrality of forms (which, in any case, they also postulate), or hastening to abstract this representational technique from the corpus in which it had been inscribed in order to give it a generalized normative validity, which would amount to granting it an intrinsic signification[1] – and maybe not the right one, as we shall see.

But without doubt a greater determining factor in choosing depth of field than the interest that André Bazin and Jean Mitry have shown in the technique is its very definition: let us recall that it is the ability offered in both photography and the cinema, using certain lenses with short focal lengths, to produce an equally clear image of an array of objects at varying distances, from the foreground to the background.[2] We have thus not left behind the problematic posed above of the regulation

1. Cf. André Bazin: "Depth of field is not a camera technique like filters or lighting styles but a seminal contribution to *mise en scène*: a dialectical advance in the history of film language." ("L'évolution du langage cinématographique," *Qu'est-ce que le cinéma?*, vol. I, *op. cit.*, p. 143 ["The Evolution of Film Language," trans. Timothy Barnard, in *What Is Cinema?*, *op. cit.*, pp. 87-106, p. 100]).

2. It is, of course, possible to obtain depth of field using lenses with "normal" focal lengths, but only when the lens is considerably stopped down, which requires either sunlight in exterior shots, or, when shooting in the studio, a substantial amount of lighting, or very sensitive film stock.

of the camera by the code of monocular perspective: the space represented by the deep-focus lens on the surface of the screen is, like that constructed by *perspectiva artificialis* in the *quattrocento*, a two-dimensional space where the *illusion* of the third dimension (depth) arises from the gradation in size of the objects (becoming smaller the further away they are supposed to be). Through an increase in lighting effects, every effort is made to bring out the different planes of this staggered field as so many "reliefs." Due to the single, centralizing eye of the camera, the deep-focus image is still organized on the basis of an axis perpendicular to the surface of the screen, as with Alberti's "central ray," which at the same time we know to be the assignation to the spectator of a *single*, rigorously fixed point of view, the real center of the spectacle. In this image, the laws of the perspectival system (with its "normality" and its censures, as well as the logocentrism that it implants) are thus reiterated, and one can even say that this is the only occurrence in the cinema (or photography) of such a reiteration, since a "flat" image, without depth of field, (such as that provided by a telephoto lens), participates in a different representational encoding, produces a different type of space, given that film has the particularity (that photography evidently does not have, unless composed in collage) of being able to depict, through the use of montage, different figurative codes in succession, with varying degrees of proximity to the *quattrocento* "model." (The possibility, which is always on offer, but very rarely exploited by filmmakers and camera operators in a scientific or systematic fashion, of varying the types of lenses – and therefore the figurative codes – leads us to relativize the remarks made by Marcelin Pleynet cited at the beginning of this study: only two or three types of lenses – those which best "imitate" normal vision, and which are therefore certainly used most frequently, or, we might say, most "naturally" – are "meticulously constructed to 'rectify' all perspectival anomalies.") Nevertheless, in the same way that the first photograph is "perspectival," the first lenses (those of the "primitive" filmmakers), doubtless because they were relatively simple, produce a deep-focus image and a perspectival vanishing point which made a not inconsiderable contribution to the "reality effects" induced, for example, by the first Lumière films. (I will return later to this primitive depth of field.)

Bazin's "surplus realism"

The reinforcement of these "reality effects" is the first and foremost reason for André Bazin's interest in depth of field. In certain famous texts,[3] and essentially concentrating on the films of Orson Welles and William Wyler (a choice which will inevitably

3. Notably: "L'évolution du langage cinématographique" and "William Wyler ou le janséniste de la mise en scène" (Bazin, *Qu'est-ce que le cinéma?*, vol. I, *op. cit.*) ["William Wyler, the Jansenist of Mise en Scène," trans. Timothy Barnard, in *What Is Cinema?*, *op. cit.*, pp. 45-72].

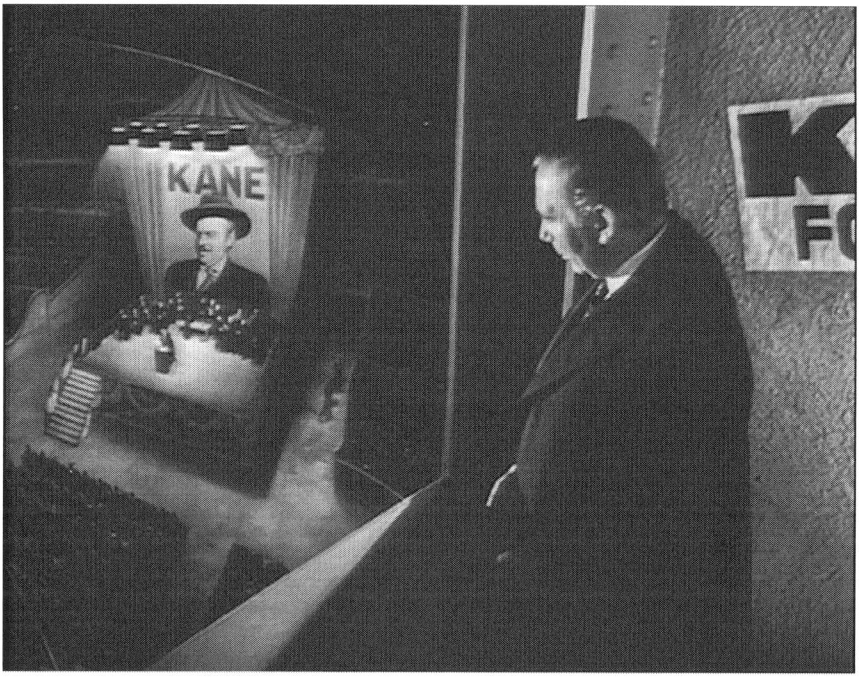

Fig. 11: Still from *Citizen Kane* (Welles, 1941).

[The use of a wide-angle lens produces three effects, combined within this shot: the creation of an "unlimited" depth of field, the deformation of those parts of the image that are on the edges of the frame, and, finally, the accentuated sense of distance between foreground and background. The frame within the frame thus indicates, as always, a *mise en abyme*, that is, a distancing or consciousness-raising effect – but one which is here reinforced. The distance between the character's look and the scene being observed appears to be excessively accentuated. Everything seems to be very close in one part of the image, and very distant in the other part. The gap produced in the image can hardly be said to be "natural." We are beyond the realm of verisimilitude, and are instead in the realm of excess and exaggeration. Like the spectator in the scene, we are "taken aback." The organization of space leads us to doubt its "reality." The shot we see is conceptual.]

overdetermine Bazin's discourse), depth of field becomes, for Bazin, both the means and the symbol of the irreversible accomplishment of the "realist vocation of the cinema" and the "realist regeneration of narrative."

But Bazin approaches the problematic from more than one angle, and more than one contradiction results. The possibility arises of a contemporary, productive re-reading of the web of contradictions yielded by the diverging and re-converging axes of interpretation in Bazin's text, which, in spite of its idealist closure, is not entirely stable, smooth or coherent. To reject this text *en bloc* in the name of a necessary antagonism toward its idealism would be to forbid ourselves from seeing relevant questions deposited in its fault lines: the unifying will of its discourse sharpens more oppositions than it reduces, and not just to the extent that the facts resist it and mark out the limits of Bazin's discourse, but also because his theoretical method itself installs contradiction as the driving principal of the history of the cinema, presenting this history as a series of conflicts between the "ontological realism of the cinematic image" – a place of "neutrality" and the "ambiguity of the real" – and the arbitrary nature of "significations imposed by montage," that is, by *writing* (the filmmakers who "put their faith in reality" are opposed to those who put their faith in "everything that the depiction of a thing on the screen can add to the thing itself"). It is on the basis of this conflict, and as one of its pivotal moments, that, for Bazin, depth of field makes its entrance. We will therefore, in turn, need to examine the account he gives of the "evolution of film language," that is, to invert or extend his questions in the direction of the determinations of this "evolution" – whether technical and aesthetic *or* ideological/economic – since Bazin attempts to constitute an autonomous history of cinematic forms, as a self-contained field of influences, styles and aesthetic concerns, from which "technical determinations" – and, as a result, ideological and economic factors – are supposedly evacuated to the greatest possible extent. It will be seen that, in fact, "the history of film form" is not determined by a similarly "autonomous" history of "technical determinations"; on the contrary, both are produced together in and through an ideological demand, which is itself determined by the socio-economic inscription of the cinema.

But let us first assure ourselves – in order to restrict the field of questions for the time being – of the pertinence of Bazin's definitions of depth of field.

To provisionally leave to one side – as much as is possible for the matter to remain clear – both the articulation between depth of field and montage, and the associated question of the historical inscription of depth of field, we shall read those passages which, in Bazin's discourse, concentrate on "the psychological and metaphysical consequences" of this technical procedure. It is in *Citizen Kane* that, as Bazin writes:

> Through the use of depth of field, entire scenes are shot in a single take; the camera doesn't even move. The dramatic effects once provided by editing derive here from the movement of actors within a single composition. [...] The narrative in Welles or Wyler is no less clear than in John Ford, but it has the advantage of not abandoning the use of precise effects made possible by the *image's unity in time and space*. It is not at all immaterial, at least in a work that creates a style, whether an event is analyzed in fragments or shown in its *physical unity*. Obviously, it would be absurd to deny the decisive advances in film language brought about through the use of editing. But these advances have been achieved *at the price of other, no less cinematic qualities* [*valeurs*]. [...] Depth of field [...] affects not only the structure of film language but also *the viewer's intellectual relationship with the image*, thereby *modifying the meaning* of the work. [...] Depth of field creates a relationship between the viewer and the image which is closer to the viewer's relationship to reality. It is thus accurate to say that its structure is

more realistic, whatever the content of the image itself; as a result, the viewer has a more active intellectual approach, and even makes a real contribution, to the *mise en scène*. With analytical editing viewers need only follow their guide and focus their attention on that of the filmmaker, who chooses for them what they should see. Here a minimum of individual choice is required. The meaning of the image depends in part on the viewer's attention and will. [...] The very nature of editing's analysis of reality confers a sole meaning upon the dramatic event. [...] Depth of field, on the contrary, re-introduces *ambiguity into the structure of the image*.[4]

Bazin insists on this last point again and again: "Despite their stylistic differences, neorealist filmmakers, like Welles, endow their films with a sense of the ambiguity of reality";[5] "to show the true continuity of reality on the screen";[6] "the concern for encompassing events in their totality";[7] "without taking the easy way out with editing, [Renoir] sought to discover the secret of a film narrative capable of expressing everything without chopping the world up into bits – to reveal the hidden meaning of beings and things without breaking up their natural unity";[8] and, finally: "because it relies upon a greater degree of realism, the image – its visual structure, its organization in time – now has more means at its disposal to inflect and modify reality from within."[9]

A series of principles are thus put into place, flowing on from what is, for Bazin, a veritable *primary principle*: "the immanent ambiguity of reality" – which montage and even classical Hollywood *découpage* reduced to a given meaning or discourse (that of the filmmaker) – "renders the event subjective in the extreme, because each little fragment is the result of the filmmaker's point of view,"[10] and that, in contrast, filming in deep focus protects this ambiguity, because it comes within an "aesthetic of reality" and lets the spectator "look from one to the other character at his own will, do his own cutting."[11]

And so: 1. reality is ambiguous; 2. to provide a representation of it chopped up by montage (that is: reworked by a writing process) is to reduce this ambiguity and replace it with a "subjectivity" (to be understood as a signification, that is, a "vision of the world," an ideology); 3. because depth of field brings the film image nearer to the "normal" retinal image of "realist" vision, and because it literally shows a surplus

4. Bazin, "L'évolution du langage cinématographique," *op. cit.*, pp. 141-144 [pp. 98-101]. Emphasis added throughout.

5. *Ibid.*, p. 145 [pp. 102-103].

6. *Ibid.*, p. 146 [p. 103].

7. *Ibid.*

8. *Ibid.* [p. 104].

9. *Ibid.*, p. 148 [p. 105].

10. Bazin, "William Wyler," *op. cit.*, p. 158 [pp. 54-55].

11. *Ibid.*, p. 159 [p. 56 – the phrase is actually a citation by Bazin from an interview with Wyler].

of objects, a *surplus of the "real,"* it once again allows this "ambiguity" to function, an ambiguity which lets the spectator be "free," that is to say, which strives to abolish the difference between film and reality, between representation and the real, to confirm the spectator in his "natural" relationship with the world, to reinforce the spontaneous conditions of his vision and ideology. It is not for nothing that Bazin writes (not without humor): "Wyler's use of depth of field is liberal and democratic, like the consciousness of American audiences and the film's characters!"[12]

On the one hand, there is a reinforcement of the ideological effects of the impression of reality, of the "normality of specular representation"; on the other hand, there is the *revelation* (in the Christian sense of the term, even) of the "natural ambiguity and unity" of the world. No more is needed, indeed, to point out the raging idealism of Bazin's discourse than the charismatic, cosmophanic attributes he lends to depth of field.

The work of "transparency"

This is what, in succession, Mitry and *Cinéthique* have denounced without much difficulty. Let us pause for a moment on the theses of the former. Critiquing the idealist currents of film theory, he ends up insisting on certain "obvious truths" both "forgotten" and masked by these currents. It may be useful to return to these, since they become unmistakably implicated in the problematic posed by depth of field and its ideological inscription.

To the "revelation," according to Bazin, of the "immanent ambiguity of reality" through depth of field, Mitry opposes "the fact that film reality is a *mediated* reality. Even when there is no evidence of a director's hand, the film, the camera, the representation, stands between us and the real world."[13] He further writes that:

> It is supremely naïve to think (as Bazin does) that the camera – because it automatically records the data of reality – is presenting an objective and impartial image of that reality.[14] [...] By the very fact that it is *presented as an image*, the reality captured by the lens is structured according to various formalizing values creating a series of new relationships and thus a new reality – or, at the very least,

12. *Ibid.*, p. 160 [p. 57, translation modified]: the film under discussion is *The Best Years of Our Lives* (Wyler, 1946).

13. Jean Mitry, *Esthétique et psychologie du cinéma*, vol. II, "Les formes" (Paris: Éditions universitaires, 1965), p. 12 [*The Aesthetics and Psychology of the Cinema* (abridged), trans. Christopher King (Bloomington: Indiana University Press, 2000), p. 170].

14. It will be noted that this passage (from 1965) critiqued Lebel's theses before they were even formulated.

> a new appearance. The *represented* is perceived via a *representation* which inevitably *transforms* it.[15]

It is on this basis that he opposes the entire current he dubs the "spiritualists" (from Roger Munier to André Bazin, Henri Agel, Éric Rohmer and Amédée Ayfre[16]):

> To consider the film image as a "statement of the real world," by virtue of its objectivity *considered as absolute*,[17] to say that it is "*cosmophanic* in it is essence," is to posit the world as "in-itself" and to posit this "in-itself" as necessarily identical (and yet "purer") with the object as we know it, without realizing that the object is the way it is only by virtue of our perception. This is to dabble in "transcendental realism."[18]

Mitry's discourse is underpinned by the fact that the film image, because it is *limited* by a spatial frame (the "frame" in the strict sense of the term) and a temporal frame (the duration of the shot), is absolutely distinct from "normal," everyday perception, such that "the mobility of our vision, our very movements, make the space around us appear homogenous and continuous."[19]

As with Bazin, the notion of the "frame" now plays a determining role for Mitry. Certainly, for Mitry this frame is not the infamous "window" opened onto the world – quite the opposite: "From that moment, the objects are literally 'cut out,' deprived of any direct association with the external world. Their associations, until then generated in space, become self-reflexive, as though the edges of the frame refer them back to the center like a parabolic mirror."[20]

Note how, in this last passage, Mitry accurately describes – but without, it seems to me, suspecting that he does so – the manner in which monocular perspective itself works: this folding inwards, this convergence into a center are precisely what perspective has come to codify and legislate. That there is a lacuna here appears symptomatic to us: what is lacking in Mitry's discourse – and this is why he will end up, in spite of everything, falling into agreement with Bazin on a point that we, by contrast, judge to be of capital importance (see below) – is any reference to what it is that comes to re-inscribe (inclusive of all their respective differences) both vision and the

15. Mitry, *op. cit.*, vol. II, p. 11 [p. 169, translation modified].

16. Roger Munier, in an article "L'image fascinante," *Diogène*, no. 61 [*sic* – the article is from *Diogène*, no. 38 (1962), pp. 91-99], Henri Agel and Amédée Ayfre in their books on the cinema, Éric Rohmer in his articles for *Cahiers*.

17. The same comment applies as in note 47, above.

18. Jean Mitry, *Esthétique et psychologie du cinéma*, vol. I, "Les structures" (Paris: Éditions universitaires, 1963), p. 129 [p. 45].

19. Mitry, *op. cit.*, vol. II, p. 10 [p. 168].

20. *Ibid.* [p. 168-169].

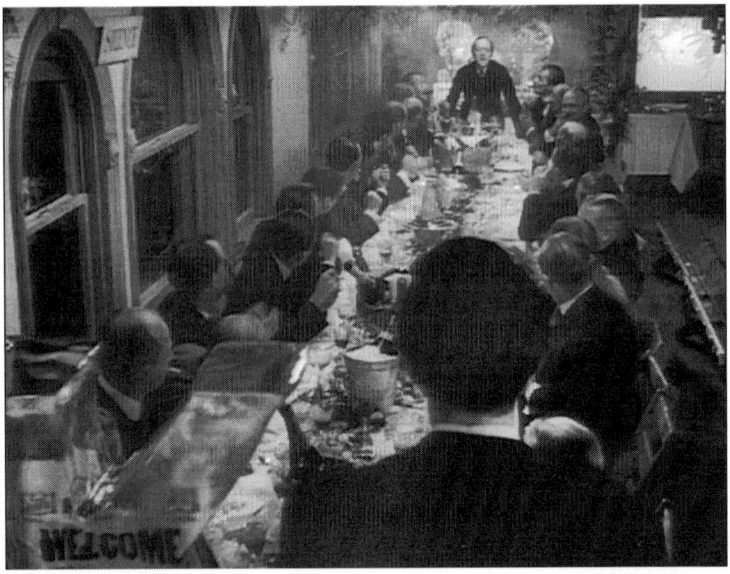

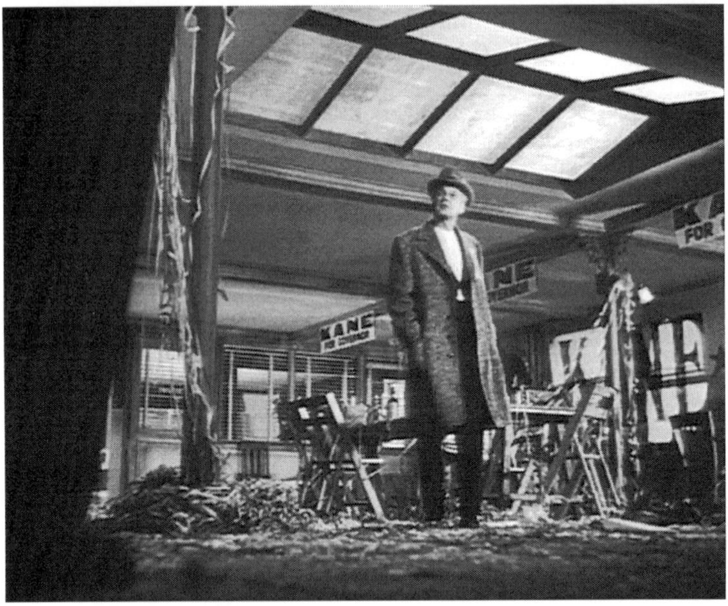

Figs. 12 and 13: Two stills from *Citizen Kane*: In the first image, we can see an accentuation of the vanishing perspective, lateral deformations (a wide-angle shot) and "depth effects" produced by the lighting (which, in a highly "abstract" manner, isolate the character in the rear of the shot). In the second image, what we shall analyze in the rest of this text is clearly inscribed. The depicted space is dramatized, in Welles' films, through the use of depth of field, such that there should be no question of a "surfeit of realism" – quite the opposite, in fact.

representation produced by the camera lens into the same specular system (and the same ideology). His following passage confirms it:

> The consequence of this is that the image records a fragment of space whose representation, limited and circumscribed (by the frame), endows the represented objects with a series of "defining characteristics" which they do not have in actual reality. The space within the frame becomes its own "entity," it forms an independent structure – any similar cuts having a similar effect. Add to this that objects within a shot are related according to their relative sizes (with no necessary connection with their actual sizes, since the most divergent views are brought together in the same fixed frame) and we may say that each shot is, as it were, a "cell," a distinct space, and that when combined into a sequence, they form a homogenous space – but one which *in no way* resembles the space from which the elements have been taken.[21]

The very imprecision of the terminology here marks a theoretical lack: fundamentally, Mitry does nothing more than empirically observe and describe one of these aforementioned "obvious truths": that, without any doubt, filmic space is different to real space, that "the film appears as a discontinuous spatio-temporal development, completely different to the univocal continuum of real space-time (that is to say, the space-time of our planet), even though it reflects its continuous schema."[22] Yet the whole problem lies in this "even though." It may indeed be apt to reverse the formulation: *even though* it is different, in fact, to the perception of "real space-time," film *appears* to reflect its "continuous schema"; *even though* it is materially discontinuous in all regards, it reproduces the very illusion of our perception elaborating "immediate" space-time as a "univocal continuum." Having insisted, in opposition to Bazin, on the difference between film and reality, Mitry forbids himself from seeing the extent to which, far from avowing this difference, the cinema tends to reduce it, by presenting itself as identical to the norms of perception, and by ceaselessly reinstating the illusion of homogeneity and continuity. This is the basis of Bazin's error, since he ascribes equal value to the unifying functions of both perception and filmic representation. (We will return to this play in and of discontinuity when, following Bazin and Mitry, we will attempt to re-read "the evolution of film language" in line with the contradictions that depth of field inscribes in it.)

At this point, it was inevitable that Mitry, in highlighting, against Bazin, the alterity between film and reality – that is, misrecognizing the process of repression whose object is this alterity, misrecognizing the place held by the spectator in this process, and thus abstracting the film from its social inscription in an absolute where the

21. *Ibid.* [p. 169].
22. *Ibid.* [translation modified].

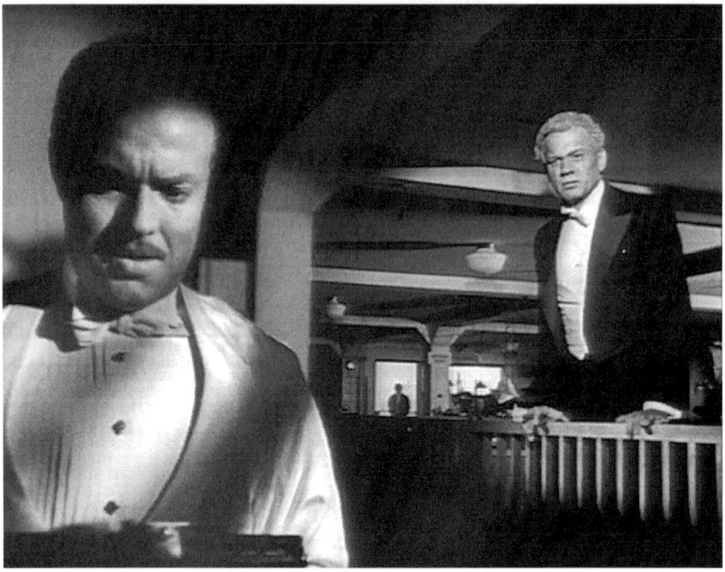

Figs. 14 and 15: In these two stills (above: *Toute la mémoire du monde* by Alain Resnais, 1956; below: *Citizen Kane*), we can see how the use of depth of field produces a space that is at once composite and composed, fragmentary and discontinuous, and distinctly coded (both through the scales of light and shadow and by the vanishing lines themselves). We could thus go so far as to reverse Bazin's hypothesis and claim that depth of field, far from manifesting a "surplus reality," actually enables the filmmaker to show less of the real, to play around with masking effects and visual tricks, as well as with the division and distortion of space...

"truth" of its nature (the "fragmentation of reality into shots and sequences") prevails over its reading (reconstituting, suturing) – also comes to recognize, with Bazin (but not without a degree of nuance, it is true), that, by reducing this "fragmentation," depth of field does indeed produce an "augmentation of realism," since it does what the classical shot does not do: that is, it captures (with its "ontological realism") "the event globally, in its real space-time," restoring "to the object and the setting their essential density, the weight of their presence,"[23] and since it resituates (with its "psychological realism") the "spectator in the true conditions of perception," that is to say, coherency, continuity and, finally, "ambiguity."[24] With the proviso that depth of field not be turned into an omnivalent principle, capable of being substituted for all other formulations of *mise en scène*, Mitry declares himself, in this matter, to be "perfectly in agreement with Bazin."[25]

Moreover, Gérard Leblanc, writing in *Cinéthique*, attests to the same agreement on the realist function of depth of field, when, in order to demonstrate the idealism *en bloc* of both Welles and the camera itself, he draws on Bazin's idealism and takes the definition that the latter gives of it for his own purposes ("Let us leave to Bazin the liberty of describing depth of field"). "What," Leblanc asks himself, "is the significance of the desire to 'create' images which have a weight of reality comparable to that of the world? For a film that, as Bazin notes, perfects the impression of reality still imperfectly produced by the 'classical camera,' this question insistently presents itself."[26] On one point, therefore, Leblanc aligns himself with Bazin's thesis, which, on this same point (and only on this point) does not contradict Mitry: "The wide-angle lens offers a field of vision comparable to that of the eye (ceilings were constructed in the studio in order to render the interior scenes more lifelike), deep focus and the long-take assure the impression of reality."[27]

It is far from certain that depth of field – particularly in the films of Welles and Wyler, who since Bazin have been the obligatory examples for this tendency – is thus responsible for an "augmentation of realism." Moreover, as I will attempt to show, this is all the more the case precisely because depth of field inscribes the representative code of linear perspective better than any other procedure for recording images.

We thus find ourselves in a moment of contradiction. If, for Bazin, the advent of deep focus photography increases the realist coefficient of the film image, this is because it accomplishes the virtues (or virtualities) *already* inscribed in it, by perfecting it (as Leblanc says), or by literally giving *more space* to its "ontological realism." For Mitry, meanwhile, this can not be the case, because, by marking out the artificiality (or alterity) of the film image, it challenges such "realism," and he only concedes

23. These are Bazinian formulations appropriated by Mitry.
24. *Idem.*
25. *Ibid.*
26. Leblanc, "Welles, Bazin et la RKO," *op. cit.*, p. 30.
27. *Ibid.*, p. 32.

to deep-focus photography, because it produces a "more global" and relatively less discontinuous space, the ability to come nearer to certain effects of common perception, that is, the ability to reinstate and re-inscribe in the image the conditions (psychologically speaking, at least) of a surplus of realism. In the first case, this *surplus* is an addition, while in the *second* case, it tends to cancel out a *deficit* and fulfill a lack. It is apparent that this contradiction between Bazin and Mitry is also a contradiction within Mitry: the specific nature of the deep-focus image does not abolish the network of differences and particularities which constitute the film image as being different to the world while presenting itself as the world's double. In his illusion, Bazin is more coherent than Mitry, despite the fact that the latter denounces the former's incoherence. After all, to insist on the constitutive differences and specific encodings of the film image could not, as the case of deep focus brings to light, do without insisting, in the same movement, on the *work* of these codes (their *raison d'être* and their aims), which is to produce their own misrecognition, to present them as "natural" and, as a consequence, to mask the role played by these differences.

It is therefore on the basis of the *positive* quality allotted to depth of field by both Bazin and Mitry that we will analyze, in the rest of this text, the *double role* of the encoding of the film image (its "transparency," since it operates on the basis of not being noticed as such[28]), insofar as the "supplementary realism" that depth of field is meant to yield can not be produced without distortion and an emphasis on the inscriptive codes of "realism," already "naturally" at work in the image. What, then, is this supplementarity, and how, precisely, does it *exceed* the system of (perspectival and cultural) norms which anchor the impression of reality and support the category of "realism"?

It is far from irrelevant that discourses which are otherwise antagonistic – or which see themselves as being antagonistic, but which at least have this recuperation (this reinforcement) in common – converge on this point: the idea that "*depth of field = surplus reality*." Specifically:

- Bazin's discourse. We have seen that his interpretation of the role of depth of field remained coherent with his entire system, to the extent that, as it happens, it is very much an *interpretation* (which the rest of this text will have the task of establishing, by *constructing* depth of field as a theoretical object), a phantasm, we would say, tautologically confirming the central illusion of the Bazinian system: that the "evolution of film language accomplishes the realist vocation of the cinema," and that it re-inscribes the "ontological realism of the film image." Let us add that this "coherence" only comes at the price of a certain number of *coups de force* that our reading, when it comes, will recognize as *indices of contradiction*, which both undermine Bazin's discourse and, by producing the other side to it

28. It is worth noting that the "theories" of the "transparency of *mise en scène*" proceed from the "transparency" of the encoding of the film image, without properly taking this fact into account.

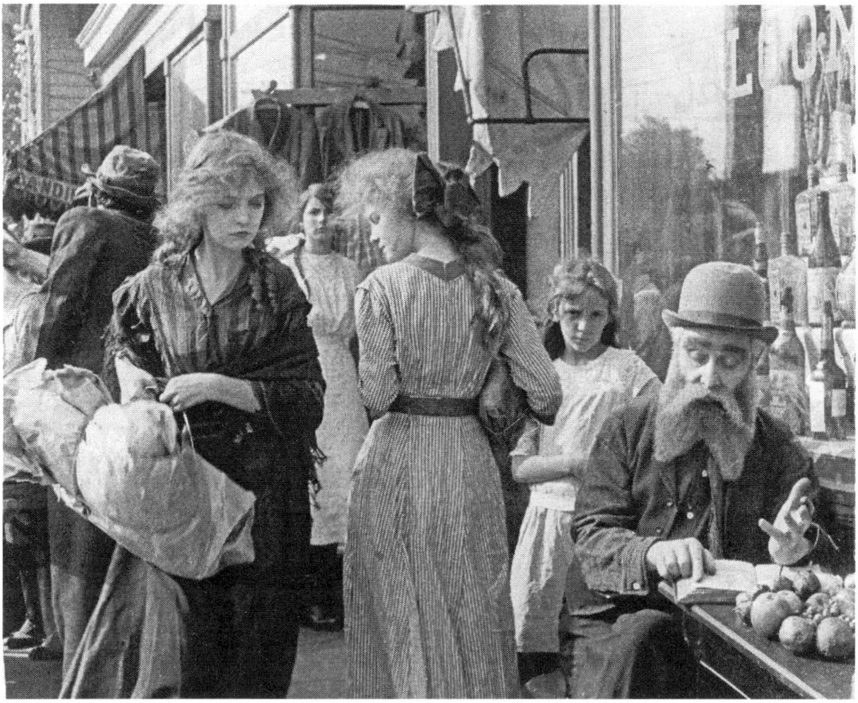

Fig. 16: *The Musketeers of Pig Alley* (Griffith, 1912). Beyond a depth of field that is "natural," "primitive" and "spontaneous," a play of gazes is noticeable here: lowered gazes for the "characters," gazes fixed on the camera lens for the two extras. Once again, this is a complex dramatic space, where the spectator is both directly implicated (through the looks-to-the-camera) and confronted with a guided pathway for *reading*.

[Here we see a new example of this "*mise en scène* of the spectator" that permits or facilitates depth of field (whether "primitive" or not). As André Bazin has written, the deployment of actions and bodies in depth – and in the duration of the shot – gives spectators the possibility (the liberty) to let their gaze wander around a complex tableau and produce a relatively aleatory reading of it, or in any case a reading that is not entirely imposed by the filmmaker. Hence in this still I can be primarily interested in the looks-to-the-camera of the two young extras, in the middle ground and the background. They tell me that film shoots have not yet fallen under the taboo of fiction. It is not only the "liberty" of the spectator that is at play, but also that of the actor.]

(its other scene), subvert it. It goes without saying that such a subversion only has the opportunity to function when the discourse which submits to it, but which also positions it (or predisposes it) shows evidence of a certain theoretical force. This is the case with Bazin, and this is why Lebel – while he never stops insisting, in his study,[29] on the kinship between Bazin and *Cahiers'* current work in order, in the name of our "father," to mark us with the indelible imprint of idealism – is wrong and misguided in wanting to base his argument on the effectiveness of this reductive operation (in "overturning the idealist problematic of Bazin," we are deemed to remain "complicit" with this problematic, and somehow inherit this idealism...). To quote Lenin, intelligent idealism is more intelligent than stupid materialism.[i]

– Mitry's discourse. There is a critique here of Bazin's idealist presuppositions and conclusions, in the name of the radical difference between the film-object and the "real" as an object of perception (the space produced by the film being different to the spatio-temporal continuum produced by perception); but there is also, since Mitry nonetheless aligns himself with the Bazinian interpretation of depth of field, a twisting of the principle governing his entire thesis. There is a flaw present here, one in which we can discern the mark of the fundamental defect of this thesis: the insufficient recognition of the *place of the spectator* in the filmic process. In order to come within the bounds of scientific knowledge, in order to even be one of the "primary generalities" of any theory of the cinema,[ii] the difference between a film and the real is no less unremittingly the site of a *disavowal* which masks it. This disavowal is linked at one and the same time to the status of the analytic subject and to the socio-historical inscription of the cinema, and thus to the "subject of ideology" (to use Kristeva's terminology[30]), whose effect is to both cover over and designate the *conflict* between the process of *signifiance*[iii] in the film's materiality and the ideological resistances which prevent this signifying materiality from being read as such, and which *obstruct the constitution of the film as* a text. Such a conflict is where what Bazin called the "evolution of film language" has a role, and it is what we prefer to designate as the production – one that is multiply and unevenly determined by and complexly articulated with the social totality (and not the linear succession, chronological chain or homogenous continuity of "forms" or "styles" that Bazin postulates) – of the filmic signifiers as

---

29. J.-P. Lebel, "Cinéma et idéologie," *op. cit.* Here, a discourse can be read which, it must be said, is hazy and confused, anchored in the "just middle" and "common sense," and, bereft of historical and dialectical materialism, proceeding from a form of empiricism that is totally blind to the ideology which speaks it, that very ideology which he strives to circumscribe, and which is, in its positivist and objectivist forms, the discourse-of-the-technicians.

30. Which makes a distinction (cf. Julia Kristeva, "Pratique analytique, pratique révolutionnaire," *Cinéthique*, no. 9-10 [1970]) between the *subject of the text*, the *subject of ideology* and the *subject of science*: "The 'subject' of the text knows the psychosis (which is characterized by the foreclosure of the subject and the real), but emerges from it and masters it in a *practice* which can only be social in nature. Inasmuch as this practice is a practice of the *signifier*, the subject of the text is also distinguished from the subject of science, which we have been able to define as being foreclosed (in a psychotic manner), in the sense that, in its metalinguistic practice, its submission to the signifier is lacking. It likewise differs from the subject of *ideology*, whose misrecognition-recognition is situated in the imaginary of the 'ego' and is structured like neurotic transference" [p. 75].

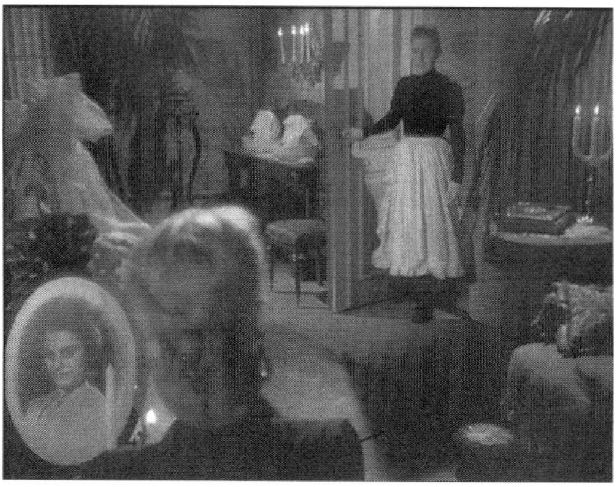

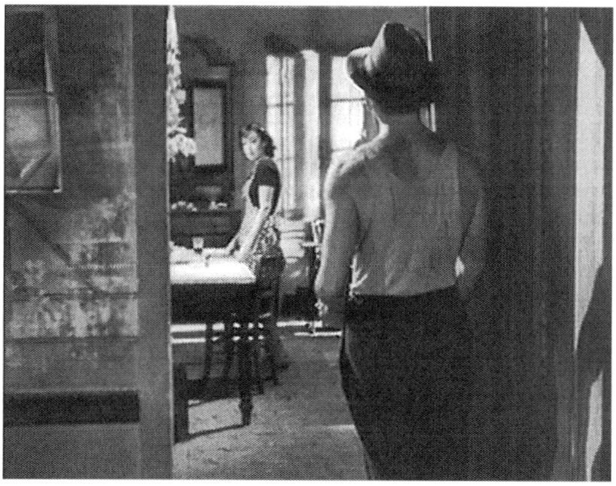

Figs. 17 and 18: Above, *Miss Julie* (Alf Sjöberg, 1951): Depth of field functions here as a form of "*mise en scène*": it inscribes the gaze of the spectator as identifying with that of the protagonist, but it also dialecticizes this axis through the homology between the face of the servant and the oval mirror in the foreground staring at the spectator.
Below, *Ossessione* (Visconti, 1943): "Neorealist" depth of field. We can see the way in which it is essentially the set that connotes the "realism" of a scene, while depth of field turns screens, panels, shadows, masks and partitions into plastic signifiers subverting any prospective "naturalism."

[In the cinema, where we are primarily concerned with *seeing*, with satisfying the scopic drive mobilized within each spectator, disturbances to the spectator's vision are precisely what implicate and activate his gaze. Obstacles – windshields, screens, areas of shadow, everything that results in the object of the gaze evading being directly seen, only able to be glimpsed at the cost of a complex visual pathway (cf. the films of Josef von Sternberg) – are there only to yield pleasure from the little that remains to be seen. In contrast to received notions, the *jouissance* of the voyeur lies in *not seeing everything*. This "not-everything" is stronger than the whole. It gives the imagination free rein. The *hors-champ* and the barred field are stimulants for it. To see the limits of the ability to see is to enjoy them all the more. The *mise en scène* of the spectator passes through his scopic implication in a *visual trap* (*mise en abyme*, for example).]

"formations of compromise," caught between ideological and textual pressures. In other words, therefore, Mitry's discourse not only lacks one of the terms of the contradiction, it does not even have this contradiction itself in view. Attentive to the "effects of form," to the alterity and specificity of filmic signifiers, to the irreducibility of the film to any "transparency" with regards to the "real" or to any transcendence by means of the "real" (in fact: to its being governed by the order of referents), he can only be embarrassed by the question of "realism" (*since cinematic realism is only produced and is only in a position to be produced as a denial of "filmic reality"*), and can only oppose it (and Bazin) with his own *formalism* – whose phenomenological roots are nothing but the *other side* of Bazinian idealism, even in the critique made of it. That, in the last instance, the task of evacuating or reducing (as "deceitful") the problematic of "realism" is devolved to this formalism explains why, even though it is wrongly "evacuated," realism ends up making its return at various points in Mitry's text (notably on the issue of depth of field), since Mitry does not hesitate to ratify Bazin's thesis, on the single condition that depth of field is reduced to one formal procedure among others, that is, that it be recuperated within his formalist discourse.

– And finally, Leblanc's discourse. The least that can be said of it is that Leblanc does not embarrass himself by constructing the notion of depth of field by himself; instead, he hurriedly takes, in a no less hurried reading of Bazin,[31] what suits him, but also, inseparably, what awaits him and what offers itself to him. We must certainly not use Bazin's opinion as an authority for submitting the ultimate proof of the cinema's congenital idealism, because the symptom that the Bazinian thesis constitutes is not *ipso facto* an index of truth, it does not necessarily point to some "truth" of the cinema, but in actual fact, as we have seen, to the truth of a conflict for which it is one of the key terms at stake. As a matter of fact, this thesis, in order to target the "being" of the cinema, is itself not divorced from history, the time and place in which it produces itself (in which it is produced) is not inconsequential. It is not possible to give a reading of Bazin without taking into account his place within ideology, the tangle of determinations which acted upon him, and even the insertion and effect of his discourse in the field of cinematic practice (Bazinian theories constituted a certain number of tendencies or styles as "models," and his condemnation of montage as "manipulation" influenced the practices of numerous filmmakers, and still does...). For example, he insists on depth of field and the long-take in the wake of (in response to) Italian neo-realism, that is to say, he is supported by a certain moment of the cinema which, still being, at that stage, of the most recent vintage, is privileged and pos-

31. The critique of idealism should not be "hurried": inasmuch as idealist discourse is always dominant in the field of cinema (as elsewhere), we should not content ourselves with replacing it with a hasty, principled repudiation, that is, with a simple repression.

tulated as a point of "progress," in order to re-stage, "on that basis," the "course" of the history of the cinema, and to project onto it, in a retrospective gesture which inscribes this history as teleological (its endpoint: "surplus realism"), the qualities of the neo-realist movement, which thus become finalities, bestowed with a prestigious genealogy (including certain distortions and *coups de force* which we will look at later, such as mobilizing Stroheim for the ranks of the "realists"). We thus see that all of Bazin's writings metonymically hark back to his global system, and that to adopt his definition of depth of field such as it is (without interrogating it or transforming it) equates more or less to sharing the vision of the history of the cinema which finds itself programmed here: a "history" which is linear (albeit riven with conflict), causal, autonomous and floating, with a tendency toward the accomplishment of a goal – namely, the appropriation of its "truth," such that the "internal necessity" of progress leads forms to succeed and perfect each other. To say, as Leblanc does without any further discussion, that "depth of field perfects the impression of reality still imperfectly produced by the 'classical camera'"[iv] amounts to endorsing an idealist (teleological) model of the history of the cinema. It is not surprising that Bazin would adhere to this model, but Leblanc?

The "history of the cinema" is not a given, it must be constructed.

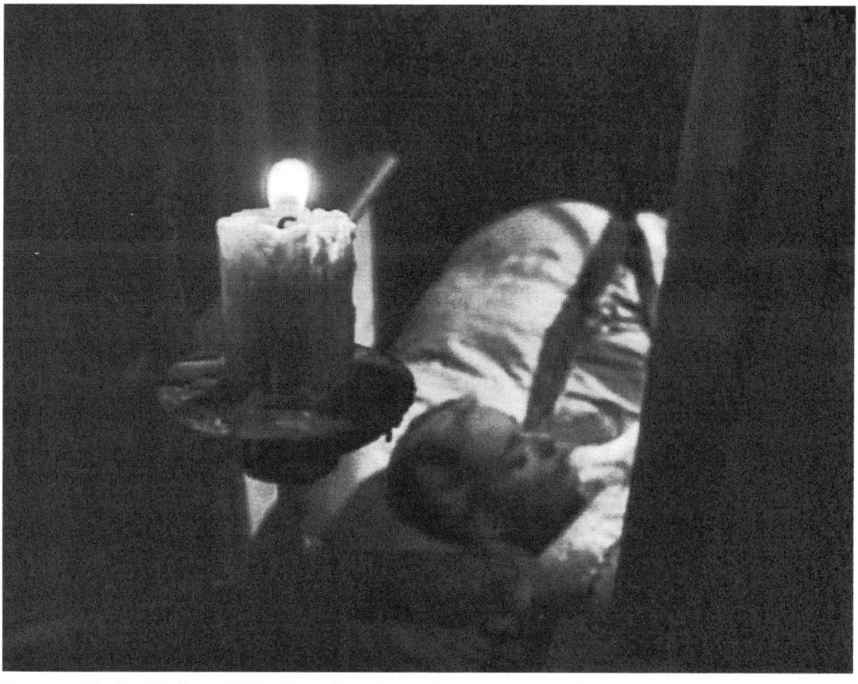

Fig. 19: *Othello* (Welles, 1952): Use of the *hors-champ* and visual composition.

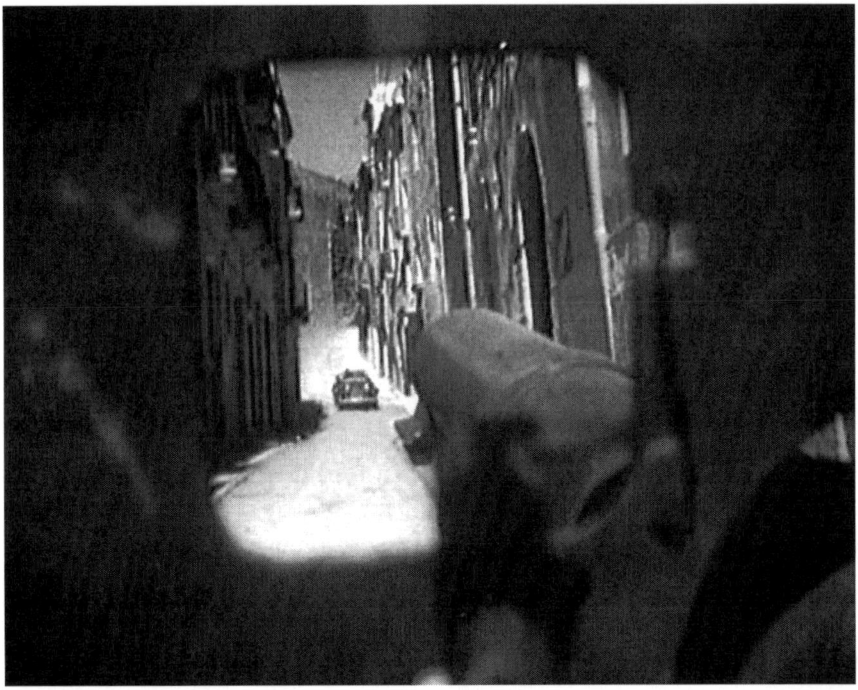

Fig. 20: *L'Espoir* (Malraux, 1939): Reinscription in a pictorial frame of linear perspective as the other space, the space of the other side: that of fiction in the documentary, for example.

For a materialist history of the cinema

It is here that lurks a question that has already been posed,[32] but now it is more forceful, even determinant; since, for Bazin, the reason why depth of field plays such a pivotal role is that – independently even of the "truth" of its nature – he makes it function as an instrument (a grid) for re-reading and re-ordering the "evolution of film language";[33] and since it thus comes to reveal a "meaning" which, subtly pro-

32. "[Bazin's] theoretical method itself installs contradiction as the driving principal of the history of the cinema. [...] We will therefore, in turn, need to examine the account he gives of the 'evolution of film language,' that is, to invert or extend his questions in the direction of the determinations of this 'evolution' – whether technical and aesthetic *or* ideological/economic – since Bazin attempts to constitute an autonomous history of cinematic forms."

33. It is in this extremely important text that Bazin attempts to apply his system to the history of the cinema, carrying out an (interpretative and tendentious) reading which insists on producing it as a "progressive" succession – albeit rife with contradictions and deferrals – of technical and stylistic acquisitions ineluctably leading to the cinema of the innate presence of the "real" in all its "mystery." And it is this very notion of the "evolution of film language" which, more or less, courses through not only Bazin's text, but those written by the majority of film historians, as well as Lebel's work. Such an "evolution" in fact proceeds from a static, non-dialectical point of view, which on the one hand sees historical time as a linear plenitude, and on the other hand only envisages films as

gramming the entire history of the cinema, returns to and insists on the question as to what should be understood by the phrase "history of the cinema," and what is actually understood by this phrase. Now, this is a question that no film theorist and/or historian has truly made the effort to pose, as they have all more or less relied on the commonplace, "obvious" (ideological) conception of history as an accumulative succession of facts and works, a chronological list of objects "already there," which itself does not cease reactivating "the empiricist ideology which, with a few exceptions, overwhelmingly dominates every variety of history (whether it be history in the wide sense, or specialized economic, social or political history, the history of art, literature, philosophy, the sciences, etc.),"[34] and which barely consists in anything other than an arrangement and re-arrangement of, or a tinkering with, a *datum* whose status is never interrogated. For the film historian, as for other historians, the empirical datum is in the position of command: over dates, films, "styles," countries, "influences" and ready-made "relations," as well as historical events in the strict sense, themselves already there, etc. A system of *direct causality* – one that is overly simplistic, elementary, and, above all, convenient because it confirms the illusion of a homogenous, full, continuous historical temporality, that is to say, one that reduces to the greatest possible extent the complex play of uneven determinations, condensing the articulation of manifold temporalities and smoothing out the gradation of deferrals and differences[35] – is unproblematically put into place as a "historical" and "concrete" base, which, for example, acts as a point of departure for Bazin to authorize himself to trace the "evolution of film language," or for Lebel to also evoke, albeit "from the point of view of a materialist reading of cinema," the "history of cinematic forms" and even "the historical progress of forms."[36] If, precisely, what separates us from Bazin is the antagonism between materialism and idealism, then it is not only

---

finished products, as literally transcended by and emptied out (envelopes, shells, sediments, fossils) of the practice which not only made them but outside of the work of which they are not legible. We should thus be wary of the ideological theme of a history of the cinema as an accumulation of films of which the latest to come out (the most recent datum) is by dint of this fact the most "modern" (a theme which we regret to see at work in Lebel).

34. Louis Althusser et al., *Lire Le Capital*, vol. I (Paris: Maspero, 1965), p. 136 [repr. Presses universitaires de France, coll. "Quadrige," 1996. For the English translation, see: *Reading Capital*, trans. Ben Brewster (London: NLB, 1977), p. 109].

35. "It is only possible to give a content to the concept of historical time by defining historical time as the specific form of existence of the social totality under consideration, an existence in which different structural levels of temporality interfere, because of the particular relations of correspondence, non-correspondence, articulation, discrepancy and torsion which obtain between the different 'levels' of the whole in accordance with its general structure." *Lire le Capital, op. cit.* p. 136 [p. 108, translation modified].

36. Jean-Patrick Lebel, *Cinéma et Idéologie*, Éditions sociales, *op. cit.*, p. 199. I cite the following passage as a fine example of conceptual and scriptural indecision: "At a precise stage in the history of cinematic forms, any given form may momentarily crystallize given ideological signifieds within itself, the reaction to which explains the rejection of these forms and the valorization of other procedures or forms, which, once 'utilized' or in turn invested by ideological signifieds, will be re-

on the aesthetic level, or on the level of film theory, that this opposition is marked out, and must be marked out, but primarily on the very question of (film) history, and of the construction of its concept. Assuredly, there would be little scope for the gesture of "rectifying" Bazin's deviations, if this involved denouncing his presuppositions and conclusions, but proceeding, in order to do so, from the same conception of history, and if it thus reaffirmed, if not the modalities, then at least the object of his discourse, unchanged. The *cinema-object*, the object of the *history of cinema*, are not the same for Bazin as they are for us, and it also seems that they are not the same for Lebel as they are for us, since, having not made the effort to theoretically establish his object (cinema and ideology: fine, but what is the value of analyzing this relationship if neither of the two terms posed are theoretically constituted?[37]), Lebel finds himself in the position of having no object apart from that which overtly pre-

---

jected in favor of new forms, or of a return to forms previously rejected and now 'scrubbed clean,' ideologically speaking, by the passage of history."

37. Lebel's book is riddled with the lack of such a theoretical elaboration: what "cinema" is he talking about, and what "ideology," if not those whose "obviousness" dispenses with a theoretical definition: those of commonsense thinking. To justify this lack, Lebel gives the pretext that Marxist theoretical research on the notion of ideology is far from being completed (but does it need to be completed?): a convenient excuse, which allows him to avoid having to advocate for a particular axis of this research, to put off theoretical work to the future, and to shirk even the slightest amount of conceptual work, which any Marxist approach toward the appropriation of the real through knowledge can not relinquish, without renouncing its Marxist character. As for us, we do not intend to evade this question, given that a major part of this study is devoted to it, treating precisely what is at stake in the title "Technique and Ideology": technicist ideology, that which speaks the "discourse-of-the-technicians," and the ideological status of film technique. Let us add that Lebel's non-definition of the objects whose relations he claims to account for leads him to describe them – in contradiction to his own project – as more or less parallel, and not articulated within the same process: on the hand the films, and on the other hand the ideology which "comes to them," phase by phase, and according to the degree of "mastery" possessed by the filmmaker, a veritable ringleader, perfecting his direction to varying degrees of success. Hence, outside of and previous to the intervention of ideology (which is doubtless waiting in the offing for a propitious moment to show its cards...), there is always a portion of the film that is ready, offering itself up to receive ideology or, by contrast, defending itself from ideology... The film/ideology relationship thus becomes a chronological successivity whose naïve schema irresistibly recalls Marx's remarks on Proudhon's schematism: "The production relations of every society form a whole. M. Proudhon considers economic relations as so many social phases, engendering one another, resulting one from the other like the antithesis from the thesis, and realizing in their logical sequence the impersonal reason of humanity. The only drawback to this method is that when he comes to examine a single one of these phases, M. Proudhon can not explain it without having recourse to all the other relations of society; which relations, however, has not yet made his dialectic movement engender. When, after that, M. Proudhon, by means of pure reason, proceeds to give birth to these other phrases, he treats them as if they were newborn babes. He forgets that they are of the same age as the first. [...] How, indeed, could the single logical formula of movement, of sequence, of time, explain the structure of society, in which all relations coexist simultaneously and support one another?" Karl Marx, *The Poverty of Philosophy*, in *The Collected Works of Karl Marx and Friedrich Engels, Vol. VI* (New York: International Publishers, 1975), pp. 166-167.

sents itself to empiricism, and which is also postulated by the empiricist idealism of Bazin.

The study that we intend to make of the variations and "utilizations" of depth of field in a certain number of films would thus be unable to deconstruct the interpretations that Bazin gives of them without being founded on a conception of film history radically different to both his own views, and to the conception established by all of the "histories of the cinema" dominant at present: causal linearity, a claim for a dual autonomy of the "specificity" of the cinema and of the model of idealist histories of "art," a teleological concern, the idea of "progress" or "increasing perfection" not only of technique but of "forms"; in short, the identification, covering over and submersion of film practice with and under the mass of films produced, already there, finished, held to be the only concrete objects, "works" which, even if they vary in terms of how "masterful" they are, have an equal *right* to establish and write this history.

Moreover, they also avoid theoretically constituting the status of depth of field in its complexity: posing the question of the *history* of what, in the beginning of the analysis, is only given as a "simple technico-stylistic procedure," which is "present" and "given" unevenly in the mass of films, and unevenly too in the text of each film, but which analysis may uncover and work on – or transform – on a double level: on the one hand its appearance-disappearance in the history of the cinema, that is, its participation in one or several series of signifying systems and its articulation in the network of determinations constituting them; and, on the other hand, the modalities, conditions and laws of the reinscription effected within films of "non-specifically" cinematic codes (photographic codes, pictorial codes, theatrical codes) whose salience, however great or small, is itself subjected to a history, and functions like film history. It is in the study of the gaps and closures, discrepancies and recoveries, which thus delineate and dynamize the inscription of depth of field into a history that overflows the specific field of the cinema in order to call forth the entirety of representative practices, thereby constituting the cinema itself as a representative practice (which is the sole basis on which a materialist theory of film, and a history of the cinema which avoids being a mere series of films, can be thought), that some responses can be formed to the questions posed by Norbert Massa[v] in *Ciné-Forum*.[38] In order to clearly show how this appeal has become an urgent matter, and not only for us, I choose to cite his article "Note sur l'histoire du cinéma" at length:

> There is still no history of the cinema. All the history books (cf. Brasillach, Ford, as well as Sadoul and Mitry) start from the simple idea that history is what has happened, that the cinema has a past and thus a history, and that the historian

38. A magazine published in Poitiers by the organizing committee of the town's film society (Marc Farina, Jean-Paul François, Norbert Massa, Jean-François Pichard and Jean-Noël Rey), and which has released five issues so far (cf. "Notes, informations, critiques," *Cahiers du cinéma*, no. 230 [1971]).

who is undoubtedly "of his time" must peer into this past with the utmost objectivity.

Objectivity, here, consists in eliminating subjective distortions to the greatest degree possible, and not in constituting an object that would be a genuine object for a science – the history of the cinema.

Now, a scientific history of the cinema is not the rediscovery, the restitution or the reconstitution of a past, even if this is not as a simple description but as an explanation.

To *carry out* the history of the cinema is to properly constitute its history. Histories of the cinema lack both history and the cinema, as both the former and the latter are self-evident for their authors. Everything occurs as if the cinema were present, as if its presence were visible in the mass of films, and as if it were simply a matter of going to take a look at it. This ideology of historical time as linear, oriented, teleological time: the time of presence, of the presence in and of itself of the essence of the cinema in its works, must give way to a scientific history which will have first of all determined its object. At the same time, the "cinema"-object and the object of a history of the cinema must be thought out. Only a theory of the cinema as a signifying practice seems to us to be able to respond to the demands of a real history of the cinema.

In other words, the constitution of a history of the cinema requires the determination of the historical moment where the filmic text appears in a reduplication designating it as such: this is the first scansion of history, and, for theory, it is the point of no return from history as science to the ideology of history.

The determination of the filmic text (i.e., its "reading") in this nodal point of history – in which it is inscribed, necessarily, like every text, like everything, and in which it also *writes history* – allows us to return to the cinema's past and to reread it as history, that is, to rewrite it as history.

[...]

A materialist history of the cinema will need to be eminently critical, that is, recursive, and it will need to constitute the past on the basis of the lines of force of the present. It will also be monumental: far from any egalitarian efforts, it will be traced along certain ridgelines, which will also be the lines of greatest tension in its writing.

A materialist history of the cinema, while attentive to the specificity of the cinema, should only consider its object in its relative autonomy, in relation to other practices. It will therefore also need to determine the specificity of this relationship.

The return of the future tense in these lines reaffirms the lack, today, of such a materialist history of the cinema, and the necessity for it. But this history is also unfeasible without the concept of signifying practice[39] (hence why it is vain to look for a foreshadowing, or even a glimpse, of it in Lebel's work, in spite of the materialist wording in a number of his chapters), or the Althusserian concept of differential historical temporality[40] – that is to say, once more, without a materialist theory of history itself, or the Marxist elaboration of the science of history, historical materialism.

---

39. "Situated within historical materialism and, *at the same time*, within dialectical materialism, the concept of the signifying practice sheds light on the fact that every social practice with an ideological function is a signifier, that the conditions of *signifiance* are within social conditions, and, inversely, that social (ideological) conditions and functions have the production of *signifiance* as their *Other Scene*. Historical materialism thus opens up to what it omits when it becomes dogmatic – that is: dialectical logic. In this perspective, to consider 'the arts,' for example, as *signifying practices* is, it seems to me, the only way to allow them to be envisaged as socio-historical formations, at the same time as designating the specificity of the functioning of meaning and of the subject in them, without reducing them to ideology, but also without alienating them as subjective-pathological experiences (sites of schizophrenization) or aesthetic experiences (sites of the pure imaginary and narcissistic *jouissance*). 'The arts'-as-signifying-practices means that they are *also* all that, as well as something else: sites for historical contradiction and participation in social history." Kristeva, "Pratique analytique, pratique révolutionnaire," *op. cit.* [p. 74].

40. "The model of a *continuous and homogenous time* which takes the place of immediate existence, which is the place of the immediate existence of this continuing presence, can no longer be regarded as the time of history. [...] We can argue from the specific structure of the Marxist whole that it is no longer possible to think the process of the development of the different levels of the whole *in the same historical time*. [...] Each of these particular histories (modes of production, relations of production, the political superstructure, aesthetic production, etc.) is punctuated with particular rhythms and can only be known on condition that we have defined the *concept* of the specificity of its historical temporality and its punctuations (continuous development, revolutions, breaks, etc.). [...] The specificity of these times and histories is therefore differential, since it is based on the differential relations between the different levels within the whole. [...] In the capitalist mode of production, therefore, the time of economic production has absolutely nothing to do with the obviousness of everyday practice's ideological time. [...] It is an invisible time, essentially illegible, as invisible and as opaque as the reality of the total capitalist production process itself. [...] [The construction of this concept of history] has nothing to do with the visible sequence of events recorded by the chronicler. [...] There is nothing in true history which allows it to be read in the ideological continuum of a linear time that need only be punctuated and divided; on the contrary, it has its specific, extremely complex, temporality which is, of course, utterly paradoxical in comparison with the disarming simplicity of ideological pre-judgement. [...] The presence of one level is, so to speak, the absence of another, and this co-existence of a 'presence' and absences is simply the effect of the structure of the whole in its articulated decentricity. [...] We should indeed by relapsing into the ideology of a homogeneous-continuous/self-contemporaneous time if we related the different temporalities I have just discussed to this single, identical time, as so many discontinuities in its continuity; these temporalities would then be thought as the backwardnesses, forwardnesses, survivals or unevennesses of development that can be assigned to this time. [...] On the contrary, we must regard these differences in temporal structure as, *and only as*, so many objective indices of the mode of articulation of the different elements or structures in the general structure of the whole. [...] To speak of differential historical temporality therefore absolutely obliges us to situate this site and to think, in its peculiar articulation, the function of such an element or such a level in the current configuration of the whole." Althusser, *Lire le Capital, op. cit.*, p. 122-133 [pp. 99-106, translation modified].

With the preceding generalities on the conditions of a materialist approach to the history of the cinema in mind, I shall now attempt two axes of application. Firstly, the obligation which seems to bind all "histories of the cinema," circulating at present (which are all embedded in empiricism in terms of their method and in idealism in terms of the conception of cinema that they inscribe and that mobilizes them: what I said above about Bazin is, in fact, just as valid for Mitry and Deslandes) to the practice of systematically, relentlessly cataloguing the long series of "first times," the chain of "inaugurations" of technical procedures and stylistic figures by this or that film. Adopting the empirical object of the "cinema" as their chosen terrain without having made the effort to transform it into a theory, they all exhaust themselves with an obsessive re-marking of the henceforth automatic proliferation of its "births," of an "origin" which can only be scattered. Certainly, this scattering should seriously shake the very notion of "origin," but these histories hasten to conjure and limit its devastating effects by turning it into the justification for their fundamental eclecticism.[41]

The second axis of verification will proceed in the opposite direction. Based on the theoretical implications of the object of depth of field – which this study, let us recall, designates as one of the scenes where the articulations of film technique, alongside its economic and ideological functions, are made to operationally function – its purpose is, on the one hand, to study its historical inscription, that is, very precisely, the variations and unevennesses of the different factors (whether economic, ideological or technological) which determine this inscription, and its modalities, contours and outlines, which explain, here and there, its occasional or systematic usage, its prominence or repression from the scene of filmic signifiers; on the other hand, and at the same time, to study what idealist histories and aesthetic theories (Bazin, Mitry) furnish as "resolutions" to these sharpened conflicts. Let us thus reread this idealist discourse from the point of view of what is primarily repressed in it – the complex of determinations (economy, politics, ideology) pulverizing any "aesthetic evolution of the cinema" (any claim for the complete autonomy of the aesthetic process). This is

41. It will be observed that what has happened to the "history" of the cinema in the strict sense had already happened to its "prehistory," the period of its invention. We noted, in fact (see above, "Birth = deferral"), that the quest for (the myth of) an origin was shattered upon encountering, *en route*, a multiplication of "inaugural inventions," that it exhausted itself by trying to place in a single causal chain (a progression) the countless acts of a dispersed production irreducible to *a single* logic. The histories of the cinema *would have liked* to find their *original, unified* object, one, in sum, that would conform to their concern for autonomy and linearity; but instead they find it to be scattered, contradictory, never entirely there. Refusing to analyze this birth and this history as one of *difference and différance*, they derisorily use their discourse to strive to suture the breaches that precisely preclude this discourse, and make themselves the scene for the contradictions that atomize any scenic singularity. In other words, their discourse produces a phantasmatic object: the "invention of the cinema," where the "cinema," in fact the absence of an object, is imperturbably denied and commented on. It is therefore the method that must be changed: only the Marxist science of history allows us to *think through* the complexity of determinations, the multiplicity of scenes where production is played out, whether it is technical, "aesthetic," or signifying production.

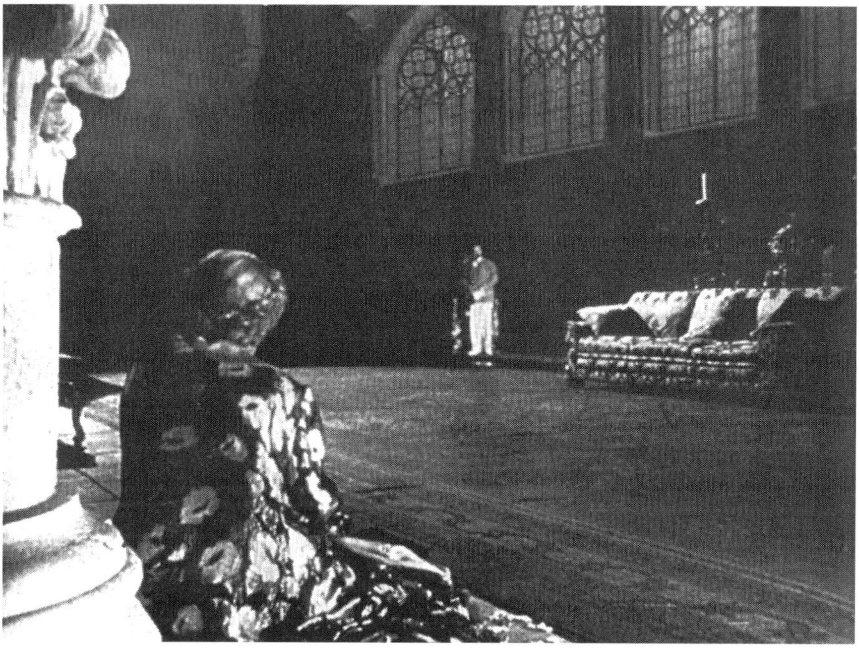

Fig. 21: *Citizen Kane* (Welles, 1941).

[Once again, the very short focal length distances the foreground from the background. The dimensions of this hall appear enormous. An abyss opens up within the gaze. There is no longer any commensurability. The two characters are separated within the very space of the frame, which seems to be a contradiction in terms. The frame can have the function of re-uniting or of separating the bodies within it. Framing, if several bodies are filmed, involves placing them together within the same frame; if it is a single body, it involves placing it in isolation. Here, the "two" united by the frame is divided by the depth of field – and we now see the role it can play in the dramatic depiction of isolation.]

nothing less than the central pillar of idealist criticism, and is the reason why this tendency will hear nothing of these determinations.

On this basis, we will here bring into play the *specific* contradictions of the concept of signifying practice in its application to the cinema. There is, notably, a wholehearted division (an antagonistic contradiction) between the mass of films which, whether "artistic" or not, are all, in idealist discourse, seen as incarnating, no matter how weakly, "the cinema" (the effect of the mass, of the wave, whose aforementioned eclecticism, precisely, is guaranteed), and which, in the last instance, are only infinite modulations, the interminable repetition (whose theoretical exposure is nonetheless unavoidable) of cinematic discourse as communication, representation, univocal signification, that is, the multiple actualizations of the cinema as an ideological apparatus, a vector and diffuser of ideological representations where the subject of ideology (the spectator of the spectacle) can not avoid recognizing himself because it is always a matter of the communication "of A Meaning always present to himself in the presence of the Subject" (this is indeed how the system of "transparency" *functions*: a denial of the work of differences, of work as difference, of meaning as work, in order to postulate meaning as an intersubjective exchange: the sign as currency) – a division, I said, between these films and the films (or practices) which, following on from Julia Kristeva,[42] we could call *films of rupture*, because the work in the signifier modifies the status of their meaning. If "this work is always a surplus exceeding the rules of communicative discourse,"[43] if it thus makes signification function on "the other scene of *signifiance*," and of the production of meaning (rather than the re-presentation of A Meaning), and if, in its capacity as work, it breaks with "the ideology of signification," insofar as the latter "censors the problematic of work," it thus constitutes this "text," on whose basis the ideological inscription of these films can be reformulated and re-founded, giving rise to *another cinema-object*, which would in no way be assigned a single, unswerving ideological function (speaking, representing, specularizing, spectacularizing, distracting without changing, ceaselessly reiterating),[44] but which, as a signifying practice, is, and re-inscribes in ideology, the "network of differences which mark and/or join the mutations of historical blocks."[45] Theorizing this new cinema-object – the "cine-signifier"[vi] – will also entail definitively dismissing the linear (literary) model of the "histories of the cinema." More precisely, it will involve:

> Smashing the conceptual mechanism which produces a historical linearity, and reading a *stratified history*: with a discontinuous, recursive, dialectical temporality, irreducible to a singular meaning, but made up of types of *signifying practices* whose plural series remains without origin or endpoint. Another history will thus be profiled, one which subtends linear history; the recursively stratified history of *signifiances*, of which communicative language and subjacent ideology (sociological, historicist or subjectivist) only represents the superficial facet. The text plays

---

42. Cf. Julia Kristeva, *Sémeiotikè: recherches pour une sémanalyse* (Paris: Seuil, 1969); "Littérature, sémiotique, marxisme," interview with Christine Glucksmann and Jean Peytard, in *La Nouvelle Critique*, no. 38 (November 1970); as well as "Pratique analytique, pratique révolutionnaire," *op. cit.*

43. Kristeva, *Sémeiotikè*, *op. cit.*, p. 16.

44. "The dialectical distinction signifier/ideology is all the more important when it is a matter of theorizing a concrete signifying practice – for example, the cinema. To substitute ideology for the signifier is, in this case, not only a theoretical error, but it also leads to a blockage of the *work* specific to the cinema, which comes to be replaced by discourses on its ideological *function*" (Kristeva, "Pratique analytique, pratique révolutionnaire," *op. cit.*, p. 72). It seems that this remark, which appeared in *Cinéthique*, no. 9/10, is also *aimed* at *Cinéthique*, no. 9-10, where the conflation of the signifier with ideology takes the form of a law. We can be assured that, on this precise point, our position is not new, as a re-reading of the programmatic text "Cinema/Ideology/Criticism" (*Cahiers du cinéma*, no. 216 [October 1969], p. 13, b, with a paragraph which equally emphasizes the importance of "films of rupture") attests [cf. infra, p. 256].

45. Kristeva, *Sémeiotikè*, *op. cit.*, p. 11.

> this role in every present-day society: it is unconsciously demanded it of it, it is forbidden to it or rendered *practically* difficult.[46]

Whatever the difficulties of this work may be (and they are considerable), it is no longer possible to keep film history and film theory hermetically sealed from one another. The new cinema-object displaces the classifications and orders established at various times by historians and aesthetic theorists, and it is in this displacement that it comes to be known and read, in the reformation of relations among signifying practices, and between these signifying practices and the social totality. Its theory does likewise, as, in order to be made, it propels this disturbance, and is constantly informed, produced and reshaped by it. A little of this dialectic is thus put into play here, at the modest level of some of the elements of film technique in which are produced, perhaps more legibly than elsewhere, the confluences and conflicts of economic pressures, forms of ideological obfuscation (masking/recuperation), scientific knowledge, relations of production, and the work of signification, that is, the emergence of *signifiance* (which is never abolished even when it is repressed or "prohibited"). In short, film technique is a double scene of *practice* and *signifying*.

"For the first time..."

When studying the existing "histories of the cinema" – not only with respect to the facts recounted, the accuracy of recollections, the number and precision of references (points on which the polemics between the authors of these "histories" are exclusively focused), but also with respect to their writing system, their rhetoric, the terminology governing them, the notions which program them and of which they are the scene – the considerable frequency with which the *fixed syntagm* "for the first time..." recurs can be read as a symptom. Ineluctably, it seems, the decisive operation of these "histories" is to evoke and give an overview of the greatest possible number of technical, stylistic and formal innovations, each one of which is presented (and sought out) as the initiation of a succession of aesthetic developments (the "progress" of a "language") whose finality, endpoint or perfection is the cinema such as it is practiced at the moment when each historian writes its history. In other words, for these historians it is the practice of contemporary cinema that, through an effect of inversion or misrecognition proper to ideological inscription, comes to program, determine and originate, as the veritable source, their search for the "sources" of this practice, for the "origins" of that which, here and now, is hypostasized as the "reality" of the cinema, as the truth of this practice, since they are contemporary to it, since they are implicated in it and since their own practice is necessarily articulated with it. It is thus in the name of a momentary, punctual film practice, which is illusorily

46. *Ibid.*, p. 13.

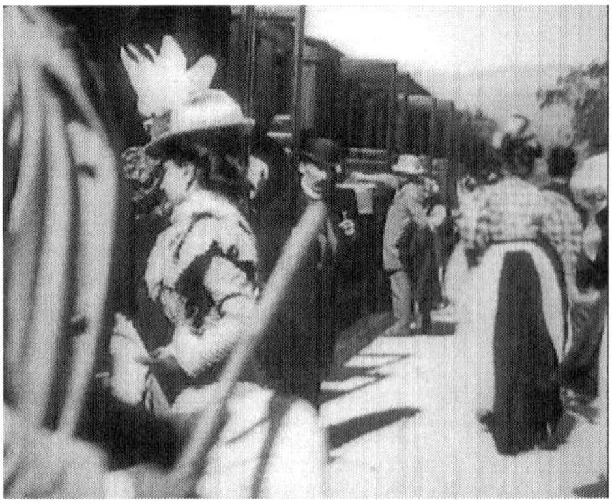

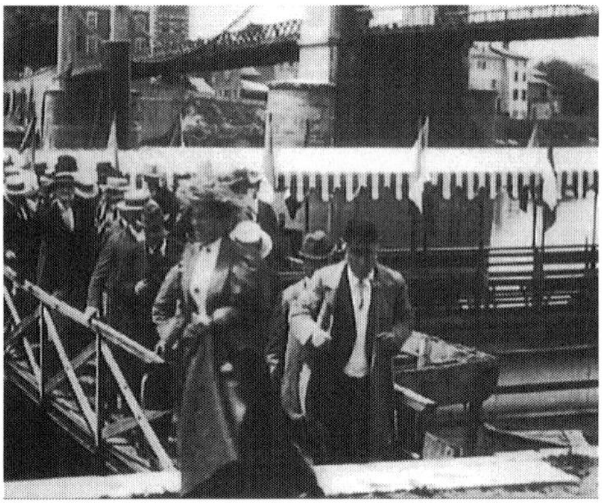

Figs. 22 and 23: Two stills from Louis Lumière films (above: *L'Arrivée d'un train à La Ciotat*, 1895): A "primitive" depth of field. That is, one that was produced and regulated outside of any special manipulation by the sole fact of the disposition to make the primitive cinematic lens conform with the "normal vision of the human eye." But "already," for *L'Arrivée d'un train*, the framing, camera angles and "*mise en scène*" are overtly determined by the depth of field that allows for the train to arrive at the station, the passengers to wait for it and the spectators to feel fright at and admiration for it. Hence, as "innocent" as it seems (because it is "automatic" and "spontaneous"), this inscription of depth also marks its ideological presuppositions and the *calculations* that determine it.

[The second still (added for the new edition), *L'Arrivée des congressistes à Neuilly-sur-Saône* (1895), shows, ironically, photographers passing in front of the Lumière camera and casually saluting the cinema, which will end up contesting their power over "reality." Depth of field here seizes an entire staging in depth of filmed bodies.

The movement of those passing close to the camera produces a "blurry," "out of focus" image: a "reality effect" which, as it happens, is due principally to the shutter speed. The artifact thus participates in the realist effect assured by depth of field, which even defines the most distant components of the scene. We should also admire the composition of the frame, which, as is often the case in the Lumières' work, uses depth to articulate several planes of action.]

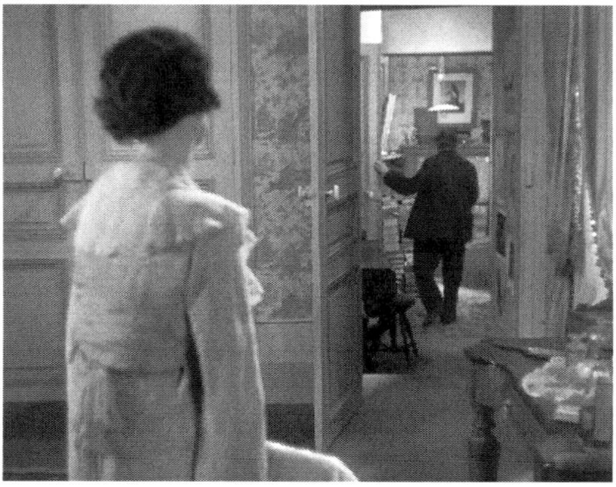

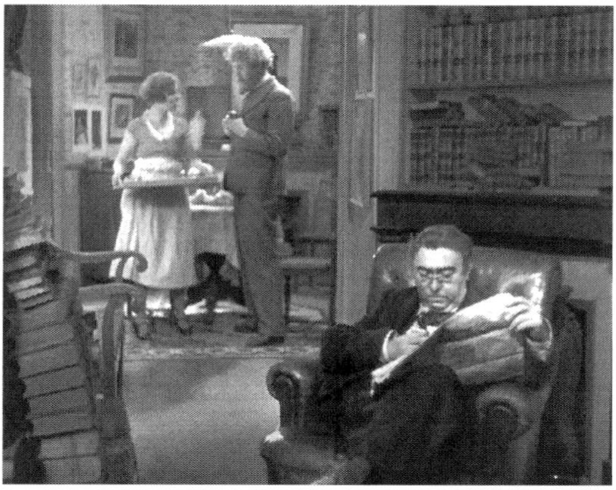

Figs. 24 and 25: Two stills from Jean Renoir (*Boudu sauvé des eaux*, 1932): A "domestic" depth of field. To a significant extent, the dramatic fabric of the film is constructed on the basis of the relationship between rooms, and the relationship between the shots of the rooms. For Bazin ("The Evolution of Film Language"), this re-appropriation by Renoir of a technical device for consciously narrative purposes acts as a gauge of the cinema's "realist vocation." Note that the depth of field shots undeniably chart the realist nature of the space of a *set*; filmed in realist fashion, this space functions not least due to its *principal* determination – that is, the fact that it is the scene of a drama. Far from depth of field functioning, as Bazin would have us believe, in an autonomous fashion as the "set," or the "reality of a set," this depth definitively centers the set as a dramatic space, and strips it of any other specificity (whether realist, naturalist or documentary), and of any function other than that of performing. It becomes, precisely, a space for the play of gazes: the gaze of Madame Lestingois (above) nabbing her husband from behind while he creeps through the doorway; and the gaze of the spectator (below), complicit in an intimate conversation and judging (more than witnessing) the exterritoriality of Lestingois, as well as the skill of the director, able to guide the trajectory of the gaze without encountering any opposition. It is not the "real" or the "world" in which the film is embedded that is "realist" here, but rather the conscious awareness of the place of the spectator within the figuration, and the solicitation of its role.

held to be the knowledge of the cinema-object, that the historian will itemize the mass of precursory signs of this practice, and it is thus in order to authenticate the moment of a practice in which the historian himself has a stake, or to *legitimize* a certain *lived experience*, which he relates *to the past*, to ancient times (on the model of the "In the beginning was..." common to all myths of origin, religions and cultures), to the prehistory and distant history of the cinema, the greatest possible number of characteristic traits of this practice today, which, finding their origin (their foundation: their law) in this manner, are all constituted in a chain with a beginning, a development and an endpoint, that is to say, with a *logic* and history that are *autonomous*, bracketed off from the determinations of the social totality. The itemization and multiplication of origins thus act as *proofs* of this autonomy: through the imperative nature of the statement "for the first time," they verify the *validity* of all the "following times," that is, precisely, the traits present in the current moment of film practice, in the "this time." The "first time" simultaneously valorizes, inscribes, encompasses, and bears with it all the other times. The eclectic nature of contemporary cinema (its apparent *de jure* equality and "value," its "diversity," its "wealth") comes to be absolved by the equally eclectic nature of its origins (there is no form which does not have its own mould, its "original" somewhere in the beginnings of the cinema), and this is all the more easily achieved because the latter is rigorously the carbon copy, the retrospective projection of the former.

Thus it is indeed an ideological discourse on (notably) the ideological place of film technique that the fixed syntagm "for the first time" does not cease to hold.

Let us return, in order to insist on its importance, to the following point: the necessity of radically distinguishing the two historical approaches confronted here, which, while being systematically opposed to each other throughout this text, nonetheless seem to have in common the fact that they both constitute the historic scene of the cinema on the basis of, and in line with, its present scene. The first is characterized by its retrospective eclecticism: incapable of being theoretically focused, and of sifting out, from the mass of traits which synchronically present themselves as being constitutive of the "cinema," the principal contradictions (articulated with the contradictions of the social scene, productive forces and relations of production) from the surface effects (the secondary contradictions functioning as both derivation and occultation), and the textual lines of force from the effects of aesthetic surplus-value, it thus receives *en bloc*, gathers together and unifies (places on the same level) under the label "cinema" everything that empirically presents itself as such, and undertakes – from among this jumble of notations and signals, questioning the pertinence of which is repressed – to historically reveal and enumerate the cinema's "birth certificates." The very recording of these historical inscriptions takes on the role of an authenticating document, and is not only the condition but also the justification of their existence today. The historical scene is thus only the duplicate, the certified copy of the contemporary scene. The second approach – evoked earlier as being "eminently critical, that is, recursive" and constituting "the past on the basis of the lines of force of the present" – proceeds in a completely different manner. Basing itself on the clarification of the principal contradictions of the current state of film practice, it is concerned with reprising and replaying the history of the cinema as (and on) the scene of its principal determinations: returning to the foreground the forces that the first approach has the effect/function of drowning in the mass of films. This second approach is therefore unthinkable outside of the incessant intervention of theory on the historical scene – with the latter no longer limited to the accumulation of "historical facts" – but breaks out on several levels where the articulations, interactions and contradictions of the productive processes are in play.

We find the *a contrario* demonstration of this necessity to keep theory and history together in the work of Mitry, which is scholastically divided into a "history of the cinema"[47] on the one hand and an "aesthetics and psychology of the cinema" on the other. Of course, these two sections can only function with reference to one another, but as the status of these references, that is, the definition of the relationship between history and theory, is never determined, they are constituted on the principle of an endless game of *back and forth* [*chassé-croisé*], with history and aesthetics lobbing the ball of the final instance back to each other at each moment of difficulty.

Symptomatic of such a never-ending pursuit in the ideological series of "first times" is, for example, the impossibility of once and for all establishing the "first close-up":

> If what we mean by *close-up* is the simple effect of magnification, then its use is as old as cinema itself. The "big heads" [*grosses têtes*], as they were then called, suddenly appearing in the midst of a uniform sequence of long shots, had been used by Méliès in his films around 1901, and the alarm bell in *The Life of an American Fireman* is, without doubt, the first close-up of an object recorded on film. The big heads, however, whose sudden appearance created an effect of surprise, were more associated with the "animated portrait" than with film expression. Only with montage, as we have seen, did shots assume a meaning relative to each other [*sic, anything else would have been a shock – JLC*]. These shots – which were almost all discovered, tried out, and applied by Griffith between 1909 and 1910 in innumerable short films – only became connected, organized and structured into a coherent whole from 1911 or 1912 onward. Thus to say that Griffith was the first to use close-ups does not mean that this magnification effect had not been used before him, merely that he was the first to turn them into a means of expression, elevating them to the level of *signs*. There is no evidence in any film (even Griffith's) before 1911 of the use of the close-up for any purpose other than description.

47. Jean Mitry, *Histoire du cinéma*, vol. I and II (Paris: Éditions universitaires, 1967-1969) [repr. 1995].

> The close-up as we know it [*? – JLC*] was to make its debut as late as 1913, in *Judith of Bethulia*.[48]

This passage alone already elicits several questions:

- What is the pertinence of the hierarchy implied by Mitry between "big heads creating an effect of surprise," "close-up of an object," "first shot used for the purpose of description" and finally "magnification effects elevated to the level of *signs*"?
- If it is a question of deciding what the "first close-up" is, why let criteria of "content" (that is, the role of these close-ups in the production of meaning) intervene, and why oppose close-ups that are only "descriptive" to those that are "expressive" (to the extent that it is difficult to maintain that descriptive close-ups – such as the fire alarm – are totally deprived of dramatic effects, denoting without connoting[49])? Either what matters is the scale of the shot, or, if its plastic or dramatic value is also important, would it not be necessary to renounce the attempt to discern a "first close-up"?
- Finally, what is to be understood by "the close-up as we know it"? The least that we can say is that "we" do not "know" one kind, one variety of close-up, but a thousand, an infinite number of them, including, of course, the "big heads" still in use and the "shots used for the purposes of description."

Nothing, therefore, authorizes Mitry to pertinently oppose the "simple effect of magnification" to the "means of expression elevated to the level of signs," because the close-up-as-sign perforce gives rise to a "magnification effect" (otherwise there is no close-up) and because any "magnification effect" can also serve as a "sign" and incorporate an "expression." Nothing, apart from the theoretical lack which leads him to preserve common usage ("as we know it") and to consider a certain normality of the close-up at the moment at which he writes to be the law and truth, since it constitutes an empirical tool for contemporary films, a tool for which Griffith serves as a guarantor by way of his quality as an "experimenter" and by way of his aesthetic,

48. Mitry, *Esthétique et psychologie du cinéma*, vol. I, *op. cit.*, p. 162-163 [pp. 69-70].

49. Which, by the way, in other passages in both the *Aesthetics* and the *History*, Mitry does not refrain from noting: "For the first time, a close-up (showing the alarm bell in a fire station) assumed dramatic significance. It was no longer the simple enlargement of a detail but the dramatic emphasis of an object which was the key to the resolution of the drama." (*Esthétique et psychologie du cinéma*, vol. I, p. 274 [p. 94]). This formula is repeated almost word for word in his *History* (*op. cit.*, vol. I, p. 235): "The close-up of the alarm bell, although shown in isolation, is no longer the simple magnification of a detail but the valorization of an object upon which the resolution of the drama depends." Between these two remarks and the passage analyzed above, such a contradiction should not be read as an "error" but as the logic of his system: for the needs of a new "first time," every new "first close-up" (those of Griffith, for example) relegates its predecessor to a lower rung on the ladder.

rather than historical, primacy. If we restrict ourselves to a single reference, the close-ups of Hollywood stars do not "descend" from the close-ups of Griffith's actors, any more than the latter "descend" from the "animated portraits" of Demenÿ (1891): we know that they are due to the contractual imperatives of the star system, with their number and quality ordered before shooting takes place, and the narrative structure of the film programmed around this stipulation. There is no kinship between the close-ups of 1913 and those of 1960 that would guarantee their equivalence, because the pertinent element of the opposition is not the parameter of the size of the shots, but the network of differences of determination between two moments of film practice, differences which, precisely, prohibit the constitution of an ahistorical chain of "close-ups" (or tracking shots, etc.), or, more literally, their being placed on the same level [*plan*]. To thus establish the "close-up as we know it" is akin to effacing the scene of contradictions where the conditions of cinematic *signifiance* function and replacing it with an autonomous series of technical procedures which, once "invented," systematized and enthroned by a pioneer (whose practice, by this very fact, perforce has nothing to do with those of earlier filmmakers) would be of the same nature that they were from the very start. Available once and for all, they are thus conceived of as universally and timelessly utilizable, abstract moulds without any modification in their nature, function or meaning (we can recognize here the consensus that backs up Lebel's technicist discourse).

Here the necessary anteriority of a theoretical definition of the "close-up" with respect to the question of its first historical appearance ("if by 'close-up' we understand [...] the close-up as we know it") is plain to see: bereft of the work of definition within our historical interrogation, we would remain, like Mitry, beholden to an empirical understanding of the close-up, which opens up to a notional vagueness and is incapable of abstract conceptual rigor, since it claims to encompass and incorporate all close-ups through the sole means of a description of their empirical existence in pre-existing films, even though they are all necessarily different to one another. To use this highly problematic, because extremely vast, "close-up as we know it" as a point of departure for establishing the "first" historical inscription of the close-up can only lead to the discovery of *more* than one of them – and, indeed, to the discovery of as many of them as one wishes (in line with his initial catch-all approach) – indeed, as many close-ups "as," in the empirical sense, we "know" them. What Mitry's text says, without its author knowing it (otherwise his entire enterprise of determining "first times" would founder), is that as long as the concept of the close-up has not been constructed there can be no "first close-up," because all close-ups, in some way, are "first";[50] that it is the very collapse of the "notion" of the close-up supported by him

50. Mitry is thus constrained by his system to mention ever new particularizations of the "first close-up." For example: "Smith was also the first to combine lighting effects with his close-ups" (*Histoire du cinéma*, vol. I, *op. cit.*, p. 227).

that he inscribes. We are thus led to interrogate, without posing any other questions, this "notion" of the close-up such as it circulates, by all rights, in technical and critical discourse, presenting itself as a "linguistic unit," even though no "close-up" is inscribed as such in filmic texts, and even though they are all not only akin to a network of signifiers, a complex set, but that they are furthermore held within signifying chains which simultaneously encompass them and traverse them, which structure them. If, for example, when he opposes the "close-up-as-simple effect of magnification" to the "close-up-as-sign," Mitry intends to claim that Griffith's close-ups have a more essential function in the production of meaning than those of Méliès were able to have (which remains to be proved), one can respond that it is the entire process of the production of meaning which has a different status in Griffith's work to that which it has in Méliès, and that to have isolated within it the "notion" of the close-up in order to bring into play textual differences rather than the parameter of the size of the shot in fact leads to an aporia. After all, either a close-up is always a close-up, or a close-up consists of its insertion into a signifying process, and the close-up is thus no longer pertinently isolatable, with the "notion" of it not producing any knowledge as to its status in the functioning of the cinema. As an operative indication in the technical practice of film production, the "notion" of the close-up thus appears to be thoughtlessly (but "naturally") deported from this field to the field of film criticism and theory, where it acts as a *false abstraction*. Is it not, indeed, its very commodity (its naturalization in technico-critical language) that masks the work of signification to a far greater extent than producing knowledge about it? By invoking, for example, the scale of the "size of shots"[51] as a syntactic category of "film language," does technico-critical discourse produce anything other than a formalist grid aimed at covering over, immobilizing and, in the end, evacuating the problematic of signifying production, or rather, carefully maintaining a mystery shrouding the mechanisms of this production, which is propitious for preserving the autonomy (the magical power) of technique?

From this point of view, it would be necessary to comb through Mitry's whole text (which is doubtless the most exemplary to the extent that it attempts, and fails, to articulate aesthetics with history) in order to systematically study the status, in the chain of "first times," of each of the basic terms of this technical discourse: "shots," "tracking shots," "pans," "sets," "montage" (instructive, for example, is the serialized ordering of "first films" instating a "narrative continuity" through montage), etc. Because it needs to be marked at all costs with a stamp of *origin*, technical terminology

51. Cf., on this point, "'Réalité' de la dénotation" by Pascal Bonitzer, *Cahiers du cinéma*, no. 229 (1971), pp. 39-41, specifically note 1 ["'Reality' of Denotation," trans. Lindley Hanlon, in *Cahiers du cinéma, 1969-1972*, *op. cit.*, pp. 248-253].

avows its incapacity to be useful as such (in terms of its most common usage: institutional) in the field of criticism and theory.[52]

---

52. Beyond the preceding statements on the "close-up, we will limit ourselves to the relatively simple example of the "first tracking shot," leaving open to a later work the important problematic of the "first" case of montage. We can read in the *Histoire du cinéma* (vol. I, p. 113): "Promio, profiting from a holiday in Italy, had the idea of placing his camera in a gondola. The shots taken were 'stationary,' as was standard practice up to 1909, but the motion of the gondola recorded wide panoramic views in such a fashion that *Le Grand Canal à Venise* (1897) was the first 'tracking shot' ever made. Proud of his discovery, Promio subsequently attached his camera to a variety of mobile elements, such as a railway carriage, the prow of a transatlantic ocean liner and the Mont-Blanc cable-car." His *Esthétique et psychologie*, meanwhile, responds to this passage with the following (vol. I, p. 151): "The traveling (or *tracking*) shot can mean several different things. It describes a 'moving' shot, i.e., one which records the countryside from a moving train, car, ski lift, whatever. The camera remains in a fixed position and moves with the vehicle on which it is fixed. This type of tracking shot is as old as cinema itself (Alexander Promio's *Le Grand Canal à Venise*, for instance, shot in 1899 [*sic* – *JLC*]. The term is used more generally, however, to describe the 'dollying' movement of the camera, mounted on a platform which moves on rails or rubber wheels. This allows the camera, for instance, to travel alongside two characters walking down a road; the camera's movement, however, is independent of the movement of the characters. In other words, it may move either in front of them or let them catch up so they are more tightly framed or, inversely, follow them and catch them up. Or else it may follow them laterally. The first director to use this kind of tracking shot – moving with the actors' movements – was Griffith in 1909. A more recent technique is the fixed-circle tracking shot, moving among static characters (in a restaurant or the stalls of a theater, for instance), in which the camera captures the behavior of some of the characters in the drama or 'picks out' the movements of one of them. It was used for the first time by Murnau in *Der letzte Mann* in 1925 [translation modified]." Returning to the *Histoire du cinéma*, however, we find a rather contradictory "rectification" (p. 407): "In *The Massacre* (Griffith, 1912), for the first time in the world, great *descriptive* tracking shots follow the characters, situate the locations, present the events (with a camera mounted on a cart three years before Pastrone's famous '*carello*')." The confusion is ultimately compounded with the note appended to this last passage: "In his *Histoire générale du cinéma* (Denoël, vol. III, p. 83) Georges Sadoul disputes the originality of these tracking shots. 'Must we recall,' he notes at the bottom of the page, 'that the first known examples of the tracking shot predate *The Massacre* by more than ten years?' We would like to know which tracking shots he is referring to. Obviously, it is *Le Grand Canal à Venise*. But is this a tracking shot? [...] A static shot taken from a mobile element – a train, a car or any other vehicle – and merely recording the landscape passing by *is not*, in the strict sense of the term, a tracking shot. No more than the forward movement of the camera toward a black backdrop in *L'Homme à la tête de caoutchouc*, which was made in order to film the enlargement, and not the approach, of the head in question. Apart from these examples and their analogues (*Attaque du grand rapide*, etc.), there is no tracking shot in any film whatsoever before 1912, the first having been attempted, as we noted earlier, in *The Sands of Dee* (Griffith, 1912)." Without worrying ourselves about the discrepancy between dates (which is nonetheless decisive for a historian who claims that he can discern "first times" – does this "descriptive tracking shot following characters" date from 1909 or, "for the first time in the world" from 1912?), let us retain the contradictions pertaining to the very definition of the procedure of the "tracking shot." We will hence be astonished by the radical distinction established by Mitry between a "stationary camera mounted on a mobile element" and a camera "carted" by a "platform mounted on rails or wheels": certainly, the mobile element supporting the camera is not of the same order, but in both cases the latter moves in identical fashion, and the shot produced by this movement is of the same type, whether the movement is due to a gondola, a train, a chariot, etc. Whatever the mobile support carrying it may be, the camera is not "stationary" and the image that it records is defined as a shot

In fact, this fetishization of the "first time" (beyond its ideological connotations: cult of the exploit, of the unique; everything that attaches itself in bourgeois ideology to the origin and the original, as a manifestation of primacy and purity, etc.) aims, in the case of technical devices, to keep them at a remove from determinations, that is, from the processes in which they find themselves captured, and to present the totality of them, eternally, as a linear, chronological and logical succession, because one could have marked the appearance of each one of them *outside of* any problematic of signifying production (that is, outside of the ideologies and economies in which this production is articulated), and outside of the cultural codes of the signifying system which governed its status in the very film where it emerged "for the first time" (emergence [*émergement*] = marginalization [*émargement*], a placing into the margins of a signature which appropriates and reduces to itself the entire signifying process. Let us take an example from Mitry: "*Mary Jane's Mishap* [*G.A. Smith, 1902 - JLC*]: for the first time the idea of continuity in the cinema"[vii]). Yet it is indeed to the separation made by the histories and aesthetic analyses of the cinema between technical processes and signifying processes that Lebel (whether he is aware of it or not) remains beholden, in order to make a claim for the autonomy of technique, its everlasting signifying availability. From the moment we read a technical procedure "for itself" ("the first tracking shot in the history of the cinema") by cutting it off from the signifying practice of which it is not only one of the factors but also one of the *effects* (not only a "form" that "acquires" or "confers" meaning, but one that is already itself a meaning, a signifier acting as a signified on the other scene of the film, its "outside": history, economics, ideology), we transform it into an empirical, ahistorical object which, subject to minor adjustments (technical refinement, etc.) will stray from film to film, always-already there, always identical to itself ("a close-up of a boss and a close-up of a worker are both the same close-up"), in spite of and in order to *mask* the system of differences in which it is necessarily inscribed; that is to say, both the signifying contradictions between one fiction and another, between one practice and

---

in motion. The care for technical precision that founds this distinction (train/camera dolly) is thus unable to alone guarantee the slightest technical and/or stylistic difference between takes brought about by one or the other techniques, both of which are mobile. In this opposition, therefore, Mitry brings in operative determinants other than those that are specifically technical: for example, the fact that in *Le Grand Canal* there is neither a fictional story nor characters, which do have a role in Griffith's films. Once more (cf. above on the "close-up"), the pertinent criteria for siding with the primacy of technique are not technical, a fact which both manifests the conceptual insufficiency of technical terms and the dependence of technical procedures on the signifying chains and narrative codes in which they take part. Let us remark once more how specious the distinction operated between a tracking shot that "approaches" and one that "magnifies" is: every forward tracking shot involves both the camera approaching its subject and the subject becoming larger within the frame. We thus see no reason why *L'Homme à la tête de caoutchouc* should not (also) be credited with a "first tracking shot," unless, once again, Mitry implicitly and probably unwittingly has allowed the context of the production of this tracking shot to intervene – namely, the fact that it was a trick effect in Méliès, and a narrative effect in Griffith.

another, and the contradictions of interests and ideologies in which the cinema is practiced and whose traces it bears, for better or worse. On this "common basis" of historical, critical and aesthetic discourses, a technical scene is erected which dominates the scene of *signifiance* – because "a close-up is always a close-up" – as well as the scene of history, because "a close-up from *Jeanne d'Arc* refers back, just as a close-up from *Battleship Potemkin,* to the 'first close-up in the history of the cinema'."[viii] In other words: that very discourse which proclaims the signifying availability of technique, its ideological "neutrality," has itself begun to dissociate technique from signifying production. Starting out as *formalist,* it can not find anything in its path other than "formal" techniques, and "universal," "neutral" forms.

III. "Primitive" Depth of Field

It is no more possible to postulate a continuous chain (or kinship) of "depth of field shots" across the "history of the cinema" than it is to do so for the "close-up." And the history of this technical device, no more than that of the "close-up" (or any other term of practice or technical metalanguage), is not possible without bringing into play a set of determinations that are *non-exclusively technical*. Rather, they are economic and ideological determinations. Hence, they spill out over the specific field of the cinematic, reworking it through a series of supplements, making it function on other scenes, and making other scenes inscribe themselves on its own scene; they burst asunder the fiction of an autonomous history of the cinema (of its "styles and techniques"); they operate the complex articulation of this particular field and history with other fields and histories; and they thus allow us to take into account, for the particular technical procedure that is depth of field, its regulation of the functions – that is to say, the *meanings* – that it assumes in the filmic signifying practice by codes which are not necessarily cinematic (in this case: pictorial, theatrical and photographic codes), and to take into account the (economic/ideological) forces which, whether positively or negatively, exert pressure on the inscription of this regulation and these codes.

In order for historian-aestheticians like Mitry, and theorists like Bazin, to allow themselves to be caught by the lure of a determination of cinematic writing and the evolution of film language through the progress of technology (the development and perfection of the cinema's means), that is to say, the lure of a technical "treasure trove" which filmmakers could "freely" pillage, in accord with the writing effects they desired, or even of an "availability" of the technical procedures whereby they are held in a zone independent of systems of meaning (histories, codes, ideologies) and "ready" to intervene in signifying production, it was actually necessary for the entirety of the technical apparatus of the cinema to appear to them as so "natural," so "self-evident," that the question of its utility and its destination (what use it is) should be totally covered over by the question of its utilization (how to use it). This naturalization of technical metalanguage into critical metalanguage, this "automatic," unthinking identification of devices and technical gestures with the "figures" of "film language" (or what Christian Metz more rigorously calls "the minimal signifying units

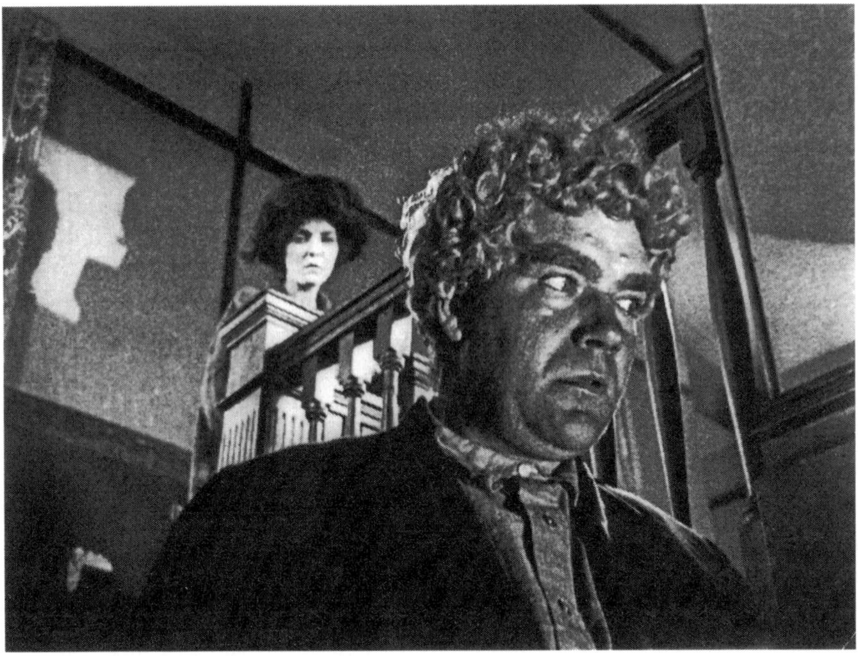

Fig. 26: *Greed* (Stroheim, 1924). The discontinuity of shots, contradiction of vanishing lines, and three-dimensional effects through the play of light and shadow all indicate the abuse present in Bazin's attempt to induct Stroheim into the camp of the "realists" (as opposed to the montage specialists, the "manipulators"). It is by no means necessary to wait for *Citizen Kane* in order to see depth of field dramatically working and being worked on, with its codes inscribed and the distorted space that it produces in play.

proper to cinematic codes"[1]) is precisely what must be the principal problem for a materialist theory of the cinema that is dissatisfied with "obvious truths" and unwilling to remain at the level of empiricism. A semiology of cinematic "figures" that would avoid interrogating the pertinence of the terms which, "consecrated by usage," designate these "figures," and that would not unravel the codes and historical/ideological strata of these "figure-terms" – in short, one that would give credence to the idea that "film language" is one and the same as technical metalanguage, itself homologous to critical metalanguage – would end up lacking the differential specificity of these three levels, and the interaction of their discrepancies and contradictions.[i] It is

1. Christian Metz, *Langage et cinéma* (Paris: Larousse, 1971 [repr. Paris: Albatros, 1992], and notably the chapter "Tendance pansémique de certaines figures" (pp. 98-103) [*Language and Cinema*, trans. Donna Jean Umiker-Sebeok (The Hague: Mouton, 1974), "The Pansemic Tendency of Certain Figures," pp. 131-137. The quote appears on p. 132].

in this direction that Christian Metz's latest work is headed,[2] and such an unraveling is also carried out in Pascal Bonitzer's recent texts (cf. "'Réalité' de la dénotation," *Cahiers*, no. 229; "Le Gros Orteil," *Cahiers*, no. 232 and "Fétichisme du plan," *Cahiers*, no. 233). It is thus on this question (and by offering a commentary on certain of Metz's analyses) that, in the next section, I will intervene in a more detailed fashion, because it does indeed seem that the idea – at present still quite dominant (and whose dominance Lebel's book strives to prolong) – of the signifying indifference (the "availability") of technique is anchored in this "naturalized," unthinking conflation of "film language" with technical metalanguage and of the latter with critical metalanguage. By insisting on banishing technical practice from systems of meaning, technicist ideology presents it as the cause that produces meaning effects in the filmic text, and not as the product, or as the effect of meaning in signifying systems, and the histories and ideologies that determine it. In my opinion, this technicist ideology draws its core strength of conviction from the (remotely) "scientific" character of those technical practices used to produce a film, a character which has acted within film criticism as the *guarantee* of the intrinsic validity of these practices, and which has favored the unquestioning, unmodified importation of their basic terms into critical metalanguage.

We must indeed speak of a "strength of conviction," of "naturalization" (and, as a corollary, of the blindness of these theorists), given that, for example, Mitry – who highlights the fact that depth of field, almost invariably used in the earliest years of the cinema, disappears (apart from some notable exceptions: such as certain of Renoir's films) from the scene of filmic signifiers for a good 20 years – is only able to explain this banishment through strictly technical motives, and thus places technique in the position of final authority, constituting a closed and autonomous circuit where technical fluctuations can only be determined by other technical fluctuations. The study of the specific historicity of depth of field, inasmuch as it is the scene of non-exclusively technical determinations – that is, of technical determinations that are themselves economically and ideologically overdetermined – will allow us to both take the measure of the relations between technical practice and the other practices which are articulated with it, and which, determining it, inscribe it in a system of meaning which enables it to signify, and, simultaneously, to theoretically formulate the *work* of this technical device – that is, the *relationship* between its signifying function in a given text or cinematic corpus and the coded signifieds that, beyond and through this function, it inscribes in these texts or corpuses. Such a relationship can be one either of reduplication or of contradiction.

---

2. Metz's concern with unscrambling the abundant terminological and conceptual confusion in critical and theoretical metalanguage invites being extended to the realm of technical metalanguage.

From the earliest films, therefore, the cinematic image was "naturally" a depth of field image. The majority of the films made by the Lumières and their cameramen bear witness to this depth, which even appears as being constitutive of these images (see above the still from *L'Arrivée d'un train à La Ciotat*). Mitry provides a number of other examples, including *The Attack on a China Mission* (Williamson, 1900), which I cite because it is also inserted in the chain of "first times," and because it recalls the manner in which Mitry is constrained by his system to make criteria that are not strictly technical intervene into his genealogy of technical innovations:

> By shooting on location in natural settings unhindered by the restrictions of the stage and the attendant scenic limitations, Williamson was able to move his actors wherever he pleased. Indeed, the actors were able to move not only from side to side but also backward and forward. In *The Attack on a China Mission* the officer who first appears at the bottom of the garden lifts the young girl up onto his horse and gallops directly toward the camera. We mentioned that this same effect was used by Lumière in *L'Arrivée d'un train en gare de La Ciotat*, but there it was used *in a documentary-type film, a real movement filmed by the cameraman and not a movement specially composed for the camera.*[3]

It is, in fact, most frequently in outdoors shooting that depth finds its field during this period. The indisputable reason for this is technical in nature: the lenses used before 1915 were, Mitry insists, "only the f. 35 and the f. 50"[4] (that is, lenses with medium focal lengths), which in order to produce a deep-focus image, had to be stopped down, and thus required a great quantity of light, which was more easily and economically obtainable outdoors than in a studio.

We must thus ask ourselves why, precisely, only lenses with "medium" focal lengths were used during the cinema's first two decades. I see no more pertinent reason for this practice than the fact that they restored the spatial proportions corresponding to "normal vision" and that by dint of this they played a role in the production of the impression of reality to which the *cinématographe* owed its success. These lenses themselves are thus governed by the codes of analogy and realism (other codes corresponding to other social demands would have produced other types of lenses). The depth of field that they authorized is thus also what authorizes them, what establishes their use and existence. It is not a supplementary "effect" which could have been blithely neglected, rather, it is what had to be obtained, and what it was necessary to strive to produce. The cinematic apparatus was made as a wager: fundamentally, it wagered on the identification (the desire to identify, to reduplicate, to specularly recognize) of the cinematic image with "life itself" (cf. the fantastic

---

3. Mitry, *Esthétique et psychologie du cinéma*, vol. I, *op. cit.*, p. 273. Emphasis added.
4. *Ibid.*, p. 149.

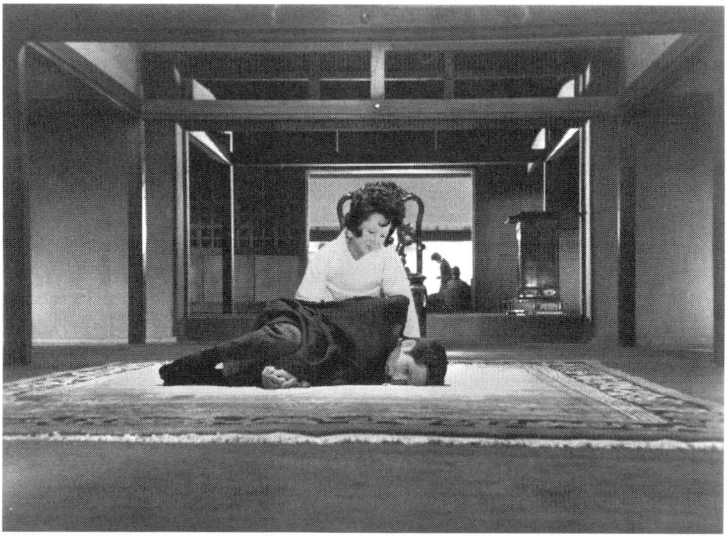

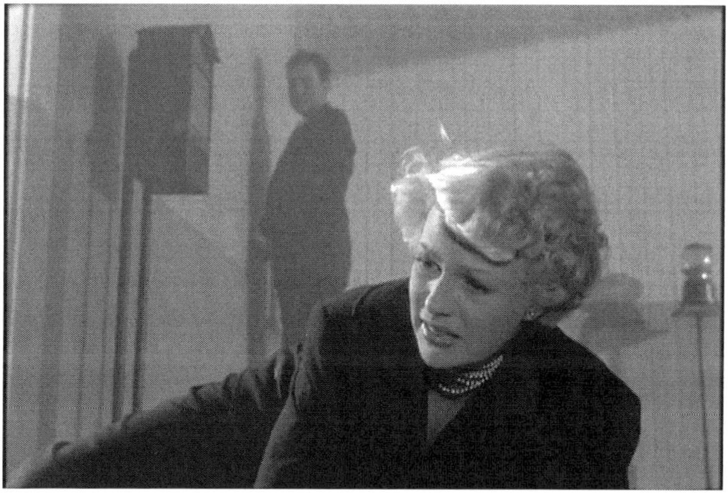

Figs. 27 and 28: In the first still, from *The Ceremony* (Oshima, 1971), the accentuation of the perspectival structure cuts up the space into a series of frames, overlapping boxes, and divided units of the theatrical scene that Oshima represents.

The second still, from *The Lady from Shanghai* (Welles, 1947), can be compared to the earlier still from *Greed*: the emphasis on the perspectival code denaturalizes the scene, the code presents itself as something to be read, it functions as a form of reading, and not as "nature" (as was the case in the early cinema).

efforts deployed for decades by hundreds of inventors in the quest for "total cinema," for complete illusion, for the duplication, including sound, color and stereoscopy, of life). Short of putting into practice the patented technique of stereoscopy, it could not do without the production of stereoscopic effects, effects of depth. These effects rely, on the one hand, on the inscription of vanishing perspective into the image, and, on the other hand, on the movement (which photography is not able to provide, and painting even less so, hence why the most perfect *trompe-l'œil*, minutely constructed according to the laws of perspective, is, as Paulhan notes,[5] incapable of fooling the eye) along these vanishing lines of figures or moving bodies (the train at La Ciotat station, for instance). These two aspects are linked: in order for characters to be able to move in a "perpendicular" fashion to the screen, the lighting must be able to follow them, there is a need for depth and the stratification of planes – in short, the code of artificial perspective. In any case, it often happened in studio shoots, where space was restricted and the lighting was not always strong enough, that scenic backdrops were, precisely, painted canvases using *trompe-l'œil* techniques, which, while unable to let the characters move in depth, at least inscribed a sense of perspective in the image.

We know what perspective brought with it, and thus what depth of field enabled to enter into the cinematic image as its *constitutive codes*: namely, the pictorial and theatrical codes of classical Western representation. As early as 1897, Méliès, a specialist in both "illusion" and the studio, said of his "workshop" in Montreuil: "In a nutshell, it is the fusion of the photographic workshop, in giant proportions, and the theatrical stage."[6] We could not be more precise in indicating the dual basis on which the cinematic image emerged, not by accident but explicitly and deliberately. Not only is depth of field the mark, in the primitive cinematic image, of its submission to these representative codes, and to the histories and ideologies that perforce determine these codes and make them function (and Lebel can not avoid the fact that these histories and ideologies are caught within the history of the rise and dominance of the capitalist bourgeoisie and its attendant ideology), but, more generally speaking, it signals that the ideological apparatus of the cinema is itself produced within these codes and by these systems of representation, as their complement, their refinement and their supersession. There is thus nothing accidental, or specifically technical, about the fact that the cinematic image adopted depth of field from the beginning, not least because it is this depth that governs it and informs it, and it is on the basis of the possibility of its restitution that optical instruments are developed. As opposed to what technicians seem to believe, the restitution of movement

5. Jean Paulhan, *La Peinture cubiste* (Paris: Denoël-Gonthier, coll. "Médiations," 1971 [repr. Paris: Gallimard, coll. "Folio essais," 1990]), p. 86.

6. Cited in Jean Vivié, *Historique et développement de la technique cinématographique* (Paris: BPI, 1946), p. 64. This work is far from realizing the program announced by its title. It is, in fact, symptomatic that there is no "history of film technique," at least in the French language: there are certainly practical manuals, overviews on the refinement of the "earliest instruments," but beyond this mythic past and the present state of practice (let alone the future of "progress"), technicians have no history.

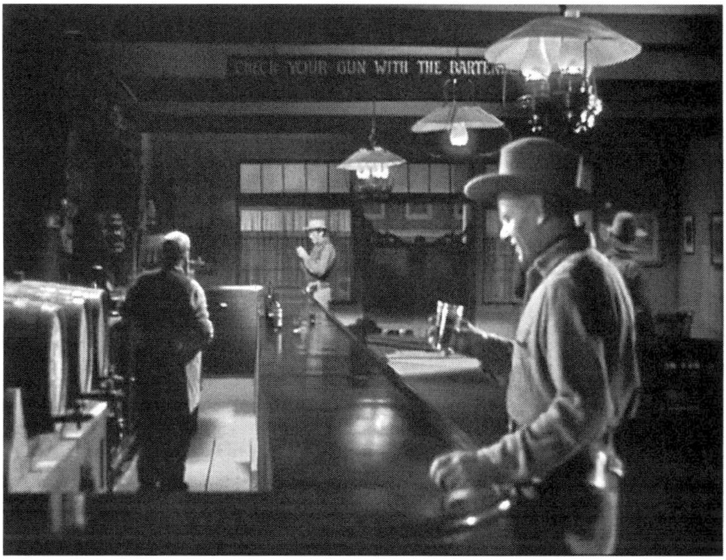

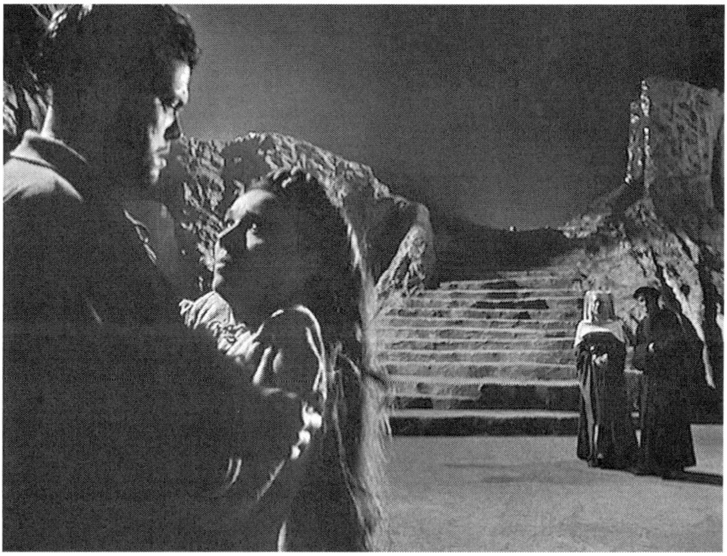

Figs. 29 and 30: The effects of *Citizen Kane* on the rest of Hollywood, *Duel in the Sun* (still 1, Vidor, 1946): here, depth and perspectival distortion are "effects," dramatico-decorative supplements perfectly integrated with the conventional space of the saloon, and in no way disrupting its "unity."

Macbeth (still 2, Welles, 1948): Here, by contrast, depth and relief (in black and white) function as a fracture, as the fragmentation of an unstable dramatic space, in a state of permanent displacement and disequilibrium.

and depth are not camera effects, rather, it is the camera itself that is both the effect of, and the solution to, the problem of this restitution.

Thus, if depth of field is indeed one of the principal determinations governing the cinematic image (or apparatus), we may be astonished that the fact that it was almost totally eclipsed for a period of 15 to 20 years has not been more of a problem for those film historians and aestheticians, such as Mitry and Bazin, who point this out, and that Mitry, as we will see, limits his analysis merely to the technical difficulties associated with it. This is in spite of the fact that, in other passages from his *Esthétique*, Mitry does not refrain from insisting on the link between perspective and movement in the production of the sensation of the third dimension in the cinema. But for Mitry it is precisely due to the fact that all these technical procedures are legally and historically equal that they are equally "valid" and can be substituted for one another without any consequences, other than the meaning-effect that the filmmaker seeks to produce. The "freedom to choose" from among the panoply of technical procedures that he postulates to be that of the contemporary filmmaker (who is, in fact, an atemporal filmmaker) is metonymically extended to those very procedures whose essence is supposedly – leaving aside only technical impossibilities – the ability to be freely chosen: a range of more or less interchangeable, and more or less recent, accessories, which may or may not be taken up by "fashion." But depth of field was not "in fashion" in 1896; rather, it was one of the factors leading to the credibility of the cinematic image (like, albeit in different ways, the faithful reproduction of movement and figurative analogy). And it is through the transformation of the conditions of this credibility, through the displacing of the codes of the cinematic verisimilitude from the level of the mere impression of reality to the more complex levels of fictional logic (narrative codes), psychological verisimilitude and the impression of homogeneity and continuity (the coherent space-time of classical drama), that we can account for the effacement of depth, and not only through technical "delays," because these "delays" are not accidental, rather, they are themselves implicated in, and effects of, this displacement and re-placement of codes.

It seems no less surprising (at least if we remain at the level of "technical causes") that a procedure that "naturally" governed a great number of films shot between 1895 and 1925[7] could disappear and fall into oblivion for such a long time, without being of the slightest concern to filmmakers – with the exception of a few figures, such as Renoir. "Primitive" depth of field had been "given" to them in tandem with the filmic image (at least in outdoors shooting), and thus did not pose a problem (save for wishing to annul it: but this implies a reflection on its effects, a mastery of its code, of which, except by omission, I see no signs in this period), and we can posit that the

7. This date is provided by Mitry. As we will see, it is not the only possible date. Brunius gives 1927 (the beginning of the "talkie"), in accordance with Bessy and Chardans' *Dictionnaire*, and the question is thus posed of the relation (whose direct or indirect nature ought to be interrogated) between the disappearance of depth of field and the advent of sound film.

codes that it inscribed were "interiorized" among filmmakers and spectators alike. Furthermore, not only did the cinematic image seem to "spontaneously" tend toward depth, but a number of filmmakers played with this circumstance and strove to reinforce its effects through the use of "deep-focus *mise en scène*." Mitry cites (apart from Williamson) Stroheim, Feuillade's *Fantômas* (1913) and Griffith's *Intolerance* (1916). We can add, at the very least, Stiller, Lubitsch and Lang. What was it that caused the reversal of fortunes which took place by 1936, such that, as J.B. Brunius would write: "In the summer of 1936, while I was preparing Jean Renoir's film *Partie de campagne* with the director, we decided that scenes could take place between figures at a distance of more than 10 metres in depth. But it was only with a great deal of bother that we managed to procure lenses so ancient that they were considered fossils: some Zeiss lenses and a Bausch and Lomb opened to 3.5..." ?[8] This is Mitry's explanation:

> We are led to wonder, therefore, why it should be that with one or two rare exceptions (notably Eric von Stroheim's films), this "depth" was abandoned between 1925 and 1940 in favor of intensive fragmentation. Some say that it had to do with fashion; others claim the influence of the Soviet cinema. Both explanations have their merit; they do not, however, explain the real reason – which had nothing to do with the almost exclusive use of lenses with wide apertures. It is nearer the mark to say that the use of such lenses was the effect of some other factor. As we have said, all the cameraman has to do is stop down [*to obtain depth of field – JLC*]. However, to keep the same quality in his photograph he must increase his lighting. And nothing was easier before 1925, using orthochromatic stock which required lighting with arcs whose candlepower was immense. But from 1925 onward, as the panchromatic emulsions became generally available, the whole approach to lighting changed. Sensitive to red and to all visible light (as the name suggests) but unevenly, panchromatic emulsions prevented cameramen from using their arcs whose spectrum, tending toward violet, coincided perfectly with the least sensitive area of the emulsion. Thus cameramen had to start using incandescent bulbs; but these were not sufficiently powerful. More than that, the first panchromatic emulsions were a long way from being as sensitive as they are nowadays. Consequently, to get the correct exposure the lens had to be "opened up," which meant sacrificing the capacity to "stop down." This explains why lenses with wide apertures (and therefore a comparatively short depth-of-field) began to be used, why composition in depth was limited, and why of necessity editing styles were much more fragmented. That this became a routine way of

8. Cited in *La Revue du cinéma*, no. 4, January 1947, p. 24 (an issue that was dedicated to the question of depth of field). The citation is taken from J.B. Brunius' book *Photographie et photographie de cinéma* (Paris: Arts et Métiers graphiques, 1938).

> shooting pictures, a fashion rather than a technique, is obviously true, but this "cause" was never more than a consequence. The minimum of technical know-how would have spared our theoreticians [*he is obviously referring to Bazin here – JLC*] looking for difficulties where there are none [*chercher midi à quatorze heures*].[9]

This is a fine example of technicist discourse (the final proclamation would have been the cause for laughter in the studios), of which the least that we can say is that it only resolves one difficulty by substituting *several others* for it.

First of all, there are the technical difficulties – on which it is worthwhile focusing for a short time (not least because Mitry lists them for us). In retracing the (interminable) chain of "technical causes" which persistently pass the final responsibility on from one to the other, there suddenly appear some of the non-technical determinations that such a back-and-forth [*chassé-croisé*] of "technical causes" had the precise function of masking.

Everything stems, Mitry assures us, from the "generalization of panchromatic stock in the years after 1925." Indeed. But to say this – as a self-evident proof – and to immediately move on to the unsuitability of lighting systems for the light spectrum of this emulsion is exactly to leave *unsaid* what necessity it was that required this "generalization," that is, what was the (new) function played by the new type of film stock, which the old type could not fulfill. Moreover, it expunges the question as to who or what *orders* the replacement of an emulsion universally used, and which (if we believe Mitry) did not appear to be all that mediocre, by another emulsion which, once again according to Mitry, was at the outset far from being its equal.

Now, it does not seem (as far as we know) to enter squarely into the technical or economic logic of the film industry (which by 1925 was already highly structured and prodigiously equipped) to adopt (or impose) a new product which initially imposes more problems than the old product, and to which an adaptation would require considerable expenditure (modification of lighting systems, lenses, etc.), *without somewhere finding an advantage, or a benefit, to it.*

The first of these advantages is that panchromatic film stock is more sensible than orthochromatic stock because – as Mitry himself states, even though he does not see the consequences of this in his text – "as the name suggests," it is "sensitive to all visible light," whereas orthochromatic stock is only sensitive to blue and violet radiations.

The *Dictionnaire du cinéma et de la télévision*[10] clarifies this gain:

---

9. Mitry, *Esthétique et psychologie du cinéma*, vol. II, *op. cit.*, p. 41 [pp. 191-192].

10. This is the only source where we can find some technical precisions and a little technical history; the chapter on "Film technique" in the *Encyclopædia universalis* has a paragraph titled "Emulsions" but only discusses film formats.

> With orthochromatic stock, the transcription of the diverse shades comprising a face, in black and white, remained unbalanced. To rectify this state of affairs, actors wore blue and ochre-tinted make-up. [...] In 1927, the first panchromatic emulsions were launched on the film market, and the range of sensitivity was considerably broadened. Make-up practices had to be reviewed, and reverted to almost normal colors. The image obtained in black and white was known as "panchromatic," that is, it reproduced all the colors of nature in a much wider range of grey, black and white shades.

It is therefore, in fact, not only a gain in sensitivity, but also a gain in *fidelity* "to the colors of nature," a *gain in realism*. The cinematic image was refined, its ability to "render" colors perfected, and it once again entered into competition with the image quality of photography, which had long used panchromatic emulsion. The reason for this "technical progress" is not only technical (it is ideological): being more sensitive to light is far less important than "being more true to life." The harsh, high-contrast image of the early cinema no longer satisfied the codes of photographic realism reworked and honed by the spread of photography. I will posit that in the production of "reality effects," depth (perspective) thus lost out in importance to shades, tones and colors. But this is not all.

We can admit, with Mitry, that during the (two or three) years of the *transition* from orthochromatic to panchromatic stock, the (bad because unsuitable) conditions for using the new emulsion prevented the full exploitation of its greater degree of sensitivity. But this mitigates Mitry's argument in two ways.

Firstly, because this period of tentative exploration was perforce very provisional (otherwise it would have compromised the industry itself), because panchromatic stock was very rapidly perfected (in 1931 Kodak launched the "super-sensitive Eastman"), and because palliatives were found for the tendency toward violet of the arc lamps (the addition of salts – fluorides of calcium, barium, strontium and chrome – to the carbon filaments). It is difficult to imagine that such an ephemeral, easily solved difficulty could have seriously prohibited working with depth of field, enough to have "lost the habit of its use."

It can be supposed that an industry capable of change (from orthochromatic to panchromatic stock, but also from the silent cinema to sound cinema) and of surmounting the obstacles posed by these changes, could undoubtedly, if it so desired – that is, if the demand existed and exerted pressure – obtain without too much difficulty the ability to film both with panchromatic stock and in depth (given that the former only secondarily and momentarily excluded the latter). And yet, if pressure was indeed required to change the type of emulsion, there was no manifest pressure to maintain depth-of-field. The deficiency of Mitry's thesis (and the reason why it is technicist) is that it explains technical changes through other technical changes, without for a moment envisaging that these changes are not "free," that they bring into play economic forces and forces of labor – in short, economically and socially programmed demands. There is no "technical firmament" where a given technique is opposed to another one.

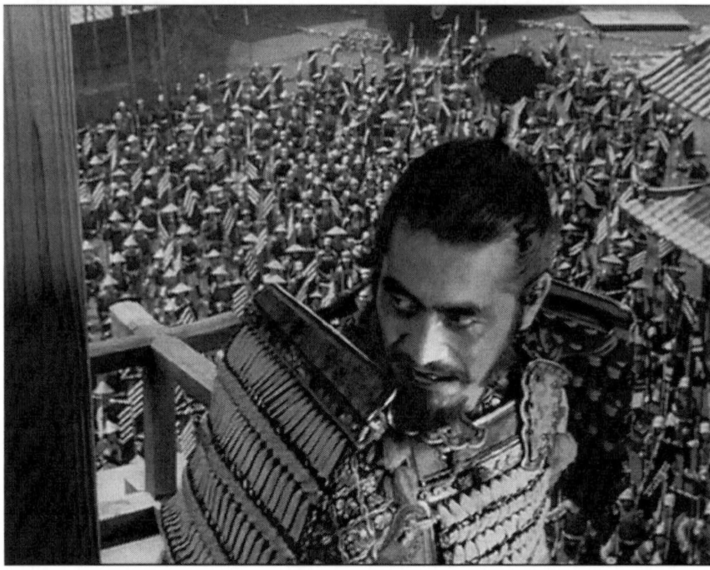

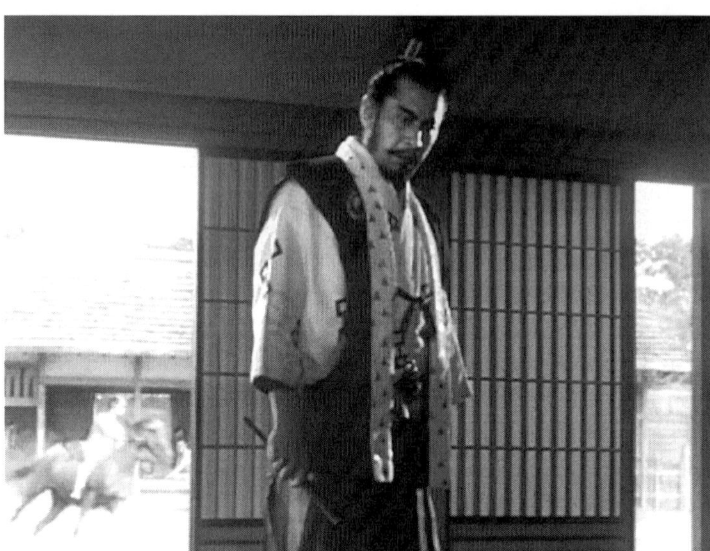

Figs. 31 and 32: Two stills from *Throne of Blood* (Kurosawa, 1957): Once again, depth of field functions as the means for producing a complex, ruptured space, where perspective no longer has a unifying, binding function, but contributes to the detachment of the shots from each other, to their *opposition* to one another. (The stills are from the collection of Vincent Pinel.)

Secondly, because, to support its cause, this argument is limited to the needs of studio filming alone (where the power of the lamps and the sensitivity of the stock used are certainly determinant), "forgetting" that it nonetheless occurred to filmmakers to leave the studios and film outdoors, in both the period immediately after 1925 and later. Here, with all the technical difficulties no longer relevant (and also because panchromatic film is more sensitive than orthochromatic film), depth of field, which had been known of since the birth of the cinema, should not have posed a problem. And yet, from the advent of sound cinema to *Citizen Kane*, when we see depth-of-field scenes, they are *generally* reduced to the state of decorative supplement in the landscapes of Westerns and adventure films, that is to say, to the *code* of the landscape in a long shot, a code of filmed "nature." While possible, and even difficult to avoid, depth of field as a whole was not developed, and remained residual. It is this "disaffection," not always linked to a material impossibility, that must be interrogated.

In fact, in classical Hollywood cinema, this decorative, residual status was not so much related to "natural" depth of field as it was to landscapes, to nature itself. The dominance of studio shooting (linked not only to practical and economic reasons, but also historical reasons – the heritage of silent cinema, and ideological reasons – the concern for "technical perfection"), even when it came to most "exterior scenes," codified the representation of nature in genre cinema. The role of landscapes was reduced to that of "decor," a decorative backdrop, a painted canvas inherited from the theater and propitious for the *découpement*[ii] of psychological drama that had been instigated by a number of silent films (even if only in the slapstick genre: *Our Hospitality*, most Keatons, the films of Lloyd and Langdon). Sending a second crew to take some "shots" of the Grand Canyon confirmed the "truth" of the painted backdrops, reinforced the code and pictorialized natural landscapes in "decor-fashion." The determination absent from Mitry's discourse is that of the ideology of studio filming, of the representation of (interior/exterior) space that it produces.

IV. Effacement of Depth/Advent of Speech

After 1925, and up until *Citizen Kane* (1941), that depth of field which was "naturally" operative in the majority of films is lost... Now, neither of these two dates is free of any attendant problems. On the one hand, work must be carried out to clarify these "years after 1925" so briskly designated by Mitry: they are articulated, synchronically, and according to a relation of determination which is yet to be analyzed, with the transition from orthochromatic to panchromatic film stock and the transition from silent to sound cinema, which was certainly more decisive and more difficult (although in the text referred to above Mitry does not mention it). With regards to these "technical" changes, we have seen that the former – and we will see that the latter – does not only involve "technical" matters, but is, albeit in an uneven fashion, ideologically and economically determined. On the other hand, if we more closely interrogate the status of "breakthrough film" [*film-coupure*] conferred on *Citizen Kane* – more by Bazin than by Mitry, but also, before Bazin, by the great majority of critics at the time – and if we concern ourselves with depth of field, we can observe that, while Welles and his director of photography Gregg Toland re-inscribe it into this film, and while this re-inscription provokes the effect of a transgression, of a true innovation, it is not because we can not find, in the very period of its greatest eclipse, a certain number of films where, exceptionally, it does have a role. Such exceptions (even if, for Renoir alone, they included *Boudu sauvé des eaux*, *Une Partie de campagne* and *La Règle du jeu*) are rare enough to confirm the rule of the demise of depth of field – whose determinations we are in the midst of elucidating. But their very existence also obliges us to interrogate the question of the "oblivion" that they suffered up until Bazin calls attention to them by attributing them with a central position in his thesis on the evolution of film language toward a "surplus realism," and which can be measured by the shock produced by the reactivation of depth in *Citizen Kane*. For it is in this way that the repression of depth of field for almost 15 years and the *coup de théatre* of its return largely exceed the mere technical scene to which Mitry strives to confine them. Instead, they involve ideological investments, practices, principles, a certain conception of the production and distribution of the film, struggles against the dominance of this conception, in short, the functioning of the cinema as an ideological apparatus and the economic conditions of this functioning.

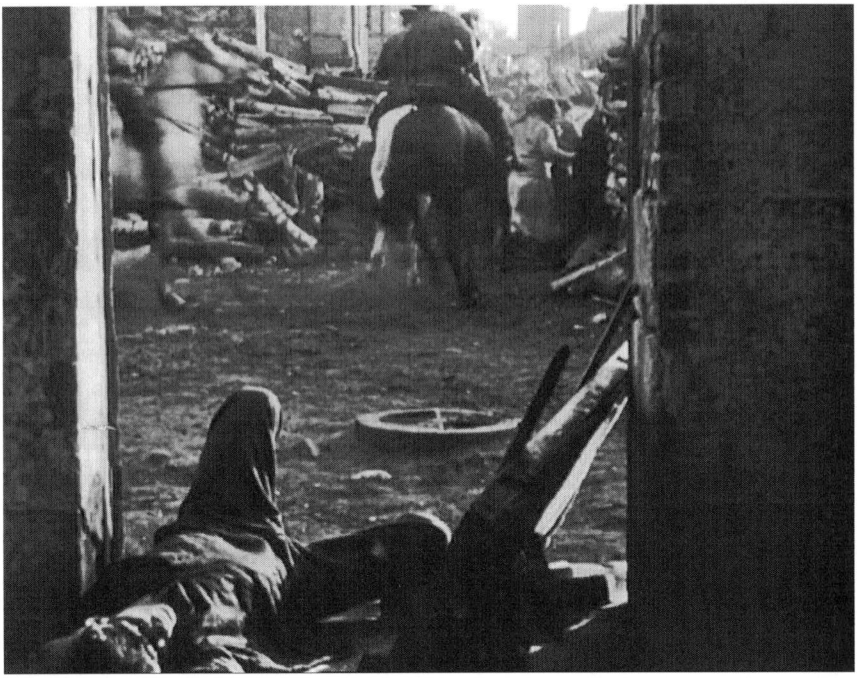

Fig. 33: *Strike* (Eisenstein, 1925). [Depth of field and framing within the frame: death in the foreground, destruction and terror in the background. Eisenstein's use of depth of field is evidently not naturalist.

Let us say that the deployment of depth of field engenders a form of *mise en scène* in the depth of the shot. This depth, certainly, is that of the lure (the image is as flat as the screen), but although it makes us believe in the depth of the projected image – a belief which is itself nourished through depth of field, which renders the depth or the spatial relief of the image in some way tangible for us (perhaps we should speak of the *haptic* dimension of depth of field) – this lure simply leads us to believe in the situation represented; that is, it leads us to believe in the cinema. The lure is not a misdeed perpetrated against the spectator, it is the very condition and the direct agent of the spectator's belief. This is the positive function of the lure.]

Whether we tackle this problem by starting with the technicist explanation provided by Mitry – radically insufficient in that, as I have shown, the replacement of orthochromatic by panchromatic stock does not determine anything in and of itself, given that the new conditions of lighting and camerawork were only very provisionally incompatible with obtaining deep-focus photography, but above all in that this replacement itself is not merely the product of "technical progress," but that this "progress" is ideologically and economically determined, that it is linked to a displacement of the codes of "realism" (leading to a redefinition of photographic realism), a displacement of codes which a strictly technical line of argument remains incapable of properly taking into account – or whether we tackle it, retrospectively, by starting with the toppling of technical norms and writing conventions produced by *Citizen*

Kane, we can not isolate its technical aspects, cut them off from the ideological and economic contradictions struggling within the total field of cinematic practice. What is at play in depth of field photography, and what is at play in the historicity of the technique, are "realism's" codes and modes of production, the transmission, circulation and transformation of the ideological systems of recognition, specularity and verisimilitude.

At this point, it could appear that I am making a return to Bazin's thesis on depth of field, which Mitry targeted by opposing to it a purely technical causality intended to "spare our theoreticians looking for difficulties where there are none."[1] Bazin indeed notes these technical determinations, but he only does so in order to immediately abandon them:

> In 1938 or 1939, therefore, talking cinema in France and the United States in particular achieved a state of classical perfection founded upon the maturity of its dramatic genres on the one hand, which had developed over the preceding decade or been inherited from silent cinema, and upon the stabilization of technological advances on the other. The 1930s were the years of both sound and panchromatic film. [*It is this conjunction – lacking in Mitry, as I have already noted – that needs to be worked on, as an articulation of technical changes with economic determinations and ideological pressures – JLC*]. Studio equipment was no doubt constantly being refined, but these improvements were only details. None of them opened up radically new possibilities for *mise en scène*. Moreover, this situation has not changed since, except perhaps in the case of cinematography, with the increased sensitivity of film stock. Panchromatic film upset the image's balanced qualities, while highly sensitive emulsion made it possible to modify the way images are created. Free to shoot in the studio with much smaller apertures, camera operators were able, in some cases, to eliminate the out-of-focus backgrounds seen in most films. But many earlier examples of depth of field exist (in the work of Jean Renoir, for example), and it has always been possible to achieve this depth outdoors and even in the studio, if exceptional measures were taken. It was enough to want do so. It was, therefore, less a technological problem, whose solution, admittedly, has been greatly facilitated, than a quest for style. [...] With technological determinants thereby practically eliminated, we must look elsewhere for the signs and principles of the evolution of film language: to the new approach to topics and, as a result, to the style necessary to express them.[2]

"It was enough to want to do so": no less than Mitry through his recourse to technique as a final authority, Bazin determines the question of the demise and rebirth of

1. Mitry, *Esthétique et psychologie du cinéma*, vol. II, *op. cit.*, p. 41 [pp. 191-192].
2. Bazin, "L'évolution du langage cinématographique," *op. cit.*, pp. 138-139 [pp. 94-95].

depth of field by turning it into a matter of the "will" or "lack of will" of a given filmmaker or technician.

Certainly, Renoir "wanted" to film *Une Partie de campagne* or *La Règle du jeu* using deep-focus photography: but I cited Brunius' remark on the extreme difficulty they had in retrieving, 15 years after they had fallen out of use, the "primitive" lenses permitting this deep-focus. Why was there such a difficulty, and why were there so few filmmakers, for a period of ten years, concerned with depth of field (if they had been numerous, there is no doubt that the technical difficulties posited by Mitry or the practices pointed out by Brunius would have been easy to resolve)? Once again: What were the forces, pressures and demands at work to produce such disaffection, and what were the exceptions that confirmed the rule? Neither Mitry nor Bazin will say. Technical problems for the former, and stylistic exploration for the latter, assume the function of ultimate justification. But where do these problems, and this exploration, come from? What produces them? On what other scenes are these "causes" themselves determined and operated on?

With respect to the technico-stylistic object of depth of field, and *in order to theoretically construct it*, we must here break open both the technical scene and the stylistic scene, each of which, in an exclusive and autonomizing manner, has been the respective domain of Mitry's and Bazin's thinking. For we could in no way concur, on the basis of the collapse of the "technical causes" of the former, with the definitive abandonment of "technical determinations" subscribed to by the latter, only too happy to be able to place the aesthetic exigencies of "stylistic exploration" and the ethical exigencies of the "realist destiny of film language" in a position of command. Firstly, because "style" or language on the one hand, and techniques on the other hand, are not at all independent, but necessarily imply each other, overlap each other (in another text on depth of field, "William Wyler, the Jansenist of *Mise en Scène*," Bazin nonetheless clearly posits this link: "improved lenses are closely linked to developments in the history of *découpage*; they were both the cause and effect of these developments"[i]). And, secondly, because this implication is precisely what a materialist theory of the cinema must demystify, inasmuch as it is also a site for the confusion of technical and critical metalanguage. Not only are the two fields not independent of each other, but, even taken together, they are not autonomous: the variations, the history of their recuperation and their (rare) moments of excess are ideologically and economically determined, in line with the points of delay and unevenness which ensure, at one and the same time, both their indissociability and their relative specificity.

Without exception, idealist histories and aesthetics pose the technical progress/stylistic innovation duality as being autonomous and self-sufficient: its two poles refer to each other in a closed circuit. What is needed, however, is not only to determine what is principal and what is secondary in this contradiction (as technicism and aestheticism both consist precisely in the primacy accorded to one of the two terms), but to see how this principal aspect and this secondary aspect can change

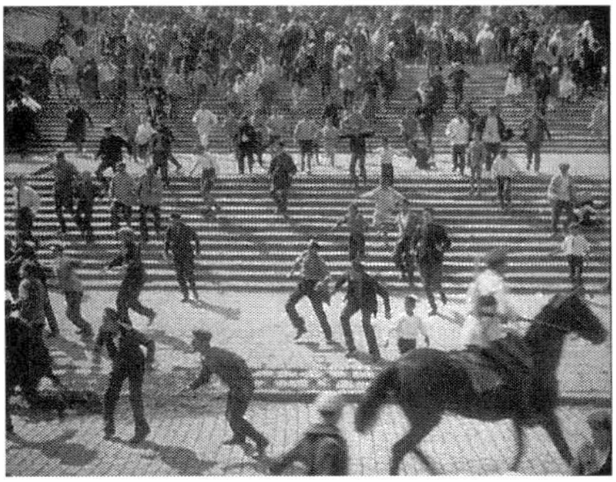

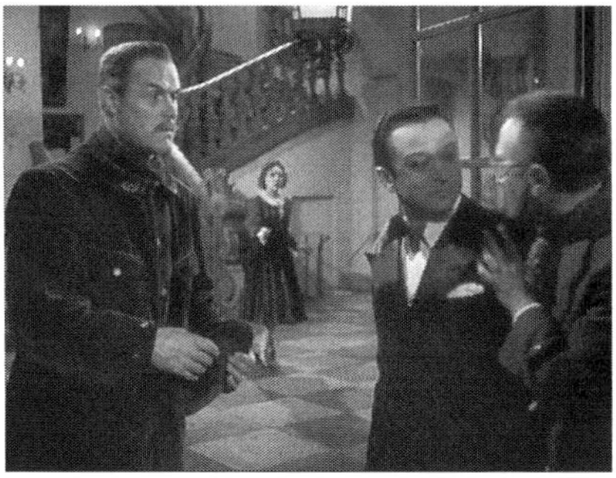

Figs. 34 and 35: Regardless of what Bazin may say, there is not the slightest incompatibility between montage and depth of field; indeed, the latter can be seen in the still from *Strike* (see the previous image) and in this still from *Battleship Potemkin* (still 1, Eisenstein, 1925), both of which have been taken from films where montage governs the production of signification. Hollywood narrative cinema in the sound era repressed both montage and depth of field, inasmuch as the inscription of depth, as soon as it ceases to be "primitive," implies a process of work and writing. In *Citizen Kane*, depth of field and montage function conjointly, in spite of Bazin's view that the inscription of the former is intended to evacuate and "transcend" the latter. On the basis of Renoir's specific practice (still 2, *La Règle du jeu*, 1939), which makes depth function within *sequence shots*, Bazin posits depth of field as being inseparable from the sequence shot, and thinks of it as a factor of "continuity" (= realism, respect for "lived reality"), negating and transcending the discontinuity of montage.

[Alongside the advent of sound – and even more so after 1960, with the possibility of recording synchronized sound in exterior shots and in the conditions of a "small-scale" shoot (with a 16mm synch-sound camera) – there arises a deployment of filmed speech that requires a certain duration, thus making the act of cutting more difficult. There are musical scansions and forms in speech, which are easy to ruin by cutting, but which, I dare say, wreak vengeance for this poor treatment by letting the spectator hear the result. Sound transitions require the know-how of an aesthetic surgeon. On the other hand, filmed speech, when it is no longer just the actors speaking a text or a dialogue written by an author, when it is the speech of their own will-to-speak, turns itself into an aesthetic form, and constructs itself through the free association of words with other words. It is this invention of a singular spoken word that is recorded by "direct cinema." From then on, any montage act becomes problematic. Montage is barred, not by depth of field, but by the act of filming the spoken word.]

places, how these variations are all the reflection – and how the duality itself is the product – of the contradictions engendered by the ideological apparatus of the cinema. The problematic of depth of field such as it is operative here has precisely the function of dividing and repartitioning the illusory singularity of the technical and aesthetic scenes, and of unraveling the contradictions which simultaneously establish and dissolve them (it is only at the expense of covering over these contradictions that idealist discourse – whether Mitry or Bazin – can be maintained).

This division is immediately played out in the lacuna which demolishes Mitry's line of reasoning: How could he have failed to notice the synchrony between the effacement of depth of field and the advent of sound cinema?

It so happens that the second of the advantages that the film industry found when it compelled itself – in spite of the practical difficulties and expense of the operation – to replace orthochromatic with panchromatic stock in the "years after 1925" is also tied to the latter's higher degree of sensitivity. Not only did this gain in sensitivity permit the realignment of the "realism" of the cinematic image in line with the photographic image,[3] but it also compensated for the loss of light due to the transition from a filming speed of 16-18 frames per second to 24 frames per second imposed by sound cinema. In light of his appeals to "technical science," it is astonishing that Mitry, in elucidating the disappearance of depth of field, could have "omitted" what happens to be the most indisputable of the possible technical explanations. As Brunius wrote in 1938: "It is the sound cinema, reducing the exposure time from 1/30th of a second to around 1/50th of a second, which led to panchromatic stock and lenses

3. I return to this point, discussed in a rather elliptical fashion earlier. I wrote: "the harsh, high-contrast image of the early cinema no longer satisfied the codes of photographic realism reworked and honed by the spread of photography." In the general re-ordering of the codes of cinematic "realism" produced by sound cinema in Hollywood (in accord, of course, with its ideological and economic norms and objectives: to its own profit and to the profit of bourgeois ideology), the codes of the properly photographic "realism" of the filmic image are redefined in a specific (but not exclusive) fashion through the relationship to the increasingly important position held by the photographic image in bourgeois societies, and its mass consumption. This position has something similar to that of gold (its fetish value): the photograph acts as a currency of the "real," of "life," it assures the "ease" of its circulation and appropriation. In this way, it is unanimously consecrated as a general equivalent, as a benchmark of all "realism." The cinematic image, therefore, could not avoid aligning itself with these norms without losing its "power" (its credibility). The "strictly technical" level of the refinements of optics and emulsions is thus totally programmed by the ideology of the "realist" reproduction of the world at work in the constitution of the photographic image as the "objective representation" *par excellence*. The image, in its turn, reaffirms ideology as a system of codification. The film thus comes to assume its position, to maintain its role in the circuit of constitution-renewal of the codes of iconic "realism" analyzed by Bourdieu: "A work appears to be 'lifelike' and 'realist' when the rules defining its conditions of production coincide with the prevailing definition of the objective vision of the world, or, more precisely, with the spectator's 'vision of the world,' that is, a system of social categories of perception and appreciation which are themselves the product of the extended exposure to representations produced according to the same rules. It is thus that, by accrediting photography with realism, our society simply confirms to itself the tautological certitude that an image conforming to its representation of objectivity is truly objective. In order to be reinforced in this *certitudo sui*, it suffices to forget that photographic representations need only appear 'lifelike' and 'objective' through their conformity to the laws of representation that society itself had produced and deployed (the use painters made of the *camera obscura* is well-known), long before it became capable of producing the means to bring them into existence through mechanical means. If it is true, as the saying goes, that 'nature imitates art,' then we can understand that photography, the 'most natural' imitation of art in our society, appears as the most faithful imitation of nature." Pierre Bourdieu, "Sociologie de la perception esthétique," in *Les Sciences humaines et l'œuvre d'art*, collective work (Brussels: La Connaissance, Brussels, 1969), p. 174.

with extremely wide apertures."[4] The chain panchromatic stock/shallow-focus lenses/sound cinema functions better as a "technical causality" than the detour through incandescent lamps proposed by Mitry.[5] The "years after 1925" (or Bazin's 1930s) are thus narrowed down to the year 1927, which witnessed the joint launch onto the market of panchromatic stock and sound cinema.

But this "better" technical explanation would only serve to re-mark the coincidence between the arrival of sound cinema and the ejection [*mise hors-jeu*] of depth of field – and it would not provide us with an underlying reason. Although certain of its effects are technical, this underlying reason is not. Moreover, as we have seen, more than one sound film before *Citizen Kane* worked with depth of field; not even the generalization of wide-angle lenses is exclusive to Welles' film. With the sensitivity of the emulsions progressively accentuated, and as long as the expense of the extra lighting could be covered, nothing was technically preventing filmmakers from stopping up the lenses (if, as Renoir did, they could not find any other types of lens). It is thus not as an ultimate "technical cause" that the advent of sound should intervene, but rather, as a precise site of production-distribution (Hollywood). It remodels not only the systems of film writing, but also, and as the guiding principle of this updating process, the ideological role of the cinema and the economic circumstances of its functioning.

It is not inconsequential that it was – in Hollywood – at the precise moment that the quality of the cinematic image had been made more fine-grained, had opened up to a diverse range of shades of grey (a monochromatic translation of the color spectrum), and had thus come closer to a more faithful imitation of the photographic image, whose promotion (fetishization) in the norms of realism I pointed to earlier, that speech, and the speaking subject, should enter the scene. As soon as they are produced,[6] sound and speech are championed as the "*truth*" *that was lacking* in silent cinema – although the fact that this was seen as a lack happened quite suddenly, and not without alarm or resistance from some quarters.[7] Moreover, this truth made all

4. Brunius, *Photographie et photographie de cinéma*, *op. cit.*

5. So much so that, if we can believe another technician, Jean Vivié, it is the sound cinema that imposed incandescent lamps, and not (only) the matter of the spectrum as affirmed by Mitry: "The lighting set-ups had to be entirely changed: in effect, the electric arcs produced a characteristic whistling sound which would have prevented any sound recording, and because a way to make the arcs silent could not be found, they were replaced by powerful incandescent lamps whose manufacturing technique had, fortunately, just been perfected." Vivié, *Historique et développement de la technique cinématographique*, *op. cit.*, p. 87.

6. 1926: *Don Juan*; 1927: *The Jazz Singer* (Warner) and *Seventh Heaven* (Fox); Finally, 1929, the "first 100% talking film": *Lights of New York*.

7. Do we need to recall, after all the "histories of the cinema" have already done so, that the majority of silent-era filmmakers were, at least for a while, hostile to sound films? For the most part, critics and theorists were too. But apart from the famous "manifesto" by Eisenstein, Pudovkin and Alexandrov, these aesthetic, formalist and elitist reactions from the opposition were quickly countered in the name of "progress." Because it demanded a more violent disavowal, silent cinema

those films not in possession of it, and not producing it, instantly obsolete.[8] This decisive supplement, this "ballast of reality" (Bazin)[ii] marked by sound and speech, thus intervenes from the start as the *refinement and redefinition of the impression of reality.*

It is at the price of a series of blind spots (of disavowals) that the silent image could be accepted as the objective reflection and duplication of "life itself": the denial of color, stereoscopy and sound. Founded on these absences (just as, incidentally, all forms of representation are founded on an absence governing them, on a fault line lying at the basis of every simulacrum – the spectator, in any case, very well knows about the artifice, but prefers to believe in it all the same[9]), filmic representation could only be produced, as I have already noted,[10] by working to attenuate their effects, and even masking their real existence. Otherwise, it would have been refused, as being too visibly factitious: it was absolutely necessary for it to facilitate the disavowal of those veritable sensorial castrations which established its specificity, and for it not to stymie this process by re-marking them. *Compromises* were needed in order for the cinema to function as an ideological apparatus, in order for it to act as a lure.

This work of suturing, of filling in the gaps, of patching up the lacks that incessantly reminded the viewer of the radical difference of the cinematic image, was not brought about in one fell swoop, but in piecemeal fashion, *through the patient accumulation of technical advances.* Directly and totally programmed by the ideology of resemblance, of the "objective" duplication of "reality," itself conceived of as a specular reflection, film technique was marshaled for the purposes of perfecting and refining the primitively imperfect (in fact, *always* imperfect) *dispositif* of the ideological lure produced by the film as the "impression of reality." Movement and the "depth" of the image immediately compensated for the absence of stereoscopy (this is the origi-

---

found that it was the site for phantasmatic investments that were stronger than those nourished by sound cinema, hence this resistance.

8. The Soviet Union reacted the most belatedly and slowly to the global propagation of sound film, and not for nothing: as late as 1934, Mikhail Romm shot his debut work, *Boule de suif,* as a silent film. There was, in fact, scant justification for a socialist nation, which was more urgently faced with other economic tasks, to replace all the equipment in its cinemas and studios (and it is also the case that the montage practices developed in the USSR had already made the representative utilization of speech outmoded). Concerning the technical "belatedness" of the USSR, due not only to economic difficulties, but also to economic *choices,* we can observe that, while capitalism can act as a brake on the development of productive forces, it can also accelerate the development of certain technologies – as long as it can make use of them. It is of no small importance that the cinema should thus be one of the fields where a mass of technical advances was accumulated in the space of a few short years, nor that this one-upmanship primarily had Hollywood (or Wall Street) as its base.

9. Cf. Octave Mannoni, *Clefs pour l'imaginaire; ou, l'autre scène* (Paris: Seuil, 1969); and, in *Cahiers du cinéma,* no. 233, Pascal Bonitzer's text ["Fétichisme de la technique: la notion de 'plan'"], which intersects with this analysis on more than one point.

10. "Cinematic 'realism' is only produced and is only in a position to be produced as a denial of 'filmic reality.'"

nal impression of reality), and they inscribe the perspectival code which, in western cultures, is seen as the principal emblem of spatial relief. The absence of color was recompensed with the use of panchromatic film stock, in anticipation of the commercial uptake of trichromatic techniques (1935-1940). The pianos and orchestras of the silent era could never really stand in for "realist sound." *Synchronous* speech and sound – in spite of their imperfections, which in truth were of little importance at a time when sound reproduction as a whole (records, the radio) was affected by background noise and static – thus considerably *displaced* the previously *strictly iconic* site and means of production of the impression of reality.

Because the *ideological* conditions of the production/consumption of the primitive impression of reality (figurative analogy + movement + perspective) changed (even if this was as a result of the spread of photography and film), it was necessary to tinker with its technical modalities, in order for the act of disavowal replenishing the lure to be able to continue to be "automatically" accomplished, in a reflex manner, without any disturbance to the spectacle and, above all, without any work or exertion on the part of the spectator. The succession and progression of technical advances can only be read as a march toward a form of Bazinian "surplus realism" (cf. supra) to the extent that they accumulate supplements of realism all aimed at reproducing the impression of reality, by reinforcing, diversifying and nuancing it – that is, by narrowing and minimizing, as much as possible, the breech that must be plugged by the "I-know-very-well-but-all-the-same."

Such is the ideological axis serving as the center for research into the "technical perfection" and "ineluctability" of "realism." This work is focused entirely on the technical instruments, and is totally monopolized by the equipment, with the goal, precisely, of sparing the spectator the slightest amount of work. Roughly speaking, we can summarize the matter by saying that it is not the spectator but technology that makes progress. Realism, made operational at great expense, in no way has as its object the cognitive appropriation of reality, but rather the reinforcement of the credibility of the spectacle, which presents itself as representing (covering over) this reality. This, at least, is the axis at work in Hollywood, the main site for not only the honing/diffusion of technical refinements, but also the dominance of the conception of cinema as spectacle.

A number of commentators have expressed their astonishment that it was at the very moment that the silent cinema had attained its highest degree of productivity, with the development of montage practices – essentially (and this is not for nothing) the development of Soviet montage practices; as other approaches (the "French school...), although they were in the "avant-garde," remained beholden to formalism – leading to talk, in the terminology of the era (Canudo, Élie Faure, etc.), of a "music of images" and "cinegraphic writing," that sound cinema suddenly made these newly discovered values obsolete, destroying a language which had just beforehand been celebrated for being admirably able to "do without" spoken language.

I will posit that it was not a matter of chance that sound cinema became dominant first in Hollywood (and then, via Germany, everywhere), that is, in an ideologically determined location which precisely refused a rightful place for montage (if we except, as a genuine – and dated – exception, some of Griffith's films). It seems to me that Hollywood's championing of sound film was overdetermined by the antagonism between the logic and the propensities of Hollywood narration (already pretty much sketched out by the end of the silent era) and the conceptions/practices of montage as a writing practice. And this is precisely due to the fact that this championing is determined not by some abstract concern for "technical progress," but rather, overwhelmingly, by an economic struggle (the competition between the trusts and the banks) *and* an ideological demand whose satisfaction turned out to be most profitable.

We know that the first procedure for the recording-reproduction of sound with auspicious commercial prospects was the Vitaphone process, property of the Western Electric trust (linked, according to Sadoul, to the Morgan bank, as well as to the major studios). Nonetheless, Western's entreaties to the majors fell on deaf ears: solidly implanted, dominating the world market at the time, they feared that the talkie, which inevitably placed an emphasis on linguistic specificity, would break up their hegemony, compromise their expansion, and considerably augment the cost of film production. A smaller company, one that was almost on the verge of collapse and thus had nothing to lose, was needed to run the risk: Warner Brothers. In August 1926, the studio released *Don Juan*, "the first sound film with songs," to great success. The competition instantly took notice: Western Electric, at the very moment that it was constructing Vitaphone equipment for Warner, also built Movietone equipment for Fox (which owned patents taken out by Lee De Forest and T.W. Case). In early 1927, Fox released some sound shorts, while Warner decisively opened the market with *The Jazz Singer*, the triumph of which led to a patent race and a commercial war. The fact that the major studios rushed to adopt sound cinema *after* it had proven its commercial superiority, rather than its technical perfection, will remind us that technical progress is definitively not the motor of the cinema's evolution, but that it is more the effect of and response to an ideological demand, and that it was the film industry's function to satisfy and replenish this demand.

We must ask ourselves whether the triumphant international distribution of the "first sound film with dialogue" was dictated more by the curiosity of the public toward a technical innovation (we know that before *The Jazz Singer* this curiosity was sated by a countless variety of experiments in synchronization and sonorization) than it was by the simultaneous revelation and filling in of a lacuna which until then had only been felt to be such in an obscure fashion, which was denied at the same time as attempts were made to alleviate it through the employment of a live orchestra or recorded accompaniments, and which brutally came to be seen as intolerable once its disavowal was no longer necessary. We will certainly need to analyze the complex and multiple determinations shaping and programming this ideological demand, and the reason for their abrupt condensation, provoking a veritable qualitative leap in this demand, because, once it had appeared on the market, the sound film negated and obliterated silent cinema in the eyes of the audience. But I insist on the fact that – as in the case of the "invention of the cinema" – it was in the years 1910-1915 that sound cinema was scientifically, technically possible (Lauste's work in 1912 "entirely resolved the problem. From 1912 on, all film production could have had synch-sound."[11]). We must account for this delay, this *différance*, which is not exhausted by the argument for a "greater" degree of refinement necessary in order to augment the technically practicable patents taken out by Lauste and De Forest in the 1910s, because it was precisely due to this delay that these multiple refinements were brought into existence.

In the industry's manifest hesitation to embark on the journey toward sound, we may be justified in seeing something other than the (inexhaustible) perfectibility of technique at play. Firstly, there are economic considerations: the intensified struggle between the trusts; the registering of patents related to the filmed image; the capitalist desire to be embedded in the mechanical reproduction of profit for the longest duration possible by renewing, with the smallest possible outlay, the original conditions of this profit; and the ideological determinations with which these factors are articulated: the industry's necessity to realign, but *after the fact*, the technical equipment with the ideological demand. Of course, it is on this ideological demand that the foundation of spectacular realism and the dominant logic of fiction film had long exerted their pressure, in the form of the repressed/denied lacks (of color, sound and stereoscopy) that the cinematic image (with its monochromes, silence and illusory depth) did not cease to inscribe – inasmuch as it persisted in presenting itself as the "objective" reproduction of the real – by placing a massive stake on the impression of reality that it produced, and by transforming this disavowal mechanism into the principle of the signifying organization of the entire cinema.

It is the extent to which they wagered on "reality effects," on the system of representation/disavowal, on "verisimilitude" and the "realism" of a spectacle where the place and the inscription of the spectator were comfortably handled, and because they counted on, and disseminated, the lure established by the impression of reality, that the types of narrative cinema dominant in Hollywood at the end of the silent era (excepting the slapstick genre) inscribed the lack of speech, and could not avoid inscribing speech (or color, or stereoscopy) as a lack. All this took place at the precise moment that montage practice – particularly in the Soviet Union – had produced another place for the spectator: that of the reader, a place for work, and it did so at the precise moment that this work had necessarily come to bar the abandonment of film to the spectacle, and of the image to the mere impression of reality.

11. Bessy and Chardans, *Dictionnaire du cinéma et de la télévision, op. cit.*

At the very minimum, all montage (even formalist montage) produces *effects of work*. It multiplies the number of traces, cuts, leaps and breakages, in short, the signs of writing which affirm it as functioning, and through which, once again at the very minimum, the fact that the work of signifying production is taking place is marked out. Montage can be *seen*. This allows the linear, continuous procession of images, hypostasized as "natural," the very "natural" quality of the "realist duration" of scenes, and "the respect for the continuity of dramatic space and, naturally, for its duration"[12] (which Bazin sees as the foundation of "realism," because the time and location of the "real" are left free to "reveal" themselves), to be barred, worked on and transformed into writing. This continuity and linearity (which Bazin, as a good idealist, represents as aspects of the real, whereas, at the very most, the impression of continuity is a product of perception), and even this duration, are disarticulated, broken, torn asunder or at least scrambled by "montage thinking." By the same token, the extension into time of the scrambled impression of reality, and its continuation through the unbroken chain of images, is contradicted, even though, in order for its lure to be implanted, and in order to play its role, this unbroken, seamless continuity is precisely what is needed. Working on the status of the image (on the succession of images, because the cinematic image is never in the singular, and because the mechanism of the impression of reality presupposes a duration in order to inscribe movement) in the signifying network redistributing their positions, reorganizing their relations according to systems of opposition and recurrence, dividing and denaturalizing their mechanical enchainment, montage *superposes* on the sequential emission of the impression of reality necessarily produced by any succession of images (whether in a montage sequence or not) another type of movement, that of meaning, of reading, which decenters it, or, more accurately, decenters it from the spectator, who is affronted by a system of discontinuity which consistently contradicts the tendency toward continuity nourished and reinforced by the impression of reality. We can thus re-write Bazin's observation:

> If film art can be reduced in essence [*and this is precisely what Bazin does not believe – JLC*] to what plasticity and editing can add to a given reality [*to an impression of reality that is always given – JLC*], silent film was a complete art. At best, sound could play only a subordinate and complementary role, as counterpoint to the image [*the Eisensteinian, or Vertovian, theory of the "counterpoint" – that is, the contradiction between sound and image – does not lead to a "subordination" of sound, but to a dialectical relationship where, at any rate, as opposed to the Hollywood talkie, sound is not always dominant – JLC*].[13]

12. Bazin, "L'évolution du langage cinématographique," *op. cit.*, p. 142 [p. 99].
13. *Ibid.*, p. 134 [p. 90, translation modified].

Exactly: montage displaces the role assigned to sound, it does not make it a complement – and, very soon, one of the central components – of the impression of reality as a fact of Hollywood narration, but a supplementary contradiction itself able to act against this impression.

There is, in fact, a major gap, and a major conflict, between, on the one hand, a conception of the cinema founded on the proliferation at all signifying levels of the institutional lure of the impression of reality, wherein speech arrives to refine and reinforce this lure, and wherein its intervention could only take this form and not that of a contradiction, and, on the other hand, a conception founded on the "realist" lure being overcome within the filmic text itself, on the film's difference to reality, on the work carried out by the spectator with this difference, to the extent that it produces contradictions, and meaning, where speech can only intervene as a supplementary contradiction at work in the text. Summoned by an ideological lack, the spoken word primarily intervenes in Hollywood cinema at the level of the mechanism of the impression of reality, giving it back its lost luster and vitality, and, at the same time, rendering its properly iconic modes of emission more negligible. This is made overt with depth of field's sudden loss of importance – the unfathomable "depth" of the presence of the spoken word advantageously replaces depth of field.

For with the Hollywood talkie it is not only sound, or noise, that synchronically returns to the image, invests it and draws it to them, but also, and above all, speech – that is, interiority, the discourse of the subject, this void, this cavity that the spoken word delimits as a replete presence, which is incessantly filled by the ideological statements that speak this subject.

V. Which Speech?

From the Hollywood fictions of the end of the silent era to those of the beginning of the sound era, a sharp decline can be detected: less complex, less elaborate, the latter are largely underpinned by the bourgeois theatrical schemas ascendant on Broadway. The reference (whether explicit or not) to musical and/or novelistic forms[1] gave way to popular theater, from which were imported not only a great part of the fictional subject matter, but an entire range of verbally determined narrative codes, which, while they did not go without exerting some pressure on filmic narration, had beforehand only done so externally and, in a certain fashion, analogously, whereas from that point on their naturalization posed no problem whatsoever, and the recourse to theatrical models even appeared as the most fitting solution to the "new" demands of the spoken word, and the most immediately profitable solution, both formally *and* economically. Two main reasons presided over this rapprochement between Hollywood and Broadway – or rather, this invasion of the former by the latter.

As long as the technical elaboration of sound cinema lasted (some 20 years), it seems – and it is astonishing – that nobody, or virtually nobody,[2] whether among technicians and scientists or filmmakers and financiers, asked questions as to what would be done with this "new instrument." The talkies would talk, and that would be that. The only difficulty had been to reach that point; once it was reached, everything else would sort itself out. As for interrogating themselves as to what this speech would be, what it would say and not say, what it would subordinate and govern, what function it would play and what specifications it would have – nothing. Or rather, life itself would speak: all that had to be done was to "capture" this speech in life in order to "put" it in the film, without any other procedure; the mimetic nature of the cinema would guarantee the success of this seizure. This ideological unthought

1. Cf. S.M. Eisenstein, "Dickens, Griffith et nous," [translated into French by Luda and Jean Schnitzer], *Cahiers du cinéma,* nos. 231, 232, 233 and 234-235 (1971-72) ["Dickens, Griffith and the Film Today," in Eisenstein, *Film Form: Essays in Film Theory,* ed. and trans. Jay Leyda (New York: Harcourt & Brace, 1949), pp. 195-255] on the role played by the model of the 19th-century English novel. As for the references to music, it suffices to recall both the critical literature on silent cinema (Élie Faure, for example), with its fetish-theme of "image music," and the aesthetic projects of the filmmakers themselves: for example, the large number of *Symphonies....*

2. Among the rare exceptions: the Soviets (Vertov on the one hand; Eisenstein-Alexandrov-Pudovkin on the other), some figures from a theatrical background (Pagnol above all).

– every spoken communication is coded, culturally and otherwise, whatever misrecognition its subjects may have of it – led to a certain number of theatrical practices coming to the aid of the initial practice of sound cinema, given that the theater was the dominant cultural codification of verbal exchanges. It is at the theater, and not "in life," that the cinema learned to speak, primarily because there was no other model for the representation of the spoken word.

As it happened, it was not only a kinship between the cinematic scene and the theatrical scene that played a role here. Another complicity was established. The technical equipment of sound cinema had to *immediately produce results*, so as to be profitable. The equipment was costly to manufacture, there were markets to conquer, as well as fierce competition, and at the time of the introduction of sound the cinema was *already* a capitalist industry, which, after 15 years of solid profits, could not afford to explore and experiment with a variety of formulae during a period of adaptation, as had been the case during the earliest years of the cinema. The enormous theatrical apparatus of Broadway (mobile and immobile sets, institutions, a repertory, funding, actors, technicians and... an audience) provided it with material that was immediately consumable, distributable, inexhaustible and proven to work. And not only material, but also a guide to usage and box office takings. Broadway helped Hollywood out at a time of need, and Hollywood returned the favor by reconfirming Broadway in its dominant role.

A curious remark by Walter Benjamin[3] focuses on this economic aspect:

> With the sound film, to be sure, a setback in its international distribution occurred at first: audiences became limited by language barriers. This coincided with the Fascist emphasis on national interests. It is more important to focus on this connection with Fascism than on this setback, which was soon minimized by synchronization. The simultaneity of both phenomena is attributable to the depression. The same disturbances which, on a larger scale, led to an attempt to maintain the existing property structure by sheer force led the endangered film capital to speed up the development of the sound film. The introduction of the sound film brought about a temporary relief, not only because it again brought the masses into the theaters but also because it merged new capital from the electrical industry with that of the film industry. Thus, viewed from the outside, the sound film promoted national interests, but seen from the inside it helped to internationalize film production even more than previously.

3. Walter Benjamin, "L'œuvre d'art a l'ère de sa reproductibilité technique," *Poésie et Révolution* (Paris: Denoël, 1971) [repr. Paris: Gallimard, coll. "Folio essais," 2000, p. 181. Translated as "The Work of Art in the Age of Mechanical Reproduction," trans. Harry Zohn, in Benjamin, *Illuminations*, ed. Hannah Arendt (New York: Schocken, 1968), p. 244].

Paradoxically, in fact, it is through the triumph of sound cinema that Hollywood's global hegemony was assured: the process of the internationalization of profits was stronger than the priority given to national cultural values. Sound cinema spoke several different languages, but soon there was only *one* sound cinema: Hollywood and its epigones.[4] This was, of course, partly due to the monopolization of patents and the concentration of financing, which gave Hollywood's bankers control over the majority of film production in the West, with their financial muscle allowing them to invade European markets. But, at the same time, it was also due to the fact that, looking to Broadway, Hollywood was quick to complete its transformation and found itself in a position to "offer" a great variety of speaking products and (with the star system also establishing itself at this time) speaking stars, who, virtually without delay, were able to take over from the leading actors of the silent era. Finally, German and Italian fascism provoked not only ideological resistance from the "liberal" nations, but also measures of economic retaliation to their protectionism and censorship. At the time, German cinema was the most robust competitor to Hollywood, whose victory was considerably facilitated by the fact that, by closing their borders to heterodox ideological products, the Nazis also closed themselves to the majority of markets.

We nonetheless need to see that the economic crisis mentioned by Benjamin – in addition to the range of economic determinations during the promotion of sound cinema that I noted above – *did not only have economic consequences* (patent wars, monopolization, extension of the control of banks, the end of international competition due to Hollywood's near-monopoly of the market). Similarly, the association between Broadway and Hollywood was not confined to the economic level, and did not only have economic effects, even if these appeared to be in the foreground. As far as the theater and the cinema are concerned, this also inseparably happened on the ideological level.

The rapid ascension of the sound cinema, after being held in abeyance for many years, is not only one of the economic repercussions of the great crisis of the capitalist system in 1929; the ideological repercussions of this crisis also played a role. Among others, and what is of principal concern for us: the brand image of triumphant capitalism was dealt a harsh blow. But the traumatisms that the crisis inflicted on the subjects of capitalist ideology, the disruption it provoked in the process of self-satisfaction in which they had been solidly established, had to be and were sealed up as rapidly as possible on the two principal scenes of representation. This was the task

4. We have not sufficiently discussed the fact that the spread of sound cinema also marked the downfall of national cinematic traditions in the sense of the "great schools" of the silent era (Swedish, Italian, French, German...). Not only were a number of their most notable filmmakers attracted to Hollywood in the later years of the silent era, but, with the advent of sound, it seemed that the specific traits of each country were largely embodied in national languages, while screenwriting became aligned with the formal and commercial norms of Hollywood.

assigned to Broadway and Hollywood: to ideologically safeguard an abruptly devalued economic system. The task prioritized by these two scenes was played out through two complementary processes.

On the one hand, there was the "headlong rush" toward spectacle, the manic recourse to dream-worlds (cf. Hollywood's musical comedies, *The Gold Diggers*[i] among others), the rise of escapist fantasy: this is indeed a case of repression, of "forgetting" and denial – never had films cost so much, and never were they seen by so many poor people. Here, speech only circulated in the form of song, and could only be futile, in accord with the morale of the period, emblematized by the "gag" of the ruined millionaire rushing toward the window of his high-rise building: "Might as well laugh it off."

On the other hand, and complementarily, there was the recuperation and anesthetizing of "problems" through the bourgeois humanist reflection on the "value" of man (resisting, for example, the collapse of stock market values), the irreplaceability of the individual, the inalienability of the American genius (cf. the films of Capra); which can be summarized as follows: man built this system, and even if the system goes wrong, man can not. It is therefore on account of the subject, more than ever put into a position of command, that these crises, limited to the ranks of "social conscience dramas," are revived, crises that can only be overcome by social conscience. At the very moment of their objective obsolescence, we witness the massive relaunch of those proven "remedies," which were – and which still are, because the social relations and the ideology that they make dominant and that reiterate them have remained unchanged, in spite of all the recent alarm, and are not permitted to be changed – the moral messages of the "struggle for life," the philosophy of the "self-made man," and the religion of individual success.[5] The advent of speech is also marked by the surge of psychology into Hollywood's archetypal fictions – those exemplary journeys where the hero, having started from nothing or having returned to a void, does not cease in his "ascent." There was, in the first wave of Hollywood talkies, a symptomatic frenzy of words, less because the repressed elements of silent cinema made a return, and more because of the immense confidence given to the sole virtues of discourse, as if the dialogues mired in intersubjectivity, the confessions of guilt, and the interminable psychological explanations had such a power of fascination that by themselves they could take the place of fictional motivations. Speech passes for something that is "naturally" owned by every individual (even when they do not own anything else). Hollywood, relaying bourgeois ideology, strove to demonstrate to the masses ruined by the acts of capitalists that, at the very least, everybody is the master of his own discourse and his own destiny. And it is precisely in these fictions that discourse and destiny are identified with one another, the right to own-

5. And, as an accessory, the warding off of "evil" and the displacement of social problems in "film noir."

ership begins with the ownership of speech – with bourgeois ideology constantly reinforcing the subjects that bolster it in the firm conviction that their speech is their property, theirs and no one else's.

This is why we must stop posing the question of sound cinema in the abstract (as has been done, as far as I know, by those film critics and historians who have analyzed the matter), only taking into consideration the fact of the spoken word, of the spoken word in the silent/sound duality, as if this spoken word was only a floating enunciation sufficient in and of itself, and without asking what this spoken word under investigation is, whence and for whom it speaks.

The place of the individual as the hero of the fiction, already solidly assured in and by Hollywood at the end of the silent era, is redoubled and reinforced by the place of the individual as the master of speech. The Hollywood talkie does not speak in itself [*en soi*]: what it says or sings and the manner in which it says it are inscribed and diffused on a vast scale by the dominant bourgeois ideological discourses and themes. It is not the case that cinematic speech in general is quintessentially reactionary or progressive, because there is no cinematic speech "in general," but rather ideological and economic inscriptions of the sound film, one of which, Hollywood, has been ideologically and economically imposed as a model.

And the fact that this model speech was constructed in Hollywood in the wake of the crisis of 1929 is a matter of no little importance. The Hollywood talkie did not fulfill a "promise" harbored all the while by the silent cinema, nor did it accomplish an abstract "realist destiny": it attained *a certain* realism determined by capitalist relations of production and the bourgeois conception of the world, and the manner in which it did so is no less determined by these factors.

A certain type of dialogue thus prevailed in Hollywood narration from the 1930s onwards, assuring the development, and soon the domination, of classical *découpage*. To the thesis that Bazin condensed as follows: "Sound images, which are much less malleable than visual images, brought editing back to realism and increasingly eliminated both visual expressionism and symbolic relations between images,"[6] we can oppose the notion that the sound cinema did not "bring editing back to realism" but rather utterly liquidated montage as a general principle of cinematic writing, *at least as far as bourgeois cinema is concerned*, inasmuch as that "realism" toward which "progress" is made (according to Bazin) is precisely not any realism whatsoever, but the realism of a specific kind of speech and ideology (whose principal determinations I noted above), which, among others, rejects montage as signifying work. From montage to *découpage* – even if we restrict our consideration to the context of Hollywood between the end of the silent era and the early sound period – there is not a harmonious evolution, an unobtrusive gradation, a transition through improvements and corrections, from a lesser to a greater degree of realism, but a rupture. There is an

6. Bazin, "L'évolution du langage cinématographique," *op. cit.*, p. 141 [p. 98].

antagonism between the two systems, the latter is not an advance on, or the conclusion or transcendence of the former, but its refusal and its censorship.

Contrary to what linear histories of the cinema may have us think, this is first of all due to the fact that there was not a passage from a silent period dominated by montage practices to a sound period dominated by the practice of *découpage*, as if the transition from montage to *découpage* could be rigorously traced onto the transition from silent cinema to sound. In fact (and Bazin picked up on this) the two systems coexisted before the advent of the sound film, and this coexistence was not a peaceful one. Sound cinema chose its camp – and this camp, too, had *already* chosen sound and prepared the way for it – in a conflict *already* opened up between montage practices (the variety of formalist avant-gardes and the Soviet cinema of the mid- to late-1920s) and the system of *découpage* which, at least in rough outline, was in place in Hollywood since Griffith and his immediate aftermath.

Film histories note (and are naïvely astonished by) the fact that Hollywood filmmakers of the silent era were able to "adapt" to sound earlier and better than their European and Soviet counterparts. On a formal level, the Hollywood talkie did not fall from the sky, but was inserted into structures and compartments which were to all intents and purposes already constituted, and of which it was at one and the same time the product and the refinement. Only a small part of Griffith's "heritage" bore fruit in Hollywood: not the experiments in montage which, via Eisenstein, were adopted and transformed in the Soviet cinema, but, exclusively, its fabled "basic grammar," the matrix of "classical *découpage*" that sound cinema only had to perfect and tweak (that is, repeat). Bazin, who thus stresses the antagonism between the two systems, errs when, in order to support his entreaties in favor of *découpage* and "surplus realism," he insists that the "synthetic conception of montage" was nigh on dominant at the end of the silent era. In fact, it undeniably remained an avant-garde practice, even if these films enjoyed more widespread distribution at the time than their counterparts do today.

It is not for nothing that the ideological determinations and investments of these two practices were in conflict, nor that one of them was principally developed in the Soviet Union, and the other in Hollywood. It would be fundamentally simplistic to place an equals sign between montage and materialism (or between montage and dialectics) on the one hand and *découpage* and idealism (or metaphysics) on the other hand. Griffithian montage reworked signifying materiality and produced formal clashes (in *Intolerance*[7]), but it is neither materialist nor dialectical. It is also not for nothing that Eisenstein and Vertov conceived, practiced and defended montage as

---

7. Cf. Pierre Baudry, "Les aventures de l'idée" (*Cahiers du cinéma*, no. 240 [1972], pp. 51-59, and no. 241 [1972], pp. 31-45), as well as Eisenstein's work on Griffith, cited above. We should stress that *Intolerance* ought today to be examined, from the perspective of the generation of Hollywood models, as a point of excess in all areas: the film contains, taken to an extreme degree, both that which was reproduced and that which was censored by the later development of Hollywood cinema.

responding to the dialectical materialist conception of film writing and the filmic scene. Nor is it an innocent fact that Bazin privileged *découpage* – even if he critiqued its Hollywood "excesses." A key component of *découpage* is its link to bourgeois representation, a metaphysical conception of the filmic scene as the reproduction and revelation of an already-there. It does not produce this scene, it does not designate it, "it allows us to see it better, emphasizing that which merits emphasis" (Bazin). It does not divide the scene, it breaks it down [*découpe*], precisely by preserving its unity, postulated as "real" or "natural," along a range of different angles (which, incidentally, is rather restricted and loaded with taboos: rules governing eyeline-matches, the 30° rule, the 180° rule, etc.). *Découpage* varies the scene, makes it *turn*, but takes care not to alter it, not to break its continuity, not to bridle its plenitude and coherence. Its function is to unify, fuse and reconcile, and this function perfectly suits the investment of Hollywood's representative scene through the bourgeois spoken word, through communication as a point of connection and reunion.

The Bazinian definition of Hollywood *découpage* – "1. The realistic nature of space, in which the character's position is always known, even when a close-up removes the decor from view; 2. The intent and effects of the *découpage* are exclusively dramatic and psychological"[8] – amply indicates the extent to which this *découpage* is subject to the structure and function of *dialogue*.

This continuous, homogenous, oriented space, where the spectator – because the scene and its dimensions are tailored to his eye ("camera at the level of the human eye") – runs no risk of being lost, nor of the actors being lost, nor of losing sight of the actors, is the space of spoken communication, the circulation zone of speech such as it has been codified by bourgeois representation (Broadway among others, as far as we are concerned), that is, as a *dialogue scene*: the shuttling back and forth of the spoken word between two or more characters reconnects and marks out the sites of the emission and reception of discourse, the place of the subjects, the *origins* and *destinations* of sounds and meaning. Because it is the scene of communication, the site where, confronting one another, discursive presences unite with each other, the unified and totalizing nature of this scene must be preserved – but not without losing sight of the agents of this confrontation, the speakers and listeners. This is the dual exigency – continuity/variation of the points of view and valorization of the subjects – that Hollywood *découpage* resolves by means of a casuistry of matching camera-angles. Inevitably, to pass from one shot to another, from one camera-angle to another, while *expunging the mark of the leap*, it is necessary to both *cut* and *efface* the cut. To do without cutting (by condensing several shots into a sequence shot) would involve formalizing and inscribing the materiality of the transition through camera-pans and disruptive re-framings, which represent signifying incidents (cf. Godard's resolution of the shot/reverse shot in *Vivre sa vie* and *Une femme est une femme*). To

8. Bazin, "L'évolution du langage cinématographique," *op. cit.*, p. 140 [p. 97, translation modified].

do without matching camera-angles would inscribe the materiality of the leap, of the gap, which is similarly intolerable. The match-cut thus accomplishes this dual, contradictory task: it makes cuts *gentle*, it lubricates them, it abolishes them in a succession of minimal, smooth transitions. *Découpage* in sound cinema is also called *invisible* editing. It is here that we once again find, extended to the entire system of narration by the insertion of the spoken word, the phantasmatic mechanism implanted by the impression of reality: enabling the spectator to see without being seen, to cut without being cut. To the "transparency" of meaning in the spoken word, and the "transparency" of the spoken word for the subject, responds the "transparency" to this meaning, this spoken word, this subject, of the functioning of the film itself. (*To be continued*)

Thus is interrupted, unfinished, "Technique and Ideology."

Appendices

Appendix I: Cinema/Ideology/ Criticism

Translator's Introduction

Although *Cahiers du cinéma* had evinced a broadly left-wing alignment for several years (a tendency which had become progressively more pronounced in the wake of May '68), Comolli and Narboni's jointly written October 1969 editorial "Cinema/ Ideology/Criticism" represents the first open avowal of Marxism as the journal's governing political orientation. The impetus for doing so was at least partially provided by a certain amount of goading from the quarters of *Tel Quel* and the newborn *Cinéthique* – in particular, Marcelin Pleynet and Jean Thibaudeau's interview with Gérard Leblanc in *Cinéthique*'s third issue (dating from April 1969, six months before Comolli/Narboni's editorial), echoes of which can be found in "Cinema/Ideology/ Criticism" at several points in the text. But it was also in line with the internal evolution of *Cahiers*, as a younger generation of writers (and readers) drawn from the student left gravitated toward the journal. The editorial thus aimed to set out the theoretical and political principles which, in spite of a number of tumultuous changes, would guide *Cahiers*' work in the following years. As such, "Cinema/Ideology/Criticism" is a crucial companion piece to "Technique and Ideology," and it is for this reason that it is included in this volume, in spite of its ready availability elsewhere.

With the editorial's strident proclamation that "every film is political" and its stress on the importance of understanding the economic and ideological determinations of films, rather than considering them as works of art autonomous from broader social conditions, Comolli and Narboni strove to mark their distances from the "*politique des auteurs*" with which *Cahiers* was still associated in the eyes of much of the French public. They also placed an emphasis, however, on the ability of films to provoke formal "discrepancies" or "ruptures" with the cinema's overarching ideological function, and the extent to which films are able do this forms the basis for the famous "seven categories" of films proposed by the *Cahiers* editors, and the fourfold "critical function" that results from this classification. Much has been made of the extent to which these categories are valid – and even the very notion of classifying films in such blanket terms may appear questionable today.[1] It should be remembered, however, that the seven categories are never presented as a definitive breakdown of cinematic production, and that the initial motivation behind them was to provide nuance to the Manichaean oppositions of much politically radical film criticism (sweepingly dividing the cinema into reactionary and revolutionary works, with the criteria for doing so usually resting on the express political content of the films in question) and to open up critical work to the formal and political ambiguities which provide the basis, above all, for categories (c) and (e). Moreover, the categories are never referred to as such in later issues of *Cahiers*, although subsequent texts will clearly hark back to this classification: their seminal article on *Young Mr. Lincoln* from August 1970 is evidently a case study of a category (e) film.

"Cinema/Ideology/Criticism" quickly appeared in translated form in *Screen*. Its publication in the English journal's Spring 1971 issue marked the onset of *Screen*'s own shift toward an Althusserian Marxist outlook, and the influence of the text was such that it has since been re-printed in a plethora of anthologies. Even now it is often seen as the single most concise encapsulation of the theoretical underpinnings of "1970s film theory," with its programmatic nature ensuring its status as an access point to this theoretical tendency for generations of film studies students. In several important respects, however, the article in its English-language form, as translated by Susan Bennett, is *not* the text as originally written by Comolli and Narboni. Bennett's translation is so freely adapted from the original article that at a number of points it departs markedly from Comolli and Narboni's own statements. As such, a few of the more glaring errors in the pre-existing translation will be addressed below.

Its deficiencies appear from the very first sentence of the text, which Bennett renders as "Scientific criticism has an obligation define its field and methods" (p. 2).[2] This quote, indeed, has been taken as gospel in some quarters, who have attributed to *Cahiers* an untempered claim that the journal practiced a "scientific" approach to film criticism. In view of the importance for the journal of the Althusserian distinction between "ideological" and "scientific" discourse, this would represent an assertion of capital importance. But the assertion is the translator's invention: in the original text, we find instead the rather wordier formulation: "D'une entreprise critique qui se veut *conséquente*, on est en droit d'attendre qu'elle délimite le plus rigoureusement qu'il se peut son champ et ses moyens d'action [emphasis added]." It is certainly tricky to find an English equivalent for the adjective "*conséquente*" – I have opted for "systematic" – but to render it as "scientific" invites a host of connotations which the authors are careful to avoid. In fact, the question as to whether film criti-

1. This, at least, is the thrust of Barbara Klinger's stance toward the text. Cf. "Cinema/Ideology/Criticism Revisited: The Progressive Text," *Screen*, vol. 25 no. 1 (1984), pp. 30-44.

2. Page references for Bennett's translation are taken from: Jean-Louis Comolli and Jean Narboni, "Cinema/Ideology/Criticism," trans. Susan Bennett, *Screen Reader 1: Cinema, Ideology, Politics*, ed. Sam Rohdie (London: BFI, 1977), pp. 2-11.

cism could be "scientific" was a vexed one for *Cahiers*; mindful of what Badiou called "the autonomy of the aesthetic process" and suspicious of the claims made by *Cinéthique* to be practicing "scientific criticism," at most they saw it as something to aim for, but not an epistemological status that could simply be attained overnight with a change of editorial line.

The problems with the translation deepen as the text continues, and often belie a lack of familiarity with the theoretical terminology being deployed by *Cahiers*. "*Système de représentation*," for instance, which occurs on a number of occasions in the text, is given as "depiction of reality," a loose rendering which thus voids the expression of its roots in Althusser's discussion of ideology in *For Marx*. This becomes particularly problematic when, in discussing "category (b)" films (those works which "operate a double action on their ideological insertion": on the level of both signified and signifiers), Comolli and Narboni refer to a "political act" that "must be linked to a critical de-construction of the system of representation." This passage is crucial for a number of reasons: its linking of the Derridean notion of "critical de-construction" to Althusser's Marxist-inflected "system of representation" denotes a moment when these two hermeneutic frameworks could still be seen as operating in tandem with one another, and the telltale retention of the hyphen in "de-construction" is a trace of the *Cahiers* writers' relatively fresh exposure to this conceptual apparatus. Moreover, it also seems to be an echo of a comment made by Thibaudeau in the interview appearing in issue no. 3 of *Cinéthique* (for more on this, cf. translator's note v to the text). But it disappears in Bennett's translation, replaced with the less theoretically inflected phrase: "a breaking down of the traditional way of depicting reality" (p. 6).

Perhaps the most flagrant inaccuracy in Bennett's translation occurs in an earlier passage, where she has the *Cahiers* editors assert: "Because every film is part of the economic system it is also a part of the ideological system, for 'cinema' and 'art' are branches of ideology. None can escape: somewhere, like pieces in a jigsaw, all have their own allotted place" (p. 4). Much of this is formulated in a far more rudimentary manner than it is in the original: Comolli and Narboni themselves speak of the "economic *insertion* of a film" and of its being "*encompassed* [*englobé*] in the dominant ideology [emphasis added]." Moreover, in this passage, the phrase "'cinema' and 'art' are branches of ideology" is nowhere to be found: it is only in the next paragraph that the *Cahiers* editors refer to the "vast field of ideology, one of whose names is 'cinema' or 'art'." Shifting a phrase from its original position and stripping it of its ambiguity, Bennett significantly transforms the meaning of the passage, and this is continued when her translation states: "The system is blind to its own nature, but in spite of that, indeed because of that, when all the pieces are fitted together they give a very clear picture" (p. 4) This reverses the thrust of the original, which speaks of the "ideological puzzle" as being "extremely coherent in its shards, despite, or because of, the fact that it is *blind* with respect to itself."

Indeed, it is notable that these citations come from a paragraph containing a single, 200-word sentence, dominated by concessive clauses, which Bennett breaks down into a series of slogan-like proclamations. This tendency recurs throughout her translation, and has the effect of creating an oversimplified text which, while influential for the readers of *Screen* and the later anthologies that included this article, did an injustice to the original. Where Bennett has them issuing brazen assertions, the *Cahiers* editors tended to be more tentative and exploratory in articulating arguments that, in many cases, they were still in the process of fully working out. On this level, it is hoped that the present translation does more justice to the original text.

This text is followed by part II of "Cinema/Ideology/Criticism," published with the subtitle "On Criticism at its Critical Point" in no. 217 of *Cahiers* (immediately before the journal was shut down by Filipacchi). In this article, Comolli and Narboni's focus shifts to a polemic with *Cinéthique*, and they commence by tackling a series of texts composed by that journal's editorial committee and printed in *Cinéthique* no. 5, before concentrating on an article submitted by Marcelin Pleynet for publication in the same number: "Le front 'gauche' de l'art: les vieux 'jeunes-hégéliens'." In spite of the apparent theoretical proximity of the journals, this exchange is a heated one – and will be continued in the same vein in *Cinéthique* no. 6. Although the *Cahiers* editors occasionally become bogged down in pedantry (typographical errors are lengthily discussed on two occasions), the text is nonetheless of great value in its discussion of a number of conceptual frameworks with which both *Cahiers* and *Cinéthique* were grappling at the time. A translation by Susan Bennett was published in two parts in *Screen*, in Summer 1971 (vol. 12 no. 2) and Spring 1972 (vol. 13 no. 1), alongside translations of the relevant *Cinéthique* articles, and was reprinted in *Screen Reader 1* (pp. 36-46, 244-255), but has not found publication since then, in spite of the numerous reprises of the first part of "Cinema/Ideology/Politics." As with the first part of the text, the translation offered here is a completely new one.

Cinema/Ideology/Criticism (I)

By Jean Narboni and Jean-Louis Comolli

It is only proper to expect of a critical undertaking which aims to be systematic that it delimit as rigorously as possible its field and its means of action: the site in which it is situated, the domain which it claims to study, and what renders it both necessary and possible. And, in this site and in view of this site, the function which it proposes to fulfill, its specific task.

As far as we – *Cahiers du Cinéma* – are concerned, such a global definition of the position we are in, and the direction we are taking, is essential at the present moment. Not that we are beginning from a blank slate: fragmentarily, our position could already be read in recent texts (articles, editorials, debates, responses to readers' letters), but in a vague and accidental manner. It has therefore been felt, by both our readers and ourselves, that there is the need for a theorization of the criticism being practiced by us, and of its field, the two being inseparable. It is not a matter of tracing out a "program" for ourselves to proclaim, nor of clutching at "revolutionary" declarations and projects, but rather, of attempting a reflection, not on what we "want" (would like) to do, but on what we *do* and what we *can* do. The analysis of the present situation is therefore an indispensable condition of implementing this reflection.

I. Where?

(A). Firstly, what site are we speaking of? *Cahiers* is a working group, one of the effects of whose work can be seen in the form of a journal.[1] A journal, that is to say: a certain product costing a certain quantity of labor (by those who write it, as well as by those who produce it, and even by those who read it), and sold at a certain price. We do not seek to hide the fact that such a product is situated very precisely in the economic system of capitalist publishing (modes of production, circuits of distribution, etc.). In any case it is hard to see how it could be otherwise today, unless we are to fall into the utopia of a "parallelism" whose first – paradoxical – effect is to consti-

1. Other effects include: the distribution, presentation and discussion of films screening in the provinces and the suburbs, film production, gatherings for theoretical work (see "Montage," *Cahiers du cinéma*, no. 210 [1969]).

tute, alongside the system from which it claims to escape, an illusory externality, a "neo-system" under the illusion that it is able to cancel out that which it is content to reject (idealist purism), and which is therefore very quickly threatened by its own "model."[2] Against this univocal "parallelism," acting on only one side – the external side – of the wound (whereas we are of the opinion that *both sides* need to be treated), and against the threat of a precipitous conjunction of the parallels in the infinite, let us affirm that we have opted for disjunction in the finite.[i]

Having affirmed this, the question is: What is our attitude toward the site in which we find ourselves situated? Given that the majority of films in France (to tell the truth: all of them, no matter what means are sought to escape this fact) are produced and distributed, like the majority of (all) books and journals, by the capitalist economic system and within the dominant ideology, it is important to know, with regard to these films, as well as these books and journals, whether they are content to be traversed by ideology such as it is, as its site of passage, its transparent mediation, its chosen language, or whether, on the other hand, they attempt to turn it back on itself, to reflect on it, to intervene *into* it, to render it visible and in doing so render its mechanisms visible – by blocking them.

(B). For the site in which we *act* is the field of cinema (*Cahiers* is a film journal);[3] and, more precisely, what we have to study is the film, in its history: its production, fabrication, distribution[4] and reading.

"What is a film today?" is the question and not (any longer) just: "What is cinema?"[ii] This is all the less the case considering that there is no theoretical knowledge or awareness constituted on "the cinema" (though we intend to contribute to this) which could fill this hollow term with a concept.[iii] And, for a film journal, the question is also: What work needs to be carried out in the field constituted by films? And for *Cahiers* in particular: What is our specific function in this field, what should mark our difference from other "film journals"?

---

2. Or tolerated, and therefore threatened by this very tolerance. Must we insist on the proven tactic of covertly repressive systems for dealing with the dissenting "fringes": that they do all they can to ignore them as vigilantly as possible? This attitude is doubly effective: in some people it instills the cautious approach of tolerance, in others the good conscience of clandestine action.

3. A field where there is no question, in a narrow-minded, corporatist gesture, of cutting ourselves off from another, infinitely vaster field, in which the political stakes are obvious. Simply put, insisting on the precise field of complex social practice is, *in this text*, a response to precise operational reasons.

4. A more and more pressing problem, which it is important to pose theoretically, and not to return to the disorder of dispersed initiatives: for now, though, we will set it aside from this text, to return to it later.

II. The Films

What is a film? On the one hand it is a particular product manufactured in a precise economic system, costing labor (money) to manufacture (and even "independent" films or films of the "new cinema" do not escape this economic determination), bringing together for this purpose a certain number of workers (including the "director," who, in the final analysis, whether it is Oury or Moullet, is a "film worker"), and thereby becoming a commodity, an exchange value, because it is sold in the form of entry tickets or contracts and determined by the circuits of amortization, distribution, diffusion, etc. On the other hand, and *consequently*, it is a product determined by the ideology of the economic system which produces and sells films – which is, in the case of films made and seen in France, the ideology of capitalism.[5]

Even if no film can of its own accord change the economic facts of its production and distribution (let us repeat that even films which want to be "revolutionary" on the level of their messages and forms can not – radically or in one fell swoop – change the economic system: deform it, yes, deviate it, partially distort it, but not negate it or overturn it from top to bottom; Godard's recent attitude, declaring his wish to no longer work in the "system," will not prevent him from having to work in another system which is only ever a reflection of the initial one: the money may no longer come from the Champs-Élysées, but it does come from London, Rome or New York, the film may no longer be exploited by the monopolies of distribution, but it is shot on the film stock of the Kodak monopoly, and so on); even if, therefore, in light of the economic insertion of a film, we are faced with a factor of constant determination; and even if films – all of which are, by means of this economic determination, encompassed in the dominant ideology – are all, through this process, from the very beginning pieces of the ideological puzzle (a puzzle which is extremely coherent in its shards, despite, or because of, the fact that it is *blind* with respect to itself), they can still play different roles in it, react differently toward it.

So the task of criticism is to make these *differences* manifest, to study the particular situations within the vast field of ideology – one of whose names is "cinema" or "art" – and to aid in its transformation (the result of which will not take place magically, all of a sudden, by the forceful blow of brutal decisions: rather, it occurs slowly yet firmly).

In passing, we will indicate a few points to which it will be necessary to return: *every film is political,* inasmuch as it is determined by the given ideology which produces it (or in which it is produced, which amounts to the same thing). This determination is all the stronger and more complete in the case of the cinema, because, as

5. "Capitalist ideology": the use we make of this term in the rest of the text (due to its clarity), without specifying it further, should not be taken as a sign that we are under any illusion that it possesses some kind of "abstract essence": we know it is historically and socially determined, multiple according to place and time, and variable throughout history.

opposed to other arts or ideological systems, it deploys substantial economic forces, even at the level of production (and not only at the level of distribution, publicity and sales, domains in which the cinema has no cause to envy "literature," or the commodity "book"). It is known that the cinema "reproduces" reality "totally naturally," because cameras and film stock are made in view of this very goal (*and within the ideology that imposes this goal*). But it is clear that this reality – susceptible to being reproduced faithfully, reflected by instruments and techniques which otherwise form a part of it – is entirely ideological. In this sense, the theory of "transparency" (cinematic classicism) is eminently reactionary: it is not the world in its "concrete reality" which is "seized" by (or, rather, impregnates) a non-interventionist instrument, but rather the vague, unformulated, untheorized, unthought world of the dominant ideology. The languages through which the world communicates to itself (including the cinema) constitute its ideology, in the sense that, speaking to itself, the world presents itself: how it is, in fact, lived and apprehended through the mode of ideological illusion. (According to Althusser's strict description: "'Ideologies' are perceived-accepted-suffered cultural objects, and they act functionally on men via a process that escapes them. [...] In ideology men do indeed express not the relation between them and their conditions of existence, but *the way* they live the relation between them and their conditions of existence: this presupposes both a real relation and an 'imaginary,' 'lived' relation."[iv]) Thus, the cinema is burdened from the very beginning, from the very first meter of film processed, by the inevitability of reproducing things not as they are in their concrete reality, but as they are when refracted through ideology; and this system of representation is present at all stages of film production – subjects, "styles," forms, meanings and narrative traditions reinforce the general ideological discourse. This is how ideology re-presents itself through the cinema. It shows itself, speaks to itself, teaches itself in this very representation. The most important task of the cinema, once we know that it is the nature of this system to turn it into an instrument of ideology, is therefore to question the system of representation itself: to question itself as cinema, in order to provoke a discrepancy or a rupture with its ideological function.

It is in relation to this demand that films today can be divided.

(A) An initial category, the largest, comprises those films which are thoroughly bathed in ideology, which express it, carry it forward without any gaps or distortions, being blindly faithful to it, and above all being blind to this very fidelity. In our opinion, the majority of films (be they "commercial" or "ambitious," "modern" or traditional," be they shown in "art houses" or on the Champs-Elysées, be they "young" or "old" cinema, all films, we have stated, are commodities and therefore objects of commerce, including those which explicitly have a political discourse – which is why the notion of a "political" cinema, today widely proclaimed,[6] should be rigorously clarified) are precisely the "unconscious" instruments of the ideology which produces them, churning them out on a daily basis. This *conformity* can be initially seen in the alignment – that is, the repetition of conformity – of public "demand" with the economic "response": ideological practice, in direct continuity with political practice (and this is a scientifically established fact, not a hypothesis) reformulates social needs and duplicates them with a discourse. Ideology speaks to itself: it has ready responses to which it furnishes false questions. (This means that there is indeed such a thing as public "demand," that is to say, the demands of the dominant ideology in a society, as it is this ideology which, in order to justify itself and perpetuate itself, creates the notion of the "public" and its tastes, a "public" which can only express itself through the ideology's modes of thought, functioning consequently in the schema of the closed circuit, of the specular mirage.)

On the other hand, in the same sense, at the level of the process of the constitution of forms, this confirmation/demand (this conformity) is *repeated* by the total acceptance in these films of the system of representation. This is the triumph of "bourgeois realism," of the arsenal of security, of the blind confidence in "life," of humanism, of "common sense," etc. This is true to such an extent that it can be a good way to arrive at the most effective definition as to which films come under the "commercial" category: not through the level of box-office takings, but through the innocent absence at every stage of production of even the slightest questioning of the representative nature of cinema. Nothing in these films causes a break with conformity and audience fascination, since, in the most reassuring manner, it is ideology itself which is being spoken in them, and which speaks to itself about itself, without any discrepancy. We can say, then, that there is no difference between the ideology in the auditorium and that of the film. Hence we could propose, as a complementary task for film criticism, an investigation, in certain cases, of the conformity (at all levels) between the products of ideology and the ideological system, and an analysis, for example, of the success of the films of Melville, Oury or Lelouch, insofar as they are monologues of ideology talking to itself.

---

6. As is the case with the category of the "militant" cinema, currently completely vague and indeterminate. What we need to do is to: (a) rigorously specify the function attributed to it, the aims intended, the effect counted on (information, awakening, critical reflection, provocation "from which something will always result"...), and *on whom* this function occurs; (b) define which strict political line these films are made and shown for, and not to be content with the vague, all-purpose qualification "revolutionary"; (c) announce if, on these terms, an activity is proposed in which cinematic practice will be the poor relation, in the illusion that the less it is exercised, the more the "militant" effect will increase in force and clarity. All this, for example, will serve to avoid the contradictions of the "parallel cinema," indefinitely mired in the problem of knowing if "underground films" should be included in this category, under the pretext that their relationships to drugs and sex, their formalistic preoccupations, are susceptible or not to instilling new modes of relations between the film and the spectator.

(B) A second category comprises those films which operate a double action on their ideological insertion. Firstly: a directly political action, at the level of the "signifieds," through the treatment of some kind of explicitly political subject ("treat" – not in the sense of discuss, reiterate, paraphrase, but to be understood as a transitive verb: an action *on* – an explicitly political subject constituting a critical return to ideology, presupposing a theoretical work which is the absolute opposite of the ideological). In order to have any effectiveness, this political act must be linked to a critical deconstruction of the system of representation.[v] At the level of the constitutive process of forms, films like *Not Reconciled, The Edge* and *Terra em Transe*[vi] operate a questioning of cinematic representation (and mark a break with the tradition constituting this representation).

We repeat that only this double action (at the level of both the "signifieds" and the "signifiers")[7] has some chance of operating *against* (in) the dominant ideology; the economic-political and formal aspects of this double action are indissoluble.

(C) Another category (where the same double action is effected, but "against the grain") comprises those films in which the signified is not *explicitly* political, but, in some way, "becomes" so; that is, finds itself re-produced as such by the "formal" critical work[8] on it – examples are *Méditerranée, The Bellboy, Persona...*[vii] For *Cahiers*, these films ((b) and (c)) are the essence of the cinema and make up the essence of the journal.

(D) Fourth case: those films (more and more numerous) which have an explicit political "content" (*Z* is not the best example, the politics in it being from the start ideo-

---

7. We do not wish to conceal the fact that the distinction between these two terms – here simply an operational one – can be static and simplistic, particularly in the case of the cinema, where the signifieds are most often nothing but the product of signifying permutations and are derived from the interaction of lexical units [*lexies*].

8. This attempt is not that of an, improbable, magical, way out from the "representative system" (particularly dominant in the cinema) but that of a rigorous, meticulous, large-scale work *on* this representation, the conditions that make it possible, the mechanisms that make it *innocent*: making it manifest by designating it, disposing of it, playing with it (making use of it to outplay it). This work ought not merely be reduced to "turning film syntax on its head" (although it may incorporate this). Even the slightest non-chronological film periodically demands to operate in the manner of this ill-defined "modernity." Without constituting "models," films as rigorously chronological as *El angel exterminador* [Luis Buñuel, 1962] or *Chronik der Anna Magdalena Bach* [Jean-Marie Straub and Danièle Huillet, 1968] can yield a subversive practice in this regard, at exactly that point where many a film with a dislocated chronology in fact overlaps with naturalistic writing. By the same token, to rely on perceptual jamming (e.g. subliminal insertions, various alterations of the film stock) sufficing to exceed the limits of representation is tantamount to being blithely unaware of the failure of the "lettrists" or the "Zaoum" movement to give infinity to language through the creation of words deprived of meaning or based on novel onomatopoeia: in both cases this involves alteration on the most superficial level of language, the immediate creation of a code of the impossible, which is then resolutely rejected, and not transgressive.

logically represented without let-up; it would be better to cite *Le Temps de vivre*[viii]), but which in fact do not operate any veritable critique of the ideological system in which they are captured, as they adopt its language and modes of figuration without question.

It will be important, then, for criticism to question the transmission of the political critique desired by these films – if they find themselves expressing, reinforcing and duplicating exactly that which they think they denounce, if they are captured by the system which they want to dismantle... (see (a))

(E) Five: those films which are apparently representative of the ideological chains to which they appear subjected, but in which, through the truthful work through and in the film, there is installed a discrepancy, a distortion, a rupture between the conditions of its appearance (the conciliatory – if not out-and-out reactionary – or feebly critical ideological project) and the end product: the ideology not being directly transposed from the intentions of the author to the film itself (these insubstantial films do not matter to us), but encountering obstacles, making detours and short cuts, seeing itself exhibited, shown up, denounced by the filmic framework in which it is captured and which *acts against it*, allowing us to see its limits but at the same time what transgresses them, and pushed by the critical work, a work which may be detected by an oblique, symptomatic reading, seizing, beyond the apparent formal coherence of the film, on its discrepancies, its fault lines, fault lines which an anodyne film is incapable of provoking. Ideology becomes an *effect* of the text, it does not persist as such; only the work of the film permits its *presentation*, its exposition. This is the case with many Hollywood films, for example, which, while being completely integrated into the system and its ideology, end up bringing about, internally, a certain dismantling of it. It is therefore necessary to know what makes possible the transformative self-designation of ideology in these films: whether it is simply the generous project of a "liberal" filmmaker (in which case the recuperation of the film by ideology is immediate and definitive) or whether, in a more complex fashion (see above), the film's deployment of a certain number of mechanisms of figuration produces these effects of discrepancy and rupture, which shatter, not the ideology which presides over the film (of course), but its reflection in the film, and the image which it gives of itself (for example, the films of Ford, Dreyer and Rossellini).

With regards to this category of films, which currently suffer from the most facile terrorism, our position is clear: being themselves the mythology of their own myths, they have no need of a judgment which, heedless of their own critical work (even if it is not inscribed in the initial project), does it for them by rejecting them with contempt. It seems more important to us to show this work in action.

(F) Films pertaining to the "direct cinema," first group: those, the most numerous, which are constituted by political (social) events or reflections, but which do not truly differentiate themselves from non-political cinema insofar as they do not question the cinema as a system of ideological representation, and so depict miners' strikes in the same formal system as *Les Grandes Familles*.[ix] The major, fundamental illusion of this cinema is to believe that once the ideological filter of classical narrative traditions (in terms of dramaturgy, construction, the domination over the component parts and the concern for visual beauty) is broken, reality will offer itself in its "truth," when in fact only a *single* filter is broken, and not even the most important one. Reality in no way contains its own *knowledge*, its theorization, its truth, like the fruit contains a stone, but rather, these must be produced (according to the strict Marxist distinction between the "real object" and the "object of knowledge": cf. *Chiefs* (Leacock),[x] and not a few of the films about May).

This is the reason why, in order to protect its function and sanction its "successes," the "direct cinema" resorts to the same idealist terminology as that of the most contrived films: "authenticity," "sense of lived experience," "snapshots captured unawares," "moments of intense truth," "transparency," and, finally, fascination. It resorts to the magical notion of the "gaze," through which ideology shows itself in order not to be denounced, in which it contemplates itself and does not criticize itself.

(G) Films of the "direct cinema," group two: those which, not satisfied with the "gaze that pierces through appearances," concentrate on the problem of representation in making the filmic material function, and thus become productive of meaning, rather than being a passive receptacle of significations which would be produced outside of itself (in ideology): *Le Règne du jour, La Rentrée des Usines Wonder*.[xi]

III. The Critical Function

Such is the field of our critical activity: films captured within ideology; their relations to it; the differences between these relations. Four functions arise out of this precisely demarcated field: 1. for the films from category (a), to shed light on what it is that they are blind to: their total determination, their *molding* by ideology. 2. for those films from types (b), (c) and (g), to proceed to a double reading, to highlight the reflexive double operation enacted by the film: on the signifieds and the signifiers. 3. for those films from types (d) and (f), to show the extent to which the (political) signifieds *always* find themselves weakened, made innocent by the absence of technical/theoretical work on the signifiers. 4. for those films from group (e): to pinpoint the ideological gap produced by the work of the film, and this work itself.

This fourfold function determines a criticism which does not intend to be of the "speculative" type (commentary, exegesis, even decryption),[xii] nor of the "idle gossip" type (the chattering of journalistic hacks), since it is founded on the study and comparison of the given facts which preside over the film's production (a given economy, ideology, demand-response mechanism), as well as over the, just as tangible, production of meanings and forms in the film.

Continuing the tenacious, persistent tradition of innumerable useless and evanescent writings on the cinema, film analysis today is overwhelmingly determined by idealist presuppositions, which are still doomed, albeit in a more and more errant manner, to empiricism. After a necessary stage – but one that it was necessary to overcome – of returning more closely to film in the materiality of its elements, in its signifying structures, its formal organization (whose first steps were taken, in spite of the reparable contradictions in his texts, by André Bazin, and whose path the model of structural linguistics continued; a path marked by the two major defects – from which we ourselves have not escaped – of phenomenological positivism and mechanistic materialism), the only possible direction for criticism is, it appears to us, to go back to the theoretical research of the Russian filmmakers of the 1920s (Eisenstein primarily) and to attempt the elaboration and application of a critical theory of the cinema, a specific mode of apprehension of rigorously determined objects, with direct reference to the method of dialectical materialism.

Let us clarify, if it is necessary, that it is not through an "immediate," magical operation that the "policy" of a journal can – or even should – be corrected, but rather through hard work to be pursued month by month. We will avoid, in our own field, all spontaneism, all "revolutionary" hastiness. It can not, therefore, at the present stage, be a matter of the proclamation of a revelatory truth (the myth of miraculous transformation, of "conversion"), but of the affirmation of a work already underway, in relation to which all of the texts published here ought to define themselves, either implicitly or explicitly.

We will briefly indicate how the various components of the journal will be inserted into this perspective. The essence of this work will obviously be effectuated in our theoretical and critical texts (the distinction between the two tending toward being more and more effaced, as we do not propose that the latter keep score of the qualities and defects of those films which we are forced to speak about due to their topicality, nor that they "peddle the merchandise," as a snide remark would have it[xiii]). On the other hand, as far as, principally, the interviews are concerned, but also the "*petit journal*" and the "film listings," whose informational function (dossiers and pieces added for potential discussion) often trumps their theoretical function, it is up to the reader to decide *when* and *how much* this distance is noticeable (or not).

Cinema/Ideology/Criticism (II): On Criticism at Its Critical Point

The premise for this article, and its motivation, lies in other texts, external to *Cahiers*, which we aim to refute. It could therefore seem to have a merely circumstantial value, worthless beyond the polemics in which it is engaging. The reader should verify its place – a normal one, following on from our previous editorial, rather than a place in some kind of "Notebook of Journals" [*Cahier des revues*]. With this article, even in its insistent negativity, we will be able to sketch out the possible basis for other texts on the cinema, to appear in later issues of *Cahiers*.

***

What film criticism is and what it is not – and what it ought to be – is the central problem facing us; here, too, much as we have undertaken to do for films themselves, it is first appropriate to provide an overview of the current state of affairs.

In section III of our previous text ("Critical function," in "Cinema/Ideology/ Criticism," *Cahiers du cinéma*, no. 216 [October 1969]), we spoke in the following terms of the form of criticism practiced today in film journals (in France – but this also applies more generally): "continuing the tenacious, persistent tradition of innumerable useless and evanescent writings on the cinema, film analysis today is overwhelmingly determined by idealist presuppositions, which are still dictated, albeit in a more and more errant manner, by empiricism." These lines demand a more ample development – but we feel it is preferable to defer this to another occasion, because there is a journal, *Cinéthique* (having already published five issues), which claims to have radically broken with the aforementioned empiricist approach, appealing to Marxist science, proposing the elaboration of a genuine theory of the cinema, claiming to be militant and in the service of proletarian struggle, and adhering to the revolution at all stages – in short, a journal which presents itself as materialist, in combat with that idealism to which most film criticism remains beholden...

This program – conforming to our own text on numerous points – should surely be welcomed by us. But, however excellent they may be, we will not limit ourselves to principles and "programs." Good intentions are not divorced from practice. As such, and because *Cinéthique* has not refrained from issuing a critical reading of *Cahiers*, we shall examine what can be read on the pages of *Cinéthique*, and whether it is anything more substantial than the proclamation of a program and the laying down of principles: whether these principles are truly put into practice, or, in contrast, whether they are merely the compensatory affirmation of their necessity-lack.

If it appears important to us to carry out this investigation without delay, then this is because *Cinéthique* claims to represent an example of "militant criticism" – which would involve tracing the path toward this criticism with *direct reference to dialectical materialism* (whose near-term advent we expressed our hopes for in our previous text), and thereby instructing filmmakers on the principles of Marxism. This is of great interest to us, and should, in fact, be of concern for any reflection on cinema and criticism in the present day.

I.

As far as the latest issue of *Cinéthique* (no. 5) is concerned, we shall initially retain, as an expression of the journal's "direction," texts written by its four regular contributors: Gérard Leblanc ("Direction"; "Godard valeur d'usage valeur d'échange?"; "L'Été"), Jean-Paul Fargier ("La Parenthèse et le détour: essai de définition théorique du rapport cinéma-politique"; "Discours-film (révolution)-mutisme: *Le Joueur de quilles* de Lajournade") and Eliane Le Grivés/Simon Luciani ("Naissance d'une théorie").[i]

Given that these four writers also form *Cinéthique*'s editorial committee, we can, without the potential risk of practicing an abusive amalgam, consider their various collaborations to be a single text, the *Text* of the journal. At any rate, this is precisely how *Cinéthique* defines its own work: "text in rupture"; "A text: *Cinéthique*"; "Of this text in becoming (not historically closed) we can say that it attempts, through the inscription of theoretical work, to subvert idealist discourse on the cinema (which has been triumphant up to now) through the systematic deconstruction of its modes of alienation and justification," and so on.[ii] Indeed, from one article to the next, we are very much faced with a single text, stating the same position, having recourse to the same examples, formulating in identical fashion the same theoretical principles, authorizing and demanding a global reading. It will thus be necessary to calculate the true gap between the distance proclaimed by this global text from that ideology which is "triumphant up to now" (that is, capitalist ideology, and its idealist discourse) and the distance that it actually practices, in order to judge whether the "rupture" whose radical effect it claims for itself is not, precisely, a *rupture effect*, an ideological speech act within general ideological discourse. We wish to know, therefore, if the militant journal *Cinéthique* is, at the same time, a *revolutionary* journal, or, by contrast, if revolution (the passage, through Marxist science, to the theory of cinema and of film criticism) is not the obligatory artifact of militant rage.

Now, this reading, once it is undertaken, comes up against a symptomatic difficulty. The Text abundantly avails itself of a certain number of notions which it does not, however, subject to theorization, which it states but does not formulate, which it uses but does so as if their simple *enunciation sufficed to think them through* (these notions include: rupture, inscription, trace, work, representation, production, deconstruction, foreclosure, mutism, theory, body, fiction, simulacrum, reflection, etc.). These notions may well be bandied about, but they are not thought out.[1] Moreover, when this Text does attempt to theoretically formulate one notion or another (the notion of "parenthesis," or the notion of "politics"), it does so in a curious (and revealing) manner: by positing that the notion in question poses a problem, that this problem had not been considered (or had been poorly considered) until that moment, by explaining why this was the case (due to ideology, etc.), and thus by feigning to discover it, by lengthily expatiating on it, and, once the problem of the notion is thus exhausted, by reverting to the original notion (unchanged, no more nor less theorized than it was before the "theoretical" detour), still undefined, and which will never end up being defined, because the effort of reflection had been expended on figuring out what had prevented the effort of reflection. Having come full circle, the problem (which had initially been posed *in order to* be resolved) leaves the very problem of its definition, of the theoretical formulation of the notion, outside of the circuit. Despite remaining unthought, this notion is then used once again. This is precisely the adventure undertaken by the notion of "parenthesis": the Text states why it was "bracketed off" for such a long time, it will also state that the lifting of this prohibition and the possibility of using the notion once more are of supreme importance in understanding the relationship between cinema and politics, but it will not state what this "parenthesis" states, nor what it "brackets off."[2]

---

1. We do not reproach *Cinéthique* for using these notions *per se*: on the contrary, they must be used; reflection today must pass through them. But only on the condition that they be ceaselessly defined and redefined in their new context, and not expediently imported into the cinema from disciplines where their usage and meaning is quite specific – and thus not specific to the cinema. Such a work of definition and, in the end, of reflection on the notions that prompt such reflection is arduous, we know, not least because we at *Cahiers* are not exempt from tentative forays of this type. At least, however, we do not claim to have resolved the problems of definition by waving a magic (ideological) wand, and to have become capable of practicing "scientific criticism" overnight. For example: p. 40, the word "foreclosed" is used in the expression "foreclosed formalism." In a footnote, we can read: "this legal term designates the situation of a person who finds himself deprived of the ability to exercise a right due to not having exercised it within a prescribed period of time. To foreclose is hence to exclude." However, if the first phrase does indeed refer to a legal definition, the second imperceptibly repositions the word within another terrain, that of the logic of the signifier, where Jacques Lacan has given it an extremely precise meaning (corresponding to the Freudian term *Verwerfung*). The author of the text, and its accompanying footnote, could not be unaware of this fact, given that the text is impregnated with the terminology specific to this "Logic." Nonetheless, he has granted himself an intolerable slippage, whose *theoretical* consequences could be serious.

2. For example, with reference to this notion of "parenthesis," it is written that the bourgeois ideology of meaning, installing a hierarchical system within the written sentence, considers what is put into parentheses as being less important than the body of the sentence, and that only a genuine materialist practice can break this hierarchy, thereby giving the parenthesis a role that is just as important as the rest of the text. In awestruck wonder at this discovery, the editor of *Cinéthique* points to the use made of the parenthesis by Sollers in *Nombres*, thus proving that he is completely

The reader thus comes up against two obstacles: on the one hand, either the analysis made by *Cinéthique* of the relationship between cinema and ideology (or cinema and politics) remains at the level of a vague, imprecise treatment, of concepts, of a terminological bidding war such that the radicality of the notions brought to the fore amounts to revolutionary verbiage, with scientific pseudo-rigor rapidly being substituted for (and masking the absence of) theoretical rigor (even the word *theory*, despite possessing a strong coefficient of frequent recurrence, is not given any theoretical formulation), in which case the Text, by dint of this imprecision and this torpid unwillingness to theorize, ends up belonging to the very domain with which it had believed it had broken, that of the dominant ideological discourse; or, on the other hand, when it does attempt to theorize its own notions, it confuses the clarification of the ideological tenets of these notions with the clarification of their scientific definition, in which case the Text, by dint of this theoretical confusion, finds itself encompassed within the confusion of the dominant ideology. Let us highlight some examples of the vague imprecision to which the Text subjects itself.

(A) "*Break*" [*coupure*] (or *rupture*). According to *Cinéthique*, which makes intensive use of these terms, they mark the divide between ideological products (films, journals) alienated from bourgeois ideology and revolutionary ideological products (films, journals). Three quotations are called for:

1. "Rupture: a certain number of texts and films, however, are irreducible to this (bourgeois) ideology: *Octobre à Madrid* (Hanoun),[iii] *Cinéthique*."
2. "This text [Cinéthique, *once again – JLC/JN*] thus establishes what could be called a "break," that is, the transformation of a neurotic ideological discourse into a scientific revolutionary discourse."
3. "Inscribed by its 'nature' and its history within idealist ideology, the cinema only allows for a single possible transgression: theoretical practice. Inscribed in theoretical practice, the cinema can really overcome its idealist ideological function. The break generally separating a theory from its anterior ideology is, in the cinema, the same break that separates the function of knowledge from the function of recognition."[iv]

The confusion, here, is ubiquitous. When Althusser speaks of a "break," he is reprising the concept of "epistemological break," as defined by Bachelard (the passage from ideology to science), and uses it to designate the gap between the writings of the young Marx and Marxist science in the strict sense, as it was later defined by Marx – that is, between those texts that were still philosophy (*The Feuerbach Theses*) and those that had become science (*Capital*).[v] When *Cinéthique*, having made an inade-

---

unaware of Roussel, not to mention the work of both Julia Kristeva ("La productivité dite texte," *Communications*, no. 11 [1968]) and Michel Foucault.

quate reading of Althusser, speaks of a "break," without defining the word any differently to Althusser, it operates a delirious extension of the notion to a domain from which, precisely, it is automatically excluded in the Althusserian definition. *The cinema is an ideological product*, its field of definition and practice is ideology, and not science. To put it simply, at present it is at the service of the dominant (bourgeois, capitalist) ideology, and we hope that in the future it will be in the service of another dominant ideology (a socialist one). But between now and the future, there will not be a transformation in the nature of the cinema. As an ideological instrument, it can not become a science; instead, there will be a transformation of how it is used and the purposes for which it is used. If we are to speak of a "break" in relation to the cinema, then we may only do so poetically (as a metaphor), and not scientifically (at the level of theory). If, therefore, *Cinéthique* makes a metaphoric, rather than scientific, use of this notion, then the journal itself is not a "text that has established a break, that is, the transformation of a neurotic ideological discourse into a revolutionary scientific discourse." Practicing confusion, having recourse to pseudo-references and phony science, the journal is still an ideological discourse blurring notions and thereby deferring the advent of scientific discourse.

(B) *Theory*. *Cinéthique* nonetheless has a confused awareness of this difficulty, and, in order to reduce it, will attempt to force the cinema to become a science. As such an operation of metamorphosis is impossible (and can not even be thought), this gives rise to a particularly grotesque "theoretical" discourse. *Cinéthique*, it seems, has read in Althusser that science and theory are contrasted with ideology. It thus sets itself the objective of converting the cinema into a "theoretical practice" of itself, in an initial stage: "the cinema only allows for a single possible transgression."[vi] We can conceive of a theoretical reflection working in tandem with film practice (and, beginning with Eisenstein, there have been several examples of this), such that the latter ceases to be carried out blindly, "innocently," in a manner entirely determined by ideology, and wherein thought is given to all the stages of its production and distribution. Such a "theoretical practice" of filmmaking may be sufficient to struggle against the ideological determinations that generally govern the cinema (see our previous text), to disrupt and counteract the dominant ideology, by trying to expel it from one of its terrains, the cinema, but in no case can it transform the cinema into a scientific system (at least insofar as the word "science" is to have any meaning, cf. Badiou[vii]).

Hence, this is not what *Cinéthique* is claiming. Having initially spoken of "theoretical practice," it ceases to head in this direction, immediately rectifies itself, and proceeds to speak of the *role* that can be played by film theory:

> In the theoretical process, the cinema can play two roles: (a) it reproduces knowledges produced in a given science (historical materialism, medicine, physics, geography, etc.). It functions as a vector in the process of the circulation of knowl-

edge. (b) It produces a specific knowledge of itself. It puts its physical and social materiality on view. It allows its ideological, political and economic function to be read in their differential specificities; and in the act of this unveiling it accedes to the level of theory, because in thus denouncing the ideology of the "impression of reality," it breaks from this ideology.

Thus, *Cinéthique*'s science-cinema is initially a means for the diffusion of scientific knowledges. The cinema can indeed play this role (and does play it) – a role which is inscribed within the domain of science (at least at the level of vulgarization or practical demonstration) – but this in no way changes the nature of the cinema as an ideological product. In this case, simply put, far from the film passing from ideology to science, the film enacts a transformation of science into ideology. But a second role will come to reinforce the first role: science-cinema can be attained by speaking about itself, by making legible its process of production and its diverse conditions of existence. The film would then unveil everything that is inscribed in it. In this case, we struggle to see how such an unveiling can be called scientific: the most we could say about it is that instead of being blind to its own nature, the film would be a discourse on itself. But, of course, it would still be a cinematic discourse. Even if the economy, the production, the ideology and the creation of the cinema are spoken of by the cinema itself, this does not make them belong any less to the cinema – quite the opposite, in fact. Once again: as an ideological product, a film can denounce its ideological nature and function, it can orient them, it can try to change its ideology, and thereby change ideology in general, but this does not turn it into a theoretical system, or a scientific discourse. Even if the film transmits a certain "understanding" of itself and the cinema, this does not entail that the means used to transmit such "understanding" is scientific, nor that this "understanding" itself is scientific. A camera filming itself (*Octobre à Madrid*) produces neither science, nor theory, nor "materialist cinema." At the most, we could say that, as a reflection of reflection, the film leads ideology to gaze at its own mirror image.[3] *Cinéthique* concludes:

---

3. It is quite obvious that *Cinéthique* suffers from a serious *theoretical* confusion with regards to the concept of *theoretical practice* (a mode of production of scientific knowledges), which it conflates with the mere "theory" of a practice (whether technical, empirical or ideological). This "theory" is only the system of determinate concepts needed by these practices to produce the end assigned to them, a system which is only ever the reflection of this end in its means of realization, and has strictly nothing to do with theoretical practice. It is a complete aberration, for example, to say that in *Octobre à Madrid* Marcel Hanoun undertakes a theoretical practice of the cinema: even if Hanoun replaces an empirical, unreflected, "inspired" cinema with a cinema that gazes at itself, mimes itself, watches itself and reflects itself, this does not mean that he has carried out any theoretical (or scientific) practice whatsoever. At the very most, he has produced a "theory" of this cinema. In contrast, it is very possible to exercise a theoretical practice on films which themselves have not carried it out, and this is the essential role of criticism. Let us not confuse matters.

We now understand that this function (b) is primordial. It conditions the ways in which function (a) is carried out. In order for knowledges to actually be able to circulate, the film must first produce itself on a theoretical level. And we end up at this decisive rule: *in the cinema the circulation of knowledges is concomitant with the production of the knowledge of the cinema.* If the two functions do not coincide, there is a relapse into ideology. When faced with a truth, conviction is swept away by virtue of the reduplication of verisimilitude and not by the force of this truth itself, known theoretically.

This conclusion is a pile of confusions:
1. Even if the film is able to "first produce itself on a theoretical level," this does not necessarily mean that it will retain traces of this theoretical work;
2. The accumulation of "knowledges" does not lead one to leave the field of ideology, because, at any rate, this accumulation takes place *within* ideology;
3. No "truth" is "known theoretically" through the cinema – known, yes, but not theoretically. There is thus, on multiple levels, an abuse of language here. Having married "theory" and "cinema" on a caprice, "cinema" and ideology" are divorced just as capriciously.

Cinéthique is sensitive to the *magic* effect of the words "science" and "theory," which, merely by dint of being used in its Text, incontestably assures the "break," the "transformation," the passage to socialism, and the rise of materialism as against idealism.

(C) *The examples.* Operating a "break," acceding to "theory," *Cinéthique* cites two films over and over again: *Octobre à Madrid* and *Le Joueur de quilles.*[viii] The former, because the film speaks of its own process of creation; the latter, because it is "mute,"[4] except for the "voice of God." Here it is not a question of the interest of the former, and the worthlessness of the latter; at issue are the "reasons" given by *Cinéthique* to support their claim that these films deserve to be classified as "materialist cinema" and that they are among those films "on the basis of which the traits of a cinema that would be 'useful' for the proletariat in its struggle for power can be outlined."

Let us look more closely at this. *Octobre à Madrid* is indeed the story of a film that was to be shot in Madrid, and its failure. Hanoun shows himself, films himself, recounts his film, feigns that he wants to shoot some sequences for it, shows that he does not shoot them, and the film is made up of these comings and goings between

4. Just like *Le Révélateur* by Garrel, although *Cinéthique* considers Garrel (like Bene) to be an idealist buffoon. So as to put an end to this blustering nonsense, we intend to return to Garrel shortly, in order to show that, in spite of its affirmation of radical struggle, Lajournade's film is the acme of complaisant, petit bourgeois cinema, and that, in spite of his messianic positions, and in opposition to them (exhaustingly at work in his films), Garrel's filmmaking is infinitely less idealist.

the film project and the discourse of the filmmaker which *prevents* it from being made. As it happens, it is easy to see why, very naïvely, *Cinéthique* confuses the work actually carried out and shown in a film with the fiction of this work, which is precisely, in *Octobre à Madrid*, the fictional story of the film. *Octobre à Madrid* is (like *Two Weeks in Another Town*, *La Fête à Henriette* or *Le Débutant*)[ix] a film that tells a story, the story of the making of a film. This story has an element of suspense (when Hanoun says, with a sly grin, "Will I end up making this film?"), and it makes the cinema a fictional element like any other. Once this fiction is made credible, it becomes precisely what *Cinéthique* violently denounces when it comes to other films, as the first step in the ideology of the cinema: the alienation of the spectator. We have thus not made our way out of confusion, and we are remote from any form of scientific criticism, which, in order to be so, ought to commence by studying the films themselves more closely than *Cinéthique* seems to do.

As for *Le Joueur de quilles*, it is supposedly "materialist" because every speech act today is ideological, because only the bourgeoisie speaks in the cinema, and because in making a mute film Lajournade escapes this ideological entrapment, and circumvents the law of the bourgeoisie! As if, in the cinema, the "speech act" of ideology was only spoken in the lines of dialogue uttered by the characters, as if being mute sufficed to be revolutionary! (Not to mention the fact that leaving speech to the bourgeoisie denotes a serious fecklessness in the ideological struggle.)

> The film's mutism is without doubt the symptom of where its allegiances lie. It is an obstinate trace of a stubborn work which ripens in silence in order to better invent an unprecedented discourse. This mutism is not an aphasic absence, but a deliberate act of silence, the refusal to speak in the *sites* invested by the enemy.[x]

On the basis of this mutism, *Cinéthique* develops a long line of reasoning intended to prove that the film, susceptible neither to a symbolic reading (it says nothing, not even through the use of symbols) nor to a "realist" reading (it only shows images), is no more nor less in a position to "change the axis of references in the cinema": because the film presents itself as a self-contained whole without any references, and because all the elements of the whole only make reference to this whole (the characters, for example, are no longer characters insofar as they only react to the "spatial modifications" of the image and not to any psychological motivations, while the author appears in his film as a deposed figure, and thus inscribes in the filmic whole the "dissolution of the author," as well as inscribing his work "metaphorically" by leaving the orders given during the shoot and the sonic frequencies produced during the mixing process on the soundtrack...). "The film's *mise en scène* is reduced to *placing* the means of production of the film *on the scene*." In doing so, the film is thus seen as breaking with "formalism" (defined curiously as the reflection of a World or of a Self): "The film does not say that the film is comprehended, but it says the entire film." (It can be seen that, perhaps specifically in order to study this film,

Cinéthique has not escaped from the most classical idealist tautology.) By declaring that formalism is "foreclosed," the film naturally enters "into the field [*champ*] and into the camp of materialist cinema" (by means of what ideological conjuring trick?)... And one day, *Cinéthique* concludes, "one day we will speak without metaphor."[xi]

What else can be said of *Le Joueur de quilles*, but that the entire film is a monstrous metaphor of its own uselessness and impotence? If all films which, like this one, bore witness to the levels of impotence reached by petit bourgeois idealism were supposed to enter the camp of materialist cinema... To say *metaphorically* that the bourgeoisie is a class condemned by history, is, on the one hand, to condemn oneself with it, and, on the other hand, to be non-metaphorically silent on what it is that condemns this class. And to regard this film as something that breaks with formalism and idealism is to regard the platitude and the conformity of a tautology (a film is a film) as a subversive event. That every film must indeed be interrogated in its materiality, and its materials, does not result in having to regard the materiality of the cinema as materialist cinema.

D) *Film theory*. We have yet to give an appreciation of the affirmation expounded on countless occasions within *Cinéthique* that the journal is in the process of elaborating a theory of the cinema that would be both scientific and materialist. If it is ridiculous to wish that a film "no longer has an ideological existence" and acquires a "theoretical" or "scientific" existence in its stead (ridiculous from a theoretical, scientific point of view, but exalting from a muddled, idealist point of view), it is nonetheless not so ridiculous to put into practice a scientific approach to film criticism. Although film is an ideological product, this does not mean that it is not susceptible to being studied scientifically – on the contrary. But the preceding passages clearly show that theoretical rigor and scientific precision exclude from the very start any conceptual vacillation and notional imprecision. Vagueness, confusion and the lack of theoretical formulation can produce nothing but that of which they are the effects: an ideological discourse, an ideological mode of criticism, even if it actively opposes this ideology. In order to be done with idealism in film criticism, more rigor is required than that shown by *Cinéthique*. And in order to embark on the path toward materialist criticism, we must strive for the same degree of rigor shown by Marx, Lenin or Althusser, and not content ourselves with borrowing a certain number of notions from them (and not even notions, but mere terms) and inserting them into the terrain of the cinema.

When, precisely, *Cinéthique* cites Marx: "In all ideology men and their circumstances appear upside-down as in a *caméra obscure*"[xii] (Marx wrote *camera obscura*)[5]

---

5. In the German edition, Marx wrote "*camera obscura.*" We can also find these words in the French translation published in the "Éditions sociales" series, with a footnote: "*chambre noire.*" In

and makes the following comment on it: "It is possibly in this remark made by Marx, which places the ideological effect and the effect of the camera under the common sign of a world seen upside down, that the authors of socialist, social or militant films have come to seek the rules for a cinema that they believe to be subversive,"[xiii] then we may ask ourselves, in view of this brusque slippage from "*camera obscura*" to the cinema camera which turns Marx into a prophet, whether *Cinéthique* knows what it is writing, or whether it is ceding to the desire to make a witty remark, on the status of which, in similar circumstances, we can not help but refer to Freud.[xiv]

As for revolution, and as for theory, *Cinéthique* exhibits the same impatience, the same haste. This frenzy doubtless has its basis in the sentiment that both revolution and theory are easy to attain and that all that is required is the necessary will. As much as they might wish the opposite to be the case, *Cinéthique*'s voluntarism denotes the very idealism that the journal claims to be combating.[xv]

II.

Among the texts – or, rather, the single text – to which we have just referred, *Cinéthique* has published, under the title "Le front 'gauche' de l'art: Eisenstein et les vieux 'jeunes-hégéliens'," a long and important article by Marcelin Pleynet.[xvi] Without interrogating, just yet, the problem posed by the presence of this article and its central place in the issue of *Cinéthique* under examination, nor to the tactical necessity to which both are responding, we will linger on it for a moment. Our reasons for doing so fall under two main categories (which are in any case difficult to divorce from one another): the first relates to its real, specific interest, when, beyond any polemical aims, it raises a certain number of questions (which are particularly pertinent at present), pronounces certain warnings, points to problems and sketches out their solutions; the second, meanwhile, pertains to the fact that we, *Cahiers du cinéma*, are directly *and* indirectly subject to scrutiny (the words "and" and "indirectly" will, as we shall see, pose a significant problem), on several issues, if not in the very core of the text, and it is for this reason that we intend to explain ourselves unambiguously by in turn questioning Pleynet.

Our intention is clear, and should be received with equal clarity: we do not wish to engage in one of those spiteful polemics whose repetitive and interminable nature is music to the ears of our profession's gossipmongers, but rather to insist on our pre-

---

the paperback volume of *The German Ideology* [*L'Idéologie allemande*] (part I, p. 36, as indicated by *Cinéthique*), the same footnote can be found, but in Marx's text itself the term is given as "*camera obscure*." The *Cinéthique* writer happily seized on a misprint, added an accent to "camera," and now Marx's expression (isolated from its context, which is absolutely not pertinent to that on which it is intended to be projected) is applied to the terrain of the cinema. A fine example of rigor, or, possibly, of humor.

sent position, whose principal theoretical line was indicated in the previous installment of our text "Cinema/Ideology/Criticism."

We shall now turn to Pleynet's text, to reiterate the main contours of his argument and position his theoretical matrix. From the opening lines, the problem is posed in all its generality: bourgeois, capitalist ideology, still dominant at present, a crucial moment in the economic and political struggles, knows, even though it remains blind to itself and its own principle of intelligibility (this being its defining trait), that it is irreversibly in decline, that it has lost momentum. And as it always does before the ascension, expansion and penetration of a rival ideological current, it tries, principally on the terrain of "culture," to annex and utilize for its own purposes, for its own benefit, those aspects of this rival ideology which appear liable to being deviated [*détournable*]. Owing to its considerable means of persuasion and diffusion, owing to its economic domination, owing to the complicity (whether voluntary or not) of "active ideologues," it feigns to inscribe its program, to stamp its signature on it and expose it as a commodity belonging to what is unswervingly hostile to it, in a double operation of obfuscation and inflation. It strives to impose a *regulated market* on socialist ideology, to inundate this market with texts characterized as "revolutionary" (texts which may indeed be revolutionary, but which are more often not authentically so, and, what is more, which tend to contradict each other and cancel each other out), in the hope both of showcasing its liberalism and of suffocating these texts through progressive saturation and reciprocal annihilation. Alongside these easily discernible attempts, there are others which are, in all good faith, "progressive," which differ in their determination but which are identical in their effects. When it comes down to it, these texts should be aligned along the same "ideological front," and should be combated for their "revolutionary" hastiness, their dearth of theorization, and their eclecticism, confusion and political fecklessness (chaotically offering up, without any specification, a *raw material* that is quickly pawned off, consumed and sanitized). To these two categories of texts (whose effects, he reminds us, are one and the same), Marcelin Pleynet opposes the necessity of unwavering work, precise theoretical research, and the ruthless subjection of texts (books, films, journals) to Marxist-Leninist science, before any attempt at using this science should be countenanced.

We believe that we have not distorted or diminished the essence of Pleynet's article, and refer those of our readers who would like to familiarize themselves with it in greater detail to issue no. 5 of *Cinéthique*.

Having thus put forth his premises, and briskly indicated the elements of a conclusion which could only flow naturally from them, Pleynet proceeds – with respect to the exceedingly complex period of Russian history comprising the years immediately preceding and following the October 1917 Revolution, and the different "cultural" currents of this era (in literature, cinema, the theater) in their intertwined, difficult relations with the historical-political-social moment – to the publication by certain "journals" of texts pertaining to these diverse currents. Now, if, as far as the general problematic of his article and his underlying principle are concerned, we are in agreement with Pleynet *on every point* (and if we are not engaging in the practice of the rhetorical flourish of concession, which he practices on more than one occasion in the course of his text), then what follows – that is, the development of his text – has nonetheless elicited very serious reserves on our part. The exposition of these reserves will be difficult, as they bear on an article which is precise in its broader framework, and which is authoritative, skilled and, for the most part, rigorous, but whose strategy nonetheless seems to warrant the same reproaches that Philippe Sollers addressed to Bernard Pingaud in his article "Le réflexe de réduction" (*Quinzaine littéraire* [January 1968], reprinted in *Théorie d'ensemble*, Éditions du Seuil, coll. "Tel Quel"[xvii]), namely: "truncated citations, conflations, accelerated dramatization, the exhortation to choose between two positions said to be 'contradictory,' the condemnation of the guilty party without appeal." Given that we are faced, here, with a text which claims to be a refusal of and an attack on conflation and confusion, "ideological conjuring tricks" and all forms of illusionism, this may be cause for surprise.

The practice of conflation is at work in Pleynet's article to such an extent that to summarize the instances in which it takes place would amount to reproducing a major part of the text. Let us at least indicate their target: they are concerned, above all, with affirming the identical nature of *Cahiers du cinéma* and the journal *Change*,[xviii] and, having done this (having affirmed it, that is – not, as we shall see, having demonstrated it), Pleynet allows himself all manner of slippages, condensations, assimilations and other textual infelicities.

Thus, an example, an argument or a sentence can begin by referring to one of the two journals, proceed to focus on the other, and then return to the first, often *without indicating* that this is what it is doing. This procedure of intensive obfuscation, this presentation of a "raw material" to readers who may not be prepared for it (or, which amounts to the same thing, who are ready to take Pleynet at his word), is jarring, we repeat, in a text that otherwise reviles "collages" and other "analogical models." Because the examples of said procedure are too numerous, we once again refer our readers to Pleynet's text itself. In particular, we will point to the last page of the text (the end of the first column and the first half of the second column), where, with reference to an article by Barthélémy Amengual in *Cahiers*,[xix] Pleynet imperceptibly passes to the affirmation of the irreducibility of the cinematic problematic to any other problematic, and concludes with a denunciation of the "universal communication" supposedly guiding the project pursued by *Change* (which remains unnamed, of course): "a narration where Homer and Alexander can, in the end, converse with Rousseau, Napoleon with Lenin, Jean Paris with Saussure, everyone with anyone and anyone with everyone."[xx] A fine example of the mimetic reduplication of the language-object through metalanguage! See also, on page 25, how "in fact, and in explicit fashion, the two journals share the enterprise, and share a willingness to be silent on the history of texts whose 'revolutionary' origins are rather vague" (where the devil did Pleynet go to draw this conclusion?), or how "the submission of *Cahiers du cinéma* to the theories of the *Change* notebooks [*cahiers*]" has come about, etc.

For our part, we can certainly object that Pleynet, globally invoking the bourgeois ideological front at the beginning of his text, has spared himself the hassle of subsequently having to distinguish *Cahiers* from *Change*, which he has designated as a participant in this field. And yet, this affiliation, this familial bond, should have been demonstrated, rather than merely being decreed in order to avoid any subsequent specifications. For, if *Cahiers* has cited *Change* on two occasions, it was not to depict it as a model, nor as an example to follow, but simply because at a given point in time it seemed to us that our respective objects of study (and neither our respective methods nor our respective projects) were shared: namely, the texts of Eisenstein, the historico-cultural currents in Russia during the 1910s and 1920s, the problematic of montage (which we understand not as any type of montage whatsoever, but as a specifically cinematic procedure, and consequently as active, dynamic and transformative).[6] The other reproach, which is of such fundamental importance that it behooves us not to evade it any longer, pertains to the common accusation of latent or manifest anti-communism. Let us be very clear here, so as to avoid any further equivocation: if, in the past, *Cahiers* could well have been accused of anti-communism, it can no longer be accused of it today. We henceforth hold this accusation to be defamatory (and relevant only to the outlook presiding over the origins of our journal, the regressive, Christian character of which has been amply demonstrated elsewhere).

We can now see the difficulty involved in responding to an author who, inattentive to the evolution of our journal, and for exclusively polemical purposes, relies on indirect accusations, paralipsis and various other rhetorical wiles. We shall thus take Pleynet's attacks *en bloc*, and act as if they were *all* aimed at us. We hope it will be believed that we are acting as if they were aimed at us *alone*, and that in our article the only journal that speaks is *Cahiers*.

(A) *Eisenstein*. If he grants us a certain methodological rigor in our publication of Eisenstein's writings over the last few months, and recognizes that we have striven to give the greatest possible number of contextual historical remarks, and an abundant system of explicatory notes, Pleynet esteems that we were found wanting in the declarations contained in our introductory paragraph to the first text we published

6. The word "montage" seems to particularly irritate Pleynet (to the extent that, it seems, he has blotted out our roundtable discussion bearing this name). At times he feigns to understand it (with *Change* in mind) as an "analogical model," "collage," or a "juggling act," juxtaposing anything with anything else in the hope that some meaning can be derived from this act; at other times he sees it as a gratuitous formal game. Now, we should remind him that the term "montage" refers to a form of work that is specific to the cinema, and that in *Cahiers* it is cinematic montage that is under consideration.

(in *Cahiers*, no. 214), explaining our project of returning to these writings, reflecting on them, repositioning them in their historical and theoretical context, and illuminating them with the light of new theoretical principles.[xxi] In a word, he reproaches us for presenting them in a chaotic, willful fashion, without sufficient specifications, and he sees some kind of underhanded ideological project of recuperation/mollification at work here. Pleynet does point to Jean-Louis Comolli's text "Le détour par le direct" (nos. 209 and 211) but is absolutely silent (not citing them at all, even if only to repudiate them *en bloc*) on our "Montage" roundtable (no. 210) and Jacques Aumont's article "Le concept de montage" (no. 211). As these are not the only omissions in a lengthy text, we shall take this opportunity to pronounce our own position.

Of the considerable, enormous, mass of Eisenstein's writings, we in France know only a tiny portion, collected under the title *Réflexions d'un cinéaste*,[xxii] and some scattered texts published in journals (we shall refrain from citing the Italian and English texts – *Film Form, The Film Sense, Essays*[xxiii] – and restrict ourselves to the French texts). The sufficiently accurate selected works of Eisenstein have been published, in a project dating back to 1964, in six volumes by the Iskusstvo publishing house in Moscow. Free of any external pressures or incitements, unaffected by passing fashions, and guided by no concealed project, *Cahiers* has undertaken to make this work known in France and thus, to start off with, to translate it. We struggle to see how we can be reproached for publishing these writings in a journal that is *primarily* focused on the cinema. Pleynet is indeed willing to accord us this specificity. As for the texts announced (if we except the text cited by Pleynet, and those that he has squarely forgotten), they will be *continued* in a special issue on "Russia in the 1920s" which we at *Cahiers* have been working on for several months, and which we have, at any rate, already publicized.

(B) *Formalists and futurists.* It would seem that these terms do not concern us directly, as they belong to an extra-cinematic domain, and *Cahiers* has not published texts by either of these tendencies. Nonetheless, because, as we explained earlier, we are responding to Pleynet's text *en bloc*, but also because formalists and futurists will play a part in our special issue on Russia, we will once again act as if Pleynet's reproaches were directed at *Cahiers*. In his view, the publication of texts by those Russian formalists and futurists under the vague label of "revolutionary" (on the pretext that they were contemporaneous with the October revolution), without interrogating the historical circumstances giving rise to them, the petit bourgeois class origins of those who had held these positions (their idealist preconceptions, their empiricism, and even their theologism), and the historical reasons why the October revolution came to distance itself from them, or even condemn them outright (Lenin, Trotsky, Stalin, Zhdanov), does indeed denote a practice of cultural obfuscation, and, as he recognizes at the beginning of his text, is the mark of the bourgeois front. But how exactly do things stand here?

In 1965, the *Tel Quel* book series published texts (until then unknown to French readers) written by the Russian formalists, in a volume edited by Tzvetan Todorov, under the title *Théorie de la littérature.*[xxiv] This publication had a considerable impact, with the texts serving as an indispensable tool for numerous researchers, and leading to greater awareness of an important movement in the history of literature (and of reflection on literature). The formalists were considered to be the founders of a science of literature. Up until 1968, even in *Tel Quel* itself, these texts were presented as both "scientific" and "revolutionary." For example, Philippe Sollers writes (in "Le réflexe de réduction"): "The endpoint of this activity [*of the journal* Tel Quel – *JLC/JN*] – beyond the intensive publication of texts – will include the constitution (by T. Todorov) of the anthology *Théorie de la littérature*, in which the writings, hitherto completely unknown, of the revolutionary (futurist and scientific) avant-garde in the Soviet Union of the 1920s and 1930s are revealed to the French public," and, further on in the same text: "The program of the Russian futurists, who were close to both structural linguistics in its nascent period and the political revolution underway, was to make each and every person an active possessor of language."[xxv]

Elsewhere – and this time no longer in the movement of a polemic able to authorize, for the practical purposes of enlightenment and conceptual precision, condensed, abrupt affirmations – Todorov writes: "Poetry and the theory of poetry are one and the same. [...] In their writings [*those of the futurists – JLC/JN*] the difference between text and metatext is effaced. Poetry is science..." or, further: "The poetic revolution proceeds in tandem with the political revolution. [...] To be a revolutionary in literature means revolutionizing poetry, not poeticizing revolt"[7] (*Tel Quel* no. 35, Autumn 1968[xxvi]).

If it is true that, today, the formalist and futurist texts are subject to a more rigorous examination, with formalism, in particular, having been "deconstructed to its very linguistic foundations" (principally in the texts of Julia Kristeva and Jacques Derrida), it is also true that a long time has elapsed between the moment when they were presented to the French public and the moment when this veritable critical and theoretical retrospection began to be sketched out. It is understood (or at least it ought to be understood), that we say this not to turn back on Pleynet a delay or a lack for which he does not refrain from reproaching us, but, rather, to insist on this fundamental point: that, when it comes to an extremely important, complex and turbulent historical-cultural period (and we are far from having the sufficient data

---

7. Although, in his introduction to *Théorie de la littérature*, and in the text from which we have just cited an extract, Todorov points to the positivism naïvely flaunted by the formalists, their proclaimed empiricism, he does so in order to conclude that they appear to proceed from a "lack of awareness of their own means, and even of the essence of their approach" (mirrored by a certain desire to escape the reproach of scientism and theoreticism), and not to interrogate their methodology or their theoretical presuppositions, let alone to link them with precision to the progression of history or to their class origins.

and time to adequately reflect on it), we all need a long period of research, learning, synthetic understanding and theorization to reach precise conclusions.[8]

(C) *Objectivity*. Having posited the petit bourgeois class origins of the formalists and the futurists, then recognized their unmitigated adherence to the October revolution, and affirmed the necessity of rigorously confronting their positions and their works with Marxist-Leninist science, in order to define them not as a "fundamental transformation of bourgeois culture, but as one effect among many of this culture, effects which should be deciphered and assimilated on the basis of the '*trans*-formational' reading of Marxism,"[xxvii] Pleynet protests against contemporary efforts to valorize these texts (by forgoing these efforts, this work), with the explicit or implicit goal of shifting the debate to the terrain of politics, since formalism in fact gains favor in the eyes of the European bourgeoisie from its censorship by Stalinism, and since this censorship nourishes the anti-communist argument put forward in the name of "artistic freedom" or "freedom of expression." Pleynet takes issue with a footnote written by Luda and Jean Schnitzer to an article by Eisenstein (*Cahiers*, no. 213, note 20),[xxviii] in which they point to Eisenstein's admiration for Meyerhold. This note contains the following comments: "Meyerhold [...] was accused of excessive formalism; arrested in 1939, he died in a camp."[9] Pleynet then writes:

> Was their idea, as I do not doubt, to give a piece of objective information and rehabilitate a man of the theater? But what real objectivity pierces out from under the ideological tissue of such an ambiguous phrasing? What comes down to us from Meyerhold (cf. *Le Théâtre théâtral*[xxix]) is theoretically worthless and can only be verified precisely through those formalist and futurist points of reference that nobody here has come to verify, and which have been entirely shifted to the terrain of politics – a terrain which, it must be said, has been amply mined.[xxx]

---

8. In any case, Kristeva and Derrida's interrogation of the idealist presuppositions of a mode of thinking founded on the sign goes well beyond (due to the breadth of their work) the specific historical problem of the Russian formalists and futurists, who *even today* still warrant research in the sense desired by Pleynet.

9. In *Cahiers*, the note states, precisely: "Meyerhold (1874-1941) was accused of excessive formalism; arrested in 1939, he died in a camp. Even his name was subject to prohibition." In *Cinéthique*: "... was accused of excessive formalism, arrested in 1939, he died in a camp." The difference can appear to be a minor detail, or merely (we hope) a printing error, but the substitution of a semi-colon with a comma can considerably alter the meaning of the note under question. In the version printed in *Cahiers*, there is certainly a relationship between the accusation of excessive formalism, the arrest and the death, given that they all pertain to the single person of Meyerhold. But, with our punctuation, it is the arrest and the death that are directly linked. In the *Cinéthique*-Pleynet version, the arrest is shifted forward, drawn closer to the accusation of formalism, and it is possible to read the sentence as a *consequential* succession. In *Cahiers* the semi-colon installs a sense of consecutive succession, but makes no claim as to cause and effect. This prudence should serve as an example.

We certainly can not prevent Pleynet from detecting, in a footnote written with honesty and objectivity, without any hidden meaning (and referring less to the point of view of Luda and Jean Schnitzer than to the relationship between Eisenstein and Meyerhold, with respect to a text written by the former and alluding to the latter), some kind of underhanded political maneuver. Conversely, it may well be possible to in turn question Pleynet's frenzied compulsion to not see an objective statement for what it is, precisely when it comes to Meyerhold and the notion of objectivity. Indeed, at one point, Pleynet writes:

> Now, if we can suppose that the young Eisenstein was shaped by his participation in the revolutionary action of the Red Army, this is by no means the case for his mentor, whose activity takes place well before the revolution; a collaborator of Stanislavsky, Meyerhold was already famous enough in 1915 that the Tsarist cinema allowed him to direct two films.[xxxi]

We should hence ask Pleynet what "real objectivity pierces through from under the ideological tissue of such an ambiguous phrasing"? Indeed.

(1) Although Meyerhold was, for a while, a collaborator of Stanislavsky's, he very quickly broke with him, for theoretical reasons (and not personal reasons), as he was opposed to the naturalist and psychologist presuppositions of the "Art Theater."

(2) Although Meyerhold directed several shows before the October revolution, and even made two films, he was never an official "Tsarist" filmmaker, nor was he celebrated or favored by the Tsarist system (we grant that the ambiguity of Pleynet's formulation is different to that of the note that he had previously incriminated). We also know that his revolutionary sympathies surfaced before the Russian October. Let us cite Nina Gourfinkel's introduction to *Théâtre théâtral*: "He [Meyerhold] was able to adapt himself for a period of several years to the environment prevailing in the heavily conservative milieus of the imperial theaters, but his revolutionary sympathies have a long provenance. Under the Tsarist regime, Penza was a center for 'politicals' under house arrest: with populists, early Marxists, Polish resisters among them, as well as a large number of students and writers..."

(3) Here we touch on an extremely important point with respect to the infamous notion of objectivity: Pleynet, directly before the citation on Meyerhold we reproduced, had signaled the immediate alignment of the formalists and futurists with revolutionary positions (in spite of their class origin). He even cites declarations made by two of *only five* representatives of the Russian "intelligentsia" who, directly after the revolution, responded to the invitation of Russia's Central Executive Committee, the supreme organ of the new regime. Let us repeat: they were two of only *five* representatives: Mayakovsky and Blok. Mayakovsky: "To accept or not to accept? For me there was no question about it. This was my revolution." Blok, a little later, responding to the same question: "Can the intelligentsia work with the Bolsheviks? – It can and it must." For these citations, Pleynet refers to an article by Dmitri Blagoi,

appearing in *Œuvres et opinions* in January 1969 in Moscow, "Aux sources de la littérature soviétique" (reprinted in *Tel Quel* no. 37).[xxxii] However, Pleynet – who either has no other point of reference at hand (and this is no excuse when he is engaged in discrediting someone by remaining silent about them) or has other, more detailed sources, but has censored these *details* (and this would be even more grave) – absolutely refrains from stating that the three individuals accompanying Blok and Mayakovsky were Rurik Ivnev, Nathan Altman and none other than *Vsevolod Meyerhold*, who immediately, unequivocally and enduringly rallied to the cause of the revolution (cf. Jay Leyda, *Kino: A History of the Russian and Soviet Film* [London: 1960]).[xxxiii] Our readers, and the readers of *Cinéthique*, can henceforth judge Pleynet's objectivity, and whether or not there is a maneuver here.

(4) As our final point on Meyerhold, we shall recall the following: Pleynet is right to note in his text that the theoretical writings of Eisenstein make constant reference to the experiments and stagings of the theater director, and that it was initially in relation to these that he "invariably defined the concepts which he would later deploy."[xxxiv] He formulates the necessity of always relating theoretical reflection to practical work, and with a particular insistence when it comes to a practice and a theory derived from heterogeneous domains, irreducible to one another (in Eisenstein's case, these are film practice and linguistic theoretical reflections). This exigency ought, it would seem, to be equally valid in the case of Meyerhold (theatrical practice and theoretical writings). And yet not only does Pleynet falsify, as we have seen, his biographical details, and aesthetic and political stances, and not only does he decree that Meyerhold's entire theoretical legacy is worthless (which is rather excessive, even if Meyerhold's texts are far from possessing a requisite rigor, breadth, clarity and terminological precision), but he also barely makes note of the considerable importance of Meyerhold's practical stagings and his theatrical work. This importance, while already manifest at the precise moment of the Revolution, would also come to bear on later theatrical practice, and even the later theatrical theories elaborated by Antonin Artaud. We shall cite a draft letter written by Artaud to René Daumal, dated July 14, 1931 (*Œuvres complètes*, vol. III, pp. 215-216, Gallimard):

> Henceforth we will have to take into account the necessities of visual harmony when staging a production, [...] just as, in the wake of Meyerhold and Appia, we have to take into account an architectural conception of the decor used, not only in depth but also in height, and deploying perspective, through masses and volumes, rather than mere flat surfaces used in *trompe-l'œil* fashion...

And: "an attempt was made, in Russia, during the revolution, to supersede this conception of man prone to ecstasy before his personal monsters with a theater of action and of the masses, and this has been the only truly theatrical attempt."

(D) This is how far we have been diverted, in referring to only a few lines from a single text, from the essence of the text and from Eisenstein himself... In fact, we have departed from neither the one nor the other, not even for an instant. But let us return, precisely, to Eisenstein, concerning whom Pleynet writes, *correctly*:

> We must now re-read the texts of the Soviet filmmaker, and establish a critical edition. [...] This must involve showing how closely linked Eisenstein's texts are to the precise historical context, and proving that, on the pain of denouncing any attempt to use them otherwise, they can not take on meaning outside of a well-documented critical reading of their relations to this context. [...] In this manner, from one text to another, and in connection with the author's biography (participation in the revolution, travels to Europe and the United States, return from the United States), the accumulation of findings, theoretical specifications, methodological rectifications and contradictions would play a role...[xxxv]

And yet, once again in contradiction with this demand for prudence and attentiveness, Pleynet – after having extracted a fragment from the text "Perspectives" (*Cahiers*, no. 209),[xxxvi] which was, we admit, rather unbridled, in a lyrico-impressionist sense, as well as a declaration made by Eisenstein at the end of his life, according to which he was yet to find a solution to his theoretical researches – authorizes himself to speak of Eisenstein's *theological* conception of the cinema, of his *metaphysical illusion*, from which he had never, supposedly, freed himself, of his Macho-Bogdanovian idealism, and of his *dependence* on Hegelian idealism. Even though these affirmations are partially true, they are far from being sufficiently defined and substantiated, while the use of the term "dependence" is not theorized enough for us to be satisfied with it. For the problem – and it is strange that, despite knowing it and formulating it, Pleynet seems to act as if he was unaware of it in its later developments – is complex for different reasons. Without mentioning the relationship between Eisenstein's "Writings" and his films, we can find in them (without forgetting that only a tiny fraction of his writings is accessible to us in France at the moment):

- Resolutely idealist concepts, formulated in idealist fashion
- Spirited proclamations of materialism, whose status should be rigorously interrogated
- Materialist notions formulated in an imprecise manner
- Materialist notions rigorously and remarkably formulated

It is not a matter, of course, of falling into the trap noted by Althusser, with respect to interpretations of the texts of the young Marx, which consists of attempting to differentiate those elements that are (still) idealist from those elements that are (already) materialist, nor is it a matter of relating a text or a textual fragment to the end or the entirety of the work of its author as if it were a revelatory truth (this would be a teleologico-analytic idealist mode of criticism), but of reading Eisenstein in the present day, as materialists, that is to say, of considering a text as a totality whose elements lose their specific characteristics in order to be understood as the *effective and living unity of the text*, of thinking through the specific problematic of this text, that is, as a *determinate structural unity* (the relations that this reflection entertains with its object, the modalities of this reflection), of subsequently relating this specific problematic to other contemporaneous problematics belonging to the ideological field, and, finally, of grasping the irruption, and the mode of irruption, of *real history* into the field of these ideologies, and the particular ideology under study. To declare that Eisenstein's texts are situated in the great history of thought running from Berkeley to Hegel, or from Mach to Bogdanov, equates to placing them in the tranquil, autonomous, self-sufficient continuity of the history of ideology, in this "nothing" of ideology which has, in the strict sense, no history; that is, in ideological immanence. In the end, it equates to adopting the same Hegelian or neo-Hegelian viewpoint that Pleynet had striven to rebuke others for.

III.

It goes without saying that Pleynet is by no means unaware of all this; in fact, his text is written precisely *in order to* say it. What mechanism, therefore, is it that leads him to destroy just as much as he advances, to contradict in its developments the material of his specific problematic, to deny in their progress the principles which determine his text, to practice conflation in order to denounce convergences, to formulate imprudent declarations at the same time that he calls for meticulousness and prudence, to resort to distortions when he summons us to be specific, to "terrorize" while under the illusion of theorizing? In our opinion, it is this: the text, which is not simply written to say what it says, but with a polemical aim in mind (which is often indirect and imbued with irony and sarcasm), is constrained to say more or less about itself, or to speak more quickly, than Pleynet would like. Certainly, Pleynet fustigates against the "alliances" which can only be sealed with theoretical concessions, but he knows (because he can not *not* know it) that he is primarily using *Cinéthique* to attack *Change*, just as *Cinéthique* is using Pleynet's wish to attack *Change* to attack *Cahiers*, and just as *Cinéthique*, in spite of its "uncompromising" proclamations, ceaselessly plays *gauchisme* against communism, Godard against Pleynet, Seban against Lajournade, syndicalism against anarchism, and *vice versa*.

Appendix II: Machines of the Visible

Translator's Introduction

As a final piece of additional material for this volume, extracts from Comolli's "Machines of the Visible" are reprinted below. The text is derived from a paper distributed in advance and then delivered at a landmark conference on "The Cinematic Apparatus" held in February 1978 at the University of Wisconsin-Milwaukee, which was then reprinted in a published overview of the conference proceedings (*The Cinematic Apparatus*, ed. Teresa de Lauretis and Stephen Heath [New York: St. Martin's Press, 1980], pp. 121-142). After a brief introduction, parts I-III reproduce scattered extracts from across "Technique and Ideology," which, seven years after their initial publication, Comolli saw no need to alter. These are then followed by two further sections which discuss the same issues in light of Comolli's experience working on *La Cecilia*, and the role of "analogical figuration" in the 17th-century English painting *The Cholmondeley Ladies*. The paper was composed in French – Comolli speaks little English – but its only published version is in English, and it is this version which is reproduced here, in spite of the fact that the unnamed translator (most likely the editors of *The Cinematic Apparatus*, who doubled as conference organizers) departs from some of the translation principles established for the other texts translated here. As parts I-III are reprised from "Technique and Ideology," and can thus be found elsewhere in this volume, they have been excised.

Machines of the Visible

By Jean-Louis Comolli

Introduction

One of the hypotheses tried out in some of the fragments here gathered together would be on the one hand that the cinema – the historically constitutable cinematic statements – functions with and in the set of apparatuses of representation at work in a society. There are not only the representations produced by the representative apparatuses as such (painting, theater, cinema, etc.); there are also, participating in the movement of the whole, the systems of the delegation of power (political representation), the ceaseless working-up of social imaginaries (historical, ideological representations) and a large part, even, of the modes of relational behavior (balances of power, confrontations, maneuvers of seduction, strategies of defense, marking of differences or affiliations). On the other hand, but at the same time, the hypothesis would be that a society is only such in that it is *driven by representation*. If the social machine manufactures representations, it also manufactures itself from representations – the latter operative at once as means, matter and condition of sociality.

Thus the historical variation of cinematic techniques, their appearance-disappearance, their phases of convergence, their periods of dominance and decline seem to me to depend not on a rational-linear order of technological perfectibility nor an autonomous instance of scientific "progress," but much rather on the offsettings, adjustments, arrangements carried out by a social configuration in order to represent itself, that is, at once to grasp itself, identify itself and produce itself in its representation.

What happened with the invention of cinema? It was not sufficient that it be technically feasible, it was not sufficient that a camera, a projector, a strip of images be technically ready. Moreover, they were already there, more or less ready, more or less invented, a long time already before the formal invention of cinema, 50 years before Edison and the Lumière brothers. It was necessary that something else be constituted, that something else be formed: the cinema machine, which is not essentially the camera, the film, the projector, which is not merely a combination of instruments, apparatuses, techniques. Which is a machine: a *dispositif* articulating between one another different sets – technological certainly, but also economic and ideological. A *dispositif* was required which would implicate its motivations, which would be the arrangement of demands, desires, fantasies, speculations (in the two senses of commerce and the imaginary): an arrangement which give apparatus and techniques a social status and function.

The cinema is born immediately as a social machine, and thus not from the sole invention of its equipment but rather from the experimental supposition and verification, from the anticipation and confirmation of its *social profitability*; economic, ideological and symbolic. One could just as well propose that it is the spectators who invent cinema: the chain that knots together the waiting queues, the money paid and the spectators' looks filled with admiration. "Never," say Gilles Deleuze and Claire Parnet, "is an arrangement-combination technological, indeed it is always the contrary. The tools always presuppose a machine, and the machine is always social before it is technical. There is always a social machine which selects or assigns the technical elements used. A tool, an instrument, remains marginal or little used for as long as the social machine or the collective arrangement-combination capable of taking it in its *phylum* does not exist."[1] The hundreds of little machines in the 19th century destined for a more or less clumsy reproduction of the image and the movement of life are picked up in this "phylum" of the great representative machine, in that zone of attraction, lineage, influences that is created by the displacement of the social co-ordinates of analogical representation.

The second half of the 19th century lives in a sort of frenzy of the visible. It is, of course, the effect of the social multiplication of images: ever wider distribution of illustrated papers, waves of prints, caricatures, etc. The effect also, however, of something of a geographical extension of the field of the visible and the representable: by journeys, explorations, colonizations, the whole world becomes visible at the same time that it becomes appropriatable. Similarly, there is a visibility of the expansion of industrialism, of the transformations of the landscape, of the production of towns and metropolises. There is, again, the development of the mechanical manufacture of objects which determines by a faultless force of repetition their ever identical reproduction, thus standardizing the idea of the (artisanal) copy into that of the (industrial) series. Thanks to the same principles of mechanical repetition, the movements of men and animals become in some sort more visible than they had been: movement becomes a visible mechanics. The mechanical opens out and multiplies the visible and between them is established a *complicity* all the stronger in that the codes of analogical figuration slip irresistibly from painting to photography and then from the latter to cinematography.

At the very same time that it is thus fascinated and gratified by the multiplicity of scopic instruments which lay a thousand views beneath its gaze, the human eye loses its immemorial privilege; the mechanical eye of the photographic machine now sees *in its place*, and in certain aspects with more sureness. The photograph stands as at once the triumph and the grave of the eye. There is a violent decentering of the place

1. Gilles Deleuze and Claire Parnet, *Dialogues* (Paris: Flammarion, 1977), pp. 126-127.

of mastery in which since the Renaissance the look had come to reign: to which testifies, in my opinion, the return, synchronous with the rise of photography, of everything that the legislation of the classic optics – that geometrical ratio which made of the eye the point of convergence and centering of the perspective rays of the visible – had long repressed and which hardly remained other than in the controlled form of anamorphoses: the massive return to the front of the stage of the optical aberrations, illusions, dissolutions. Light becomes less obvious, sets itself as problem and challenge to sight. A whole host of inventors, lecturers and image showmen experiment and exploit in every way the optical phenomena which appear irrational from the standpoint of the established science (refraction, mirages, spectrum, diffraction, interferences, retinal persistence, etc.). Precisely, a new conception of light is put together, in which the notion of wave replaces that of ray and puts an end to the schema of rectilinear propagation, in which optics thus overturned is now coupled with a chemistry of light.

Decentered, in panic, thrown into confusion by all this new magic of the visible, the human eye finds itself affected with a series of limits and doubts. The mechanical eye, the photographic lens, while it intrigues and fascinates, functions also a *guarantor* of the identity of the visible with the normality of vision. If the photographic illusion, as later the cinematic illusion, fully gratifies the spectator's taste for delusion, it also reassures him or her in that the delusion is in conformity with the norm of visual perception. The mechanical magic of the analogical representation of the visible is accomplished and articulated from a doubt as to the fidelity of human vision, and more widely as to the truth of sensory impressions.

I wonder if it is not from this, from this lack to be filled, that could come the extreme eagerness of the first spectators to *recognize* in the images of the first films – devoid of color, nuance, fluidity – the identical image, the double of life itself. If there is not, in the very principle of representation, a force of disavowal which gives free rein to an analogical illusion that is yet only weakly manifested by the iconic signifiers themselves? If it was not necessary at these first shows to forcefully deny the manifest difference between the filmic image and the retinal image in order to be assured of a new hold on the visible, subject in turn to the law of mechanical reproduction...

[...]

IV. Denaturalizing Depth

The theater in *La Cecilia* as tipping over of the fiction, as superimposition, disphasing, dislocation of two representations, one over the other, one against the other.

This doubling-splitting of the scene that the inscription of the theater produces in the film is produced in the shot by deep focus. The decision was taken with the cameraperson Yann Le Masson to use almost throughout short focal length lenses which give a field that is sharp in its distance, a space divided into planes set out in depth, backgrounds as legible as foregrounds. Paradoxically, this was not in order to strengthen the realism of the image (deep focus as "more real" but in order to make the shot theatrical: to act along the verticality of the image in the same way that in the theater one can perform along the vertical axis of the stage, in its depth, making dramatic use of what is the central condition of the Italian stage (governed by linear perspective): a theatrical space that is immediately and totally perceptible, a set given over straightaway and entirely to vision. With the proviso that what is arranged on the theatrical stage in the real depth of the given space necessarily becomes in the filmic image a spacing out in the plane of the frame, a lateral-vertical decentering of the "subjects" (otherwise what is in the foreground would always mask what comes behind). With the proviso also that the short focal lengths, which alone allow the apprehension of this depth, which do so with a forceful emphasis on perspective, bring with them at the same time as the background depth a more or less considerable deformation of the lateral edges of the field. This is why cinematic deep focus does not slip into the "naturalness" of linear perspective, but inevitably stresses that perspective, accentuates it, indicates its curvature, denounces the visual field it produces as a construction, a composition in which there is not simply "more real" but in which this more visible is spatially organized in the frame, dramatized. Deep focus does not wipe out perspective, does not pass it off as the "normality" of vision, but makes it readable as coding (exteriorization of the interiorized code); it de-naturalizes and dramatizes it. The relationship which is established within the frame and in the duration of the scene between the actions or figures in the foreground and those in the backgrounds functions not only as a "montage within the shot" (opposed by Bazin to classic Hollywood editing) but also as the reinscription of a theatrical space and duration, in which the legibility of meanings goes via a movement of the eye, in which the playing of the actors is a playing of relationship to the others and to the elements of the decor, in which the bodies are always held in space and time, never abstract. (The abstraction is the method and the result of the analysis of concrete contradictions: a body in a space, in relation to other bodies; speech first of all as accent, delivery, diction; a discourse as mode of behavior, symptom, relational crisis; political conflicts as dramatic conflicts – the political, in other words, not as [autonomous, free floating] discourse or [magisterial] lesson, but as movement, as trace, mark on faces, gestures, words; in short, theater).

V. Notes on Representation

The most analogical representation of the world is still not, is never, its reduplication. Analogical repetition is a false repetition, staggered, disphased, deferred and different; but it produces *effects* of repetition and analogy which imply the disavowal (or the repression) of these differences and which thus make of the *desire* for identity, identification, recognition, of the desire of the *same*, one of the principal driving forces of analogical figuration. In other words the spectator, the ideological and social subject, and not just the technical apparatus, is the operator of the analogical mechanism.

There is a famous painting of the English school, *The Cholmondeley Sisters* (1600-1610),[i] which represents two sisters side by side, each holding a baby in her arms. The two sisters look very much alike, as do the babies, sisters and babies are dressed almost identically, and so on. Confronted with this canvas, one is disturbed by a repetition that is not a repetition, by a contradictory repetition. What is here painted is the very subject of figurative painting: repetition, *with*, in this repetition, all the play of the innumerable differences which at once *destroy* it (from one figure to the other, nothing is identical) and *assert* it as violent *effect*. Panic and confusion of the look doubled and split. The image is in the image, the double is not the same, the repetition is a fiction: it makes us believe that it repeats itself just because it does not repeat itself. It is in the most "analogical" representation (never completely so), the most "faithful," the most "realistic," that the *effects of representation* can be most easily read. One must be fooled by the image in order to see it as such (and no longer as a projection of the world).

Is it that cinema begins where *mise en scène* ends, when is broken or left behind the machinery of performance, of the actor and the scenario, when technical necessity takes off the mask of art? That is roughly what Vertov believed and what is repeated more or less by a whole avant-garde in his wake – with categories such as "pure cinema," "live cinema," "*cinéma vérité*" – right up to certain experimental films of today. It is not very difficult to see, however, that what is being celebrated in that tradition of "non-cinema" is a visible with no original blemish that will stand forth in its "purity" as soon as the cinema strips itself of the "literary" or "theatrical" artifices it inherited at its birth; a visible on the right side of things, manifesting their living authenticity. There is, of course, no visible not held in a look and, as it were, always already framed. Moreover, it is naïve to locate *mise en scène* solely on the side of the camera: it is just as much, and even before the camera intervenes, everywhere where the social regulations order the place, the behavior and almost the "form" of subjects in the various configurations in which they are caught (and which do not demand the same type of performance: here authority, here submission; standing out or standing aside; etc.; from one system of social relation to another, the place of the subject changes and so does the subject's capture in the look of others). What Vertov films without *mise en scène* (as he believes) are the effects of other *mises en scène*. In other words, script, actors, *mise en scène* or not, all that is filmable is the changing, historical, determined relationship of men and things to the visible, the dispositions of representation.

However refined, analogy in the cinema is a deception, a lie, a fiction that must be straddled – in disavowing, knowing but not wanting to know – by the *will to believe* of the spectator, the spectator who expects to be fooled and wants to be fooled, thus becoming the first agent of his or her own fooling. The spectacle, and cinema itself, despite all the *reality effects* it may produce, always gives itself away *for what it is* to the spectators. There is no spectator other than one *aware* of the spectacle, even if (provisionally) allowing him or herself to be taken in by the fictioning machine, deluded by the simulacrum: it is precisely *for that* that he or she came. The certainty that we always have, in our heart of hearts, that the spectacle is not life, that the film is not reality, that the actor is not the character and that if we are present as spectators, it is because we know we are dealing with a semblance, this certainty must be capable of being doubted. It is only worth its risk; it interests us only if it can be (provisionally) canceled out. The "yes, I know" calls irresistibly for the "but all the same," includes it as its value, its intensity. We know, but we want something else: to believe. We want to be fooled, while still knowing a little that we are so being. We want the one and the other, to be both fooled and not fooled, to oscillate, to swing from knowledge to belief, from distance to adherence, from criticism to fascination. Which is why realist representations are successful: they allow this movement to and fro which ceaselessly sets off the intensity of the disavowal, they sustain the spectator's pleasure in being prisoner in a situation of conflict (I believe/I don't believe). They allow it because they lay out a contradictory, representative space, a space in which there are both effects of the real and effects of fiction, of repetition and difference, automatic devices of identification and significant resistances, recognition and seizure. In this sense, analogical fiction in the cinema is bound up with narrative fiction, and all cinematic fictions are tightened, more or less forcefully, by this knot of disavowal which ceaselessly stops and starts again with the continual *petitio principii* of the "impression of reality." The capturing power of a fiction, whether the fiction of the analogical reproduction of the visible, or the fictions of cinematic narrative, depends always on its self-designation as such, on the fact that its fictive character is known and recognized from the start, that it presents itself as an artificial arrangement, that it does not hide that it is above all an apparatus of deception and thus that it postulates a spectator who is not easily but *difficultly* deceivable, not a spectator who is blindly condemned to fascination but one who is complicit, willing to "go along."

Fictional deceits, contrary to many other systems of illusions, are interesting in that they can function only from the clear designation of their deceptive character. There is no uncertainty, no mistake, no misunderstanding or manipulation. There is ambivalence, play. The spectacle is always a game, requiring the spectators' participation not as "passive," "alienated" consumers, but as players, accomplices, masters of the game even if they are also what is at stake. It is necessary to suppose spectators to be total imbeciles, completely alienated social beings, in order to believe that they are thoroughly deceived and deluded by simulacra. Different in this to ideological and political representations, spectatorial representations declare their existence as simulacrum and, on that contractual basis, invite the spectator to *use* the simulacrum to fool him or herself. Never "passive," the spectator works. But that work is not only a work of decipherment, reading, elaboration of signs. It is first of all and just as much, if not more, to play the game, to fool him or herself out of pleasure, and in spite of those knowledges which reinforce his or her position of non-fool; it is to maintain – if the spectacle, its play make it possible – the mechanism of disavowal at its highest level of intensity. The more one knows, the more difficult it is to believe, and the more it is worth it to manage to.

If there is in iconic analogy as operative in cinema the contradictory work of difference, non-similitude, false repetition which at once found and limit the deception, then it is the whole edifice of cinematic representation that finds itself affected with a fundamental lack: the negative index, the restriction the disavowal of which is the symptom and which it tries to fill while at the same time displaying it. More than the representative apparatuses that come before it (theater, painting, photography, etc.), cinema – precisely because it effects a greater approximation to the analogical reproduction of the visible, because it is carried along by that "realist vocation" so dear to Bazin – is no doubt more profoundly, more decisively undermined than those other apparatuses by everything that separates the real from the representable and even the visible from the represented. It is what resists cinematic representation, limiting it on all side and from within, which constitutes equally its force; what makes it falter makes it go.

The cinematic image grasps only a small part of the visible; and it is a grasp which – provisional, contracted, fragmentary – bears in it its impossibility. At the same time, film images are only a small part in the multiplicity of the visible, even if they tend by their accumulation to cover it. Every image is thus doubly racked by disillusion: from within itself as machine for simulation, mechanical and deathly reproduction of the living; from without as single image only, and not all images, in that what fills it will never be but the present index of an absence, of the lack of another image. Yet it is also, of course, this structuring disillusion which offers the offensive strength of cinematic representation and allows it to work against the completing, reassuring, mystifying representations of ideology. It is that strength that is needed, and that work of disillusion, if cinematic representation is to do something other than pile visible on visible, if it is, in certain rare flashes, to produce in our sight the very blindness which is at the heart of this visible.

Glossary of Terms

To aid the reader, a glossary of terms specific to Comolli's articles is included here, arranged in alphabetical order of the French. His texts pose two main lexical challenges for the reader of English: firstly, the adoption of specialized terminology from Marxist, semiotic and psychoanalytic theory; and, secondly, the use of film-specific French vocabulary, which does not always have precise equivalents in English. Throughout the text, care has been taken to follow existing conventions in the English translation of French theoretical terms, when these are relatively uncontested. The exceptions, and the occasions in which the present text markedly differs from Matias' translation, are given explanations either here or in the translator's footnotes. Existing glossaries provided by Ben Brewster (in his translation of Althusser's *For Marx*) and Leon S. Roudiez (in Kristeva's *Desire in Language*) have been consulted. For many of the entries, however, the glosses provided below can perforce only offer the briefest of introductions to concepts of considerable complexity.

Comolli also has occasional recourse to devising neologisms, but these are generally only used on a one-off basis, and are glossed in the translator's footnotes.

Appareil, dispositif (*apparatus, dispositif*). The considerable confusion in English translations of French texts between *appareil* and *dispositif* continues to the present-day. Both are frequently rendered as "apparatus," despite the fact that in French a distinction is often drawn between the two terms. Matters become even murkier because Comolli uses both *appareil* and *dispositif* in a dual sense: firstly (and more commonly) as a technical term to describe film equipment (in which case I have opted for *apparatus, device, equipment* or *instrument* where appropriate), and secondly as a theoretical concept. In the latter case, *appareil* has been rendered as *apparatus,* while *dispositif* has been retained as a loanword, in line with recent practice. When speaking of the *apparatus,* Comolli is primarily referring to Althusser's text "Ideology and Ideological State Apparatuses," in which the Ideological State Apparatus is conceived of as the material embodiment of and conduit for the preservation of the prevailing dominant ideology (bourgeois ideology in the case of capitalist state formations), but also as a site of struggle between contending ideologies. The term was also used in a more specific sense in relation to the cinema, most notably in Jean-Louis Baudry's text "Ideological Effects of the Basic Cinematographic Apparatus" (a polemical target in "Technique and Ideology"), to refer to the governing system of representation in the vast majority of films (based on the "impression of reality") as well as the ideological determination of the various social codes and practices surrounding the act of viewing a film (the darkened room, the rectangular, frontal screen, the projected beam of light, etc.). As for the *dispositif*, its distinction from the *appareil* was not solidified until after the initial publication of "Technique and Ideology" (cf. Michel Foucault, "The Confession of the Flesh," in *Power/Knowledge: Selected Interviews and Other Writings*, ed. Colin Gordon [New York: Pantheon, 1980], pp. 194-228; Jean-Louis Baudry, "Le dispositif: approches métapsychologies de l'impression de réalité," *Communications*, vol. 23 no. 23 [1975], pp. 56-72, translated as "The Apparatus: Metapsychological Approaches to the Impression of Reality in the Cinema," trans. Jean Andrews and Bertrand Augst, *Camera Obscura*, no. 1 [1976], pp. 104-128). There is only one case of its use in a non-technical sense in Comolli's original text, but its use as a theoretical concept does occur more frequently in both "Machines of the Visible" and "Cinema against Spectacle."

Barrer (*bar*). Comolli's use of the verb *barrer* invokes the inflection given to it by Lacan, who uses the term in the dual sense of "prohibit, forbid" and "divide, bisect" – most notably in his notion of the "*sujet barré*" (barred subject). Comolli himself emphasizes the dialectical aspect of the term, describing it as follows: "In other words: to negate, but to do so by conserving the term that is negated, hence barred. Under the bar that negates, there subsists the (barred) term or notion that one wishes to negate without abolishing it, by maintaining its ghostly trace" (private communication, September 2013). In all cases, I have followed existing convention and used the verb *to bar*.

Cache, masque (*mask*). In his landmark text "Théâtre et cinéma," Bazin argues against seeing the film screen as a strict analogue to the painting, delimited by the frame (*cadre*), and instead prefers to see it as a "*cache*," analogous to a "window on the world" (cf. translator's note vii "Cinema against Spectacle," chapter I). The opposition *cadre/cache* was frequently referred to, and hotly disputed, by *Cahiers* during their radicalized period. No precise equivalent exists to the French term *cache*, as used by Bazin, but I have followed existing translations (both Hugh Gray and Timothy Barnard are in unison on this matter) by rendering it as *mask*. To obviate the otherwise unavoidable confusion with *masque* (also regularly used by Comolli, and in quite a different sense to Bazin's use of *cache*), I have added the original term in brackets when warranted.

Connaissance (*knowledge*). Brewster gives the following definition of Althusser's use of the term *connaissance*, which is rigorously adhered to by Comolli: "Knowledge is the product of theoretical practice. [...] As such it is clearly distinct from the practical recognition of a theoretical problem" (*For Marx*, p. 252). Comolli frequently uses the term in the plural (*connaissances*), a distinction which has been maintained here, even if *knowledges* comes across as slightly stilted in English.

Décalage (*discrepancy, dislocation*). In his translations of Althusser, Brewster originally chose (in *Reading Capital* and *Lenin and Philosophy*) to translate *décalage* as *dislocation*, but in "Rousseau: The Social Contract" he opted for *discrepancy*, explaining the change as being one that shifts "from a more mechanical to a more mental metaphor" of a term whose meaning "is something like the state of being 'staggered' or 'out of step'," as well as being more in line with conventional translations of Lenin (cf. Althusser, *Politics and History: Montesquieu, Rousseau, Marx*, trans. Ben Brewster [London: NLB, 1972], p. 113, fn. 2). Comolli often uses *décalage* in a temporal sense, where *lag* may be an appropriate English equivalent, but to maintain the link with Althusserian theory (and to distinguish the term from Comolli's own use of the French word *dislocation*), I have opted to follow Brewster's practice and render it as *discrepancy*.

Découpage. From the 1930s onwards, French film theory has maintained a rigid distinction between two forms of shot construction: *découpage*, whereby the articulation of shots is defined prior to the shoot, and which is primarily associated with the editing method in classical Hollywood cinema; and *montage*, whereby shots are assembled after the filming process, a technique most readily identified with 1920s Soviet cinema (and the work of Eisenstein and Vertov in particular). Whereas in *découpage* the editing of a film seeks to be as unobtrusive (or "invisible") as possible, by following rigorous rules of continuity, pacing and spatial relations, in *montage* the editing calls attention to itself, and is even theorized as being the primary site for the creation of meaning or aesthetic impact in a film. Unfortunately, whereas *montage* was quickly adopted into the English language, no such process took place for *découpage* (which literally refers to the shot-breakdown, or storyboard, used in studio filmmaking), and the various efforts at rendering the term as "cutting," "editing," "continuity," etc., have resulted in many English translations of French texts veering into the nonsensical. Barnard, in his 2009 translation of Bazin's writings, insists on the viability of retaining the original term in the English, and offers a 20-page footnote in defense of his decision, which discusses the issue in a much more detailed fashion than is possible here (cf. *What Is Cinema?*, pp. 261-281). I have thus followed his practice.

Dénier, déni, désavouer, dénegation (*deny, denial, disavow, disavowal*). Comolli uses these terms in their Freudian sense, wherein a denial/disavowal of an event or personality trait can be seen as a tacit confession of its existence. Although roughly interchangeable, I have generally maintained consistency with Comolli's usage, with *dénier/déni* given as *deny/denial* and *désavouer/dénegation* given as *disavow/disavowal* (these last two terms are not etymologically linked in the French, but their meaning is close enough to authorize this option in English).

Déplacement, replacement (*displacement, re-placement*). These terms, and their associated verb forms, are used by Comolli to denote the symptomatic shifting of the terms of an argument or theoretical treatment of an object (and the reverse operation correcting this shift). The concept is derived from Freud's discussion, in *The Interpretation of Dreams*, of the technique of displacement operative in the dreamwork. Care should thus be taken not to confuse the hyphenated term *re-placement* with the more common word *replacement* (*remplacement* in the French).

Différence, différance (*deferral/difference, différance*). Cf. translator's note i to "Technique and Ideology," chapter I.

Diffuser (*diffuse, distribute, broadcast*). Comolli uses *diffuser* in two distinct ways: in the media-specific sense (equivalent to *distribute* in the cinema, and *broadcast* in television), and in a more theoretical sense to refer to the secretion and propagation of ideology through signifying practices, in which case I have opted for the English cognate *diffuse*.

Disponibilité (*availability*). Although Matias goes to great lengths to avoid rendering *disponibilité* as *availability*, there seems no reason not to simply adopt the common English translation of the French term, as long as heed is taken that when Comolli speaks of the "*availability*" of a given film technique, he is using the expression in a specific (and invariably ironic) sense, which he defines as its "signifying indifference."

Dispositif – cf. *appareil*.

Dissemblance, resemblance (*dissemblance, resemblance*). Although largely absent in "Technique and Ideology," this pair of terms is frequently deployed in "Cinema against Spectacle" to refer to the specificities of the *lure* (cf. the entry for *leurre*) of cinematic representation, involving both similitude between the referent and the representation (the impression of reality produced through on-screen movement and the indexical realism of photography), and the marked dissimilarities between cinematic vision and everyday human perception (the two-dimensionality of the image, its delimitation by the screen's framelines, the flicker effect, etc.).

Écriture, lecture (*writing, reading*). *Écriture,* the common French term for the process of writing (as opposed to the result of this process, which is rendered as *écrit* or *écrits*) has been given a range of theoretical inflections, most notably by Barthes, Derrida and Kristeva, referring mainly to the encoding activity of the writer, as a non-authorial subject. English usage is divided between rendering the term as *writing,* adopting a neologism such as *scription,* or maintaining the original French. This last option was favored by Nick Browne in the edited collection *Cahiers du cinéma, 1969-1972,* but doing so here is complicated by the fact that it is not always unambiguous when Comolli is using the term in its theoretical sense, as opposed to the everyday use of the word, and it is unlikely that he always had such a sharp distinction in mind. I have thus given *écriture* as *writing,* while occasionally opting for *writing process* or *writing practice* when the specification was felt to be necessary. Much the same applies for Comolli's use of the term *lecture* (*reading*), indicating an inversion/repetition of the process of *écriture* on the part of the reader of a text.

Effacer, effacement (*efface, effacement*). The English cognate of *effacer* has been preferred over the more common *erase,* in order to highlight Comolli's specific use of the term to denote the disavowal of the inscription of the film production process onto the film itself (for example, the conventions of Hollywood editing are used to *efface* the real spatial disjunctions between shots, creating a sense of continuity from an assemblage of discontinuous film fragments).

Énoncé, énonciation (*statement, enunciation*). This pair of terms was devised by the French linguist Émile Benveniste in the early 20th century, and was widely adopted by structuralist thinkers (as well as *Cahiers*) in the 1960s. To put it briefly, the *énoncé* refers to the abstract content of a verbal or written communication, while *énonciation* designates the specific, contextualized act of communication. English conventions when translating these terms vary (and it is a common option to maintain the French), but here I have opted for *statement* and *enunciation*.

Évidence (*obvious truth*). Care has been taken to avoid rendering *évidence* as *evidence*, which has a subtly different meaning in English. Instead, the more accurate, although slightly more unwieldy, paraphrase *obvious truth* is given.

Filiation (*kinship*). To denote the twin qualities denoted by Comolli's use of the term *filiation* (that is, both surface resemblance and common origins), it has been translated as *kinship* throughout.

Forclusion, forclos (*foreclosure, foreclosed*). *Forclusion* is Lacan's translation of Freud's term *Verwerfung* (referring to the defense mechanisms of the psyche), and was eagerly adopted as a concept in his *Séminaires*, although its status as a fully fledged concept in Freud has been open to debate. The conventional English equivalent is *foreclosure*, and this has been retained here. In both French and English (but not German), the term is originally a legal expression designating the abrogation of ownership rights on a mortgaged property, and this semantic provenance notably led *Cahiers*, in part II of "Cinema/Ideology/Criticism" to issue a harsh rebuke to *Cinéthique* for its ill-defined use of the term. Cf. supra, p. 263, fn. 1.

Hors-champ. This term is first used by Noël Burch in *Praxis du cinéma* (1969), devised on the model of the *hors-scène* (which refers to the offstage space in the theater). It was quickly adopted by *Cahiers*, and in particular Pascal Bonitzer in the article "Hors-champ" (*Cahiers du cinéma*, no. 234-235, pp. 15-26). Bonitzer, however, critiqued Burch for his "empiricist" use of the concept, and widened its theoretical breadth to such an extent that the English term *off-screen space* used in the translation of Burch's work (*Theory of Film Practice* [New York: Praeger, 1973]) is inadequate to convey its meaning. It has thus been decided to retain *hors-champ* in the French where possible, and to indicate its use in brackets when a translation is used. More generally, the word *champ* in French denotes the visible area represented in a film image, and so is employed where English usage is particularly variable, with *shot*, *field*, *screen* and *space* all possible. The editing technique known in English as *shot/reverse shot*, for instance, is rendered as *champ-contrechamp* in French. In "Cinema against Spectacle," Comolli makes prodigious use of wordplay involving variations on the expression *hors-champ*, resulting in terms such as *hors-film*, *hors-temps* and *jeu hors jeu*. A range of strategies has been adopted to reproduce the semantic subtleties at work here.

Impensé (*unthought*). English does not permit the straightforward conversion of participles into abstract nouns to the same extent that French does, so using *unthought* in its nominal form as an equivalent to *l'impensé* – a term Comolli borrows from Lacan to describe an object, concept or phenomenon that is symptomatically *not* subjected to theorization or conscious thought processes – inevitably comes across as the stilted concoction of a translator. *Unthought* has nonetheless made its way into English by dint of existing translations of Lacan, and in the absence of a more fitting rendition, is also used here.

Jouer, jeu. One of the striking stylistic markers of "Technique and Ideology" is the particularly frequent recurrence of the verb *jouer*, and its related noun form *jeu*. Unfortunately, there is no single English equivalent capable of conveying the various shades of meaning Comolli imparts on the terms, and so I have had to opt for a large number of equivalents, including: *play, act, function* and *work* for *jouer*; and *role, performance, play, game, interplay, interaction* and *functioning* for *jeu*.

Jouissance. The word *jouissance* was in common use in English during the Renaissance, but its modern usage derives from Lacan's notion of *jouissance* as a form of infinite, totalizing pleasure. In *Cahiers*, it was readily deployed by writers such as Jean-Pierre Oudart, Serge Daney and Pascal Bonitzer (indeed, a key text co-authored by Oudart and Daney is entitled "Travail, lecture, jouissance"). Comolli, however, was far more reserved when it comes to using the term. It only appears once in "Technique and Ideology" (in a citation of Kristeva), but occurs more frequently in "Cinema against Spectacle," where it is generally left untranslated.

Lecture – cf. *écriture*.

Leurre (*lure*). Another adoption from Lacan's idiosyncratic vocabulary, *leurre* was widely used by all the major *Cahiers* writers to denote the process of spectatorial investment in the reality of the diegetic events depicted in a film, most notably with respect to the empathetic identification with on-screen characters. They were careful, however, to insist that this credence in the "impression of reality" is never a totalizing conviction, but is always constrained by a *lack* (the perceptual differences between a film screening and everyday vision), and is thus exemplary of the divided subjectivity encapsulated by the Lacanian phrase "*Je sais bien... mais quand même...*" (*I know very well... but all the same...*). Cf., in particular, Pascal Bonitzer's "Hors-champ" (*Cahiers du cinéma*, no. 234-235, pp. 15-26). Existing translations of *Cahiers* texts have rendered *leurre* in a number of ways, including *snare* and *illusion*, but here I have followed accepted practice in the translation of Lacan into English and opted for the etymologically related word *lure*.

Lieu, place (*site, place/position*). Comolli uses *lieu* and *place* in a generally interchangeable fashion, but for the sake of consistency I have rendered the former as *site* and the latter as *place* (or, occasionally, as *position*). When used with a theoretical inflection, in particular in the phrase *la place du spectateur* (*the place of the spectator*) the terms are used to denote the positioning of a subject within a given ideological formation.

Manque (*lack*). One of the terms most readily associated with Lacanian psychoanalysis, *manque* refers to the sense of absence or loss felt by a subject whose desire can never, strictly speaking, be fulfilled, because this desire is not for a specific object, but for desire itself. It is rendered as *lack* throughout.

Parole (*speech, the spoken word*). *Parole* is a term in the Saussurean linguistic triad *langue-langage-parole* designating the individual act of using language (and can thus be spoken, written or conveyed through a variety of other means). It is also, however, a word in everyday French that covers a range of meanings in English, usually rendered by either *speech* or *word*. Comolli makes particularly frenetic use of the term in his passages on the advent of sound cinema (*le film parlant* in his French), and it has been given here as either *speech* or *the spoken word* where appropriate (to retain the ambiguities of Comolli's usage, I have avoided the more specialized form *speech act*).

Passage à l'acte (*passage to the act*). Freud's original term *agieren* – referring to the propensity to cede to the impulse to perform a normally repressed activity – is usually rendered in English as *acting out* and in French as *passage à l'acte*. In *Le Séminaire*, vol. X ("L'Angoisse"), Lacan, however, drew a distinction between the two, considering *passage à l'acte* to be inadequate to convey Freud's *agieren* and bestowing new meaning on the term. Lacan likens the difference between the two concepts to a gushing tap: "What is the symptom? It is the gush of water from the tap. The passage to the act is akin to turning the tap on, but turning it on without knowing what you are doing. [...] As for acting-out [...] it is not the deed of turning the tap on, it is simply the presence or not of the spurt of water" (*Le Séminaire*, vol. X, p. 372). Comolli deploys the term rather freely in "Cinema against Spectacle," but it is clear that his usage refers back to the Lacanian sense of the term. It has thus been literally translated as *passage to the act*.

Photogramme (*frame, still, still-image*). The French term *photogramme* refers to the individual *frame* in a strip of film, as well as to a *still* (or *still-image*) from a film reproduced in printed form. The English term *photogram* is a false friend, and pertains to images produced using photo-sensitive paper, but without the use of a camera. Nonetheless, when Comolli, in "Cinema against Spectacle," speaks of the *squelette photogrammatique* to describe the physical chain of still images making up a film, there is no other viable option than to opt for the phrase *photogrammatic skeleton*.

Place – cf. *lieu*.

Plus de réel, plus de réalisme (*surplus reality, surplus realism*). A central plank of Bazinian theory contested by Comolli is the notion that deep-focus photography, and an editing system based on the uninterrupted long-take, heighten the fidelity of a film's depiction of reality by more closely approximating the norms of human perception. Comolli dubs this idea the theory of the *plus de réel* or *plus de réalisme*, on the basis of an expression used by Bazin in his monograph on Orson Welles. Matias renders these as *supra-realism*, but this gives the misleading sense of a transcendence of realism (as in the term *surrealism*). Instead, I have followed in the footsteps of Rosenbaum by opting for *surplus reality* or *surplus realism* (cf. André Bazin, *Orson Welles: A Critical View*, trans. Jonathan Rosenbaum [London: Elm Tree Books, 1978],

p. 80). *Surplus realism* has the additional value of retaining the Marxist echoes of Comolli's use of the term (*surplus value*, or *Mehrwert*, is rendered in French translations of Marx as *plus-value*). Comolli also uses a variety of synonyms for this notion, including *supplément de réalisme* (*supplementary realism* – also used by Bazin), *surcroît de réalisme* (*augmentation of realism*) and *gain de réalité* (*gain in reality*).

Pratique signifiante (*signifying practice*). The term is originally Kristeva's, who defines it as follows: "I shall call signifying practice the establishment and the countervailing of a sign system. Establishing a sign system calls for the identity of a speaking subject within a social framework, which he recognizes as a basis for that identity. Countervailing the sign system is done by having the subject undergo an unsettling, questionable process; this indirectly challenges the social framework with which he had previously identified, and it thus coincides with times of abrupt changes, renewal, or revolution in society" (*Desire in Language*, p. 18). Comolli tends to use the term in a broader sense, to denote any social practice that produces communicable meaning or *signification*, but his debt to Kristeva is unmistakable.

Réconnaissance, méconnaissance (*recognition, misrecognition*). A central component of Lacan's theory of the mirror stage. The infant who first *recognizes* their own image in a reflected image of themselves is in fact subject to a process of *misrecognition*, whereby they mistake the whole, unitary subject visible to them in the mirror image for the divided subject that they themselves are. This concept was readily imported into film theory to account for spectatorial identification with on-screen characters (or, in Metz's version, with the camera itself), with texts by Oudart, Bonitzer and Baudry playing key roles in this process.

Récouvrir (*cover over, overlap*). The term *récouvrir* (and its noun form *récouvrement*) is used frequently by Comolli, most often to denote a process of ideological masking or *covering over*, and more rarely to refer to the *overlapping* between two different aspects of a *signifying practice*.

Régler (*regulate, govern, order*). Like *jouer*, *régler* is used with unerring regularity in "Technique and Ideology," for the most part to refer to the process whereby the development of film technique is dictated by the ideological demands required of it. No single English word quite encapsulates the breadth of meanings generated by *régler*, so *regulate, govern* or *order* have been used where appropriate.

Relief, Cinéma du (*stereoscopy, relief, the third dimension*). The standard French word for three-dimensional cinema is *cinéma du relief*, but *le relief* on its own can be used to denote the more abstract sense of *stereoscopy*, or *the third dimension* in a three-dimensional image.

Replacement – cf. *déplacement*.

Resemblance – cf. *dissemblance*.

Retard (*delay, belatedness*). Comolli frequently deploys this term to refer to the temporal disjunction between the scientific possibility of the adoption of a film technology or technique and its actual generalized take-up, ascribing this disjunction to the twin factors of ideological need and economic demand. It has been rendered as either *delay* or *belatedness* where appropriate.

Signifiance. Cf. translator's note iii to "Technique and Ideology," chapter II.

Signifiant, signifié (*signifier, signified*). Standard usage in translating Saussure's terms *signifiant* and *signifié* as *signifier* and *signified* has been followed in this volume. For Saussure every linguistic sign can be divided into the *signified* (the abstract concept to which the sign refers) and the *signifier* (the "acoustic image" of a word), and he stressed the generally arbitrary relationship between the two. *Cahiers* frequently used the Saussurean distinction between *signifier* and *signified* as an analogy for the form/content duality of traditional aesthetic theory, but also warned against a "static and simplistic" distinction between the two terms (cf. supra, p. 256, fn. 7).

Speculaire (*specular*). An adjective frequently used in Lacanian and Althusserian theory to refer to the processes of identification associated with the mirror stage, *speculaire* has generally been rendered as *specular* in English translations (although some translators opt for the variant *speculary*), reviving a rare word that has nonetheless been in use in English since the 16th century. This practice has been maintained here.

Suture. In French, as in English, *suture* is a surgical term for the stitching together of open wounds. It was introduced into psychoanalytic discourse by the Lacanian Jacques-Alain Miller in the 1967 article "Suture (éléments de la logique du signifiant)" to describe the process by which a subject is integrated into a social totality through discourse, and soon imported into film theory by Jean-Pierre Oudart, in the 1970 article "La Suture," to refer to the process that allows the spectator to create a synthetic sense of space from the fragmentary shots of a film sequence. Taken up by theorists such as Daniel Dayan and Kaja Silverman, it has since become a key concept in film studies, although it is only referred to sparingly by Comolli.

Technique (*technique, technology*). The French term *technique* is used to mean both *technique* and *technology*, and it is clear that Comolli has both meanings in mind in the title "Technique et idéologie." This ambiguity is such that a recent translation of Bernard Stiegler's *Technique et temps* has opted for the rarer form *technics*, but Comolli's text is so widely known under the title "Technique and Ideology" that it would be unproductive to try to alter it at this stage. As for the body of the text, *technique* has generally been rendered as *technique*, and on occasion as *technology* when the more specific sense of the term seems appropriate.

Transparence (*transparency*). This is the term used in *Cahiers* to designate the common ideological basis to the theories of representation in both the advent of Renaissance perspective (by figures such as Leon Battista Alberti and Leonardo da Vinci) and Bazin's notion of photographic realism: specifically, the idea that the representation should be akin to a "window onto the world," as close as possible to the human visual field. Although Bazin himself shied away from using the term *transparence*, it was taken up with gusto by the *macmahoniens*, who spoke of "transparent *mise en scène*" as being the key characteristic of their favored directors. As Comolli notes in "Cinema against Spectacle," however, this is not a formal quality readily associated with most of the work of their "four aces": Lang, Walsh, Preminger and Losey (cf. supra, p. 61). For a fascinating debate between the later *Cahiers* and a continued adherent of the Bazinian outlook (namely, Éric Rohmer), cf. "Nouvel entretien avec Éric Rohmer," *Cahiers du cinéma*, no. 219 (1970), pp. 46-55 (translated as "New Interview with Éric Rohmer," trans. Daniel Fairfax, *Senses of Cinema*, no. 54 [2010]).

Travail, travailler (*work, rework, transform*). With its origins in the literary theory dominant at *Tel Quel*, the notion of *travail* was of extreme importance to *Cahiers*, and while its precise meaning was complex and often obscure, it was generally used to refer to the processes of transformation of the signifying material enacted by both the filmmaker and the spectator, and specifically counterposed to the "naïveté" of the theories of *transparency* between the representation and the reality depicted. The notion of *travail* tended to be understood in an overly literal manner in *Screen*, however, with spectators urged to "work" during the screening of a film. Cf., in particular, their special issue on Brecht (*Screen*, vol. 16 no. 4 [1975-76]). *Tel Quel*, meanwhile, understood *travail* in a sense much closer to Freud's concept of the dream-work (cf. Kristeva, "Pratique analytique, pratique révolutionnaire," *Cinéthique* no. 9-10 [1971], p. 74), or the Greek term ποιειν (meaning *craftwork*, but also used to denote poetic activity – cf. Kristeva, *Séméiotikè*, p. 7). Comolli himself would note, in "Machines of the Visible," that, "Never 'passive,' the spectator works. But that work is not only a work of decipherment, reading, elaboration of signs. It is first of all and just as much, if not more, to play the game, to fool him or herself out of pleasure, and in spite of those knowledges which reinforce his or her position of non-fool; it is to maintain [...] the mechanism of disavowal at its highest level of intensity" (cf. supra, p. 288-289). In translating the term I have opted either for *work* or, as a verb, *rework*, and occasionally for *transform/transformation* when *work* would give rise to ambiguity.

Publication History

Publication History of "Technique and Ideology"

Note: Although Comolli's article has since come to be known as "Technique et idéologie" ("Technique and Ideology"), it is unclear from the initial publication of the text in *Cahiers du cinéma* whether this title was to refer to his article alone, or a section of the journal devoted to texts on the broader theme it denoted. The first mention of the article appears in an advertisement on page 70 of issue no. 218 for articles that "*Cahiers* will publish," giving its title as "Idéologie de la technique (collectif)." Unlike similar undertakings, when the first article did appear 11 issues later it was not as a collective effort, but under Comolli's name alone, and with the subtitle "Caméra, perspective, profondeur de champ." In subsequent issues, however, the table of contents pages include a range of articles under the heading "Technique, idéologie," not all of which were written by Comolli (these include Pascal Bonitzer's "Le gros orteil" in no. 232, "Fétichisme de la technique: la notion de 'plan'" in no. 233, and "Hors-champ" in no. 234-235, and Christian Metz's "Ponctuation et démarcation dans le film de diégèse" in no. 234-235). Nonetheless, common usage would soon refer to Comolli's texts alone as "Technique et idéologie," and even Comolli himself is happy to adopt this practice.

"Technique and Ideology" was first published in six "installments" (from issue no. 229 to no. 241), but these do not correspond precisely to the five "parts" into which the text is divided: the first installment covers parts I and the beginning of part II, the second installment is composed of the middle segment of part II, the third installment completes part II, while the fourth, fifth and sixth installments correspond to parts III, IV and V respectively. The division into parts I to V was standardized in the article's reprinting in *Cinéma contre spectacle*. When English publications refer to the "parts" of "Technique and Ideology," however, they generally refer to the installments in the series, rather than the sections of the text properly speaking.

In French

First Installment: "Technique et Idéologie: Caméra, perspective, profondeur de champ," *Cahiers du cinéma*, no. 229 (May 1971), pp. 4-21.

To: "... the system of (perspectival and cultural norms which anchor the impression of reality and support the category of 'realism'?" (p. 182)

Second Installment: "Technique et Idéologie: Caméra, perspective, profondeur de champ," *Cahiers du cinéma*, no. 230 (July 1971), pp. 51-57.

From: "It is far from irrelevant that discourses which are otherwise antagonistic..." (p. 182)

To: "... that is to say, once more, without a materialist theory of history itself, or the Marxist elaboration of the science of history, historical materialism." (p. 193)

Third Installment: "Technique et Idéologie (3): Caméra, perspective, profondeur de champ," *Cahiers du cinéma*, no. 231 (August-September 1971), pp. 42-49.

From: "With the preceding generalities on the conditions of a materialist approach to the history of the cinema..." (p. 194)

To: "...it can not find anything in its path other than 'formal' techniques, and 'universal,' 'neutral' forms." (p. 207)

Fourth Installment: "Technique et Idéologie (4): Caméra, perspective, profondeur de champ," *Cahiers du cinéma*, no. 233 (November 1971), pp. 39-45

From: "[III.] 'Primitive' Depth of Field" (p. 209)

To: "...that of the ideology of studio filming, of the representation of (interior/exterior) space that it produces." (p. 221)

Fifth Installment: "Technique et Idéologie (5): Caméra, perspective, profondeur de champ," *Cahiers du cinéma*, no. 234-235 (December 1971-January-February 1972), pp. 94-100.

From: "[IV.] Effacement of depth/advent of speech" (p. 223)

To: "...as a replete presence, which is incessantly filled by the ideological statements which speak this subject." (p. 235)

Sixth Installment: "Technique et idéologie, 6. II. Caméra, perspective, profondeur de champ," *Cahiers du cinéma*, no. 241 (September-October 1972), pp. 20-24.

"From "[V.] Which speech?" (p. 237)

Repr. as "Technique et idéologie: Caméra, perspective, profondeur de champ." In Jean-Louis Comolli, *Cinéma contre spectacle*. Lagrasse: Verdier, 2009, pp. 123-243.

In English

"Technique and Ideology: Camera, Perspective, Depth of Field," trans. Diana Matias, *Film Reader*, no. 2 (1977), pp. 128-140.

To: "it is under the effects of an economic demand – that is, within ideology and as an instrument of ideology – that the cinema is progressively imagined, made and purchased." (p. 169)

Extracts reprinted in Comolli, "Machines of the Visible." Trans. [Teresa de Lauretis and Stephen Heath]. In *The Cinematic Apparatus*, ed. Teresa de Lauretis and Stephen Heath. New York: St. Martin's Press, 1980, pp. 121-142. Repr. in *Film Theory and Criticism: Introductory Readings*, ed. Gerald Mast and Marshall Cohen, 3rd edition. Oxford: Oxford University Press, 1985, pp. 741-760.

"Technique and Ideology." Trans. Diana Matias. In *Movies and Methods*, ed. Bill Nichols, 2 vols. Berkeley: University of California Press, 1985, vol. 2, pp. 40-57.

To: "it is under the effects of an economic demand – that is, within ideology and as an instrument of ideology – that the cinema is progressively imagined, made and purchased." (p. 169)

"Technique and Ideology: Camera, Perspective, Depth of Field (Parts 3 and 4)." Trans. Diana Matias (with revisions by Marcia Butzel and Philip Rosen). In *Narrative, Apparatus, Ideol-*

ogy: A Film Theory Reader, ed. Philip Rosen. New York: Columbia University Press, 1986, pp. 421-443.

From: "With the preceding generalities on the conditions of a materialist approach to the history of the cinema..." (p. 194)

To: "...that of the ideology of studio filming, of the representation of (interior/exterior) space that it produces." (p. 221)

"Technique and Ideology: Camera, Perspective, Depth of Field." Trans. Diana Matias (with revisions by Nick Browne). In *Cahiers du cinéma, 1969-72: The Politics of Representation*, ed. Nick Browne. London: BFI, 1990, pp. 213-247.

To: "... that is to say, once more, without a materialist theory of history itself, or the Marxist elaboration of the science of history, historical materialism." (p. 193)

Publication History of "Cinema/Ideology/Criticism"

In French

Part I: "Cinéma/Idéologie/Critique," *Cahiers du cinéma*, no. 216 (October 1969), pp. 11-15.

Part II: "Cinéma/Idéologie/Critique (2): D'une critique à son point critique," *Cahiers du cinéma*, no. 217 (November 1969), pp. 7-14.

In English

Part I: "Cinema/Ideology/Criticism," trans. Susan Bennett, *Screen*, vol. 12 no. 1 (Spring 1971), pp. 27-38.

Part II: "Cinema/Ideology/Criticism (2): Examining a Critique at its Critical Point," trans. Susan Bennett, *Screen*, vol. 12 no. 2 (Summer 1971), pp. 145-155, and *Screen*, vol. 13 no. 1 (Spring 1972), pp. 120-131.

Parts I and II reprinted in *Screen Reader 1: Cinema, Ideology, Politics*, ed. Sam Rohdie. London: BFI, 1977, pp. 2-11, 36-46 and 244-255.

Part I reprinted in:

Movies and Methods, ed. Bill Nichols, 2 vols. Berkeley: University of California Press, 1976, vol. 1, pp. 22-30.

Cahiers du cinéma, 1969-1972: The Politics of Representation, ed. Nick Browne. London: Routledge, 1990, pp. 58-67.

Film Studies Reader, ed. Joanne Hollows, Peter Hutchings and Mark Jancovich. Oxford: Oxford University Press, 2000, pp. 197-200.

Film Theory and Criticism: Introductory Readings, ed. Gerald Mast, Marshall Cohen and Leo Braudy, 6th edition. Oxford: Oxford University Press, 2004, pp. 812-819.

Critical Visions in Film Theory: Classic and Contemporary Readings, ed. Timothy Corrigan, Patricia White and Meta Mazaj. Boston: Bedford/St. Martins, 2011, pp. 478-486.

Filmography

Les Deux Marseillaises (co-directed with André S. Labarthe – 1968, 120', Argos). With Albin Chalandon, Roger Hanin and Claude Denis. Screened at the 1969 Venice film festival.

La Cecilia (1976, 100', Filmoblic/NEF). With Maria Carta, Massimo Foschi and Vittorio Mezzogiorno. Screened at the London, Brussels, Taormina, Montreal and Hong Kong film festivals.

Totò, une anthologie (1979, 110', Dramaturgie). With Totò and Dario Fo. Screened at the 1980 Paris film festival.

On ne va pas se quitter comme ça (1981, 55', A2/INA). Part of the series *Carnets de bal*, written by Alain-Ilan Chojnow. With La Boule Rouge and Simone Réal. Screened at the Rotterdam film festival, the Festival dei popoli (Florence) and the Cinéma du réel festival (Paris).

L'Ombre rouge (1981, 110', MK2/La Cecilia). With Claude Brasseur, Jacques Dutronc, Nathalie Baye, Andréa Ferréol, Alexandre Arbatt and Stephan Meldegg. Screened at the Brussels and New York film festivals.

Balles perdues (1982, 90', La Cecilia/Gaumont). With Andréa Ferréol, Serge Valletti, Maria Schneider, Capucine, Alexandre Arbatt, André Dupont and Stephan Meldegg.

Harmonie (1982, 50', A2/INA). Part of the series *Carnets de bal*. A ball at Wissembourg.

Les Chemins du retour (1982, 55', A2/INA). Part of the series *Carnets de bal*. Italians in Paris.

L'École des chefs (1985, 55', INA/Canal+). With Marc Meneau, Michel Lorain, Jacques Cagna, Gérard Vié.

La France à la carte (1986, 13 x 26', Initial/FR3/CEL). With Pierre Salinger and Jean-Marie Amat, Jean Bardet, Georges Blanc, Paul Bocuse, Michel Bras, Alain Ducasse, Jean-Paul Lacombe, Michel and Jean-Michel Lorain, Jacques Maximin, Marc Meneau, Roger Vergé, etc. Screened at the Rotterdam and Salsomaggiore film festivals.

Le Bal d'Irène (1987, 90', FR3). Part of the series *Cinéma-16*. With Anne Brochet, Francine Bergé, Bernard Freyd, Jean-François Perrier, Clovis, Yves Lambrecht, Stephan Meldegg.

Tabarka 42-87 (1987, 82', Médiations/INA/La Sept/CNC). With Claude Grenié and the European and Tunisian inhabitants of Tabarka. Screened at Vidéo-Réalités (Brussels, 1988).

Pétition (1987, 45', La Cecilia/INA). Based on the Vaclav Havel play, with Daniel Gélin and Stephan Meldegg. Nominated for best short film at the "Césars."

Kataev, la classe du maître (1988, 60', INA/La Sept). With Vitaly Kataev. Screened at the FIPA (Cannes).

Tous pour un! (1988, 2 x 60', Méli-Mélo/Centre Pompidou/CNC/Télévision Suisse Romande). With activists from the Parti socialiste in Neuilly-sur-Marne and the RPR in Bois-Colombes. Screened at the Cinéma du réel festival (Paris) and the États Généraux du Documentaire (Lussas).

Marseille de père en fils (co-authored with Anne Baudry and Michel Samson – 1989, 2 x 82', Archipel 33/La Sept/FR3 "Océaniques"/INA/CNC). First installment of the series *Marseille contre Marseille*. With Michel Samson, Jean-Claude Gaudin, Michel Pezet, Robert Vigouroux, Philippe Sanmarco, Loïc Fauchon, Claude Bertrand, Charles-Émile Loo, Lucien Weygand, Voudia Slimani, Jean Kéhayan, Zohra Maaskri... and the specter of Gaston Deferre. Screened at the Cinéma du réel festival (Paris).

Belep danse autour de la terre (1990, 52', Méli-Mélo/La Sept/CNC). With Eymard Bouénaoué and the dancers of the island of Belep. Screened at the FIPA (Cannes).

Paul-Émile Victor: un rêveur dans le siècle (1990, 3 x 52', Éliane Victor for Anabase/INA/FR3/La Sept/CNC). With Paul-Émile Victor, Jean Audouze, Claude Lévi-Strauss, Claude Lorius, Joëlle Robert-Lamblin. Screened at the Festival européen de télévision (Reims).

Naissance d'un hôpital (1991, 67', INA/La Sept/CNC). Based on *Journal d'un architecte* by Pierre Riboulet, and with Pierre Riboulet. Awarded prizes at the Biennale du documentaire (Marseilles, 1991), the FIFA (Paris, 1993) and the FIFARC (Bordeaux, 1993). Screened at the Montreal festival, the Festival dei popoli (Florence) and the États généraux du documentaire (Lussas).

La Campagne de Provence (co-authored with Anne Baudry and Michel Samson – 1992, 92', Vidéo 13/FR2/INA/Télévision Suisse Romande/RTBF). Second installment of the series *Marseille contre Marseille*. On the regional elections in Provence, with Michel Samson and Messieurs Gaudin, Léotard, Le Pen, Mégret, Pezet, Tapie. Screened at the États généraux du documentaire (Lussas).

Une semaine en cuisine (1992, 60', INA/La Sept). On and with Alain Ducasse (Restaurant "Le Louis XV," Hôtel de Paris, Monte-Carlo). Screened at the Festival dei popoli (Florence).

La Jeune Fille au livre (filmed opera; music: André Bon; libretto: Michel Beretti – 1993, 67', INA/Arte). With Sophie Marin-Degor, Jean-Marc Saltzmann, Christine Schweitzer, Monte Jaffe. Screened at the Locarno and Aix film festivals (1994), FIPA (1995), INPUT (1995).

Chahine & Co. (1993, 55', AMIP/INA/La Sept). Part of the series *Cinéma de notre temps* supervised by Janine Bazin and André S. Labarthe. A portrait of Youssef Chahine. Screened at the Locarno (1993) and Jerusalem (1994) film festivals.

La Vraie Vie (dans les bureaux) (1993, 88', 13 Production/C. Otzenberger/La Sept-Arte/CNC/Centre Pompidou). On low-level office work at the Caisse Régionale d'Assurances Maladie in the Île de France. Screened at the Cinéma du réel festival (Paris, 1993).

Marseille en mars (co-authored with Anne Baudry and Michel Samson – 1993, 52', 13 Production/Archipel 33/INA). Third installment in the series *Marseille contre Marseille*. On the March 1993 legislative elections. Screened at the États généraux du documentaire (Lussas), "Vive le cinéma français" (1994).

Un Américain en Normandie (Le Jour J de Samuel Fuller) (1994, 52', GMT Production/La Sept-Arte/Centre Pompidou). Director Samuel Fuller recounts the disembarkation of Corporal Samuel Fuller at Omaha Beach, June 6, 1944, and the subsequent Normandy campaign (the "war of the sharks"). Screened at the Festival dei popoli (Florence, 1994).

Musiques de films: Georges Delerue (1994, 60', Les Films d'Ici/Alternate Current (New York)/Arte/Centre Pompidou/France 3/RTBF/La Chaîne). With Georges Delerue, Oliver Stone, Ken Russell, Claudine Bouché, Yan Dedet, Russell Lloyd, Leslie Hodgson. Screened at the Festival dei popoli (Florence, 1994) and the Locarno film festival (1995).

Rêve d'un jour (co-authored with Anne Baudry – 1995, 86', Com'une Image/Collectif Arcobaleno/Planète Câble/Telessonne). One year later, the editors of the ephemeral daily newspaper *Le Jour* relive their experiences. With Catherine Delgado, Jean-Christophe Notias, Christian Perrot, Jean-Michel Decugis, Aziz Zemouri, Yannick Bourg, Cheikh M'Baye, Florence Pinaud, Jérôme Brézillon, Laure Tran. Screened at the Cinéma du réel festival (Paris, 1996).

Marseille contre Marseille (co-authored with Anne Baudry and Michel Samson – 1995, 87', Archipel 33/13 Production/INA/La Sept-Arte). Fourth installment in the series *Marseille contre Marseille.* Pro- and anti-Tapie forces during the June 1995 Marseilles municipal elections. Screened at the Locarno film festival (1996) and the États généraux du documentaire (Lussas, 1996).

De mère en filles (1996, 22', MAB productions/FR3/Sagacités). With Zahia, her daughters and Myriam in a kitchen in the *banlieue*, faced with bread, couscous, cakes – and life, suffering, sacrifice and revolt.

Le Concerto de Mozart (co-authored with Francis Marmande – 1996, 80', INA/La Sept-Arte). With Michel Portal and musicians from the Orchestre du Conservatoire. Screened at the Festival du film d'art (UNESCO, Paris, 1998).

La Question des alliances (co-authored with Michel Samson – 1997, 90', 13 Production/INA/Archipel 33/Planète). Fifth installment in the series *Marseille contre Marseille.* The May 1997 legislative elections, with Michel Samson, Christian Rossi, Renaud Muselier, Bruno Mégret, Claude Bertrand, Jean-Claude Gaudin, Henri D'Attilio, René Olmeta, etc.

Jeux de rôles à Carpentras (1998, 95', 13 Production/La Sept-Arte/INA). From May 1990 (the desecration of the Jewish cemetery at Carpentras) to July 1996 (when the neo-Nazis who committed the act turned themselves in), the Front national peddled a rumor accusing "children of distinguished figures" of the crime. Its version of the facts – that there had been a "socialist conspiracy" hatched by Pierre Joxe – quickly made inroads with the media and public opinion. An analysis of the effects of this manipulation through the use of archival footage and interviews. With some of the individuals who resisted the pressure of the media: the magistrate Sylvie Mottes, the journalists Nicole Leibowitz, Marcel Trillat, Michel Henry, and the political analyst Nonna Mayer. Screened at Vue sur les Docs (Marseilles, 1998).

Buenaventura Durruti, anarchiste (co-authored with Ginette Lavigne – 1999, 115', INA-Mallerich (Barcelona)/Arte/Televisión Española). The troupe of Catalan actors "Els Joglars" (directed by Albert Boadella) embarks on a process of reflection, writing and staging on the basis of four episodes from the life Buenaventura Durruti, notably in the five years preceding the Spanish Civil War (1931-1936). Screened at the Valladolid, Malaga, Marseilles, Cannes (ACID), Yamagata and Belo Horizonte film festivals (1999-2001). Awarded the Euromedia Prize at Strasbourg (2001).

L'Affaire Sofri (co-authored with Ginette Lavigne – 2001, 65', 13 Production/INA/La Sept-Arte/Telepiù). The historian Carlo Ginzburg debunks the first trial of Adriano Sofri and Lotta Continua in 1990, which ended in a sentence of 22 years in prison. A story of judicial error and political conspiracy. Based on *Le Juge et l'historien* (Carlo Ginzburg, French translation: Verdier, 1997). Screened at the Venice, Belo Horizonte and Buenos Aires film festivals (2001-2002).

Nos deux Marseillaises (co-authored with Ginette Lavigne, Michel Samson – 2001, 52', 13 Production/INA/La Cinquième). Sixth installment in the series *Marseille contre Marseille.* The municipal and cantonal elections of May 2001, Socialist Party activists present themselves to the electorate. Samia Ghali, in the 15th and 16th districts, on the list of the communist Guy Hermier; she will be elected to the municipal council. Nadia Brya in a canton in the northern districts, against the communist Jeanine Porte: even though it is her first campaign, she will only lose by a few dozen votes. As the children of immigrants, what effects are these new candidates having on the Marseilles political scene?

Miquel Barcelò, des trous et des bosses (co-authored with Jean-Michel Mariou – 2002, 71', Les Films à Lou/La Sept-Arte). Painting, sculpture, food, the body and its gestures... according to Miquel Barcelò, filmed in his workshops in Majorca and Paris. Screened at the Festival dei popoli, Florence (2003).

Rêves de France à Marseille (co-authored with Ginette Lavigne and Michel Samson – 2002, 105', 13 Production/INA). Seventh and final installment in the series *Marseille contre Marseille*. The ups and downs of the 2001 municipal elections, with candidates descended from Maghrebine and Comorian immigrants: Tahar Rahmani, Samia Ghali, Rebia Benarouia, Noredine Haggoug, Salah Barik. But also a woman who has no desire to enter politics, the founder and president of the association Sheba: Zoubida Megheni. A new visit, 12 years after the first film, to Marseilles, where ethnic minorities are now integrated into the political scene. Released in French cinemas on November 26, 2003.

Jours de grève à Paris Nord (co-directed with Ginette Lavigne – 1995-2003, 95', ISKRA/INA/Citizen TV). For ten days, we followed a small group of train drivers from the Gare du Nord (Paris) during the December 1995 strike. A retrospective look at a major turning point in the nation's political history. Screened at the Festival international du documentaire (Marseilles, 2003), Traces de vie (Clermont-Ferrand, 2003) and the Belo Horizonte film festival (2003).

Les Esprits du Koniambo (en terre kanak) (co-authored with Alban Bensa – 2004, 90', Archipel 33/La Sept-Arte). Kanaks confronting globalization. Screened at the Cinéma du réel festival (Paris, 2004).

Le Peintre, le poète et l'historien (2005, 26', Arte/INA). In the Cappella degli Scrovegni in Padua, Carlo Ginzburg evokes the world of Dante and Giotto. Includes a sequence shot lasting 24 minutes. Screened at the Festival dei popoli (Florence, 2005).

La Dernière Utopie (la télévision selon Rossellini) (co-authored with Ginette Lavigne – 2006, 90', INA/Vivo Films/Ciné Classic/RAI Trade/Sky TV). How to understand, from the present day, the radical nature of the choice made by Rossellini in 1964, to side with television over cinema, with the project of an audiovisual encyclopedia taking in all fields of human knowledge? With Silvia d'Amico, Adriano Aprà, Claudio Bondì, Gianni Bonicelli, Bepe Cino, Mario Fioretti, Giusto Puri Purini and Renzo Rossellini. Screened at the Cinéma du réel (Paris, 2006), the États généraux du documentaire (Lussas, 2006) and Meacvad (Buenos Aires, 2006).

Reproduction/Reproduction ("Ars imitatur naturam") (co-authored with Carlo Ginzburg and Ginette Lavigne – 2003-2007, INA). Focusing on Dante and the *Divine Comedy*, Carlo Ginzburg launches an investigation into what separates us from Aristotle's statement that "art imitates nature" – and what still links us to it. Six shooting sessions over a three-year period, with the use of some miniature models and illustrations, in order to accompany a long working process in all its bifurcations, and to closely follow the *research process* of a historian. A book and five episodes (lasting seven hours in total) are envisaged for release on DVD and DVD-ROM.

Le Monde dans l'arène (co-authored with Michel Samson – 2007, 55', Arte/INA). Reportage on the first round of the 2007 presidential election, from March 22 to April 22, as seen through the eyes of the journalists from the political bureau of *Le Monde*.

Les Clés de Marseille (co-authored with Michel Samson and Ginette Lavigne – 2008, 60', INA/ Public Sénat/La Chaîne Marseille). A postscript to the series *Marseille contre Marseille* (included in the DVD box set released by Doriane Films). The 2008 municipal elections in Marseilles, where Michel Samson catches up with some of our characters: Jean-Claude Gaudin, of course; and Samia Ghali, Claude Bertrand, Bruno Gilles, Jean-Noël Guérini, Patrick Mennucci, Roger Ruzé...

Lettre à une jeune fille kanak (2008, 17', HOYA B/La Poste). A video letter addressed to Outène, the eldest daughter of Samy Goromido (from *Les Esprits du Koniambo*), living in Netchaot, in the North Province of New Caledonia, a corner of the world bereft of the cinema. Screened at the États généraux du documentaire (Lussas, 2009).

Face aux fantômes (co-authored with Sylvie Lindeperg – 2009, 109', INA). Based on Sylvie Lindeperg's research on the genesis of *Nuit et brouillard* (Alain Resnais, 1954). A meticulous exploration of the circumstances and documents that were used to construct the film, as well as the contradictions and questions it confronted and opened up. A journey through history, based on the pioneering work of Olga Wormser and Annette Wieviorka. How should we think about the intersection between historical research and archival images? It appears that Resnais' film is more two-sided than we had thought, with its soundtrack referring to the system of concentration camps, and its image-track showing an awareness of the extermination of European Jews during World War II. Screened at the États généraux du documentaire (Lussas, 2009).

Lettre aux aveugles (2009, 18', HOYA B/Éducation Nationale). A video letter featuring a reading of Denis Diderot's "Letter on the Blind" by students from the Lycée Maurice Ravel in Paris, in conjunction with the "Braille Workshop." With Anne Chotin and Yola Le Caïnec.

Lettre à Bob. (2009, 18', HOYA B). Video letter addressed to Gérard Bobillier (founder of Éditions Verdier, my publisher) after his death. Music by Jean-Philippe Rameau, played by Marc Minkowski's Musiciens du Louvre. Screened at the États généraux du documentaire (Lussas, 2009).

À voir absolument (si possible). 1963-1973: Dix années aux Cahiers du cinéma (co-authored with Jean Narboni and Ginette Lavigne, 2011, 90', INA/ Cinécinéma). Return to the period 1963-1973 at *Cahiers du cinéma*. With Jean Narboni, Jacques Bontemps, Jacques Aumont, Pascal Bonitzer, André S. Labarthe, Bernard Eisenschitz, Sylvie Pierre, Pascal Kané and Jean-Louis Comolli. Screened at the La Roche-sur-Yon film festival (2011).

Chemins d'enfance (co-authored with Doriane Roditi-Buhler – 2012, 80', Agalma/Agora Films). Young children and their teachers at the Jardin Thérapeutique in Geneva.

À Fellini, d'un spectateur amoureux (co-authored with Jean-Paul Manganaro – 2013, 110' INA/ Ciné-cinémas). A fresh look at a series of stills from *La dolce vita* (1960) and *8½* (1962). The early 1960s shook things up. Television was posing a threat to the cinema. Fellini was the first of the great filmmakers to feel the pressure. He responds to it in these two films, analyzed by Manganaro, on the basis of his book *Federico Fellini Romance* (Paris: POL, 2011).

Bibliography

Books by Comolli

Free Jazz/Black Power (with Philippe Carles). Paris: Champs Libre, 1971. Repr. Paris: Folio, 2001.

Tecnica e Ideologia (Italian translation of "Technique et idéologie"). Parma: Pratiche Editrice, 1982.

Dictionnaire du jazz (with Philippe Carles and André Clergeat). Paris: Laffont, 1989.

Regards sur la ville (with Gérard Althabe). Paris: BPI/Centre Pompidou, 1994.

Arrêt sur histoire (with Jacques Rancière). Paris: BPI/Centre Pompidou, 1997.

Les Années pop: cinéma et politique, 1956-1970 (with Gérard Leblanc and Jean Narboni). Paris: BPI/Centre Pompidou, 2001.

Filmar para ver (Spanish translation of selected articles by Comolli). Buenos Aires: Simurg-Catedra La Ferla, 2002.

Voir et pouvoir: l'innocence perdue: cinéma, télévision, fiction, documentaire. Lagrasse: Verdier, 2004.

Cinéma contre spectacle. Lagrasse: Verdier, 2009.

Vedere et potere: il cinema, il documentario e l'innocenza perduta (Italian translation of *Voir et pouvoir*). Rome: Donzelli, 2006.

Ver y poder (Spanish translation of *Voir et pouvoir*). Buenos Aires: Aurelia Rivera, 2007.

Cine contra espectáculo (Spanish translation of *Cinéma contre spectacle*). Buenos Aires: Manantial, 2011.

Corps et cadre: cinéma, éthique, politique, 2004-2010. Lagrasse: Verdier, 2012.

Articles and Other Texts by Comolli

Note: Comolli's writings from 1987 to 2012 have been gathered in the volumes *Voir et pouvoir* (hereafter VP) and *Corps et cadre* (hereafter CC). These anthologies contain an exhaustive collection of his published articles on the cinema in this period, along with a number of previously unpublished texts. Only a tiny fraction of this output has been translated into English. Details of texts published elsewhere are provided below. Where they have been reprinted in the above two volumes, these details are given.

Texts given below are only those in which Comolli's name appears as one of the authors. Much of the output of Cahiers in the period from 1970 to 1973 was published either anonymously or under the name of collective entities. It is certain that Comolli had a major part to play in the composition of many of these texts, but the desire for the attribution of collective texts not to fall on the shoulders of individuals has been respected here. Similarly, many minor notices in the "Petit journal" or other sections of *Cahiers*, as well as Comolli's articles for *Jazz Magazine*, are not included in this bibliography.

"La grandeur du simple (*Sergent York*)," *Cahiers du cinéma*, no. 135 (1962), pp. 54-58.

"La mort blanche (*Tempête à Washington*)," *Cahiers du cinéma*, no. 137 (1962), pp. 43-47.

"Vivre le film," *Cahiers du cinéma*, no. 139 (1963), pp. 14-29.

"La présence et l'absence (*Le Petit Soldat*)," *Cahiers du cinema*, no. 139 (1963), pp. 54-58.

"Vanité de l'art (*La Flèche et le Flambeau, L'Or et l'Amour*)," *Cahiers du cinéma*, no. 142 (1963), pp. 54-57.

"L'autre ailleurs (*Le Procès de Jeanne d'Arc*)," *Cahiers du cinéma*, no. 143 (1963), pp. 42-49.

"Le divorce accompli (*Les 55 jours de Pékin*)," *Cahiers du cinéma*, no. 146 (1963), pp. 50-54.

"Feux croisés (*Duel in the Sun*)," *Cahiers du cinéma*, no. 147 (1963), pp. 58-62.

"Venise 63," *Cahiers du cinéma*, no. 148 (1963), pp. 21-32.

"Les Malheurs de *Muriel*" (with Jean Domarchi, Jean-André Fieschi, Pierre Kast, André S. Labarthe, Claude Ollier, Jacques Rivette and François Weyergans), *Cahiers du cinéma*, no. 149 (1963), pp. 20-37. Translated as "The Misfortunes of *Muriel*." Trans. Diana Matias. In *Cahiers du cinéma, 1960-1968: New Wave, New Cinema, Re-evaluating Hollywood*, ed. Jim Hillier. London: Routledge, 1986, pp. 68-81.

"Paralipomènes aux *Oiseaux*" (with Jean Douchet, Jean-André Fieschi, Fereydoun Hoveyda, Jean Narboni and Claude Ollier), *Cahiers du cinéma*, no. 149, pp. 38-44.

"Poème et plaisir (*Adieu Philippine*)," *Cahiers du cinéma*, no. 149 (1963), pp. 55-58.

"L'Amérique à découvert," *Cahiers du cinéma*, no. 150-151 (1963), pp. 215-222.

"L'affaire Eva," *Cahiers du cinéma*, no. 153 (1964), pp. 11-14.

"Cléopâtre, le jeu, l'échec," *Cahiers du cinéma*, no. 153 (1964), pp. 32-40.

"Papa Daves," *Cahiers du cinéma*, no. 153 (1964), pp. 54-55.

"Yin, Yang and Co. (*Bye Bye Birdie*)," *Cahiers du cinéma*, no. 153 (1964), pp. 61-62.

"L'ésprit d'aventure," *Cahiers du cinéma*, no. 154 (1964), pp. 11-14.

"La fêlure (*Light on the Piazza*)," *Cahiers du cinéma*, no. 154 (1964), pp. 70-72.

"Le Journal entre les lignes" (with Michel Delahaye, André S. Labarthe, Jean Narboni and Jacques Rivette), *Cahiers du cinéma*, no. 154 (1964), pp. 35-42.

"Bergman anonyme (*Les Communiants, Le Silence*)," *Cahiers du cinéma*, no. 156 (1964), pp. 30-39.

"Retour en Italie (*Prima della rivoluzione, I fidanzati*)" (with Jean Narboni), *Cahiers du cinéma*, no. 157 (1964), pp. 29-37.

"La Terreur à l'enchère (*La Bataille de France*)," *Cahiers du cinéma*, no. 157 (1964), pp. 56-59.

"L'amour sans larmes (*Alta Infedelta*)," *Cahiers du cinéma*, no. 158 (1964), p. 67.

"Venise 64" (with François Weyergans), *Cahiers du cinéma*, no. 159 (1964), pp. 16-31.

"H.H., ou l'ironique," *Cahiers du cinéma*, no. 160 (1964), pp. 49-52. Translated as "The Ironical Howard Hawks." Trans. Norman King. In *Cahiers du cinéma, 1960-1968: New Wave, New Cinema, Re-evaluating Hollywood*, ed. Jim Hillier. London: Routledge, 1986, pp. 181-186.

"Un film par omission (*Toutes ses femmes*)," *Cahiers du cinéma*, no. 161-162 (1964), p. 144.

"Amères victoires" (with Jacques Bontemps, Jean-André Fieschi, André S. Labarthe, Luc Moullet and Jean Narboni), *Cahiers du cinéma*, no. 161-162 (1964), pp. 99-109.

"Signes de piste" (*Les Cheyennes*)," *Cahiers du cinéma*, no. 164 (1965), pp. 75-76. Translated as "Signposts on the Trail." Trans. Norman King. In *Theories of Authorship*, ed. John Caughie. London: Routledge, 1981, pp. 109-116.

"L'a-critique," *Cahiers du cinéma*, no. 164 (1965), pp. 59-61.

"Les miettes de l'existence (*La Vieille Dame indigne*)," *Cahiers du cinéma*, no. 166-167 (1965), pp. 126-129.

"À rebours? (*Alphaville*)," *Cahiers du cinéma*, no. 168 (1965), pp. 86-87. Translated as "Alphaville," *Cahiers du Cinéma in English*, no. 3 (1966).

"La canne du tambour-major (*Première victoire*)," *Cahiers du cinéma*, no. 169 (1965), p. 68.

"Fou de Catherine (*La Bugiarda*)," *Cahiers du cinéma*, no. 170 (1965), p. 59.

"Trois masques pour un visage de l'oubli (*Shock Corridor*)," *Cahiers du cinéma*, no. 171 (1965), pp. 68-69.

"Vingt ans après: le cinéma américain et la politique des auteurs" (with Jean-André Fieschi, Gérard Guégan, Michel Mardore, Claude Ollier and André Téchiné), *Cahiers du cinéma*, no. 172 (1965), pp. 18-31. Translated as "Twenty Years On: A Discussion about American Cinema and the *politique des auteurs*." Trans. Diana Matias. In *Cahiers du cinéma, 1960-1968: New Wave, New Cinema, Re-evaluating Hollywood*, ed. Jim Hillier. London: Routledge, 1986, pp. 196-209.

"Au royaume des sourds (*Paris vu par...: La Muette*)," *Cahiers du cinéma*, no. 172 (1965), pp. 53-54.

"Magots entre eux (*Paris vu par...: Saint-Germain-des-près*)," *Cahiers du cinéma*, no. 172, p. 54.

"Une proche limite du cinéma (*La Cage de verre*)," *Cahiers du cinéma*, no. 173 (1965), pp. 121-123.

"La danse des images: kaleidoscopie de Busby Berkeley," *Cahiers du cinéma*, no. 174 (1966), pp. 24-26. Translated as "Dancing Images," *Cahiers du Cinéma in English*, no. 2 (1966).

"Situation du nouveau cinéma, 1," *Cahiers du cinéma*, no. 176 (1966), p. 5.

"Retour à Tours ou Vanité du portrait," *Cahiers du cinéma*, no. 177 (1966), pp. 17-19.

"Notes sur le nouveau spectateur," *Cahiers du cinéma*, no. 177 (1966), pp. 66-69. Translated as "Notes on the New Spectator." Trans. Diana Matias. In *Cahiers du cinéma, 1960-1968: New Wave, New Cinema, Re-evaluating Hollywood*, ed. Jim Hillier. London: Routledge, 1986, pp. 210-215.

"Une tempête au fond des yeux (*Une Balle au cœur*)," *Cahiers du cinéma*, no. 177 (1966), p. 73. Translated as "*Une Balle au coeur*," *Cahiers du Cinéma in English*, no. 6 (1966).

"Tous dans le même cul-de-sac (*Viva Maria, Les Grandes Geueles*)," *Cahiers du cinéma*, no. 177 (1966), p. 75. Translated as "*Viva Maria* and *Les Grandes Geueles*," *Cahiers du Cinéma in English*, no. 6 (1966).

"Une semaine comme une autre," *Cahiers du cinéma*, no. 178 (1966), p. 66.

"L'œil du maître (*Bunny Lake Is Missing*)," *Cahiers du cinéma*, no. 178 (1966), pp. 77-78.

"Cherchez l'Hawks (*Red Line 7000*)," *Cahiers du cinéma*, no. 180 (1966), pp. 24-27.

"Table ronde sur *Au hasard Balthazar*" (with Michel Delahaye, André S. Labarthe, Jean Narboni and François Weyergans), *Cahiers du cinéma*, no. 180 (1966), pp. 32-35, 76-79.

"Lelouch, ou la bonne conscience retrouvée," *Cahiers du cinéma*, no. 180 (1966), pp. 67-69. Translated as "Lelouch, or the Clear Conscience." Trans. Diana Matias. In *Cahiers du cinéma, 1960-1968: New Wave, New Cinema, Re-evaluating Hollywood*, ed. Jim Hillier. London: Routledge, 1986, pp. 100-105.

"Tu n'as rien vu sur la Vistule (*Mourir pour Varsovie*)," *Cahiers du cinéma*, no. 180 (1966), pp. 74-75.
"Jack le Fataliste," *Cahiers du cinéma*, no. 181 (1966), pp. 31-32. Translated as "Jack le Fataliste," *Cahiers du Cinéma in English*, no. 11 (1967).
"Dé-composition," *Cahiers du cinéma*, no. 182 (1966), pp. 14-20.
"Ford et les autres," *Cahiers du cinéma*, no. 183 (1966), p. 55.
"L'auteur, les masques, l'autre (*Fahrenheit 451*)," *Cahiers du cinéma*, no. 184 (1966), p. 64. Translated as "The Auteur, the Masks, the Other," *Cahiers du Cinéma in English*, no. 9 (1967).
"Le rideau soulevé, retombé (*Torn Curtain*)," *Cahiers du cinéma*, no. 186 (1967), pp. 36-39. Translated as "The Curtain Lifted, Fallen Again," *Cahiers du Cinéma in English*, no. 10 (1967).
"Le médecin malgré lui (*Three on a Couch*)," *Cahiers du cinéma*, no. 186 (1967), pp. 67-68. Translated as "*Three on a Couch*," *Cahiers du Cinéma in English*, no. 11 (1967).
"Dictionnaire du nouveau cinéma français" (with Jacques Bontemps, Michel Delahaye, Jean-André Fieschi and Jean Narboni), *Cahiers du cinéma*, no. 187 (1967), pp. 53-64.
"Le Fantôme de Personne (*Persona*), *Cahiers du cinéma*, no. 188 (1967), p. 20. Translated as "The Phantom of Personality," *Cahiers du Cinéma in English*, no. 11 (1967).
"L'aveugle et le miroir, ou l'impossible cinéma de Douglas Sirk," *Cahiers du cinéma*, no. 189 (1967), pp. 14-19.
"Au cœur des paradoxes," *Cahiers du cinéma*, no. 190 (1967), p. 18.
"Contingent 67 1 A, ou les insoumis du nouveau cinéma," *Cahiers du cinéma*, no. 190 (1967), pp. 58-61. Part II translated as "A Morality of Economics." Trans. Diana Matias. In *Cahiers du cinéma, 1960-1968: New Wave, New Cinema, Re-evaluating Hollywood*, ed. Jim Hillier. London: Routledge, 1986, pp. 290-293.
"Un catéchisme travesti," *Cahiers du cinéma*, no. 191 (1967), pp. 24-25.
"A l'assaut de l'image (*Anticipation*)," *Cahiers du cinéma*, no. 191 (1967), pp. 67-68. Translated as "Anticipation." In *Focus on Jean-Luc Godard*, ed. Roy Brown. Englewood Cliffs, NJ: Prentice-Hall, 1972.
"L'envers de l'Éden (*El Dorado*)," *Cahiers du cinéma*, no. 192 (1967), pp. 22-23.
"La remontée d'Orphée: à propos de *La Barrière*," *Cahiers du cinéma*, no. 192 (1967), p. 41.
"Le point sur l'image (*La Chinoise*)" *Cahiers du cinéma*, no. 194 (1967), pp. 28-30. Translated as "*La Chinoise*." In *The Films of Jean-Luc Godard*, ed. Ian Cameron. London: Studio Vista, 1969.
"*L'Île*, ou l'exemplarité d'un cinéma de combat," *Cahiers du cinéma*, no. 194 (1967), pp. 56-58.
"Pourquoi, où, comment, quand," *Cahiers du cinéma*, no. 195 (1967), p. 38.
"Des migrations exemplaires," *Cahiers du cinéma*, no. 196 (1967), pp. 24-27.
"Chacun son soi," *Cahiers du cinéma*, no. 197 (1967), pp. 51-54.
"Première semaine," *Cahiers du cinéma*, no. 199 (1968), pp. 32-33.
"Postface (*L'heure du loup*)," *Cahiers du cinéma*, no. 203 (1968), p. 58. Translated as "Postscript: *Hour of the Wolf*." Trans. David Wilson. In *Cahiers du cinéma, 1960-1968: New Wave, New Cinema, Re-evaluating Hollywood*, ed. Jim Hillier. London: Routledge, 1986, pp. 313-316.
"Les films des IV Rencontres de Hyères" (with Jacques Aumont), *Cahiers du cinéma*, no. 203 (1968), pp. 14-20.
"Objet parmi d'autres," *Cahiers du cinéma*, no. 204 (1968), pp. 40-41.
"Dos à dos (*Faces*)," *Cahiers du cinéma*, no. 205 (1968), p. 39. Translated as "Back to Back." Trans. Annwyl Williams. In *Cahiers du cinéma, 1960-1968: New Wave, New Cinema, Re-evaluating Hollywood*, ed. Jim Hillier. London: Routledge, 1986, pp. 325-327.

"Rêves mouvants (*Baisers volés*), *Cahiers du cinéma*, no. 205 (1968), p. 57.
"*Jusqu'au cœur*," *Cahiers du cinéma*, no. 206 (1969), p. B.
"Rhétorique de la terreur," *Cahiers du cinéma*, no. 207 (1968), pp. 42-44.
"Folie et autres rêves," *Cahiers du cinéma*, no. 208 (1969), pp. 32-35.
"Le Cahier des autres," *Cahiers du cinéma*, no. 209 (1969), p. 4.
"Le détour par le direct (1)," *Cahiers du cinéma*, no. 209 (1969), pp. 48-54.
"Le détour par le direct (2)," *Cahiers du cinéma*, no. 211 (1969), pp. 40-45.
"Développements de la ligne Jancsò," *Cahiers du cinéma*, no. 212 (1969), pp. 32-33.
"Dernier acte, encore (*La Honte*)," *Cahiers du cinéma*, no. 215 (1969), pp. 55-58.
"*La vie est à nous*, film militant" (with Pascal Bonitzer, Serge Daney, Jean Narboni and Jean-Pierre Oudart)," *Cahiers du cinéma*, no. 218 (1970), pp. 44-51.
"Autocritique," *Cahiers du cinéma*, no. 219 (1970), pp. 40-45.
"Film/politique (2): *L'Aveu*: Quinze propositions," *Cahiers du cinéma*, no. 224 (1970), pp. 48-51. Translated as "Film/Politics 2: *L'Aveu*: 15 Propositions." Trans. Nancy Kline Piore. In *Cahiers du cinéma, 1969-1972: The Politics of Representation*, ed. Nick Browne. London: Routledge, 1990, pp. 163-173.
"Débat (*Ice*)" (with Jacques Aumont, Pascal Bonitzer, Jean-André Fieschi, Jean Narboni and Sylvie Pierre), *Cahiers du cinéma*, no. 225 (1970), pp. 17-27.
"La pratique didactique de S.M.E.," *Cahiers du cinéma*, no. 226-227 (1971), pp. 111-114.
"Le réalisateur a vingt têtes: la pratique didactique de S.M.E. (II)" *Cahiers du cinéma*, no. 228 (1971), pp. 46-50. Repr. as preface to S.M. Eisenstein, *Mettre en scène*. Paris: UGE/Cahiers du cinéma, 1973, pp. 5-27.
"Cinéma/idéologie/politique: présentation pour Porretta Terme" (with Pascal Bonitzer and Jean Narboni), *Cahiers du cinéma*, no. 232 (1971), pp. 54-55. Translated as "Cinema, Ideology, Politics: For Porretta Terme." Trans. Alan Williams. In *Cahiers du cinéma, 1969-1972: The Politics of Representation*, ed. Nick Browne. London: Routledge, 1990, pp. 287-290.
"Cinéma/idéologie/politique: Porretta Terme (2)," (with Pascal Bonitzer and Jean Narboni), *Cahiers du cinéma*, no. 233 (1971), pp. 46-48.
"L'animateur, l'appareil, les masses (1)," *Cahiers du cinéma*, no. 244 (1973), pp. 16-24.
"L'animateur, l'appareil, les masses (2)," *Cahiers du cinéma*, no. 247 (1973), pp. 56-65.
"Les luttes, l'appareil," *Cahiers du cinéma*, no. 249 (1974), pp. 52-54.
La Cecilia: une commune anarchiste au Brésil en 1892. Film press kit. Paris: Daniel et Cie, 1976.
"Éditorial: la censure libérale avancée," *Cahiers du cinéma*, no. 262-263 (1976), pp. 5-8.
"*La Cecilia*: présentation," *Cahiers du cinéma*, no. 262-263 (1976), pp. 69-78.
"L'image absente (sur *L'Olivier*)," *Cahiers du cinéma*, no. 265 (1976), pp. 44-47.
"Le passé filmé," *Cahiers du cinéma*, no. 277 (1977), pp. 5-14.
"Un corps en trop," *Cahiers du cinéma*, no. 278 (1977), pp. 5-16. Translated as "Historical Fiction – A Body Too Much," trans. Ben Brewster, *Screen*, vol. 19 no. 2 (1978), pp. 41-54.
"On the Practice of Political Film" (interview), *Ciné-Tracts*, vol. 1 no. 4 (1978), pp. 44-47.
"L'arbre a bougé," *Cahiers du cinéma* (*hors série*, 1978).
"Deux fictions de la haine (1): *Les Bourreaux meurent aussi*" (with François Géré), *Cahiers du cinéma*, no. 286 (1978), pp. 30-36.
"Deux fictions de la haine (2): *To Be or Not to Be*" (with François Géré), *Cahiers du cinéma*, no. 288 (1978), pp. 4-15.

"Deux fictions de la haine (3): *To Be or Not to Be*" (with François Géré), *Cahiers du cinéma*, no. 290-291 (1978), pp. 91-98.
"La real-fiction du pouvoir" (with François Géré), *Cahiers du cinéma*, no. 292 (1978), pp. 24-27.
"L'amour de Renoir," *Cahiers du cinéma*, *Jean Renoir: entretiens et propos* (*hors série*, 1979), pp. 163-165.
"Le cinéma de Totò" (with François Géré), *Cahiers du cinéma*, no. 297 (1979), pp. 17-18.
"Le mannequin, la poule et le totem" (with François Géré), *Cahiers du cinéma*, no. 298 (1979), pp. 7-10.
"En revoyant *Une partie de campagne*," *Cahiers du cinéma*, no. 299 (1979), pp. 39-40.
"Note sur la profondeur de champ," *Cahiers du cinéma*, *Photos de films III: Scénographie* (*hors série*, 1980), pp. 88-89.
"Anton et Léo dans les griffes de *L'Ombre rouge*" (with Gérard Guicheteau), *Cahiers du cinéma* (*hors série*, 1981), pp. 6-79.
"Entretien avec Jean-Louis Comolli" (with Alain Bergala and Alain Philippon), *Cahiers du cinéma*, no. 333 (1982), pp. 23-31.
"Ceux que l'on filme: notes sur la mise en scène documentaire," *Lignes*, no. 3 (1988). Repr. VP, pp. 31-40.
"Violence d'*Accatone*," *Pariscope* (1988). Repr. VP, pp. 41-42.
"Daney chez Kinu," *Cahiers du cinéma*, no. 458 (1992), p. 21.
"Comment s'en débarrasser?," *Trafic*, no. 10 (1994). Repr. VP, pp. 111-134.
"Plus vrai que le vrai: le cinéma de John Cassavetes et l'illusion de la vie." In catalogue for the Festival dei Popoli, Florence (1994). Repr. VP, pp. 135-140.
"*In Calabria* de Vittorio De Seta." In catalogue for the Cinéma du réel festival, Paris (1994). Repr. VP, 141-142.
"Montage comme métamorphose," *Images documentaires*, no. 17 (1994). Repr. VP, pp. 143-148.
"Lettre de Marseille sur l'auto-mise en scène." In *La Mise en scène documentaire*. Paris: Ministère de la Culture et de l'éducation nationale, 1994. Repr. VP, pp. 149-154.
"Dox-Journal," *DOX*, no. 1 (1994). Repr. VP, pp. 155-161.
"Fin d'une histoire d'amour: la disparition de la critique de télévision signifie-t-elle la disparition de la télévision?" In catalogue for the *États généraux de Lussas* (1994). Repr. VP, pp. 169-173
"L'œil était dans la boîte," *Trafic*, no. 12 (1994). Repr. VP, pp. 174-193.
"Éloge du ciné-monstre." In catalogue for the Cinéma du réel festival, Paris (1995). Repr. VP, pp. 202-208.
"L'homme essentiel: *Man of Aran* de Robert Flaherty," *Images documentaires*, no. 20 (1995). Repr. VP, pp. 222-228.
"L'avenir de l'homme: autour de *L'Homme à la caméra*. Dziga Vertov." In *Trafic*, no. 15 (1995). Repr. VP, pp. 229-255
"Lumière éclatante d'un astre mort," *Images documentaires*, no. 21 (1995). Repr. VP, pp. 256-262.
"'No lipping!,'" *Images documentaires*, no. 22 (1995). Repr. VP, pp. 263-271.
"Mon ennemi préféré?," *Images documentaires*, no. 23 (1995). Repr. VP, pp. 272-282.
"Musiques noires pour films noirs," *Cahiers du cinéma*, *Musiques au cinéma* (*hors série*, 1995). Repr. VP, pp. 283-285.
"Passages entre musique et cinéma," *Cahiers du cinéma*, *Musiques au cinéma* (*hors série*, 1995), pp. 90-93.

"L'idiot à la manivelle." In catalogue for the Festival dei Popoli, Florence (1995). Repr. VP, pp. 290-297.
"Marionnettes sans théâtre," *Cahiers du cinéma*, no. 503 (1996), pp. 108-109.
"Jouer à la Russie: le corps projeté de Godard," *Trafic*, no. 18 (1996). Repr. VP, pp. 307-323.
"Prisons du regard," *Lignes*, no. 27 (1996). Repr. VP, pp. 324-337.
"Corps mécaniques de plus en plus célestes...," *Images documentaires*, no. 24 (1996). Repr. VP, pp. 338-346. Translated as "Mechanical Bodies, Ever More Heavenly," trans. Annette Michelson, *October*, no. 83 (1998), pp. 19-24.
"Les rushes de *Terre sans pain* à Valence," *Le Monde*, February 17 (1996). Repr. VP, pp. 353-355.
"Âmes héroïques cherchent corps érotiques," *Images documentaires*, no. 25 (1996). Repr. VP, pp. 356-366.
"Du réalisme comme utopie," preface to Gérald Collas, *Cinéma européen: le défi de la réalité*. Paris: Coordination européenne des Festivals, 1997. Repr. VP, pp. 380-386.
"Comment filmer l'ennemi?," *Trafic*, no. 24 (1997). Repr. VP, pp. 387-400.
"Rétrospective du spectateur," *Images documentaires*, no. 31 (1998). Repr. VP, pp. 405-413.
"Ceux qui (se) perdent," *Images documentaires*, no. 32-33 (1998). Repr. VP, pp. 414-428.
"Voyage documentaire chez les réducteurs de têtes," *Images documentaires*, no. 32-33 (1998). Repr. VP, pp. 431-451. Translated as "Journey to the Land of the Head Shrinkers," trans. Annette Michelson, *October*, no. 90 (1999), pp. 36-49.
"L'absente de tout miroir." In catalogue for the Festival dei Popoli, Florence (1998). Repr. VP, pp. 459-465.
"La ville de l'impossible oubli," *L'image, le monde*, no. 1 (1999). Repr. VP, pp. 480-488.
"Au nom de Personne," *Images documentaires*, no. 35-36 (1999). Repr. VP, pp. 489-497.
"Les archives du futur," *Le Monde*, February 5 (1999). Repr. VP, pp. 498-501.
"Au risque du réel." In catalogue for the "Le documentaire c'est la vie" program (1999). Repr. VP, pp. 507-517.
"À propos d'un torchon-manifest," *Le Monde*, December 1 (1999). Repr. as "Un se divise en deux," VP, pp. 520-522.
"Travail au noir," *Images documentaires*, no. 37-38 (2000). Repr. VP, pp. 526-544.
"La ville filmée." In catalogue for the Thessaloniki Film Festival (2000). Repr. VP, pp. 545-551.
"Suspension du spectacle," *Images documentaires*, no. 39 (2000). Repr. VP, pp. 552-564.
"Puissances du vide et pleins pouvoirs," *Images documentaires*, no. 40-41 (2001). Repr. VP, pp. 568-579.
"L'évadé: *Le Moindre Geste*, de Fernand Deligny, Jo Manenti et Jean-Pierre Daniel, 1959-1970," *L'image, le monde* (2001), no. 2. Repr. VP, pp. 582-588.
"Le silence des tours," *L'image, le monde*, no. 2 (2001). Repr. VP, pp. 589-591.
La police des images: droit à l'image, droit des auteurs (with Claudine Bories and Patrice Chagnard). Paris: L'Harmattan, 2002.
"Jean-Louis Comolli, le cinéma pour utopie," *Le Monde*, January 26 (2002), p. 32.
"La part de l'ombre." In *Dictionnaire des utopies*, ed. Michèle Riot-Sarcey. Paris: Larousse, 2002. Repr. VP, pp. 597-606.
"L'anti-spectateur: sur quatre films mutants," *Images documentaires*, no. 44 (2002). Repr. VP, pp. 607-633.
"Pour un cinéma pauvre," *Cahiers du cinéma*, no. 583 (2003), pp. 78-80.

"Un film sobre et cruel sur la politique," interview with Nadia Tazi and Fethi Benslama, *Cahiers du cinéma*, no. 585 (2003), pp. 34-35.
"L'œil contrôle, le corps écoute (Filmer le free)." In *All that Jazz*, catalogue for the Locarno Film Festival (2003). Repr. VP, pp. 652-662.
"Lettre à Jean-François Chevrier," *Trafic*, no. 48 (2003). Repr. VP, pp. 677-684.
L'âge des aiguilles: Mimi, de Claire Simon," *L'image, le monde*, no. 4 (2003). Repr. VP, pp. 685-692.
"La disparition: *Disneyland, mon vieux pays natal*, d'Arnaud Des Pallières," *L'image, le monde*, no. 4 (2003). Repr. VP, pp. 693-699.
"L'attente du prochain coup," *Cahiers du cinéma*, no. 593 (2004), pp. 70-71.
"Laura Betti, vivement," *Cahiers du cinéma*, no. 593 (2004), pp. 53-54.
"Je ne sais pas bien mais quand même," *Trafic*, no. 50 (2004). Repr. CC, pp. 41-47.
"Destin cinématographique du journaliste." In *Print the Legend – Cinéma et journalisme*, catalogue for the Locarno Film Festival (2004). Repr. CC, pp. 48-62.
"L'action parlée," *Cahiers du cinéma*, no. 595 (2004). Repr. CC, pp. 110-115.
"Salut à l'homme de Varan," *Cahiers du cinéma*, no. 600 (2005), p. 73.
"À bout de forces (autour de l'excès)," *Théâtre Public*, no. 178 (2005). Repr. CC, pp. 119-124.
"Après, avant l'explosion: le cinéma d'Avi Mograbi," *Cahiers du cinéma*, no. 606 (2005). Repr. CC, pp. 125-130.
"Corps à corps dans le bureau du juge," *Images documentaires*, no. 54 (2005). Repr. CC, pp. 138-157.
"Entamer le monde (pour une histoire du cinéma sous influence documentaire)," *Images documentaires*, nos. 54, 55-56 and 59-60 (2005-2006). Repr. CC, pp. 63-109.
"En temps réel," *La Vangardia* (2005). Repr. CC, pp. 158-160.
"Les raisons de la colère," *Trafic*, no. 56 (2005). Repr. CC, pp. 164-173.
"Marseille, ville ouverte." In *La Ville au cinéma*, ed. Thierry Paquot and Thierry Jousse. Paris: Cahiers du cinéma, 2005. Repr. CC, pp. 177-184.
"Les villes invisibles." In *La Ville au cinéma*, ed. Thierry Paquot and Thierry Jousse. Paris: Cahiers du cinéma, 2005. Repr. CC, pp. 185-198.
"Du promeneur au spectateur." In *La Ville au cinéma*, ed. Thierry Paquot and Thierry Jousse. Paris: Cahiers du cinéma, 2005. Repr. CC, pp. 199-208.
"La pensée dans la machine" (with François Roussel), *Rue Descartes*, no. 53 (2006), pp. 72-99.
"Un séminaire en Kanaky," *Communications*, vol. 79 no. 1 (2006), pp. 247-270.
"Suspens et désirs," *Les Lettres françaises*, May 6 (2006).
"Menaces sur Lussas," *Cahiers du cinéma*, no. 617 (2006), p. 61.
"Beauté de l'horizon: un voyage au Brésil en novembre 2005," *Trafic*, no. 58 (2006). Repr. CC, pp. 211-228.
"L'oral et l'oracle: séparation du corps et de la voix," *Images documentaires*, no. 55-56 (2006). Repr. CC, pp. 229-250.
"Élan et retour: le théâtre de Tchekhov au temps du cinéma," In *LEXI/textes 10*. Paris: L'Arche/Théâtre national de la Colline, 2006. Repr. CC, pp. 251-258.
"Fin du hors-champ?," *Images documentaires*, no. 57-58 (2006). Repr. CC, pp. 259-291.
"Dans la chambre de Moebius," *Images documentaires*, no. 61-62 (2007). Repr. CC, pp. 304-311.

"Une lecture de *Close-up* d'Abbas Kiarostami au moyen de *Lignes de temps*: frustration et délivrance." Published on the Pompidou Center website, in conjunction with the exhibition "Erice-Kiarostami, regards croisés" (2007). Repr. CC, pp. 312-350.
"Post-scriptum sur Rossellini," *Trafic*, no. 63 (2007). Repr. CC, pp. 366-378.
"Fatal rendez-vous." In *Le Cinéma et la Shoah: un art à l'épreuve du 20e siècle*, ed. Jean-Michel Frodon. Paris: Cahiers du cinéma, coll. "Essais," 2007, pp. 69-84. Repr. CC, pp. 379-394. Translated as "Fatal rendezvous." Trans. Anna Harrison and Tom Mes. In *Cinema and the Shoah: An Art Confronts the Tragedy of the Twentieth Century*, ed. Jean-Michel Frodon. Albany: State University of New York Press, 2010.
"La pensée dans la machine" (interview with François Roussel), *Rue Descartes*, no. 53 (2007), pp. 72-99.
"Mauvaises fréquentations: document et spectacle," *Images documentaires*, no. 63 (2008). Repr. CC, pp. 398-418 (abridged).
"Passage à l'acteur," *Trafic*, no. 65 (2008). Repr. CC, pp. 419-429.
"Incidence du moindre geste," *Les Lettres françaises*, June 7 (2008). Repr. CC, pp. 433-435.
"Un cinéma hors de lui," *Mouvements* (2008). Repr. CC, pp. 438-442.
"Mai 1968 au miroir du cinéma," *Le Monde diplomatique*, no. 106 (2008). Repr. CC, pp. 445-449.
"Chenille et papillon." DVD booklet for *9m2 pour deux* (2008). Repr. CC, pp. 466-469.
"Bandes à part." DVD booklet for *L'Image à paroles* (2008). Repr. CC, pp. 470-472.
"L'acteur de passage: esquisse d'une renaissance." First published in English translation. Trans. Timothy Barnard. In *Actors and Extras*, ed. Paul Willemsen and Thomas Trummer. Brussels: Argos, 2009. Repr. CC, pp. 480-502.
"Cadres et corps. Notes sur trois films de Pedro Costa: *Ossos, Dans la chambre de Vanda, En avant, jeunesse!*," *Trafic*, no. 77 (2010). Repr. CC, pp. 535-547. Translated as "Frames and Bodies – Notes on Three Films by Pedro Costa: *Ossos, No Quarto da Vanda, Juventude em Marcha*," trans. Timothy Barnard, *Afterall*, no. 24 (2010), pp. 62-70.
"Le nom dit," *Images documentaires*, no. 67-68 (2010). Repr. CC, pp. 548-554.
"*Les yeux ne veulent pas en tout temps se fermer*," *Les lettres françaises* (2010). Repr. CC, pp. 555-557.
"Au présent, parcours documentaire," prologue to Marianne Thys (ed.), *Mémoires du monde*. Crisnée: Yellow Now, 2011, pp. 7-34.
"Humiliés et offensés: éthique et maquis," *Images documentaires*, no. 69-70 (2011). Repr. CC, pp. 558-577.
"Langue de sable. *La Belle Journée*, de Ginette Lavigne," *Trafic*, no. 80 (2012). Repr. CC, pp. 578-585. Translated as "*La Belle Journée* by Ginette Lavigne," trans. Daniel Fairfax, *Senses of Cinema*, no. 62 (2012), online.
"D'une critique à venir," *Images documentaires*, no. 75-76 (2012), pp. 81-100.
"*À l'ouest des rails*: suite de voyage," *Images documentaires*, no. 77 (2013), pp. 23-34.

Works Cited in "Cinema against Spectacle"

Adorno, Theodor W. *Minima Moralia: Reflections from Damaged Life*. Trans. E.F.N. Jephcott. London: NLB, 1974.
Alberti, Leon Battista. *De la peinture – De pictura* [1435]. Translated from Latin into French by Jean Louis Schefer (Paris: Macula, 1992) and Danielle Sonnier (Paris: Allia, 2007). Translated

into English as *On Painting: A New Translation and Critical Edition*. Trans. Rocco Sinisgalli. Cambridge: Cambridge University Press, 2011.

Amengual, Barthélemy. *Que viva Eisenstein!* Lausanne: L'Âge d'homme, 1990.

Auerbach, Erich. *Mimesis*. Berne: C.A. Francke, 1946.

St. Augustine, *Soliloques*, Book II. Translated from Latin into French by Denis Marianelli. Paris: Migne, 1999. Translated into English as *Soliloquies*, Book II. Trans. Gerard Watson. Warminster: Aris & Phillips, 1990.

Aumont, Jacques. *À quoi pensent les films?* Paris: Séguier, 1996.

Bajac, Quentin, and Dominique Planchon de Font-Réaulx, eds. *Le Daguerréotype français, un objet photographique*, exhibition catalogue. Paris: Musée d'Orsay, 2003.

Banda, Daniel, and José Moure, eds. *Le Cinéma: naissance d'un art 1895-1920*. Paris: Flammarion, coll. "Champs arts," 2008.

Bataille, Georges. "Le 'Jeu lugubre,'" *Documents*, no. 7 (1929), pp. 297-302.

Baudrillard, Jean. *L'Échange symbolique et la mort*. Paris: Gallimard, 1976. Translated as *Symbolic Exchange and Death*. Trans. Iain Hamilton Grant. London: Sage Publications, 1993.

---. *Le Système des objets*. Paris: Gallimard, 1978. Translated as *The System of Objects*. Trans. James Benedict. London: Verso, 1996.

---. *Pourquoi tout n'a-t-il pas disparu?* Paris: L'Herne, 2007. Translated as *Why Hasn't Everything Already Disappeared?* Trans. Chris Turner. London: Seagull, 2009.

Bazin, André. "À propos de *Pourquoi nous combattons*," *Esprit*, no. 123 (1946), pp. 1022-1026. Translated as "On *Why We Fight*." Trans. Alain Piette and Bert Cardullo. In *Bazin at Work: Major Essays and Reviews from the Forties and Fifties*, ed. Bert Cardullo. New York: Routledge, 1997, pp. 187-192.

Bellour, Raymond, ed. *Le Cinéma américain: analyses de films*, vol. I and II. Paris: Flammarion, 1980.

---. *Le Corps cinéma*. Paris: P.O.L., 2009.

Benjamin, Walter. "L'Œuvre d'art à l'époque de sa reproductibilité technique" [1939]. Translated from German into French by Maurice de Gandillac, Rainer Rochlitz and Pierre Rusch. In Benjamin, *Œuvres*, vol. III. Paris: Gallimard, coll. "Folio essais," 2000. Translated into English as "The Work of Art in the Age of Mechanical Reproduction." Trans. Harry Zohn. In Benjamin, *Illuminations*. Ed. Hannah Arendt. New York: Schocken, 1968, pp. 217-251.

Bergounioux, Pierre. *Où est le passé?* Paris: Éditions de l'Olivier, 2007.

Bergson, Henri. *Matière et Mémoire*, 7th edition. Paris: PUF, 1939. Translated as *Matter and Memory*. Trans. Nancy Margaret Paul and W. Scott Palmer. New York: Macmillan, 1913.

Blanchot, Maurice. *Écrits politiques, 1953-1993*. Ed. Éric Hoppenot. Paris: Gallimard, 2008.

Boltanski, Luc. *La Souffrance à distance*. Paris: Gallimard, coll. "Folio Essais," 2007.

Bonitzer, Pascal. *Éric Rohmer*. Paris: Cahiers du cinéma, 1999.

Brossat, Alain. *Le Sacre de la démocratie*. Paris: Anabet, 2007.

Brunet, François. *La Naissance de l'idée de photographie*. Paris: PUF, 2000.

Chardère, Bernard. *Les Images des Lumière*. Paris: Gallimard, 1995.

Chevrier, Jean-François. *Jeff Wall*. Paris: Hazan, 2006.

Coetzee, J.M. *Elizabeth Costello: Eight Lessons*. London: Secker & Warburg, 2003.

Dagognet, François. *E.-J. Marey, la passion de la trace*. Paris: Hazan, 1987. Translated as *Etienne-Jules Marey: A Passion for the Trace*. Trans. Robert Galeta and Jeanine Herman. New York: Zone Books, 1992.

Daney, Serge. *La Rampe*. Paris: Cahiers du cinéma-Gallimard, 1983. Repr. Paris: Cahiers du cinéma, coll. "Petite bibliothèque," 1996.

De Baecque, Antoine. *La Caméra-histoire*. Paris: Gallimard, 2009. Translated as *Camera Historica: The Century in Cinema*. Trans. Ninon Vinsonneau and Jonathan Magidoff. New York: Columbia University Press, 2012.

De Font-Réaulx, Dominique, Thierry Lefebvre and Laurent Mannoni, eds. *E.-J. Marey, Actes du colloque du centenaire*. Paris: Arcadia, 2006.

De France, Claudine. *Cinéma et Anthropologie*. Paris: Maison des scienes de l'homme, 1982.

Debord, Guy. *Œuvres*. Paris: Gallimard, coll. "Quarto," 2006.

Deleuze, Gilles. *Cinéma 1: l'image-mouvement*. Paris: Minuit, 1983. Translated as *Cinema 1: The Movement-Image*. Trans. Hugh Tomlinson and Barbara Habberjam. London: Athlone Press, 1986.

---. *Cinéma 2: l'image-temps*. Paris: Minuit, 1985. Translated as *Cinema 2: The Time-Image*. Trans. Hugh Tomlinson and Robert Galeta. London: Athlone Press, 1989.

Didi-Huberman, Georges. *Invention de l'hysterie, Charcot et l'iconographie photographique de la Salpêtrière*. Paris: Macula, 1982. Translated as *The Invention of Hysteria: Charcot and the Photographic Iconography of the Salpêtrière*. Trans. Alisa Hartz. Cambridge, MA: MIT Press, 2003.

---. *La Ressemblance informe ou le gai savoir visuel selon Georges Bataille*. Paris: Macula, 2003.

---. *Images malgré tout*. Paris: Minuit, 2004. Translated as *Images in Spite of All: Four Photographs from Auschwitz*. Trans. Shane B. Lillis. Chicago: University of Chicago Press, 2008.

---. *L'Image survivante*. Paris: Minuit, 2005.

Douchet, Jean. *Art d'aimer*. Paris: Cahiers du cinéma, 1987.

Eisenschitz, Bernard. *Le Cinéma allemand*. Paris: Nathan, 1999.

Eisenschitz, Bernard, and Christian Bourgois, *Roman américain, les vies de Nicholas Ray*. Paris: Cahiers du cinéma, 1990. Translated as *Nicholas Ray: An American Journey*. Trans. Tom Milne. London: Faber and Faber, 1993.

Eisner, Lotte H. *Fritz Lang*. Trans. Gertrud Mander. New York: Da Capo, 1976.

Foucault, Michel. *Surveiller et punir*. Paris: Gallimard, 1975. Translated as *Discipline and Punish: The Birth of the Prison*. Trans. Alan Sheridan. London: Allen Lane, 1977.

Freud, Sigmund. *Beyond the Pleasure Principle* [1920]. In *The Complete Psychological Works of Sigmund Freud*, vol. XVIII. Ed. James Strachey. London: Hogarth Press, 1976.

Gallagher, Tag. *The Adventures of Roberto Rossellini: His Life and Films*. New York: Da Capo, 1998.

Glissant, Édouard. *Les Entretiens de Baton Rouge*. Paris: Gallimard, 2008.

Guénon, Denis. *Livraison et délivrance: théâtre, politique, philosophie*. Paris: Belin, 2009.

Ibarz, Mercè. *Luis Buñuel y los nuevos caminos de las vanguardias*. Valencia: IVAM, 1999.

Ishaghpour, Youssef. *Orson Welles, une caméra visible*. Paris: La Différence, 2001.

Lacan, Jacques. "Le séminaire sur *La Lettre volée*." In Lacan, *Écrits*. Paris: Seuil, 1966, pp. 11-61. Translated as "Seminar on *The Purloined Letter*." In Lacan, *Écrits*. Trans. Bruce Fink. New York: W.W. Norton, 2006, pp. 6-50.

Legendre, Pierre. "Analecta: L'attaque nazi contre le principe de filiation." In Alexandra Papageorgiu-Legendre, *Filiation: leçons 4, suite 2*. Paris: Fayard, 1990, pp. 205-209.

Leutrat, Jean-Louis. *Le Cinéma en perspective: une histoire*. Paris: Nathan, 1992.

Lindeperg, Sylvie. *Nuit et brouillard, un film dans l'histoire*. Paris: Odile Jacob, 2007.

Mannoni, Laurent. *Le Grand Art de la lumière et de l'ombre, Archéologie du cinéma*. Paris: Nathan Université, 1995. Translated as *The Great Art of Light and Shadow: Archaeology of the Cinema*. Trans. Richard Crangle. Exeter: University of Exeter Press, 2000.
Mannoni, Laurent, and Georges Didi-Huberman. *Mouvements de l'air – Étienne-Jules Marey*. Paris: Gallimard, 2004.
Metz, Christian. *Le Signifiant imaginaire*. Paris: Union générale d'éditions, 10/18, 1977. Translated as *The Imaginary Signifier: Psychoanalysis and the Cinema*. Trans. Celia Britton et al. Bloomington: Indiana University Press, 1982.
Milner, Jean-Claude. *L'Arrogance du présent*. Paris: Grasset, 2008.
Mitry, Jean. *Histoire du cinéma*, vol. I and II. Paris: Éditions universitaires, 1967-1969. Repr. Paris: Éditions universitaires, 1995.
Mondzain, Marie-José. *L'Image naturelle*. Paris: Le Nouveau Commerce, 1995.
---. *Le Commerce des regards*. Paris: Seuil, 2003.
---. *Homo spectator*. Paris: Bayard, 2007.
Moullet, Luc. *Politique des acteurs: Gary Cooper, John Wayne, Cary Grant, James Stewart*. Paris: Cahiers du cinéma, 1993.
Nancy, Jean-Luc. *Vérité de la démocratie*. Paris: Galilée, 2008.
Narboni, Jean. "Les futurs antérieurs." In *Les Années pop: cinéma et politique, 1956-1970*, by Jean-Louis Comolli, Gérard Leblanc and Jean Narboni. Paris: BPI/Centre Pompidou, 2001.
Narboni, Jean. *Mikio Naruse, les temps incertains*. Paris: Cahiers du cinéma, 2006.
Ossola, Carlo. "Variations sur l'écriture," preface to Roland Barthes, *Le Plaisir du texte*. Paris: Seuil, 2000.
Oudart, Jean-Pierre. "La Suture," *Cahiers du cinéma*, no. 211 (1969), pp. 36-39, and no. 212 (1969), pp. 50-55. Translated as "Cinema and Suture," trans. Kari Hanet, *Screen*, vol. 18 no. 4 (1977-78), pp. 35-47.
Rancière, Jacques. *La Parole ouvrière*. Paris: 10/18, 1976. Repr. Paris: La Fabrique, 2007.
---. *La Nuit des prolétaires: archives du rêve ouvrier*. Paris: Fayard, 1981. Repr. Paris: Hachette, coll. "Pluriel," 1997. Translated as *The Nights of Labor: The Workers' Dream in Nineteenth-Century France*. Trans. John Drury. Philadelphia: Temple University Press, 1989.
---. *Le Spectateur emancipé*. Paris: La Fabrique, 2008 Translated as *The Emancipated Spectator*. Trans. Gregory Elliott. London: Verso, 2011.
Ricœur, Paul. *Temps et récit*, vol. I. Paris: Seuil, Essais, 1983. Translated as *Time and Narrative*, vol. I. Trans. Kathleen McLaughlin and David Pellauer. Chicago: University of Chicago Press, 1984.
Rohmer, Éric. *L'Organisation de l'espace dans le Faust de Murnau*. Paris: Cahiers du cinéma, 1977.
---. *Le Goût de la beauté*. Ed. Jean Narboni. Paris: Cahiers du cinéma, 1984. Repr. Paris: Cahiers du cinéma, 2004. Translated as *The Taste for Beauty*. Trans. Carol Volk. Cambridge: Cambridge University Press, 1989.
Rosenthal, Victor, and Yves-Marie Visetti, "Sens et temps de la *Gestalt*," *Intellectica*, no. 28 (1999), pp. 147-227.
Roudinesco, Élisabeth. *La Part obscure de nous-mêmes: une histoire des pervers*. Paris: Albin Michel, 2007. Translated as *Our Dark Side: A History of Perversion*. Trans. David Macey. Cambridge, MA: Polity, 2009.

Sanbar, Elias. *Figures du Palestinien. Identité des origines, identité de devenir.* Paris: Gallimard, 2004.

Sansot, Pierre. *Du bon usage de la lenteur.* Paris: Payot, 1998.

Starobinski, Jean. *L'Invention de la liberté.* Paris: Gallimard, 2006. Translated as *The Invention of Liberty, 1700-1789.* Trans. Bernard C. Swift. Geneva: Skira, 1964.

Stiegler, Bernard. *La Technique et le temps.* Paris: Galilée, 1994-2001. Translated *Technics and Time.* Trans. Richard Beardsworth and George Collins. Stanford, CA: Stanford University Press, 1998-2011.

---. *Mécréance et discrédit.* Paris: Galilée, 2004-2006.

---. *La Télécratie contre la démocratie.* Paris: Flammarion, 2006.

Tarkovsky, Andrei. *Sculpting in Time.* Trans. Kitty Hunter-Blair. Austin: University of Texas Press, 1989.

Virilio, Paul. *Vitesse et politique: essai de dromologie.* Paris: Galilée, 1977.

Virilio, Paul. *La Machine de vision: essai sur les nouvelles techniques de représentation.* Paris: Galilée, 1988. Translated as *The Vision Machine.* Trans. Julie Rose. Bloomington: Indiana University Press, 1994.

Wajcman, Gérard. *L'Objet du siècle.* Lagrasse: Verdier, 1998.

---. *Fenêtre, Chroniques du regard et de l'intime.* Lagrasse: Verdier, 2004.

Wieviorka, Annette. *L'Ère du témoin.* Paris: Hachette, coll. "Pluriel," 2002. Translated as *The Era of the Witness.* Trans. Jared Stark. Ithaca, NY: Cornell University Press, 2006.

---. *Déportation et génocide. Entre la mémoire et l'oubli.* Paris: Hachette, coll. "Pluriel," 2003.

---. *Auschwitz, la mémoire d'un lieu.* Paris: Hachette, coll. "Pluriel," 2005.

Works Cited in "Technique and Ideology"

Althusser, Louis, et al. *Lire Le Capital,* vol. I. Paris: Maspero, 1965. Repr. Paris: PUF, coll. "Quadrige," 1996. Translated as *Reading Capital.* Trans. Ben Brewster. London: NLB, 1977.

Aumont, Jacques. "Le concept de montage," *Cahiers du cinéma,* no. 211 (1969), pp. 46-51.

Baudry, Jean-Louis. "Cinéma: effets idéologiques produits par l'appareil de base," *Cinéthique* no. 7-8 (1970), pp. 1-8. Translated as "Ideological Effects of the Basic Cinematographic Apparatus." Trans. Alan Williams. In *Narrative, Apparatus, Ideology: A Film Theory Reader,* ed. Philip Rosen. New York: Columbia University Press, pp. 286-298.

Baudry, Pierre. "Les aventures de l'idée," *Cahiers du cinéma,* no. 240 (1972), pp. 51-59, and no. 241 (1972), pp. 31-45.

Bazin, André. "Ontologie de l'image photographique." In Bazin, *Qu'est-ce que le cinema?,* vol. I, "Ontologie et langage." Paris: Cerf, 1958, pp. 11-20. Translated as "Ontology of the Photographic Image." Trans. Timothy Barnard. In Bazin, *What Is Cinema?,* ed. Timothy Barnard. Montreal: Caboose, 2009, pp. 3-12.

---. "L'évolution du langage cinématographique." In Bazin, *Qu'est-ce que le cinéma?,* vol. I, "Ontologie et langage." Paris: Cerf, 1958, pp. 131-148. Translated as "The Evolution of Film Language." Trans. Timothy Barnard. In Bazin, *What Is Cinema?,* ed. Timothy Barnard. Montreal: Caboose, 2009, pp. 87-106.

---. "Le mythe du cinéma total." In Bazin, *Qu'est-ce que le cinéma?,* vol. I, "Ontologie et langage." Paris: Cerf, 1958, pp. 21-26. Translated as "The Myth of Total Cinema." Trans. Timothy

Barnard. In Bazin, *What Is Cinema?*, ed. Timothy Barnard. Montreal: Caboose, 2009, pp. 13-21.
---. "William Wyler ou le janséniste de la mise en scène." In Bazin, *Qu'est-ce que le cinéma?*, vol. I, "Ontologie et langage." Paris: Cerf, 1958, pp. 149-174. Translated as "William Wyler, the Jansenist of Mise en Scène." Trans. Timothy Barnard. In Bazin, *What Is Cinema?*, ed. Timothy Barnard. Montreal: Caboose, 2009., pp. 45-72.
Benjamin, Walter. "L'œuvre d'art a l'ère de sa reproductibilité technique." In Benjamin, *Poésie et Révolution*. Paris: Denoël, 1971. Repr. Paris: Gallimard, coll. "Folio essais," 2000. Translated as "The Work of Art in the Age of Mechanical Reproduction." Trans. Harry Zohn. In Benjamin, *Illuminations*, ed. Hannah Arendt. New York: Schocken, 1968, pp. 217-251.
Bessy, Maurice, and Jean-Louis Chardans. *Dictionnaire du cinéma et de la télévision*. Paris: Jean-Jacques Pauvert, 1965-1971.
Bonitzer, Pascal. "Film/politique," *Cahiers du cinéma*, no. 222 (1970), pp. 33-38.
---. "'Réalité' de la dénotation," *Cahiers du cinéma*, no. 229 (1971), pp. 39-41. Translated as "'Reality' of Denotation." Trans. Lindley Hanlon. In *Cahiers du cinéma, 1969-1972: The Politics of Representation*, ed. Nick Browne. London: Routledge, 1990, pp. 248-253.
---. "Le Gros Orteil," *Cahiers du cinéma*, no. 232 (1971), pp. 14-23.
---. "Fétichisme de la technique: la notion de 'plan,'" *Cahiers du cinéma*, no. 233 (1971), pp. 4-10.
Bourdieu, Pierre. "Sociologie de la perception esthétique." In *Les Sciences humaines et l'œuvre d'art*, collective work. Brussels: La Connaissance, Brussels, 1969, pp. 161-176.
Brunius, J.B. *Photographie et photographie de cinéma*. Paris: Arts et Métiers graphiques, 1938.
[*Cinéthique* editors]. "Texte collectif," *Cinéthique*, no. 9 (1970), pp. 1-70.
Comolli, Jean-Louis. "Le détour par le direct," *Cahiers du cinéma*, no. 209 (1969), pp. 48-54, and no. 211 (1969), pp. 40-45.
Daney, Serge, and Jean-Pierre Oudart, "Travail, lecture, jouissance," *Cahiers du cinéma*, no. 222 (1970), pp. 39-54. Translated as "Work, Reading, Pleasure." Trans. Diana Matias. In *Cahiers du cinéma, 1969-1972: The Politics of Representation*, ed. Nick Browne. London: Routledge, 1990, pp. 115-136.
Da Vinci, Leonardo. *La Peinture*, texts collected and translated into French by André Chastel. Paris: Hermann, coll. "Miroirs de l'art," 1964.
Deslandes, Jacques. *Histoire comparée du cinéma*, vol. I. Brussels: Casterman, 1966.
De Vaucouleurs, Gérard. *La Science de la photographie*. Paris: Elzévir, 1947.
Eisenstein, S.M. "Dickens, Griffith et nous," translated into French by Luda and Jean Schnitzer, *Cahiers du cinéma*, no. 231 (1971), pp. 16-22, no. 232 (1971), pp. 24-26, no. 233 (1971), pp. 11-18, and no. 234-235 (1971-1972), pp. 27-42. Translated into English as "Dickens, Griffith and the Film Today." Trans. Jay Leyda. In Eisenstein, *Film Form: Essays in Film Theory*, ed. Jay Leyda. New York: Harcourt & Brace, 1949, pp. 195-255.
Fargier, Jean-Paul. "La parenthèse et le détour," *Cinéthique*, no. 5 (1969), pp. 15-21. Translated as "Parenthesis or Indirect Route," trans. Susan Bennett, *Screen*, vol. 12 no. 2, pp. 131-144.
Francastel, Pierre. *Peinture et Société*. Paris: Gallimard, coll. "Idées-arts," 1965.
Kristeva, Julia. *Séméiotikè, Recherches pour une sémanalyse*. Paris: Seuil, 1969.
---. "Littérature, sémiotique, marxisme," *La Nouvelle Critique*, no. 38 (1970), pp. 28-35.
---. "Pratique analytique, pratique révolutionnaire," *Cinéthique*, no. 9-10 (1970), pp. 71-79.

Lebel, Jean-Patrick. "Cinéma et idéologie," *La Nouvelle Critique*, nos. 34, 35, 37 and 41. Repr. Paris: Éditions sociales, 1971.

Leblanc, Gérard. "Direction," *Cinéthique*, no. 5 (1969), pp. 1-8. Translated as "Direction," trans. Susan Bennett, *Screen*, vol. 12 no. 2 (1971), pp. 121-130.

---. "Welles, Bazin et la RKO," *Cinéthique*, no. 6 (1970), pp. 27-32.

Marx, Karl. *The Poverty of Philosophy* [1847]. In *The Collected Works of Karl Marx and Friedrich Engels*, vol. VI. New York: International Publishers, 1975.

Mannoni, Octave. *Clefs pour l'imaginaire ou l'Autre Scène*. Paris: Seuil, 1969.

Massa, Norbert. "Note sur l'histoire du cinéma," *Ciné-Forum*, no. 5 (1971).

Metz, Christian. *Langage et cinéma*. Paris: Larousse, 1971. Repr. Paris: Albatros, 1992. Translated as *Language and Cinema*. Trans. Donna Jean Umiker-Sebeok. The Hague: Mouton, 1974.

Mitry, Jean. *Esthétique et psychologie du cinéma*, vol. I, "Les structures," and vol. II, "Les formes." Paris: Éditions universitaires, 1965. Repr. Paris: Éditions du Cerf, 2001 (abridged). Abridged version translated as *The Aesthetics and Psychology of the Cinema*. Trans. Christopher King. Bloomington: Indiana University Press, 2000.

---. *Histoire du cinéma*, vol. I and II. Paris: Éditions universitaires, 1967-1969. Repr. Paris: Éditions universitaires, 1995.

Munier, Roger. "L'image fascinante," *Diogène*, no. 38 (1962), pp. 91-99.

Narboni, Jean. "La vicariance du pouvoir," *Cahiers du cinéma*, no. 224 (1970), pp. 43-47. Translated as "Vicarious Power." Trans. Leigh Hafrey. In *Cahiers du cinéma, 1969-1972: The Politics of Representation*, ed. Nick Browne. London: Routledge, 1990, pp. 150-162.

Narboni, Jean, Sylvie Pierre and Jacques Rivette, "Montage," *Cahiers du cinéma*, no. 210 (1969), pp. 16-35. Translated as "Montage." Trans. Tom Milne. In *Cahiers du cinéma, 1969-1972: The Politics of Representation*, ed. Nick Browne. London: Routledge, 1990, pp. 21-44.

Oudart, Jean-Pierre. "La Suture," *Cahiers du cinéma*, no. 211 (1969), pp. 36-39, and no. 212 (1969), pp. 50-55. Translated as "Cinema and Suture," trans. Kari Hanet, *Screen*, vol. 18 no. 4 (1977-78), pp. 35-47.

---. "L'effet de réel," *Cahiers du cinéma*, no. 228 (1971), pp. 19-27. Translated as "The Reality Effect." Trans. Annwyl Williams. In *Cahiers du cinéma, 1969-1972: The Politics of Representation*, ed. Nick Browne. London: Routledge, 1990, pp. 189-202].

Paulhan, Jean. *La Peinture cubiste*. Paris: Denoël-Gonthier, coll. "Médiations," 1971. Repr. Paris: Gallimard, coll. "Folio essais," 1990.

Pleynet, Marcelin, and Jean Thibaudeau, "Économie, idéologique, formel...," *Cinéthique*, no. 3 (1969), pp. 7-14. Translated as "Economic-Ideological-Formal." Trans. Elias Noujaim. In Sylvia Harvey, *May '68 and Film Culture*. London: BFI, 1978, pp. 149-164.

Sadoul, Georges. *Histoire générale du cinéma*, vol. I, "L'Invention du cinéma (1832-1897)." Paris: Denoël, 1946.

---. *Histoire générale du cinéma*, vol. III, "Le cinéma devient un art (1909-1920)." Paris: Denoël, 1950.

Schefer, Jean Louis. *Scénographie d'un tableau*. Paris: Seuil, 1969.

Vigneau, André. *Une brève histoire de l'art de Niépce à nos jours*. Paris: Robert Laffont, 1963.

Vivié, Jean. *Historique et développement de la technique cinématographique*. Paris: BPI, 1946.

Works Cited in "Cinema/Ideology/Criticism"

Althusser, Louis. "Marxism and Humanism." In Althusser, *For Marx*. Trans. Ben Brewster. London: NLB, 1969, pp. 219-248.

Artaud, Antonin. *Œuvres complètes*, vol. III. Paris: Gallimard, 1961.

Badiou, Alain. "L'autonomie du processus esthétique," *Cahiers marxistes-léninistes*, no. 12-13 (1966), pp. 77-89.

Blagoi, Dmitri. "Aux sources de la littérature soviétique," *Tel Quel*, no. 37 (1970), pp. 95-103.

Eisenstein, S.M. *Réflexions d'un cinéaste*. Translated into French by Lucia Galinskaia and Jean Cathala. Moscow: Progress Publishers, 1958.

Fargier, Jean-Paul. "La parenthèse et le détour," *Cinéthique*, no. 5 (1969), pp. 15-21. Translated as "Parenthesis or Indirect Route," trans. Susan Bennett, *Screen*, vol. 12 no. 2, pp. 131-144.

---. "Discours-film (révolution)-mutisme: *Le Joueur de quilles* de Lajournade," *Cinéthique*, no. 5 (1969), pp. 37-40.

Le Grivés, Eliane, and Simon Luciani, "Naissance d'une théorie," *Cinéthique*, no. 5 (1969), pp. 45-47.

Kristeva, Julia. "La productivité dite texte," *Communications*, no. 11 (1968), pp. 59-83.

Leblanc, Gérard. "Direction," *Cinéthique*, no. 5 (1969). Translated as "Direction," trans. Susan Bennett, *Screen*, vol. 12 no. 2 (1971), pp. 121-130.

Leyda, Jay. *Kino: A History of the Russian and Soviet Film*. London: Allen and Unwin, 1960.

Marx, Karl. *L'Idéologie allemande* [1846]. Translated into French by Émile Bottigelli. Paris: Éditions sociales, 1952. Translated into English as *The German Ideology*. In *The Collected Works of Marx and Engels*, vol. V. New York: International Publishers, 1975.

Meyerhold, Vsevolod. *Le Théâtre théâtral*. Translated into French by Nina Gourfinkel. Paris: Gallimard, 1963.

Narboni, Jean, Sylvie Pierre and Jacques Rivette. "Montage," *Cahiers du cinéma*, no. 210 (1969), pp. 16-35. Translated as "Montage." Trans. Tom Milne. In *Cahiers du cinéma, 1969-1972: The Politics of Representation*, ed. Nick Browne. London: Routledge, 1990, pp. 21-44.

Sollers, Philippe. *Nombres*. Paris: Seuil, 1968.

---. "Le réflexe de réduction," *Quinzaine littéraire*, no. 43 (1968). Repr. in *Théorie d'ensemble*, ed. Philippe Sollers. Paris: Éditions du Seuil, coll. "Tel Quel," 391-398.

Todorov, Tzvetan, ed. *Théorie de la littérature* (Paris; Seuil, 1966).

---. "Formalistes et futuristes," *Tel Quel* no. 35 (1968), pp. 42-45.

Other Works Cited

Allen, Richard. *Projecting Illusion: Film Spectatorship and the Impression of Reality*. Cambridge: Cambridge University Press, 1995.

Althusser, Louis. *Lenin and Philosophy and Other Essays*. Trans. Ben Brewster. New York: Monthly Review Press, 1971.

---. *Politics and History: Montesquieu, Rousseau, Marx*. Trans. Ben Brewster. London: NLB, 1972.

---. *The Future Lasts a Long Time*. Trans. Richard Veasey. London: Chatto & Windus, 1993.

–––. *Sur la reproduction*. Paris: PUF, 1995. Translated as *On the Reproduction of Capitalism: Ideology and Ideological State Apparatuses*. Trans. Geoffrey Goshgarian. London: Verso, 2014.

Amengual, Barthélémy. "À propos du *Pré de Béjine*," *Cahiers du cinéma*, no. 203 (1968), pp. 6-12.

Andrew, Dudley. "The 'Three Ages' of Cinema Studies and the Age to Come," *PMLA*, vol. 115 no. 3 (2000), pp. 341-351.

Andrew, Dudley, and Hervé Joubert-Laurencin. *Opening Bazin*. Oxford: Oxford University Press, 2011.

[Anon.]. "Réponses à 'Politique Hebdo'," *Cahiers du cinéma*, no. 229 (1971), pp. 61-63.

[Anon.]. "Intervention à Avignon: premier bilan critique," *Cahiers du cinéma*, no. 241 (1972), pp. 7-16.

Barker, Jason. *Alain Badiou: A Critical Introduction*. London: Pluto, 2002.

Barthes, Roland. *Sade Fourier Loyola*. Paris: Seuil, 1971. Translated as *Sade Fourier Loyola*. Trans. Richard Miller. Berkeley: University of California Press, 1989.

Bataille, Georges. "Human Face," trans. Annette Michelson, *October*, no. 36 (1986), pp. 17-21.

Baudry, Jean-Louis. "Le dispositif: approches métapsychologies de l'impression de réalité," *Communications*, vol. 23 no. 23 (1975), pp. 56-72. Translated as "The Apparatus: Metapsychological Approaches to the Impression of Reality in the Cinema," trans. Jean Andrews and Bertrand Augst, *Camera Obscura*, no. 1 (1976), pp. 104-128.

Bazin, André. "Renoir français," *Cahiers du cinéma*, no. 8 (1952), pp. 9-29. Translated as "French Renoir." In Bazin, *Renoir*. Trans. W.W. Halsey and William H. Simon. London: W.H. Allen, 1974, pp. 74-91.

–––. "Théâtre et cinéma." In Bazin, *Qu'est-ce que le cinéma?*, vol. II, "Le cinéma et les autres arts." Paris: Éditions du Cerf, 1959, pp. 69-118. Translated as "Theatre and Film." In Bazin, *What Is Cinema?* Trans. Timothy Barnard. Montreal: Caboose, 2009, pp. 161-214.

–––. *Orson Welles: A Critical View*. Trans. Jonathan Rosenbaum. London: Elm Tree Books, 1978.

Bickerton, Emilie. *A Short History of* Cahiers du cinéma. London: Verso, 2009.

Bonitzer, Pascal. "Ciné-Forum," *Cahiers du cinéma*, no. 230 (1971), p. 61.

–––. "Note sur une note de Comolli et sur un cinéma tordu," *Cahiers du cinéma*, no. 279-280 (1977), pp. 94-97.

–––. "Nos années non-légendaires" [1998]. In *Cinéma 68*, ed. Antoine de Baecque, Stéphane Bouquet and Emmanuel Burdeau. Paris: Cahiers du cinéma, 2008, pp. 143-156.

Bonitzer, Pascal, and Serge Daney, "L'écran du fantasme," *Cahiers du cinéma*, no. 236-237 (1972), pp. 30-41.

Bordwell, David. "Historical Poetics of Cinema," *Georgia State Literary Studies*, no. 3 (1989), pp. 369-398.

Bordwell, David, Janet Staiger and Kristin Thompson. *The Classical Hollywood Cinema: Film Style and Mode of Production to 1960*. New York: Columbia University Press, 1985.

Bordwell, David, and Noël Carroll, eds. *Post-Theory: Reconstructing Film Studies*. Madison: University of Wisconsin Press, 1996.

Bourseiller, Christophe. *Les Maoïstes: la folle histoire des gardes rouges français*. Paris: Plon, 1996.

Britton, Andrew. "The Ideology of *Screen*," *Movie*, no. 26 (1978-79), pp. 2-28.

Browne, Nick, ed. *Cahiers du cinéma, 1969-1972: The Politics of Representation*. London: Routledge, 1990.

Burch, Noël. *Theory of Film Practice*. Trans. Helen R. Lane. New York: Praeger, 1973.
Buscombe, Edward, Christine Gledhill, Alan Lovell and Christopher Williams. "Statement: Psychoanalysis and Film," *Screen*, vol. 16 no. 4 (1975-76), pp. 119-130.
---. "Why We Have Resigned from the Board of *Screen*," *Screen*, vol. 17 no. 2 (1976), pp. 106-109.
[*Cahiers* editors]. "Politique et lutte idéologique de classes: Intervention 1," *Cahiers du cinéma*, no. 234-235 (1971-72), pp. 4-12.
[*Cahiers* editors]. "À propos de la traduction plus ou moins pirate des *Cahiers*," *Cahiers du cinéma*, no. 279-280 (1977), p. 2.
Cameron, Ian. "Editorial," *Movie*, no. 26 (1978-79), p. 1.
Carroll, Noël. "Address to the Heathen," *October*, no. 23 (1982), pp. 89-163.
---. "A Reply to Heath," *October*, no. 27 (1983), pp. 81-102.
[*Cinéthique* editors]. "Du bon usage de la valeur d'échange," *Cinéthique*, no. 6 (1970), pp. 1-12.
[Collective text]. "*Young Mr Lincoln* de John Ford," *Cahiers du cinéma*, no. 222 (1970), pp. 29-47. Translated as "John Ford's *Young Mr. Lincoln*," trans. Helen Lackner and Diana Matias, *Screen*, vol. 13 no. 3 (1972), pp. 5-43.
Croombs, Matthew. "Pasts and Futures of 1970s Film Theory," *Scope*, no. 20 (2011).
Daney, Serge "Chantez le code!," *Cahiers du cinéma*, no. 264 (1976), pp. 52-54.
---. "Les Journées de Damas," *Cahiers du cinéma*, no. 290-291 (1978), pp. 73-78.
---. *L'Exercice a été profitable, monsieur*. Paris: POL, 1993.
Dayan, Daniel. "The Tutor-Code of Classical Cinema," *Film Quarterly*, vol. 28 no. 1 (1974), pp. 22-31.
De Baecque, Antoine. *Cahiers du cinéma: histoire d'une revue*, vol. I, "À l'assaut du cinéma," and vol. II, "Cinéma, tours détours." Paris: Cahiers du cinéma, 1991.
Deleuze, Gilles. *Proust et les signes* (Paris: PUF, 1964). Translated as *Proust and Signs: The Complete Text*. Trans. Richard Howard. Minneapolis: University of Minnesota Press, 2000.
---. "Postscript on the Societies of Control," *October*, no. 59 (1992), pp. 3-7.
Deleuze, Gilles, and Claire Parnet. *Dialogues*. Paris: Flammarion, 1977.
Derrida, Jacques. "Différance." In Derrida, *Margins of Philosophy*. Trans. Alan Bass. Chicago: University of Chicago Press, 1982.
Derrida, Jacques, and Michael Sprinker, "Politics and Friendship: An Interview with Jacques Derrida." In *Althusser's Legacy*, ed. E. Ann Kaplan and Michael Sprinker. London: Verso, 1993, pp. 183-231.
Douzinas, Costas, and Slavoj Žižek, eds. *The Idea of Communism*, 2 vols. London: Verso, 2010-2013.
Eisenschitz, Bernard. "Le Cahier des autres," *Cahiers du cinéma*, no. 211 (1969), p. 59.
Fairfax, Daniel. "Conference Report: The Impact of Technological Innovations on the Historiography and Theory of Cinema," *Cinema Journal*, vol. 52 no. 1 (2012), pp. 127-131.
Fargier, Jean-Paul. "Pour le dépérissement du cinéma militant," *Cinéma d'aujourd'hui*, no. 5-6 (1976), pp. 163-168.
Foucault, Michel. "The Confession of the Flesh." In Foucault, *Power/Knowledge: Selected Interviews and Other Writings*, ed. Colin Gordon. New York: Pantheon, 1980, pp. 194-228.
Freud, Sigmund. *Jokes and Their Relation to the Unconscious* [1905]. In *The Complete Psychological Works of Sigmund Freud*, vol. VIII. London: Hogarth Press, 1975.
---. *The Interpretation of Dreams* [1911]. In *The Complete Psychological Works of Sigmund Freud*, vol. IV. London: Hogarth Press, 1975.

Gaudreault, André. *Film and Attraction: From Kinematography to Cinema.* Trans. Timothy Barnard. Urbana: University of Illinois Press, 2011.

Godard, Jean-Luc. *Introduction à une véritable histoire du cinéma.* Paris: Albatros, 1980.

Grieveson, Lee, and Haidee Wasson, eds. *Inventing Film Studies.* Durham, NC: Duke University Press, 2008.

Harvey, Sylvia. *May '68 and Film Culture.* London: BFI, 1978.

Heath, Stephen. "Le Père Noël," *October*, no. 26 (1983), pp. 63-115.

Heidegger, Martin. *Chemins qui ne mènent nulle part.* Translated from German into French by Wolfgang Brokmeier. Paris: Gallimard, 1962. Translated from German into English as *Off the Beaten Track.* Trans. Julian Young and Kenneth Haynes. Cambridge: Cambridge University Press, 2002.

Hillier, Jim, ed. *Cahiers du cinéma, The 1950s: Neo-Realism, Hollywood, New Wave.* Cambridge, MA: Harvard University Press, 1985.

---. *Cahiers du cinéma, 1960-1968: New Wave, New Cinema, Re-evaluating Hollywood.* London: Routledge, 1986.

Hoveyda, Fereydoun, and Jacques Rivette. "Entretien avec Roberto Rossellini," *Cahiers du cinéma*, no. 94 (1959), pp. 1-11. Translated as "Interview with Roberto Rossellini." Trans. Annapaola Cancogni. In Rossellini, *My Method: Writings and Interviews*, ed. Adriano Aprà. New York: Marsilio, 1995, pp. 100-113.

Kané, Pascal. "Le detour par l'enfance," *Cahiers du cinéma*, no. 265 (1976), pp. 19-22.

Klinger, Barbara. "Cinema/Ideology/Criticism Revisited: The Progressive Text," *Screen*, vol. 25 no. 1 (1984), pp. 30-44.

Kristeva, Julia. *Desire in Language.* Trans. Thomas Gora, Alice Jardine and Leon S. Roudiez. New York: Columbia University Press, 1980.

Lacan, Jacques. *Le Séminaire*, vol. X, "L'Angoisse." Paris: Seuil, 2004.

---. *Le Séminaire*, vol. XI, "Les quatre concepts fondamentaux de la psychanalyse." Paris: Seuil, 1973. Translated as *The Four Fundamental Concepts of Psychoanalysis.* Trans. Alan Sheridan. London: Hogarth Press, 1977.

Lenin, V.I. *Imperialism: The Highest Stage of Capitalism* [1917]. In *Collected Works of Lenin*, vol. XXII. Moscow: Progress Publishers, 1976.

---. *Philosophical Notebooks.* In *Collected Works of Lenin*, vol. XXXVIII. Moscow: Progress Publishers, 1976.

Leys, Simon. *Les Habits neufs du Président Mao.* Paris: Éditions Champ Libre, 1971. Translated as *The Chairman's New Clothes: Mao and the Cultural Revolution.* Trans. Carol Appleyard and Patrick Goode. New York: St. Martin's Press, 1977.

MacCabe, Colin. *Godard: Images, Sounds, Politics.* London: BFI, 1980.

---. *Theoretical Essays: Film, Linguistics, Literature.* Manchester: Manchester University Press, 1985.

---. *Godard: Portrait of the Artist at 70.* New York: Farrar, Strauss and Giroux, 2003.

Macciochi, Maria-Antonia. *La Chine.* Paris: Maspero, 1970.

Macherey, Pierre. *Pour une théorie de la production littéraire.* Paris: Maspero, 1966. Translated as *A Theory of Literary Production.* Trans. Geoffrey Wall. London: Routledge, 1978.

Mao Tse-tung, "On Contradiction" [1937]. In *Mao: On Practice and Contradiction*, ed. Slavoj Žižek. London: Verso, 2007, pp. 67-102.

Mitry, Jean. "De quelques problèmes d'histoire et d'esthétique du cinéma," *Cahiers de la Cinémathèque*, no. 10-11 (1973), pp. 112-141.

Musser, Charles. *The Emergence of Cinema: The American Screen to 1907*. New York: Scribner, 1990.

Oddos, Christian. "Lettre de Lecteur," *Cahiers du cinéma*, no. 229 (1971), pp. 54-56.

Pasolini, Pier Paolo. "The Cinema of Poetry." In *Movies and Methods*, ed. Bill Nichols, 2 vols. Berkeley: University of California Press, 1976, vol. I, pp. 542-558.

Rivette, Jacques. "De l'abjection (*Kapò*)," *Cahiers du cinéma*, no. 120 (1961), pp. 54-55.

Rodowick, D.N. *The Crisis of Political Modernism*, 2nd edition. Berkeley: University of California Press, 1993.

Rohdie, Sam. "Editorial," *Screen*, vol. 13 no. 1 (1972), pp. 2-4.

–––, ed. *Screen Reader 1: Cinema, Ideology, Politics*. London: BFI, 1977.

Rohmer, Éric. "Le Celluloïd et le marbre": Part I: "Le Bandit philosophe," *Cahiers du cinéma*, no. 44 (1955), pp. 32-37; Part II: "Le Siècle des peintres," *Cahiers du cinéma*, no. 49 (1955), pp. 10-15; Part III: "De la métaphore," *Cahiers du cinéma*, no. 51 (1955), pp. 2-9; Part IV: "Beau comme la musique," *Cahiers du cinéma*, no. 52 (1955), pp. 4-12; Part V: "Architecture d'apocalypse," *Cahiers du cinéma* no. 53 (December 1955), pp. 22-30. Repr. *Le Celluloïd et le marbre*. Paris: Éditions Léo Scheer, 2010.

–––. "Nouvel entretien avec Éric Rohmer," *Cahiers du cinéma*, no. 219 (1970), pp. 46-55. Translated as "New Interview with Éric Rohmer," trans. Daniel Fairfax, *Senses of Cinema*, no. 54 (2010), online.

Philip Rosen, "*Screen* and 1970s Film Theory." In *Inventing Film Studies*, ed. Lee Grieveson and Haidee Wasson. Durham, NC: Duke University Press, 2008, pp. 264-297.

Ross, Kristin. *May 1968 and Its Afterlives*. Chicago: University of Chicago Press, 2002.

Spellerberg, James. "Technology and Ideology in the Cinema," *Quarterly Review of Film Studies*, vol. 2 no. 3 (1977). Repr. in *Film Theory and Criticism: Introductory Readings*, ed. Gerald Mast and Marshall Cohen, 3rd edition. Oxford: Oxford University Press, 1985, pp. 761-775.

Toubiana, Serge. "Les Arpenteurs," *Cahiers du cinéma*, no. 264 (1976), pp. 41-43.

Valente, Joe. "Lacan's Marxism, Marxism's Lacan (from Žižek to Althusser)." In *The Cambridge Companion to Lacan*, ed. Jean-Michel Rabaté. Cambridge: Cambridge University Press, 2003, pp. 153-172.

Willemen, Paul. "On Realisms in the Cinema," *Screen*, vol. 13 no. 1 (1972), pp. 37-44.

Williams, Christopher. "The Deep Focus Question: Some Comments on Patrick Ogle's Article," *Screen*, vol. 13 no. 1 (1972), pp. 73-78.

Wilson, David, ed. *Cahiers du cinéma, 1973-1978: History, Ideology, Cultural Struggle*. London: Routledge, 2000.

Translator's Notes

Cinema against Spectacle

Introduction

i. Langlois was sacked as head of the Cinémathèque in February 1968, with André Malraux centrally involved in the decision. Ongoing protests led to a backdown by de Gaulle's government and his reinstatement. The *États généraux du cinéma* were held in the École Louis Lumière in May 1968, and involved the entire gamut of the French film industry, which was on strike at the time. *Cahiers* participated in the drafting of resolutions, although most of its own formulations did not win majority support at the mass meetings. Despite airing a spate of utopian proposals, the *États* had few lasting repercussions on the functioning of the French film industry.

ii. The French original, "*jardins de soucis*" is an untranslatable pun based on *jardin de délices* (garden of delights): *souci* is the common term for worry or concern, while *souci des jardins* is the name of a type of flower (the pot marigold). The phrase was previously used by Victor Ségalen in his series of poems *Stèles*, but Comolli affirms that, at most, this is an "unconscious citation" (private communication, September 2013).

iii. Here, and on subsequent occasions that Comolli uses the phrase, he retains the original English.

iv. The French original, "*peau des apparences*" is a common poetic expression used to denote the strip of celluloid.

v. In 2009, shortly before the publication of *Cinéma contre spectacle*, the Sarkozy government banned commercial advertising on French public television networks during prime-time hours. The controversial legislation led to stations such as FR2 and FR3 making significant changes to their broadcast schedules.

vi. Mireille Dumas is a French television personality widely known for her confessional-style interviews, particularly in the programs *Bas les masques* (1992-1996) and *Vie privée, vie publique* (2000-2011). Comolli provides a critical analysis of her interviewing style in the 1993 text "*Nous deux*: la forme de l'entretien," in *Voir et pouvoir*, pp. 90-102.

I. Opening the Window?

i. An allusion to the 1755 novel *La Nuit et le moment ou les matines de Cythère: dialogue* by Claude-Prosper Jolyot de Crébillon.

ii. "Amateur" in French can mean both "amateur" and "fan."

iii. Rossellini's quote comes from a 1959 interview with *Cahiers du cinéma*. Cf. Fereydoun Hoveyda and Jacques Rivette, "Entretien avec Roberto Rossellini," *Cahiers du cinéma*, no. 94 (1959), p. 6. An English translation of the interview has been published in Roberto Rossellini, *My Method: Writings and Interviews*, ed. Adriano Aprà (New York: Marsilio, 1995), pp. 100-113, but the quote is given as "Everything is there – particularly in this film. Why fiddle with anything?" (p. 106).

iv. Arte is the primary cultural television network in France, and is funded through a joint agreement with Germany.

v. The analogy between the functioning of the cinema and Lacan's mirror stage was first explored at length in Oudart's "La Suture" and Baudry's "Notes on the Basic Cinematographic Apparatus," before being further discussed (with different conclusions) in Christian Metz's *The Imaginary Signifier*. More generally, the dichotomy between the cinema screen as mirror and Bazin's notion of film as a "window on to the world" has become one of the key tropes of film theory.

vi. The phrase "destruction of the old must precede construction of the new" was a central slogan of Maoism, in both China and Western Europe.

vii. For the Bazin quote, cf. André Bazin, "Théâtre et cinéma," in Bazin, *Qu'est-ce que le cinéma?* (Paris: Éditions du Cerf, 1959), vol. 2, p. 100; translated as "Theatre and Film," trans. Timothy Barnard, in Bazin, *What Is Cinema?* (Montreal: Caboose, 2009), p. 193.

viii. Alexis Grüss (1909-1985) was a well-known French circus performer.

ix. "Left-wing fiction" (*fiction de gauche*) was the term used by *Cahiers* in the mid-1970s, under Daney's editorship, to refer to fiction films with a left-liberal political line and conventional formal and narrative structures.

x. Cf. André Bazin, "Renoir français," *Cahiers du cinéma*, no. 8 (1952), p. 29. This text was translated into English as part of Bazin's Renoir book (cf. André Bazin, *Renoir*, trans. W. W. Halsey and William H. Simon [London: W.H. Allen, 1974], pp. 74-91). While the translators of this volume rendered the phrase "*robe sans couture de la réalité*" as "simple cloak of reality" (p. 91), the far more common (and more precise) English equivalent is "seamless fabric of reality."

xi. *Relève* is the term suggested by Derrida as an equivalent for Hegel's notoriously untranslatable concept *Aufhebung*. As with *Aufhebung* it has a double sense, meaning both "continuation" and "replacement" (as in "the changing of the guard"). No English analogue is adequate, but "sublation" has been used in translations of Hegel since the early 20th century. Translators of Derrida generally leave *relève* in the original. Cf. Jacques Derrida, "Différance," in Derrida, *Margins of Philosophy*, trans. Alan Bass (Chicago: University of Chicago Press, 1982).

II. Inventing the Cinema?

i. La Salpêtrière was a notable hospital and mental asylum in Paris, where the French neurologist Jean-Martin Charcot (1825-1893) practiced and taught.

III. Filming the Disaster?

i. *Qualunquismo* was a demagogic movement in post-war Italy, founded by the right-wing journalist Guglielmo Giannini, which rejected all political parties, whether communist, social-democratic or conservative. A parallel phenomenon in France was the Poujadist movement in the 1950s. The term is now used in Italian as a general description for political cynicism and has passed into French as *qualunquisme*. Interestingly, Bernard Eisenschitz accused *Positif* of this tendency in 1969 (cf. "Le Cahier des autres," *Cahiers du cinéma*, no. 211 [1969], p. 59).

ii. In February 1962, nine PCF sympathizers were killed by the French police in Charonne metro station during a protest against the French occupation of Algeria. The deaths caused outrage in the French media, as opposed to the October 1961 massacre of more than 200 Algerian protestors in Paris, which was barely reported at the time.

IV. Cutting the Figure?

i. The expression "*lest de réalité*" ("ballast of reality") derives from Bazin's "Evolution of film language," and is also referred to in "Technique and Ideology." Cf. André Bazin, "L'évolution du langage cinématographique, in Bazin, *Qu'est-ce que le cinéma?* (Paris: Éditions du Cerf, 1958), p. 135. Barnard's translation paraphrases Bazin at this point, and so does not offer a suitable equivalent term. Cf. Bazin, *What Is Cinema?*, op. cit., p. 91.

ii. Bataille's phrase "*la figure humaine*" has been translated into English as "human face," but "human figure" is used here to denote the broader meaning that Comolli gives to the term. Cf. Georges Bataille, "Human Face," trans. Annette Michelson, *October*, no. 36 (1986), pp. 17-21.

iii. JC Decaux is a French corporation specializing in the manufacture of street furniture and billboards, whose products are omnipresent in France.

iv. In Deleuze's gloss of Foucault's *Discipline and Punish*, he claims that the societies of discipline that marked classical 19th-century capitalism have given way to "societies of control," which rely less on organs of state repression and more on the programming of human behavior through the new forms of subjectivity inherent to contemporary capitalism. In some ways this argument recasts Althusser's notion of the Ideological State Apparatus in post-structuralist terms. Cf. Gilles Deleuze, "Postscript on the Societies of Control," *October*, no. 59 (1992), pp. 3-7.

v. Comolli alludes, here, to Heidegger's *Holzwege*, the title of which was translated in French as *Chemins qui ne mènent nulle part* ("Paths that lead nowhere"). Cf. Martin Heidegger, *Chemins qui ne mènent nulle part*, translated into French by Wolfgang Brokmeier (Paris: Gallimard, 1962); Martin Heidegger, *Off the Beaten Track*, trans. Julian Young and Kenneth Haynes (Cambridge: Cambridge University Press, 2002).

V. Changing the Spectator?

i. Comolli uses the neologism "*cinécroyance*," a portmanteau of "*cinéma*" and "*croyance*" (belief).

ii. Here Comolli puns on the words "*spectateur*" and "*sectateur*" (sect-follower).

iii. Located on the Right Bank of the Seine, Les Halles was the main fresh food market for the Paris area from as early as the 12th century. Its most recent pavilions were erected in 1863 under the auspices of the architect Victor Baltard, and were demolished in 1971 to make way for a commuter railway station and shopping mall, with market activities relocated to the suburb of Rungis.

Technique and Ideology: Camera, Perspective, Depth of Field

Introduction

i. The term "scientificity" (*scientificité*) is used in the Althusserian tradition to denote those qualities separating scientific knowledge from ideological discourse, in line with Althusser's notion of the "epistemological break" between the ideological writings of the early Marx and the scientific outlook of his later work.

I. On a Dual Origin

i. The correct translation for Comolli's "*différence*" (here given as "deferral") has been open to dispute. Matias' original translation gave it as "postponement," but, in his editorial notes to "Technique and Ideology," in *Narrative, Apparatus, Ideology*, Rosen insisted that Comolli actually had Derrida's notion of *différance* in mind, and gives the following lengthy footnote explaining the concept: "A comment on a term used here might be helpful for understanding Comolli's project. *Différance* is a neologism developed by Jacques Derrida. The French verb *différer* means both to differ and to defer. *Différance* is an invented noun form marking the combination of the two senses in a single word. This term is part of a complex philosophical argument which includes the notion that a neologism is necessary to point toward – though it can never adequately name or signify – the principle underlying the differentiated structure of language as well as that which drives language and knowledge toward an impression of adequacy or 'presence.' Here we may say very briefly that, for Derrida, something which manifests a meaning or identity can never be fully present in its manifestation; it is always mediated. Hence, any manifestation or experience is always *different* from what it 'professes' to be, and an experience of its full presence is 'always already' *deferred*. As Derrida's translator Gayatri Chakravorty Spivak puts it, '*differance* – being the structure (a structure never quite there, never by us perceived, itself deferred and different) of our psyche – is also the structure of "presence," a term itself under erasure. For *differance*, producing the differential structure of our hold on "presence," never produces presence as such.' Comolli mobilizes Derrida's term as part of his critique of film scholars who, explicitly or implicitly, see the historian's task as devising an account of 'firsts.' For example, Comolli attacks the illusion that if one can name the first time cinema appeared, one has focused on the generative identity of cinema itself. Comolli wishes to stress the discursive and differential character both of the historian's task and of historical 'material' itself. Instead of assuming a punctual, unified source of all cinema history (the 'birth' of cinema), Comolli argues for the dispersed quality of historical phenomena and events. In previous installments, Comolli argued that if one searches for the birth of cinema, one will continually find side paths, a complex of events, factors, and determinations not reducible to a single, unified origin. Hence, for the historian the birth of cinema should be constantly found in difference and as deferred; therefore 'birth = *différance*'." (Philip Rosen, commentary on Jean-Louis Comolli, "Technique and Ideology: Camera, Perspective, Depth of Field [Parts 3 and 4], in *Narrative, Apparatus, Ideology*, ed. Rosen [New York: Columbia University Press, 1986], pp. 438-439, fn. 2) In this case, however, while correctly pinpointing the inadequacies of Matias' "postponement," Rosen offers an over-reading of Comolli's use of the term "*différence*." "*Différance*" in the Derridean sense (with the telltale alternate spelling), *does* appear in "Technique and Ideology," but only on two isolated occasions (both given in the present volume as "*différance*"). Elsewhere, and above all in his lapidary chapter heading "*Naissance = différence*," Comolli is not referring to Derrida, but is relying on the more common French use of the term, which can mean both "difference" and "deferral." For the most part, it is the latter term which is used in this translation, as the emphasis in Comolli's text is primarily on the sense of temporal disjunction. The reader should nonetheless keep in mind the fact that the French term is more polyvalent than its English equivalent.

ii. Comolli neglects to provide citations for the Deslandes and Bazin quotes here. For the Deslandes quote, cf. Jacques Deslandes, *Histoire comparée du cinéma*, vol. I, p. 26. For the Bazin quote, cf. André Bazin, "Le mythe du cinéma total"/"The Myth of Total Cinema," in Bazin, *What Is Cinema?, op. cit.*, p. 15, translation modified.

II. Depth of Field: The Double Scene

i. The Lenin quote actually reads "Intelligent idealism is closer to intelligent materialism than stupid materialism," and derives from a 1915 marginal note written with respect to Hegel's *History of Philosophy*. Cf. V.I. Lenin, *Philosophical Notebooks*, in *Collected Works of Lenin*, vol. XXXVIII (Moscow: Progress Publishers, 1976), p. 274.

ii. Comolli makes reference, here, to Althusser's classification of the three "generalities" representing different levels of theoretical knowledge, first proposed in "On the Materialist Dialectic." Generality I (the primary generality) constitutes, for Althusser, the "raw material that the science's theoretical knowledge will transform into specified 'concepts'." In contrast, Generality II refers to the state of a scientific field at a given historical moment, while Generality III represents a point of "concrete" theoretical knowledge, and is produced, in Althusser's view, by "the work of Generality II on Generality I." Cf. Althusser, *For Marx*, trans. Ben Brewster (London: Verso, 1979), pp. 183-185.

iii. Kristeva has defined *signifiance* as "this work of differentiation, stratification and confrontation that is practiced in language, and that deposes on the line of the speaking subject a communicative and grammatically structured signifying chain" (*Sémeiotikè* [Paris: Seuil, 1969], p. 9). Rosen, meanwhile, gives the following explicatory note for the term: "*Signifiance* is a special term introduced by Julia Kristeva. It is equivalent neither to signifier (*signifiant*) nor signified (*signifié*) nor significance. Kristeva explains *signifiance* as a force subtending all signification, but which is exploited especially by modernist texts. As Comolli indicates, these underlying processes of signification are what produce the possibility of meaning. Therefore, in any instance of signification the existence of *signifiance* may be more heavily or less heavily marked (which can serve as an account of the relations between classical and modernist textuality). But if *signifiance* is the underlying processes which enable meaning, this is precisely why it is in some sense other than and outside meaning. In Kristeva, it has a number of associations: with *work* on the signifier (rather than deemphasizing the characteristics of the signifier in order to stress the signified/meaning), with textual excess, with a psychoanalytic conceptualization of the drives and the unconscious. It designates a certain 'alterity,' something beyond meaning in the very processes that produce 'communication.' Comolli's use of the concept of *signifiance* allies itself with his use of the concept of *différance*: they both function in his argument to signal a resistance to any quick unification of history or films around meaning ('the' meaning of history, or films taken solely from the perspective of their 'meanings'); and both terms support a dialectic between meaning and/or signifying system on the one hand, and the non-speakable processes and forces underlying discursive 'surfaces' that produce those surfaces on the other. Since *signifiance* both is necessary to 'ordinary communication,' and is there repressed, it can provide the basis for kinds of 'countersignification,' where its existence would be figured. Furthermore, as Comolli will argue, one can construct a history of *signifiances* – the various modes of repressing signifiance and/or figuring and exploiting it at different times and places. Comolli's reference is to Kristeva's essay 'Le Texte et sa science' in her collection *Sémeiotikè*. In that essay, pp. 8-12 provide a general, schematic introduction to the concept of *signifiance* on which this note has drawn" (Rosen, *op. cit.*, pp. 439-440, fn. 5).

iv. Cf. Gérard Leblanc, "Welles, Bazin et la R.K.O.," *op. cit.*, p. 30.

v. Little is known about Norbert Massa, or the mimeographed film magazine *Ciné-Forum* (based out of the *maison de la culture* at Poitiers), beyond the glowing references to it in the pages of *Cahiers*. The note on the journal in issue no. 230 of *Cahiers* (by Pascal Bonitzer), speaks of it as: "one of the most rigorous attempts at present to produce a *theory/criticism* of cinematic practice. Avoiding the pitfalls most frequently encountered in this field – dogmatism and eclecticism (or dogmatic eclecticism) – the magazine has produced, in the five issues that have come out so far, a certain number of analyses founded on the incipient theory of signifying practices, and based in dialectical and historical materialism. [...] Works such as this represent, in the current ideological struggle (particularly within the *maisons de la culture* and the *ciné-clubs*, so massively invested, as they are, with petty-bourgeois eclecticism and regressive cinephilia), an important strategic force. They must be multiplied." Cf. Pascal Bonitzer, "*Ciné-Forum*," *Cahiers du cinéma*, no. 230 (1971), pp. 61, 63.

vi. Comolli uses the neologism "*ciné-signifiant*" here, an evident portmanteau of "*cinéma*" and "*signifiant*."

vii. The quote is from Jean Mitry, *Histoire du cinéma*, vol. I (Paris, Éditions universitaires, 1967), p. 228.

viii. "*Jeanne d'arc*" refers to Dreyer's 1929 film *La Passion de Jeanne d'arc*. This quote appears to be from Mitry, but is not to be found in his *Histoire* or his *Esthétique et psychologie*, although the latter work does discuss the role of the close-up in Dreyer's film (cf. vol. I, pp. 409-410).

III. "Primitive" Depth of Field

i. "Differential specificity" is a key term introduced by Louis Althusser in *Reading Capital*, trans. Ben Brewster (London: NLB, 1969) to refer to the relationship between different forms of historical temporality (most notably those of the economic "base" and the various ideological "superstructures"), which are, in his view, "relatively autonomous" from each other. The concept was introduced to film theory in a brief comment by Marcelin Pleynet in "Économique, idéologique, formel...," *op. cit.*, p. 7.

ii. "*Découpement*" is a term devised by Comolli, related to but distinct from the more common term *découpage*. He describes it as "a neologism that emphasizes the cut [*coupe*], the acting of cutting [*découpe*], whereas *découpage* in the cinematic lexicon tends to signify an organization into sequences and shots. *Découpement* thus manifests a desire to cut up [*découper*] what appears to be continuous, while *découpage* aims more to organize a more or less continuous whole from a segmentation" (private communication, September 2013). Rosen gave the term as "cutting-up/assemblage operations," and appended the following extensive footnote, which broadly goes in the same direction as Comolli's view, albeit with some differences: "'Cutting-up/assemblage operations' is a rendering of Comolli's term *découpement*. There seems to be no English term which captures the implications of the French. Briefly, a possible sense of the verb *découper* is not only to cut into pieces, but also to carve out. Thus one of Comolli's points is that the psychological dramas in silent film involve a 'carving out,' whereby the most pertinent elements of the psychological drama occur in the foreground and are played out against the scenic background. (This can be quite evident for some films in the use of process shots.) But for cinema the noun *découpage* has specialized meanings. To begin with, it is rooted in the verb *couper*, to cut, which as in English can denote the activity of editing a film. However, *découpage* itself means something like the English terms 'shooting script,' 'storyboard,' or 'shot breakdown.' In addition, in his *Theory of Film Practice*, trans. Helen R. Lane (New York: Praeger, 1973), Noël Burch glosses the French term, pointing out some of its further potential not captured in English renderings. As Burch puts it on p. 4: 'Formally, a film consists of a succession of fragments excerpted from a spatial and temporal continuum. *Découpage* in its [further] meaning refers to what results when the spatial fragments, or, more accurately, the succession of spatial fragments excerpted in the shooting process, converge with the temporal fragments whose duration may be roughly determined during the shooting, but whose final duration is established only on the editing table.' Thus, the noun *découpage* implies the synthetic organizational structure underlying and governing the spatiotemporal composition of a film – the specific mode by which a film cuts up and joins together time and space. It seems, then, that with the term *découpement* Comolli is not solely highlighting the codified and organized stratification and sectioning ('cutting-up/assemblage') of the dramatic scene in terms of the spatial organization of a given *frame*. In addition, he is simultaneously (if somewhat implicitly) indicating that this 'synchronic' construction of space is tied to the *temporal* organization of spatial fragments ('cutting-up/assemblage') in the classical cinematic system of signification. That is, Comolli suggests that relations of temporal fragments (often highlighted in discussions of editing) are tied to another axis of the partitioning of space, one which (for the period he is interested in) gives much emphasis to the organization of depth planes; and that the history of the classical cinematic construction of space is to be theorized along both these axes. Their mobilization as part of the heritage of the 'psychological drama' of the silent period provides one avenue of thinking through their interrelation. Perhaps it is to emphasize his doubled use of the term that Comolli uses *découpement* rather than the more usual *découpage* here" (Rosen, *op. cit.*, pp. 442-443, fn. 26). For a more detailed discussion of the concept of *découpage*, cf. Timothy Barnard's relevant footnote in *What Is Cinema?*, *op. cit.*, pp. 261-281.

IV. Effacement of Depth/Advent of Speech

i. Cf. André Bazin, "William Wyler ou le janséniste de la mise en scène," in Bazin, *Qu'est-ce que le cinéma?*, *op. cit.*, p. 157 ("William Wyler, the Jansenist of Mise en Scène," in Bazin, *What Is Cinema?*, *op. cit.*, p. 54).

ii. Cf. translator's note i to "Cinema against Spectacle," chapter IV.

V. Which Speech?

i. *The Gold Diggers* was a series of musical comedies made in the 1930s based on the 1919 Broadway play of the same name, whose most well-known episode was *The Gold Diggers of 1933* (Mervyn Le Roy, 1933).

Appendices

Cinema/Ideology/Criticism (I)

i. The denunciation of "parallelism" in this paragraph is an unmistakable rebuttal to *Cinéthique*, whose editors, in editorial statements on the inside covers of issues no. 3 and 4 of the journal, vaunted their economic independence from the monopolistic practices of France's commercial press and espoused the creation of parallel distribution circuits to circulate both their journal and the films it championed.

ii. While the obvious reference point here is the title of Bazin's collection of articles *What Is Cinema?* (*Qu'est-ce que le cinéma?*), a more immediate polemical target is Marcelin Pleynet, who, in his interview with *Cinéthique* (Marcelin Pleynet and Jean Thibaudeau, "Économique, idéologique, formel...," *Cinéthique*, no. 3 [1969], pp. 7-14), asserted: "Nobody has answered the question: 'What is cinema?' It remains suspended" (p. 13).

iii. This is likely an echo of a comment made by Althusser in "On the Materialist Dialectic" to the effect that, "The Marxist theoretical practice of *epistemology*, of the history of science, of the history of ideology, of the history of philosophy, of the history of art, has yet in large part to be constituted. Not that there are not Marxists who are working in these domains and have acquired much real experience there, but they do not have behind them the equivalent of *Capital* or of the revolutionary practice of a century of Marxists. Their practice is largely *in front of them*, it still has to be developed, or even founded, that is, it has to be set on correct theoretical bases so that it corresponds to a *real* object." Althusser, *For Marx*, *op. cit.*, p. 169.

iv. The quote from Althusser is taken from "Marxism and Humanism," in *For Marx, op. cit.*, p. 233 (translation modified).

v. The deficiencies of Bennett's rendering of this passage have been discussed in the introduction. It should also be noted that *Cinéthique* saw the phrase as a tacit citation of Jean Thibaudeau – who spoke of the "systematic de-construction of representative phenomena" ("Économique, idéologique, formel...," op. cit., p. 7) – and commented that, "As the project is rather unprecedented on the terrain of film criticism (but not elsewhere: Roland Barthes, Umberto Eco, Jacques Derrida), it is astonishing that *Cahiers*, so careful on other occasions to establish their sources, did not judge it useful to refer to him." Cf. [*Cinéthique* editors], "Du bon usage de la valeur d'échange," *Cinéthique*, no. 6 (1970), p. 3.

vi. *Nicht versöhnt* (Jean-Marie Straub and Danièle Huillet, 1965), *The Edge* (Robert Kramer, 1968), *Terra em transe* (Glauber Rocha, 1967).

vii. *Méditerranée* (Jean-Daniel Pollet and Philippe Sollers, 1963), *The Bellboy* (Jerry Lewis, 1960), *Persona* (Ingmar Bergman, 1968).

viii. *Z* (Constantin Costa-Gavras, 1969), *Le Temps de vivre* (Bernard Paul, 1969).

ix. *Les Grandes Familles* (Dènys de La Patellière, 1958).

x. *Chiefs* (Richard Leacock and Noel E. Parmentel, Jr., 1969).

xi. *Le Règne du jour* (Pierre Perrault, 1969), *La Reprise du travail aux usines Wonder* (Jacques Willemont, 1968).

xii. The opposition to "speculative" film criticism is likely a reference to the text "La notion de production," in *Cinéthique* no. 4, which asserted, "If there is a habit that must be radically overcome, it is the *speculative* practice of film critics." Cf. Gérard Leblanc, Jean-Paul Fargier and Jacques Mondolin, "La notion de production," *Cinéthique*, no. 4 (1969), p. 25.

xiii. The "snide remark" was made by Pleynet, when he stated: "Look at what has happened to *Cahiers du cinéma*, which, objectively speaking, has never ceased to, as they say, 'peddle the merchandise,' and which will end up disappearing without ever having been a film journal – or by only ever having been a film journal, as in just another one" ("Économique, idéologique, formelle...," *op. cit.*, p. 13).

Cinema/Ideology/Criticism (II): On Criticism at Its Critical Point

i. Of the four *Cinéthique* editors at the time, only Gérard Leblanc and Jean-Paul Fargier proved to be long-term contributors and editors for the journal in the following years. The Le Grivés/Luciani text ("Naissance d'une théorie," *Cinéthique*, no. 5 (1969), pp. 45-47) is written in a markedly different register to Leblanc/Fargier's work, coming close to concrete poetry. Later in the 1970s, Fargier would make a Damascene conversion by leaving *Cinéthique* and joining the *Cahiers* editorial board, leaving Leblanc to oversee the journal alone, which continued to appear sporadically until its demise in 1985. For Fargier's distancing from the militant cinema he had previously advocated in *Cinéthique*, cf. "Pour le dépérissement du cinéma militant," *Cinéma d'aujourd'hui*, no. 5-6 (1976), pp. 163-168.

ii. These quotes are taken from "Naissance d'une théorie," *op. cit.*, p. 47

iii. *Octobre à Madrid* (Marcel Hanoun, 1969). Hanoun was the founder of *Cinéthique* and briefly a member of its editorial board; his film is held up as a model for revolutionary film practice throughout issue no. 5 of the journal.

iv. The first two quotes derive from "Naissance d'une théorie," *op. cit.*, p. 47, while the last is taken from Jean-Paul Fargier, "La parenthèse et le détour," *Cinéthique*, no. 5 (1969), p. 20.

v. Cf. Louis Althusser, "On the Young Marx," in Althusser, *For Marx*, *op. cit.*, pp. 49-86.

vi. For this, and the following quotes, cf. Fargier, "La parenthèse et le détour," *op. cit.*, p. 20.

vii. The text in question is: Alain Badiou, "L'autonomie du processus esthétique," *Cahiers marxistes-léninistes*, no. 12-13 (1966), 77-89. Badiou's text notably contains a passage – "Art is not the reflection of reality but the reality of reflection" – which would be quoted by Godard in *La Chinoise*, and which has since been commonly ascribed to the filmmaker. Later, during their "*front culturel*" period in 1972-1973, the *Cahiers* writers would have close relations with the small Maoist group with which Badiou was involved, the Union des communistes français.

viii. *Le Joueur de quilles* (Jean-Pierre Lajournade, 1969).

ix. *Two Weeks in Another Town* (Vincente Minnelli, 1962), *La Fête à Henriette* (Julien Duvivier, 1952), *Le Débutant* (Daniel Däert, 1969).

x. Jean-Paul Fargier, "Discours-film (révolution)-mutisme," *Cinéthique*, no. 5 (1969), p. 38.

xi. *Ibid.*, p. 40.

xii. *The German Ideology*, in *The Collected Works of Marx and Engels*, vol. V (New York: International Publishers, 1975), p. 36. For the edition that was the source of contention in footnote 5, cf. *L'idéologie allemande*, trans. Émile Bottigelli (Paris: Éditions sociales, 1952; repr. 1966, 1969). This edition, as *Cahiers* point out, gave Marx's *camera obscura* (which should be the same in German, English and French, although French also has the option of rendering it as *chambre noire*) as *camera obscure*, which was likely a misprint.

xiii. Fargier, "La parenthèse et le détour," *op. cit.*, p. 19.

xiv. Comolli and Narboni are referring, of course, to Freud's *Jokes and Their Relation to the Unconscious.*

xv. In the Marxist-Leninist tradition, voluntarism denotes an excessive emphasis on the subjective ability of revolutionary parties to transform a given conjuncture, and a downplaying of the objective political conditions.

xvi. Cf. Marcelin Pleynet, "Le front 'gauche' de l'art: Eisenstein et les vieux 'jeunes-hégéliens'," *Cinéthique*, no. 5 (1969), 23-32. This was translated as "The 'Left' Front of Art," trans. Susan Bennett, in *Screen*, vol. 13 no. 1 (1972), pp. 101-119.

xvii. Philippe Sollers, "Le reflèxe de reduction," in *Théorie d'ensemble* (Paris: Seuil, 1965), p. 391. Pleynet notes that *Cahiers* mistakenly dated this text as being published in 1968, when it actually appeared three years earlier. Cf. Marcelin Pleynet, "Le point aveugle," *Cinéthique*, no. 6 (1970), p. 19.

xviii. *Change* was a literary journal founded in 1968 by Jean-Pierre Faye after his break with *Tel Quel*. Faye and Sollers entertained a bitter, ongoing polemic with each other throughout the late 1960s. *Cahiers* entertained a brief flirtation with the journal in 1969, with Comolli praising their special issue on montage in issue no. 209 of *Cahiers* ("Le Cahier des autres," *Cahiers du cinéma*, no. 209 [1969], p. 4). *Cahiers*' collaboration with *Change* was thus bound to incur the wrath of the *Tel Quel* editors, but Pleynet nonetheless noted that the publication of Eisenstein's writing was "envisaged with a much greater degree of methodological rigor in *Cahiers du cinéma* than in the *Change* notebooks [*cahiers*]." Pleynet, *op. cit.*, p. 30.

xix. The article in question is Barthélémy Amengual's "À propos du *Pré de Béjine*," *Cahiers du cinéma*, no. 203 (1968), pp. 6-12.

xx. Pleynet, "Le front 'gauche' de l'art," *op. cit.*, p. 32.

xxi. The text in question, a short introductory paragraph, can actually be found in *Cahiers du cinéma*, no. 209 (1969), p. 21.

xxii. This was a collection of Eisenstein's writings published in Moscow for a French readership. Cf. S.M. Eisenstein, *Réflexions d'un cinéaste*, translated into French by Lucia Galinskaia and Jean Cathala (Moscow: Progress Publishers, 1958).

xxiii. Cf. Sergei Eisenstein, *Film Form*, ed. and trans. Jay Leyda (New York: Harcourt and Brace, 1949); Sergei Eisenstein, *The Film Sense*, ed. and trans. Jay Leyda (New Yorl: Harcourt and Brace, 1947); *Film Essays, with a Lecture*, ed. and trans. Jay Leyda (London: Dobson, 1968).

xxiv. *Théorie de la littérature*, ed. Tzvetan Todorov (Paris; Seuil, 1966).

xxv. Sollers, *op. cit.*, pp. 392, 393.

xxvi. Tzvetan Todorov, "Formalistes et futuristes," *Tel Quel*, no. 35 (1968), pp. 42-45.

xxvii. Pleynet, "Le front 'gauche' de l'art," *op. cit.*, p. 29.

xxviii. Cf. S.M. Eisenstein, "*La non-indifférente nature* (2)*: Encore une fois de la nature des choses*," translated into French by Luda and Jean Schnitzer, *Cahiers du cinéma*, no. 213 (1968), pp. 36-42. The incriminating footnote is on p. 42. Luda and Jean Schnitzer were a husband-and-wife couple of Russian nationality living in France. In addition to their translations for *Cahiers du cinéma*, they also wrote several books on Russian cinema.

xxix. Vsevolod Meyerhold, *Le Théâtre théâtral*, translated into French by Nina Gourfinkel (Paris: Gallimard, 1963).

xxx. Pleynet, "Le front 'gauche' de l'art," *op. cit.*, p. 29.

xxxi. *Ibid.*, p. 25.

xxxii. Cf. Dmitri Blagoi, "Aux sources de la littérature soviétique," *Tel Quel*, no. 37 (1970), pp. 95-103.

xxxiii. Leyda discusses this matter on p. 121.

xxxiv. Pleynet, "Le front 'gauche' de l'art," *op. cit.*, p. 30.

xxxv. *Ibid.*, pp. 28, 31.

xxxvi. Cf. S.M. Eisenstein, "Perspectives," trans. Luda and Jean Schnitzer, *Cahiers du cinéma*, no. 209 (1969), pp. 22-29. The (long) passage in question appears on p. 26.

Machines of the Visible

i. More commonly known as *The Cholmondeley Ladies*, the painting, of unknown provenance, presently hangs in the Tate Gallery in London.

Index of names cited by Comolli

Film Theory in Media History

Sarah Keller and Jason N. Paul (eds.)
Jean Epstein: Critical Essays and New Translations, 2012
ISBN 9789089642929

Mattias Frey
The Permanent Crisis of Film Criticism: The Anxiety of Authority, 2015
ISBN 9789089647177

Daniel Fairfax (trans. and ed.)
Jean-Louis Comolli. Cinema against Spectacle: Technique and Ideology Revisited, 2015
ISBN 9789089645548

Naum Kleiman and Antonio Somani (eds.)
Sergei M. Eisenstein: Notes for a General History of Cinema, Forthcoming 2015
ISBN 9789089648440

14W88573/ T2/ 9789089645548